Informal Institution

Informal Institutions and Democracy

Lessons from Latin America

Edited by

GRETCHEN HELMKE

STEVEN LEVITSKY

The Johns Hopkins University Press

Baltimore

The Johns Hopkins University Press
2715 North Charles Street
Baltimore, Maryland 21218-4363
www.press.jhu.edu

Library of Congress Cataloging-in-Publication Data
Informal institutions and democracy : lessons from Latin America /
edited by Gretchen Helmke and Steven Levitsky.
p. cm.
"The volume emerged out of two conferences on informal institutions. The first,
entitled 'Informal Institutions and Politics in the Developing World,' was held at
Harvard University in April 2002. . . . The second conference, entitled 'Informal
Institutions and Politics in Latin America: Understanding the Rules of the Game,'
was held at the Kellogg Institute for International Studies, University of Notre
Dame, in April 2003"—Pref.
Includes bibliographical references and index.
ISBN 0-8018-8351-2 (hardcover : alk. paper)
ISBN 0-8018-8352-0 (pbk. : alk. paper)
1. Political culture—Latin America—Congresses. 2. Democratization—Latin
America—Congresses. 3. Democracy—Latin America—Congresses. 4. Politics,
Practical—Latin America—Congresses. 5. Latin America—Politics and
government—1980– I. Helmke, Gretchen, 1967–
II. Levitsky, Steven, 1968–
JL966.I55 2006
306.2098—dc22
2005032064

A catalog record for this book is available from the British Library.

Contents

Preface

Political reality can be compelling. The sweeping regime changes of the 1980s and 1990s brought democratic institutions to virtually every country in Latin America, but the quality or performance of those institutions has disappointed both scholars and policymakers alike. Military coups have largely disappeared, but presidents continue to be forced from office before the end of their mandate; constitutional liberties have been restored, but security forces kill some citizens with impunity; legislators seem more interested in making money than in making policy; corruption and clientelism remain widespread, and in many rural (and some urban) areas, the rule of law effectively does not exist. This book contends that in order to understand how—and how well—democratic institutions work in Latin America, scholars must go beyond the study of formal institutions and take seriously informal "rules of the game." The book presents a conceptual and theoretical framework for analyzing how formal and informal institutions interact in new democracies. Although it focuses on Latin America, its lessons are broadly applicable throughout the developing and postcommunist worlds.

The idea for this volume emerged out of a series of conversations that began nearly a decade ago. As researchers beginning fieldwork in Argentina during the mid-1990s, we were struck by the vast gap between the formal institutions we had come to study (political parties in one case, courts in the other) and the informal realities we encountered on the ground. Our respective efforts to make sense of these patterns were heavily influenced by the work and teaching of Guillermo O'Donnell. O'Donnell, who has written an afterword to this volume, is a major intellectual inspiration behind it.

We have incurred many debts in bringing this project to fruition. The volume emerged out of two conferences on informal institutions. The first, entitled "Informal Institutions and Politics in the Developing World," was held at Harvard University in April 2002. It was generously funded by the Weatherhead Center for International Affairs and the David Rockefeller Center for Latin American Studies. We

are particularly grateful for the support of Weatherhead Center director Jorge Domínguez, and for the dedicated organizational work of Jeana Flahive. Our own
conceptual and theoretical ideas about informal institutions were heavily informed
by this conference, and we thank participants Kathleen Collins, Keith Darden, Jorge
Domínguez, Dennis Galvan, Robert Gay, Kathryn Hendley, Jim Johnson, Jack
Knight, Hans-Joachim Lauth, Melanie Manion, José Luis Medina, María Victoria
Murillo, Andreas Schedler, Rudra Sil, Lily Tsai, and Lucan Way.

The second conference, entitled "Informal Institutions and Politics in Latin
America: Understanding the Rules of the Game," was held at the Kellogg Institute
for International Studies, University of Notre Dame, in April 2003. The conference
was generously supported by the Kellogg Institute, through a grant from the Coca
Cola Foundation. We are particularly thankful for the support of Frances Hagopian
and Scott Mainwaring, as well as Christopher Welna, Holly Rivers, and Dawn
Dinovo, and to conference participants Rebecca Bill Chavez, Martín Böhmer, Jorge
Buendia, Michael Coppedge, Jack Knight, Miriam Kornblith, Susan Stokes, Ignacio
Walker, and Kurt Weyland for their insightful comments.

In addition, we have received extremely useful comments along the way from
Jorge Domínguez, Anna Grzymala-Busse, Peter Hall, Goran Hyden, Lisa Martin, María Victoria Murillo, Shannon O'Neil Trowbridge, Benjamin Smith, Hillel
Soifer, Lucan Way, and Jason Wittenberg. Maria Koinova, Elena Plaxina, and Hillel
Soifer provided critical research and editorial assistance. We also thank the staff at
the Johns Hopkins University Press, and particularly Henry Tom, for their careful
assistance in bringing the book to press.

Excerpts from the Introduction are taken from "Informal Institutions and Comparative Politics: A Research Agenda," by Gretchen Helmke and Steven Levitsky, in
Perspectives on Politics, vol. 2, no. 4, December 2004, pp. 725–740. Copyright © 2004
by the American Political Science Association. Reprinted with the permission of
Cambridge University Press.

Finally, Steve Levitsky thanks his wife, Liz Mineo, and daughter, Alejandra Sol
Mineo-Levitsky, for keeping him focused on the rules of the game that really matter.
Gretchen Helmke thanks Mitch Sanders and her father, Stephen Helmke, for their
support and encouragement.

Informal Institutions and Democracy

Introduction

GRETCHEN HELMKE AND STEVEN LEVITSKY

Over the past two decades, a scholarly consensus has emerged around the centrality of political institutions. In Latin America, recent research on executive-legislative relations, electoral and party systems, judicial politics, bureaucracies, and federalism has shed new light on how institutional design affects the stability and quality of democracy.[1] Nevertheless, persistent problems of corruption, clientelism, executive-legislative conflict, and the "unrule of law" cast doubt on whether an exclusive focus on "parchment"[2] institutions is sufficient for understanding what drives politics in the region (O'Donnell 1996a, 1999c; Weyland 2002a). Scholars such as Guillermo O'Donnell and Douglass North have argued that *informal institutions*—or rules and procedures that are created, communicated, and enforced outside the officially sanctioned channels—are often as important as their formal counterparts in structuring the "rules of the game."

Informal rules coexist with formal democratic institutions throughout Latin America. In Mexico during much of the twentieth century, presidents were selected not according to rules laid out in the constitution, the electoral law, or the statutes of the governing Party of the Institutional Revolution (PRI), but rather by means of the *dedazo* ("finger tapping"), an unwritten code that gave the sitting president the right to choose his successor, specified the candidate pool, and prohibited potential candidates from openly seeking the job. In Chile, notwithstanding a constitution that created one of the most powerful presidencies in the world, informal power-sharing arrangements in place since democratization have induced presidents to systematically underutilize that power. As a result, Chile is viewed as an exception in a region characterized by presidential dominance (O'Donnell 1994). In parts of Bolivia, Ecuador, Mexico, Peru, and Guatemala, where state judicial institutions are often absent or ineffective, local communities solve conflict through indigenous law and other informal justice systems. And throughout Latin America, established patterns of clientelism, corruption, and patrimonialism challenge the efficacy of elections and the rule of law (O'Donnell 1996b).

Informal rules shape how democratic institutions work. They reinforce, subvert, and sometimes even supersede formal rules, procedures, and organizations. Analyses of democratic institutions that focus exclusively on formal rules thus risk missing much of what shapes and constrains political behavior, which can yield an incomplete—if not wholly inaccurate—picture of how politics works. Hence, it is imperative that the institutionalist turn in Latin American politics be grounded in an understanding of what O'Donnell calls "the actual rules that are being followed" (1996a, 10; see also Weyland 2002a).

Taking up O'Donnell's call, this volume examines the relationship between informal institutions and democracy in Latin America. Building on a large but heretofore disparate body of research,[3] the book provides a conceptual and theoretical foundation for informal institutional analysis. The volume brings together scholars of Latin American political institutions, from diverse theoretical and methodological traditions, who converge around a simple observation: political actors respond to a mix of formal and informal incentives (North 1990), and, consequently, the degree to which formal rules actually enable and constrain politicians varies considerably. Although formal rule-based incentives predominate in many instances, they may also compete with—and even be trumped by—informal incentives. In some cases, formal rules exist only on parchment, and actors are guided almost entirely by unwritten rules. In these cases, political behavior can be expected to deviate substantially from that prescribed by (or expected from) the formal rules.

The implications for institutional analysis are far-reaching. Even in areas that have traditionally been the exclusive domain of formal institutional analysis, research has found that informal rules have a powerful—and, at times, systematic—effect on institutional outcomes. For example, although earlier work on presidentialism in Latin America centered mainly on issues of formal institutional design (Linz 1990; Shugart and Carey 1992; Linz and Valenzuela 1994), recent studies suggest that the dynamics of presidentialism cannot be fully understood in strictly constitutional terms. Studies have shown how norms of patrimonialism produce a degree of executive dominance that far exceeds that prescribed by the constitution (O'Donnell 1994, 1996b; Hartlyn 1998; Sandbrook and Oelbaum 1999). At the same time, other scholars have shown how informal institutions may *limit* presidential power, even in cases of "hyper-presidentialist" constitutions (Peter Siavelis, this volume). Similar informal institutional effects have been found in studies of legislative politics, judicial politics, electoral systems, party politics, political regimes, federalism, and public administration.[4]

Informal institutions also shape formal institutional outcomes in a less visible, but equally important, way: by creating or strengthening incentives to comply with formal rules. In other words, they may do the enabling and constraining that we usually attribute to the formal rules. As Susan Stokes argues in this volume, formal institutions often work because they are embedded in implicit and informally shared expectations, or "grammatical rules," about the particular behavior governed by the explicit formal or "game" rules. For example, the effectiveness and stability of the United States' presidential democracy is not only a product of the rules laid out in the Constitution, but is also rooted in a set of "paraconstitutional" rules that prevent formal checks and balances from deteriorating into severe interbranch conflict (Riggs 1988). The absence of such norms of restraint and accommodation may help explain why similarly designed presidentialist systems have often proven more crisis-prone in Latin America.

By bringing informal institutions more centrally into the picture, this book seeks to lay a better foundation for understanding how political institutions in Latin America work. The essays in the volume cover a diverse array of informal institutions, including the Mexican *dedazo*, clientelism in Brazil and Honduras, legislative "ghost coalitions" in Ecuador, norms of executive-legislative power-sharing in Chile, illicit campaign finance in Brazil, norms of electoral accountability in Argentina, indigenous law in the Andes, norms underlying police violence in Brazilian cities, and informal mechanisms of electoral dispute resolution (*concertacesiones*) in Mexico. The chapters explore how these informal rules of the game affect the quality and stability of democracy. They find myriad, complex, and often unexpected effects: whereas some informal rules compete with and subvert democratic institutions, others complement and even help sustain them.

The chapters also explore a set of conceptual, theoretical, and methodological questions that are critical to advancing a research agenda on informal institutions.

- In the *conceptual* realm, they address the question of what informal institution are and, crucially, what they are not.
- In the *theoretical* realm, the chapters explore four central questions: (1) What are the distinct ways in which formal and informal institutions interact? (2) What are the effects of informal institutions, particularly with respect to the quality, performance, and stability of democracy? (3) What are the origins

of informal institutions, and specifically, why—and how—are they created? (4) What are the sources of informal institutional stability and change?

- In the *methodological* realm, the chapters explore the crucial questions of how to identify, measure, and compare "rules of the game" that are unwritten and, in many cases, hidden from public view.

This introductory chapter provides an overview of these questions. The first section examines the concept of informal institution. It makes the case for a narrow definition that permits scholars to distinguish between informal institutions and other informal phenomena, such as weak institutions, culture, and non-rule-bound behavior patterns. In the second section we provide an overview of how informal institutions affect the performance and quality of democracy in Latin America. The third section develops a typology of formal-informal institutional interaction. Expanding on the work of Hans-Joachim Lauth (2000), we distinguish among four types of informal institution: complementary, accommodating, competing, and substitutive. The fourth section explores a set of theoretical issues at the frontier of research on informal institutions, including the critical, but underresearched, questions of informal institutional emergence and change. Finally, we discuss some challenges related to research on informal institutions, such as issues of identification, measurement, and comparison.

CLARIFYING THE CONCEPT:
WHAT IS AN INFORMAL INSTITUTION?

This book focuses on informal *political* institutions, leaving aside a range of informal social (e.g., the handshake; the rules of dating) and economic (e.g., black markets) institutions. Yet even in the narrower realm of politics, informal institution is an ambiguous concept. The term has been applied to a broad diversity of phenomena, including culture, civil society, personal networks, clans and mafias, corruption and clientelism, and bureaucratic and legislative norms.[5] Such conceptual ambiguity has serious analytic costs, for it limits our capacity to build and test theories.

In this section, we attempt to clarify the concept of informal institution and to develop a more precise and analytically useful definition. In our view, such a definition should capture as much of the universe of informal rules as possible, but it must be narrow enough to distinguish informal rules from other, noninstitutional, informal phenomena.

Formal versus Informal Institutions

We begin with a fairly standard definition of institutions as rules and procedures that structure social interaction by constraining and enabling actors' behavior. This definition is generally thought to encompass both formal and informal rules (North 1990, 3–4; J. Knight 1992, 2; Carey 2000,735). There is less agreement, however, on how to distinguish between formal and informal institutions. Some scholars treat informal institutions as synonymous with culture or tradition. For example, Svetozar Pejovich defines them as "traditions, customs, moral values, religious beliefs, and all other norms of behavior that have passed the test of time . . . Thus, informal institutions are the part of a community's heritage that we call *culture*" (1999, 166). Other scholars employ a state-societal distinction, characterizing state agencies and state-enforced rules as formal institutions and the norms and organizations that constitute civil society—including religious, ethnic, kinship, and civic associations—as informal institutions (Boussard 2000; Manor 2001; L. Tsai 2002). A third group of scholars distinguishes between informal norms, which are self-enforcing, and formal rules, which are enforced by a third party, often the state (Ellickson 1991; J. Knight 1992; Calvert 1995).

In our view, each of these conceptualizations is problematic. Although some informal institutions may be rooted in cultural tradition, many informal rules (legislative norms, illicit patterns of party finance) have little to do with a community's larger values and attitudes. The state-societal distinction fails to capture the many informal rules—from organized corruption to bureaucratic norms to intragovernmental power-sharing arrangements—that are embedded within state institutions.[6] It also fails to capture what Ellickson (1991, 31) calls "organization rules," or the official rules that govern nonstate organizations such as political parties and corporations. Finally, although the self-enforcing definition is analytically useful, it fails to account for the fact that certain informal rules may be externally enforced (e.g., by clan and mafia bosses), in some cases by the state itself (Joy Langston, this volume).

We define informal institutions as *socially shared rules, usually unwritten, that are created, communicated, and enforced outside officially sanctioned channels.*[7] By contrast, formal institutions are rules and procedures that are created, communicated, and enforced through channels that are widely accepted as official.[8] A key element of this definition, to which we return later in the chapter, is that informal institutions must be enforced in some fashion.[9] In other words, actors must believe that breaking the rules carries some form of credible sanction—be it physical punishment, loss of employment, or simply social disapproval. As several of the chapters in this volume show, informal rules are often enforced—albeit unofficially—by actors and institutions within the state itself.[10]

A Second Distinction: Informal Rules versus Other Informal Phenomena

Distinguishing between formal and informal institutions, however, is only half the conceptual task. One of the dangers of our "parchment"-based definition is that *informal institution* may become a residual category, or a term used to describe virtually any behavior that departs from, or is not accounted for by, the written-down rules. To avoid this pitfall, it is essential to distinguish informal institutions from several other informal phenomena. In other words, we must elaborate further what an informal institution *is not*.

Four distinctions are worth noting. First, informal institutions should be distinguished from *weak institutions*. Many formal institutions are ineffective, in that the rules that exist on paper are, in practice, widely circumvented or ignored. Yet formal institutional weakness does not necessarily imply the presence of informal institutions. It may be that no stable or binding rules—formal or informal—exist. For example, in his seminal article on delegative democracy, O'Donnell (1994) argued that in much of Latin America, the formal rules of representative democracy are weakly institutionalized. In the absence of institutionalized checks on executive power, the scope of permissible presidential behavior widened considerably, which resulted in substantial abuse of executive authority. In subsequent work, O'Donnell (1996b) highlighted how particularistic informal institutions such as clientelism undermined the effectiveness of representative institutions. O'Donnell's work points to two distinct patterns of formal institutional weakness that should not be conflated. Clientelism and abuses of executive authority both depart from formal rules, but whereas the former pattern is an informal institution, the latter is best understood as noninstitutional behavior.

Second, informal institutions must be distinguished from other informal behavioral regularities. Not all patterned behavior is rule-bound, or rooted in shared expectations about others' behavior (Hart 1961, 53–56; J. Knight 1992, 66–72). Behavioral regularities may be a product of a variety of other incentives. To cite an example offered by Daniel Brinks (2003b, 4), removing one's hat in church is an informal institution, whereas removing one's coat in a restaurant is simply a behavioral regularity. In the latter case, leaving one's coat on may bring physical discomfort, but it is not expected to trigger social disapproval or sanction. To be

considered an informal institution, a behavioral regularity must respond to an established rule or guideline, the violation of which generates some kind of external
sanction. To take another example, public graft is clearly informal behavior, but not
all patterns of graft should be considered institutional. Where graft is organized and
enforced from above (Waterbury 1973; Darden 2002), or where it is rooted in widely
shared expectations among citizens and public officials (and a refusal to go along
risks incurring important costs) (Manion 1996; Della Porta and Vannucci 1999),
corruption may indeed be an institution. By contrast, where graft is neither externally sanctioned nor rooted in shared expectations, but rather is a response to low
public sector salaries and ineffective enforcement, it may be best characterized as an
informal behavior pattern.

Third, informal institutions should be distinguished from *informal organizations.*
Although scholars often incorporate organizations into their definition of institution,[11] it is useful, following North (1990, 4–5), to separate the "rules" from the
"players." Just as formal organizations (such as political parties or unions) may be
distinguished from formal rules, informal organizations (such as clans or mafias)
should be distinguished from informal institutions. Nevertheless, just as parties and
other organizations are routinely studied under the broader rubric of "institutionalism," informal organizations—such as the informal party structures analyzed by
Flavia Freidenberg and Steven Levitsky in their contribution to this volume—may
be usefully incorporated into informal institutional analysis.

Finally, we return to the distinction between informal institutions and culture.
Although the border at which culture ends and informal institutions begin can admittedly be difficult to discern, it is essential to avoid conflating these two phenomena. Our approach to this problem is to cast informal institutions in narrow
terms, defining them in terms of shared expectations or beliefs rather than shared values. Shared expectations among a particular set of actors may or may not be rooted in
broader societal values. For example, whereas particularistic norms embedded in
kinship or clan networks may be plausibly traced to broader societal values (Price
1975; Dia 1996), elite power-sharing norms that emerge in deeply divided societies
(e.g., Dutch consociationalism, Chile's consensus democracy) cannot. This point is
clearly made in Donna Lee Van Cott's chapter on indigenous justice institutions.
Although indigenous institutions are often assumed to be deeply embedded in culture or tradition, Van Cott shows that this is not always the case. Whereas some
indigenous institutions draw on preexisting tradition, others are recent inventions—
in some cases, modeled on modern state institutions—that cannot be traced back to
earlier traditions. Not least of all, distinguishing between shared values and shared

expectations permits us to analyze potential causal relationships *between* culture and informal institutions, such as the conditions under which shared societal values engender, reinforce, or undermine particular informal rules.

WHY INFORMAL RULES MATTER

Informal institutions merit our attention because they shape how democracy works—for both good and ill. Perhaps not surprisingly, much of the existing literature on informal institutions in new democracies focuses on their negative effects. In particular, studies have highlighted ways in which corruption, clientelism, and patrimonialism undermine the effectiveness of democratic, state, and market institutions.[12] The chapters in this volume tell a more mixed story. Although several essays provide systematic evidence of how informal institutions erode the quality of democratic institutions, others point to the ambiguous, double-edged, and even positive effects of informal rules. Particularly where formal state and regime institutions are weak, ineffective, or insufficiently democratic, informal rules may enhance the performance and stability of democracy. In this section we examine the effects of informal institutions in four key areas of democratic politics: representation, accountability, governability, and citizenship and the rule of law.

Political Representation

Several of the essays in this volume grapple with issues of political representation. Evidence of a growing gap between citizens and politicians in Latin America is abundant: it includes declining party identification and voter turnout (Hagopian 1998, 114–21), high levels of electoral volatility (Mainwaring and Scully 1995; Roberts and Wibbels 1999), the rise of personalistic or "neopopulist" outsiders (Roberts 1995; Weyland 1996, 1999), and, in a few countries, large-scale protest against the entire political elite. Scholars have linked this "representation gap" to informal institutions such as clientelism, patrimonialism, and corruption (Fox 1994; O'Donnell 1996b; Mainwaring 1999; Brusco et al. 2004). These particularistic institutions are thus said to erode or prevent the establishment of programmatic linkages between parties and citizens.

The chapters in this volume find new evidence in support of these claims. For example, in his comparative analysis of state-level legislative politics in Brazil, Scott Desposato finds that clientelism erodes legislative parties' capacity to represent voters on programmatic issues. In the highly clientelistic state of Piauí, he finds that party discipline is low, individual legislators rarely take public positions on issues, and opposition parties are frequently co-opted by governors. By contrast, in São Paulo, where clientelism is less pervasive, Desposato discovers the same parties to be more cohesive, more willing to take public positions on programmatic issues, and less vulnerable to co-optation. The chapters by Freidenberg and Levitsky, Andrés Mejía Acosta, and David Samuels also suggest that informal—and especially particularistic—rules erode the quality of programmatic representation.

Yet the effects of informal institutions on representation are not uniformly negative. Where formal mechanisms of representation are weak or ineffective, informal institutions—even particularistic ones—may yield some positive benefits in terms of representation. In her chapter on clientelism and pork-barrel politics in Honduras, Michelle Taylor-Robinson argues that due to Honduras's closed-list proportional representation system, the electoral incentives for legislators to represent local interests are weak. She finds that elected representatives from poor rural areas who sponsor locally targeted (usually pork-barrel) legislation do so mainly in response to established norms of clientelism. In the absence of such norms, the legislative process might have ignored poor rural localities entirely.

Democratic Accountability

Recent evidence from Latin America suggests that democratic elections are often insufficient mechanisms for ensuring government accountability and responsiveness. Using O'Donnell's terms (1994), accountability has been found wanting in two key areas: vertical accountability, or the degree to which citizens are able to reward or punish officials for their performance in office (O'Donnell 1994; Stokes 2001), and horizontal accountability, or the degree to which public officials are responsible to (or checked by) other agencies and institutions of the state (O'Donnell 1994, 1999b; Schedler et al. 1999; Mainwaring and Welna 2003). In much of the region, citizens and their representatives are said to lack effective mechanisms to oversee and, when necessary, punish officeholders who abuse power. As a result, elected officials routinely betray their mandates, abuse their authority, and ignore constituents' demands.

Here, too, informal institutions are widely viewed as obstacles to normatively desirable outcomes, and for good reason. Because they are unwritten and unregulated, informal rules generally lack the transparency or public oversight that is often essential to accountability. It is difficult to use the law or public agencies to hold a politician accountable for breaking rules that—by definition—are not on the books. Several chapters in this volume explore the link between the nontransparent nature of informal institutions and deficits of accountability. For example, in their essay on informal party organization, Freidenberg and Levitsky argue that informal finance, decision-making, and other intraparty processes widen the gap between parties' public faces and their "real" power structures, which limits the capacity of activists and voters to hold party leaders accountable. In line with this analysis, Langston argues in her chapter that PRI elites preferred to govern through informal institutions such as the *dedazo* (rather than create formal authoritarian rules) in part because they helped prevent local party activists from holding them accountable. Had the *dedazo* system been written into PRI statutes or the constitution, it would have been open to public scrutiny—and thus more vulnerable to public challenge.

Informal institutions need not always undermine accountability, however. As Stokes's chapter shows, informal norms may also *reinforce or sustain* formal institutions of accountability. For elections to function effectively as mechanisms of vertical accountability, Stokes argues, certain shared expectations about how citizens will evaluate politicians are essential. Only when it is widely believed that citizens will follow an informal decision rule to vote retrospectively, weighing a politician's past performance in deciding how to vote (as opposed to, say, exchanging their votes for particularistic favors), will politicians act responsively and citizens expect such responsiveness. Drawing on a comparison of cities and provinces in Argentina, Stokes finds that democratic institutions work better where such shared expectations exist (Mar del Plata) than where they do not (Misiones).

Of course, informal institutions may also ensure accountability in less appealing ways. As Samuels shows in his analysis of campaign finance in Brazil, particularistic relationships are critical to sustaining illicit campaign finance contracts, for they help overcome the credible commitment problems inherent in illegal transactions. By providing trust, familiarity, reputations, and repeated interaction, particularistic norms help business leaders and politicians hold each other accountable in a context in which no legal recourse is available. Hence, they serve as the "glue" that sustains informal campaign finance contracts. Todd Eisenstadt's chapter on informal mechanisms of postelectoral conflict resolution (*concertacesiones*) also finds an ambiguous effect with respect to accountability. On the one hand, negotiated agreements between Mexico's ruling PRI and the opposition National Action Party (PAN) brought a degree of vertical accountability in that they removed from power ruling party candidates who had won elections through fraud. On the other hand, choosing mayors and governors though backroom bargaining completely severed the (however fictitious) link between the voting process and electoral outcomes, which can hardly be said to enhance vertical accountability.

Taken together, these chapters thus show that informal rules may provide the bases for credible commitment and some degree of accountability. However, as Samuels points out, they are less likely to provide the "right" kind of credible commitments (i.e., those that enhance *public* accountability) needed for democratic consolidation.

Democratic Governance

A third set of problems facing contemporary Latin American democracies lies in the area of democratic governance (Domínguez and Shifter 2003). Notwithstanding the virtual absence of military coups since 1980, the region has experienced widespread and often severe problems of executive-legislative conflict. In many countries, the result has been policy failure, periods of governmental paralysis, severe institutional crises (including executive efforts to circumvent and close congress, and extra-constitutional efforts to remove presidents), and, in extreme cases, democratic breakdown.[13]

Democratic governance is an area in which informal institutions are frequently seen to have a positive effect. For example, studies have shown that key features of presidential systems, particularly when combined with multiparty or fragmented party systems, increase the likelihood of governability crises rooted in executive-legislative conflict.[14] In some cases, however, informal norms of accommodation, power-sharing, and coalition building have helped prevent many of the problems associated with multiparty presidentialism. Nowhere is this clearer than in post-Pinochet Chile. In his chapter, Siavelis shows how informal power-sharing arrangements ensured smooth executive-legislative relations in a context of Chile's multiparty system and "hyper-presidentialist" constitution. Similarly, John Carey and Siavelis show how the practice of "electoral insurance" helped maintain the cohesion of the governing Concertación coalition despite an electoral system that is ill-suited to multiparty coalitions. Informal institutions also contributed to democratic governance in Ecuador. As Mejía Acosta's chapter argues, Ecuador's fragmented party system (which virtually ensures that presidents will lack legislative majorities) made it a "least likely" case for successful economic reform under democracy. Yet Ecuadorian presidents managed to push substantial economic reforms through the legislature during the 1990s. Mejía Acosta attributes this legislative success to informal "ghost coalitions," sustained by widely known and accepted practices of legislative vote-buying. In both the Chilean and Ecuadorian cases, however, the authors note that informal institutions of power-sharing have a double-edged effect: governability is achieved through means that reduce transparency and public accountability.

Informal institutions may also enhance governability in authoritarian regimes, as the two chapters on Mexico demonstrate. Langston's chapter shows how the *dedazo* served as the basis for one of the few institutionalized nondemocratic mechanisms of succession in the modern world. Similarly, Eisenstadt's essay suggests that the PRI's use of *concertacesiones* may have helped prevent large-scale political conflict during the 1990s. Although these informal mechanisms of governability probably slowed Mexico's democratic transition, they may also have contributed to the relative stability of that transition.

Citizenship and the Rule of Law

Finally, scholars of Latin American democracies have called attention to serious deficiencies in the area of citizenship rights. Notwithstanding the enshrinement of a variety of civil and human rights in democratic constitutions, many Latin American states have failed to consistently uphold or enforce the rule of law and, as a result, many citizens, particularly poor citizens and members of ethnic or racial minorities, do not possess these rights in practice (O'Donnell 1993, 1999c; Holston and Caldeira 1998; Méndez et al. 1999; Yashar 1999). The result, in many countries, is what O'Donnell has called "brown areas": territories characterized by "low-intensity citizenship" and the "unrule of law" (1993, 1999c).

The chapters in this volume suggest that informal institutions both violate *and* advance citizenship rights in such "brown areas." Daniel Brinks's chapter on police violence is a clear example of the former. Brinks shows that in major Brazilian cities, a set of norms exists within the justice system that not only permits but encourages extrajudicial executions of suspected violent criminals. It is widely known and accepted that those who kill suspected violent criminals will be protected from prosecution and perhaps even rewarded with a promotion or bonus. Hence, the extraordinarily high levels of extrajudicial killing by police in Brazil's major cities are not simply a product of sheer lawlessness, but rather are reinforced by a complex system of informal rules and incentives within the Brazilian state. However, as Van Cott's contribution shows, informal institutions may help protect citizenship rights where the state fails to do so. For example, in parts of the Andes in which state legal institutions either do not exist or are widely viewed as corrupt or ineffective, informal systems of justice such as indigenous law, *rondas campesinas* (community patrols; Peru) and *juntas vecinales* (neighborhood juntas; Bolivia) have been used to resolve disputes, provide security, and dispense justice. Where they are effective, informal justice systems may offer some partial remedies for low-intensity citizenship.

In sum, these chapters provide new evidence of how informal rules of the game may undermine the quality and performance of new democracies. However, they also point to ways in which informal institutions may strengthen or enhance the quality of democracy. These institutions seem to be particularly important where formal institutions are ineffective or insufficiently democratic. Such performance-enhancing effects of informal institutions have been underexamined in recent studies of Latin American democracies.

A TYPOLOGY OF INFORMAL INSTITUTIONS

As the previous section makes clear, formal and informal institutions interact in diverse ways, with diverse consequences. To make sense of these various patterns, in this section we develop a typology of formal-informal institutional relationships. The typology is based on two dimensions.[15] The first is the degree of convergence between formal and informal institutional outcomes. The distinction here is whether following the informal rules produces a result substantively similar to or different from that expected from a strict and exclusive adherence to the formal rules. Where following the informal rule leads to a substantively different outcome, formal and informal institutions may be said to diverge. Where the two outcomes are not substantively different, formal and informal institutions converge. The second dimension is that of the effectiveness of the relevant formal institutions. By *effectiveness* we mean the extent to which rules and procedures that exist on paper are enforced or complied with in practice.[16] Where formal institutions are effective, actors believe there is a high probability that noncompliance will be sanctioned by official authorities. Where formal rules and procedures are ineffective, actors believe the probability of enforcement (and hence the expected cost of violation) to be low. These two dimensions produce the fourfold typology shown in figure I.1.

Complementary Informal Institutions. The left side of the figure corresponds to informal institutions that coexist with effective formal institutions, such that actors expect the rules that exist on paper to be enforced. The upper left cell combines effective formal rules and convergent outcomes, producing what Lauth (2000, 25) calls *complementary* informal institutions. Complementary informal institutions shape behavior in ways that neither violate the overarching formal rules nor produce substantively different outcomes. Often, they are seen to enhance the efficiency or effectiveness of formal institutions.

Complementary informal institutions may be broken down into two types. One type simply "fills in gaps" within formal institutions, either by addressing contingencies that are not dealt with in the formal rules or by helping actors pursue their goals more effectively within a given formal institutional framework. Like many of the informal norms, routines, and operating procedures that pervade bureaucracies,

Outcomes/ Effectiveness	Efffective Formal Institutions	Ineffective Formal Institutions
Convergent	Complementary	Substitutive
Divergent	Accommodating	Competing

Figure I.1. A Typology of Informal Institutions

legislatures, and other complex organizations, such informal institutions facilitate coordination and ease decision-making.[17] A clear example of this type is the system of "electoral insurance" developed by Chile's democratic Concertación in response to the country's distinctive M=2 (two-member district) electoral system (Carey and Siavelis, this volume). Because two legislators are elected per district, parties or coalitions must double the vote of their nearest competitor to capture both seats, which requires that they run two strong candidates. Because a "doubling" outcome is highly uncertain, however, politicians are often reluctant to share a ticket with another high-quality candidate. Electoral insurance helped resolve this problem by assuring strong but unsuccessful candidates that they would be compensated with a government appointment. By reducing the risk of joining a strong ticket, this norm enhanced both the Concertación's competitiveness and its cohesion.

The second type of complementary informal institution serves as the underlying foundation for formal institutions. These informal norms create incentives to comply with formal rules that might otherwise exist merely as pieces of parchment. Thus, compliance with formal rules is rooted not in the formal rules per se, but rather in shared expectations created by underlying (and often preexisting) informal norms. For example, the success of the U.S. Constitution has been attributed not only to institutional design but also to reinforcement by a complementary set of shared beliefs and expectations among citizens (e.g., North et al. 2000). Likewise, Stokes (this volume) posits that elections serve as an effective mechanism of democratic accountability only where voters and politicians believe that citizens will weigh politicians' past behavior when casting their votes. Where such a shared expectation exists, as in the Argentine city of Mar del Plata, elections will induce politicians to be accountable to voters, and citizens will be more likely to find governments' promises credible. Where it is absent, as in many other parts of Argentina, elections are unlikely to bring the kind of governmental responsiveness that they were designed to ensure.

Accommodating Informal Institutions. The lower left cell of figure I.1, which combines effective formal institutions and divergent outcomes, corresponds to what we call *accommodating* informal institutions. These informal institutions create incentives to behave in ways that alter the substantive effects of formal rules, but without directly violating them. In other words, they contradict the spirit, but not the letter, of the formal rules. Accommodating informal institutions are often created by actors who dislike outcomes generated by the formal rules but are unable to change or openly violate those rules. As such, these institutions often help reconcile these actors' interests with the existing formal institutional arrangements. A classic example is Dutch consociationalism, a set of "informal, unwritten rules" of cross-party accommodation and power-sharing that included extensive consultation in policymaking, mutual vetoes, and a proportional distribution of government jobs (Lijphart 1975, 122–38). Although consociational arrangements violated the democratic spirit of the Dutch constitution by limiting the power of the vote, they enhanced regime stability by dampening class and religious conflict (Lijphart 1975, 137–38).

Siavelis's contribution to this volume offers another example of an accommodating informal institution. According to Siavelis, the 1980 Chilean constitution was "among the least conducive to effective democracy in Latin America." A powerful presidency and majoritarian electoral rules "create disincentives for cooperation, coalition formation and political accommodation," which threatened the quality, if not the stability, of Chile's post-1989 democracy. Lacking the political strength to abolish or reform the Pinochet-era constitution, elites within the governing democratic Concertación developed a set of informal procedures that counteracted its effects. Informal mechanisms such as the *cuoteo, partido transversal,* and *democracia de los acuerdos* created incentives for interparty and interbranch cooperation and consultation, which "mitigated the most negative characteristics of exaggerated presidentialism."

Competing Informal Institutions. To the right side of figure I.1 are instances of informal institutions that coexist with ineffective formal institutions. The lower right cell combines ineffective formal rules and divergent outcomes, producing *competing* informal institutions. These informal institutions structure incentives in ways that are incompatible with the formal rules: to follow one rule, actors must violate another. Competing informal institutions trump their formal counterparts, generating outcomes that diverge markedly from what is expected from the formal rules. An example is systemic corruption. In postwar Italy, norms of corruption were "more powerful than the laws of the state: the latter could be violated with impunity, while anyone who challenged the conventions of the illicit market would meet with certain punishment" (Della Porta and Vannucci 1999, 15). Similarly, particularistic norms such as clientelism and patrimonialism are often said to subvert formal state, market, and electoral institutions (O'Donnell 1996b; Borozc 2000; Lauth 2000).

Brinks's chapter on police violence offers an example of a competing informal institution. Although Brazilian law prohibits police officers from killing suspected violent criminals, it is routinely trumped by norms (within the law enforcement community itself) that encourage extrajudicial killing and protect those who engage in it. Van Cott's chapter on informal systems of justice administration in the Andes offers additional examples. State law prohibits some acts (e.g., marital violence, marriage of minors) that are permitted by indigenous law, and some transgressions in indigenous law, such as gossip and religious dissent, are not crimes according to state law. In these latter cases, community efforts to punish transgressors clearly infringe upon individuals' constitutionally enshrined rights.

Substitutive Informal Institutions. Finally, the upper right cell of figure I-1, which combines ineffective formal institutions and compatible outcomes, corresponds to *substitutive* informal institutions.[18] Like complementary institutions, substitutive informal institutions are employed by actors who seek outcomes compatible with formal rules and procedures. Like competing institutions, however, they exist in environments where the formal rules are not routinely enforced. Hence, substitutive informal institutions achieve what formal institutions were designed, but failed, to achieve.

Substitutive institutions generally emerge where state structures are weak or ineffective. For example, as Eisenstadt's chapter shows, Mexico's formal institutions of electoral dispute resolution—such as the electoral courts—lacked credibility and were frequently bypassed during that country's protracted democratic transition. In this context, *concertacesiones*, or "gentleman's agreements," thus served as a "way station" for government and opposition elites until formal institutions of electoral dispute resolution became credible. Similarly, in rural northern Peru, where state weakness resulted in inadequate police protection and ineffective courts during the late 1970s, citizens created informal *rondas campesinas* to defend their communities and *ronda* assemblies (informal courts) to resolve local disputes (Starn 1999, 49–71, 106–32; Van Cott, this volume). These informal structures served a state-like function, dispensing community-level justice in areas in which the state had virtually disappeared (Van Cott, this volume).

A few final points regarding this typology merit mention. First, whereas much of the political science literature casts informal institutions as either entirely *functional* (i.e., providing solutions to problems of social interaction and coordination)[19] or wholly *dysfunctional* (i.e., particularistic norms such as clientelism, corruption, and patrimonialism),[20] the typology helps capture more complex and double-edged relationships between formal and informal rules. Thus, although substitutive informal institutions such as *concertacesiones* and *rondas campesinas* lead actors to bypass formal rules and procedures, they may also help achieve results (resolution of post-electoral conflict, public security) that the formal rules failed to achieve. And although accommodating informal institutions such as power-sharing norms violate the spirit of the formal rules, they may generate outcomes (democratic stability) that are viewed as broadly beneficial.

Second, as many of the essays in this volume demonstrate, categorizations of informal institutions are not always mutually exclusive. Indeed, as Brinks points out in his chapter, informal rules may fall into different categories in relation to different formal institutions. For example, mafias directly violate certain state laws, but they may also substitute for ineffective state agencies that fail to deliver public goods.[21] Similarly, clientelism may violate liberal democratic procedure (O'Donnell 1996b, 40), but as Taylor-Robinson (this volume) notes, it may also substitute for weak formal mechanisms of local representation.[22] This point is made particularly manifest in Van Cott's chapter, which shows how indigenous laws may fall into all four of our categories.

Third, formal-informal institutional relationships are dynamic (Farrell and Héritier 2002; K. Tsai 2003; Galvan 2004). Informal institutions often serve as catalysts for formal institutional change. For example, formal rules may be created to entrench informal norms that actors find beneficial, as when the twenty-second amendment to the U.S. Constitution formalized the norm of a two-term presidency.[23] Alternatively, formal rules may be modified to close loopholes exploited through informal institutions (Farrell and Héritier 2002, 6), as when Argentine President Carlos Menem's extensive use of pseudo-constitutional executive decree authority led politicians to formalize (and regulate) such decree authority in the 1994 constitution (Ferreira Rubio and Goretti 1998, 56–57). Informal institutions may also lead to formal institutional *collapse*. By drawing public attention to the ineffectiveness of formal rules, for example, competing informal institutions may trigger efforts to dismantle them.[24]

Yet informal institutions may also contribute to formal institutional *stability*. By enhancing the performance of formal institutions or increasing the benefits gained by working within them, complementary informal institutions may strengthen actors' commitment to the formal rules. Along similar lines, accommodating informal institutions may dampen pressure for formal institutional change by blunting the negative effects of formal institutions. This dynamic can be seen in Chile (Siavelis, this volume), where informal power-sharing arrangements helped attenuate the effects of the Pinochet-era constitution, which in turn softened opposition to it within the democratic Concertación. In such cases, the collapse of previously existing informal rules may trigger pressure for formal institutional change. For example, Carey and Siavelis suggest in their chapter that the collapse of "electoral insurance" may generate pressure to modify Chile's electoral system.

Finally, informal institutions may have a "crowding out" effect on formal institutions. Thus, substitutive informal institutions may inhibit the development of effective formal institutions by dampening demands for the service provided by the formal structure and encouraging actors to invest in (and thus gain a vested interest in the preservation of) the informal rules of the game.[25] For example, citizen investments of time, energy, and resources into informal justice systems in Andean communities may contribute to the further neglect of (already weak) state-backed legal systems.[26]

This typology provides a useful starting point for categorizing the interaction between formal and informal institutions.[27] However, at least two alternative types of distinctions among informal institutions deserve mention. One is based on the origins of informal institutions relative to formal ones. Some informal institutions emerge endogenously from formal institutional arrangements, in that their origins are directly related to particular formal rules. As we elaborate in the next section, actors create informal rules in an effort to subvert, mitigate the effects of, substitute for, or enhance the efficiency of formal institutions. Examples include many legislative, judicial, and bureaucratic norms. Other informal institutions develop independent of formal institutional structures, in response to conditions that are largely unrelated to (and, in many cases, pre-date) the formal institutional context. Many indigenous or customary laws fall into this latter category (Galvan 2004; Van Cott, this volume).

A second distinction, also discussed below, revolves around *how* informal institutions emerge.[28] Some informal institutions are created in a "top-down" fashion by a small number of elites. Among the informal institutions discussed in this volume, the *dedazo*, as described by Langston, and the legislative and cross-party power-sharing norms described by Carey and Siavelis, Siavelis, and Mejía Acosta fall into this category. Other informal institutions emerge in a decentralized, "bottom-up" manner that involves a much larger number of societal actors. Clientelism (Desposato, Taylor-Robinson), many indigenous laws (Van Cott), and norms of police violence (Brinks) fit this pattern. Whereas the dynamics of top-down or elite-created informal institutions are in many ways similar to those of formal institutions, bottom-up, "societal" informal institutions are often seen as linked to broader societal values or cultural patterns.

THEORETICAL FRONTIERS: ISSUES OF EMERGENCE AND CHANGE IN INFORMAL INSTITUTIONS

At the cutting edge of research on formal institutions lie questions of institutional emergence, stability, and change.[29] To date, the comparative politics literature on informal institutions has largely neglected these issues.[30] Studies of phenomena such as clientelism, patrimonialism, clan politics, and indigenous or custom law often take those institutions as historically given, treating them as part of a static cultural landscape, but without specifying the mechanisms by which they are sustained. Other studies treat informal institutions in purely functionalist terms, explaining their emergence solely in terms of their purported effects (e.g., the efficiency gains they yield).[31] The chapters in this volume pose challenges to both static and functionalist accounts, examining the particular mechanisms underlying why and how informal institutions are created, as well as the sources of informal institutional stability and change.

Origins of Informal Institutions

By definition, the creation of informal institutions differs markedly from formal rule-making processes. Whereas formal rules are created through official channels (such as executives and legislatures) and communicated and enforced by state agencies (such as the police and courts), informal rules are created, communicated, and (usually) enforced outside public channels. They are rarely publicly debated or written down, and the actors who create and enforce them may deny doing so. Hence, their origins are often murky and disputed.[32] Why and how, then, do informal institutions emerge?

Building on the previous section, we can identify four reasons for informal institutions to emerge. One is the "incompleteness" of formal institutions.[33] Formal rules set general parameters for behavior, but they cannot cover all possible contingencies or provide guidelines for what to do in all circumstances. Consequently, actors operating within a particular formal institutional context develop norms and procedures that expedite their work or address problems not contemplated by the formal rules. Thus, ambiguities in the formal rules governing relations between the European Parliament and the European Council gave rise to a variety of informal institutions—such as *trialogues*—that facilitated the codecision process within the European Union (Farrell and Héritier 2002). Likewise, ambiguities in the statutes governing the U.S. Federal Reserve gave rise to the 1951 "Accord," an informal agreement that specified the nature of the Fed's responsibilities toward the Treasury Department (Keech 1995, 190, 200–201).

Second, actors may also create informal institutions because they lack the power to carry out formal institutional change, or because they deem such change to be too costly (Mershon 1994, 50–51). In these cases, informal rule creation can be seen as a "second-best" strategy for actors who are unable to achieve certain goals through formal institutions. This is the logic suggested by the two chapters on post-Pinochet Chile. Concertación leaders created "electoral insurance" and other power-sharing arrangements as means of adapting to a constitution and electoral system that they disliked but—due to the power of the military and the right—could not change.[34]

A third source of creation of informal institutions is formal institutional weakness, or the fact that formal rules lack credibility or are not enforced. Thus, Mexican opposition leaders participated in *concertacesiones* because they did not view the formal electoral courts as credible or fair (Eisenstadt, this volume), and Peruvian villagers created *rondas campesinas* because the state judicial system failed to uphold the rule of law (Van Cott, this volume). In these cases, then, actors do not develop informal institutions in order to weaken their formal counterparts: actors turn to them because formal institutions are *already* weak.

Finally, actors may create informal rules to pursue publicly (or internationally) unacceptable goals. Because they are relatively inconspicuous, informal institutions allow actors to pursue activities—ranging from the unpopular to the illegal—that cannot stand a test of public scrutiny.[35] For example, as Samuels argues in his chapter, the explicit exchange of money for political influence is not publicly acceptable in any democracy in the world. Unable to turn to the law to enforce campaign finance contracts, then, Brazilian politicians and firms routinely turn to informal institutions. Similarly, although norms permitting the killing of suspected violent criminals by police seem to enjoy substantial public support in Brazil, they grossly violate prevailing domestic and international human rights standards and thus cannot be legalized. Along similar lines, Langston suggests that one of the reasons why PRI leaders never formalized the rules of the *dedazo* was that such openly authoritarian practices were more likely to meet with public and international disapproval.

Identifying the incentives that actors face to create informal institutions, however, is not sufficient to explain how they are established. "Incompleteness" cannot explain how the need for additional rules translates into their creation. Where informal institutions are a second-best strategy, it remains to be explained why actors who lack the capacity to change the formal rules are nevertheless able to establish and enforce informal ones. And where actors share certain illicit goals, it must be explained how they are able to agree on informal norms that enable them to circumvent the formal rules.

Along these lines, several of the volume's chapters explore the creation of informal institutions through the lens of coordination. Because coordination often takes place in a context in which power and resources are unevenly distributed, informal institutions are cast as the culmination of a bargaining process in which actors seek to maximize their benefits, given their beliefs about the strategies available to other actors (J. Knight 1992). This is the gist of the arguments in the chapters by Langston, Eisenstadt, Mejía Acosta, and Samuels.

Alternatively, the emergence of informal institutions may be explained as a historically contingent, and ultimately path-dependent, process.[36] In these cases, informal rules are less a product of actor design than the (often unintended) consequence of a particular historical experience that creates certain socially shared expectations.[37] For example, as Stokes suggests in her chapter, norms of democratic accountability may emerge out of an early felicitous experience with good government, which sets in motion a virtuous cycle in which citizens believe that politicians can be held accountable and, because of this, politicians are willing to act more responsibly.

Explaining how informal rules emerge and persist also requires specifying how they are communicated to the relevant actors. Two mechanisms of the transmission and enforcement of informal rules emerge out of the chapters. One is personal networks, often operating through organizations such as political parties. Thus, political parties played an important role in diffusing *rondas campesinas* in Peru (Starn 1999, 116–17; Van Cott, this volume) and *concertacesiones* in Mexico (Eisenstadt, this volume), and in consolidating electoral clientelism in Honduras (Taylor-Robinson, this volume).

Informal rules may also be communicated through highly visible (if infrequent) episodes of rule-breaking and sanction. Widely observed efforts to punish deviations from informal rules can effectively signal the costs of noncompliance. For example, as Langston's chapter shows, the Mexican *dedazo* was institutionalized during the 1940s and 1950s through a process of "learning by example." PRI leaders who defied the incumbent president's right to choose his successor suffered political marginalization, while those who played by the rules were rewarded with better posts. Likewise, in his chapter Brinks suggests that the murder of investigators into (or witnesses of) police crime communicated the norms of police impunity, effectively discouraging others from taking such actions.

Informal Institutional Change

Informal institutions are often portrayed as highly resistant to change. Like culture, they often are assumed to possess a "tenacious survival ability" (North 1990, 45), which allows them to endure regardless of the formal institutional context. When change occurs, it is expected to be slow and incremental (North 1990, 45; Lauth 2000, 24–25). Lauth, for example, argues that because informal rules "do not possess a center which directs and co-ordinates their actions," informal institutional change is bound to be an "extremely lengthy" process (2000, 24–25). The chapters in this volume, however, suggest that informal institutional change—both in highly centralized and in decentralized instances—may be more frequent than we often assume. As Langston's and Eisenstadt's chapters on Mexico make clear, informal institutions can collapse quite quickly. And, as Van Cott argues in her essay, many indigenous institutions that are widely assumed to be long established as unchanging have in fact been repeatedly transformed—and even reinvented—over time.

One possible explanation for variation in the stability of informal institutions lies in the type of institution being examined. For example, "top-down" or elite-created informal institutions, which are usually a product of strategic interaction among a relatively small number of actors, may be more susceptible to change than "bottom-up," society-wide informal institutions, which emerge in a more decentralized (and less conscious) manner through repeated interaction.[38] Because coordination is often harder to achieve in larger groups, once an informal norm is in place, reorienting expectations around a new set of rules may prove more difficult. This may be too neat a dichotomy, however. Under certain conditions, even deeply rooted and decentralized societal norms may change relatively quickly (e.g., foot-binding in China; see Mackie 1996). Moreover, community size can cut both ways. As J. Knight (1992) points out, informal institutions may actually be less stable in larger communities, given higher relative costs of sanctioning and increased opportunities for the development of multiple interpretations of the norm.

There is a clear need, then, for greater attention to the questions of why and how informal rules change. Explorations into informal institutional change will almost certainly force scholars to think more seriously about their foundation. Identifying potential sources of change in informal institutions is, in effect, the flip side of specifying the mechanisms of institutions' reproduction or stability (cf. Thelen 1999, 399).[39]

This volume's essays consider three sources of informal institutional change: (1) formal institutional change, (2) changes in the underlying distribution of power and resources, and (3) changes in shared beliefs and collective experiences.

Formal Institutional Change. Because many informal rules are endogenous to formal institutional structures (in that they emerge in response to incentives created by those institutions), formal institutions often serve as a catalyst for informal institutional change. This impact should not, of course, be overstated: informal institutions have often proven resilient even in the face of large-scale legal or administrative reform.[40] Nevertheless, when changes in the formal rules affect the relative costs and benefits of playing by informal rules, they may have an important effect on the stability of informal institutions.

In evaluating how formal rules affect informal institutional stability and change, it is useful to disaggregate formal institutional change into two types. The first is a change in formal institutional *design*. Particularly in the case of complementary and accommodating informal institutions, formal rule changes may alter the nature of problems that the informal institution had addressed, thereby creating incentives for actors to modify or abandon the informal rule.[41] For example, the elimination of Chile's $M=2$ electoral system would almost certainly undercut the informal institution of electoral insurance. Or in Ecuador, electoral reforms that reduced the number of political parties would potentially eliminate the need for ghost coalitions, while institutional reforms that limited the executive's discretion in making political appointments would undermine a president's capacity to sustain them.

Informal institutional change may also be driven by a change in formal institutional *strength* or effectiveness. For example, changes in the level of enforcement of formal rules may alter the costs and benefits adhering to informal institutions that compete with or substitute for those rules. Compliance with competing informal institutions becomes more costly as enforcement of the formal rules increases, and, at some point, these costs will lead actors to abandon the informal rules. Thus, the increased judicial enforcement triggered by the Mani Pulite investigations undermined some forms of corruption in Italy (Della Porta and Vannucci 1999, 265–69), and federal enforcement of civil rights legislation weakened Jim Crow institutions in the U.S. South. Or, to take an example from this volume, reforms to Salvador's (Brazil) juvenile justice system that enhanced enforcement in the area of child homicides seem to have weakened informal norms encouraging killing of children by police (Brinks, this volume).

Increased effectiveness of formal institutions may also weaken substitutive informal institutions. When the credibility of previously ineffective formal structures is enhanced, the benefits associated with the use of substitutive institutions may diminish, potentially to the point of their dispensability. For example, the increased credibility of Mexico's electoral courts over the course of the 1990s reduced the incentive of opposition leaders to work through informal *concertacesiones* (Eisenstadt, this volume), and the increased effectiveness of Peru's public security and judicial systems led to the eventual collapse of many *rondas campesinas* (Starn 1999, 265–68; Van Cott, this volume).

The destruction of informal institutions does not always result in a stable new formal institutional equilibrium, however. It may also lead to chaos. In Guatemala, for example, state attempts to impose national legal institutions in rural Mayan communities during the 1970s and 1980s disrupted preexisting patterns of customary law, but the failure to consolidate a new legal system left rural residents uncertain over which laws and authorities prevailed (Handy 2004, 555–60). As a result, "much of Guatemala was essentially left lawless," leading to a sharp increase in violence and vigilantism (Handy 2004, 558–60; see also Galvan 2004).

Change in the Distribution of Power and Resources. Formal institutions are not the only impetus for informal institutional change. An alternative source of change is an alteration of the status quo conditions that had previously sustained the institution (J. Knight 1992; see also Greif and Laitin 2004). Developments in the external environment may change the distribution of power and resources among actors, weakening those who benefit from a particular informal institution and strengthening those who seek to change it. This dynamic can be seen in Langston's analysis of the collapse of the *dedazo*. Mexico's increasingly competitive electoral environment during the 1990s strengthened local PRI leaders and activists vis-à-vis the national leadership, which allowed them to contest and eventually dismantle the *dedazo* system. In this case, the relative pay-offs to PRI politicians were transformed by the leadership's growing inability to credibly threaten those members who challenged the president's prerogatives. Similarly, Eisenstadt argues that the shift in the balance of power created by the PAN's capture of the presidency in 2000 put an abrupt end to *concertacesiones*. Informal postelection bargaining tables had always been a second-best strategy for PAN leaders, and when the power asymmetries created by the PRI's control of the presidency disappeared, the PAN was free to abandon them. Finally, Carey and Siavelis argue that the viability of the Concertación's "electoral insurance" hinges on the continued electoral success of the coalition. Were the Concertación to lose the presidency, it would lose its capacity to reward unsuccessful legislative candidates.

Changes in Shared Beliefs and Experiences. A third source of informal institutional change lies in actors' beliefs about the opportunities and threats they face. If actors' shared expectations about the costs or benefits of an informal rule should change (due to a particular event or collective experience, a gradual accumulation of experiences, or the existence of a mechanism through which to coordinate expectations), then informal institutions—even long-established ones—may change quickly. As Gerry Mackie (1996) argues in the case of foot-binding in China, the move to end the centuries-old practice hinged on convincing a critical mass of people of the existence of an alternative marriage market that allowed sons to marry daughters with natural feet. Along similar lines, Siavelis (this volume) argues that a shared perception of the threat of a coup helped ensure adherence to informal norms of interbranch cooperation in post-Pinochet Chile. As this perceived threat fades, Siavelis argues, actors' willingness to sustain those norms may erode. Finally, Stokes's suggestion that positive experiences with democratic government create and reinforce norms of accountability suggests that the converse—for example, a particularly corrupt or abusive government—may contribute to their breakdown.[42]

RESEARCH CHALLENGES: ISSUES OF IDENTIFICATION, MEASUREMENT, AND COMPARISON

Research on informal institutions confronts a set of practical challenges that are quite distinct from those of formal institutional analysis. One challenge lies in simply identifying the existence of an informal institution. If a rule is unwritten, just how do we demonstrate that it exists? Because formal rules are usually written down and officially communicated and sanctioned, their identification and measurement often requires little more than a glance at a country's constitution or electoral law. Identifying informal institutions is different. Whereas a constitution tells us whether a country has a presidential or parliamentary system of government, it tells us little about the pervasiveness of clientelism, patrimonialism, or power-sharing norms. Although identifying such informal patterns lends itself to case-oriented ethnographic research, the chapters in this volume demonstrate that a range of other methodological tools—including small-n comparison, statistical analysis, and rational choice models —may also be employed fruitfully in this endeavor.

The contributors to this volume employ three distinct strategies for establishing the existence of informal institutions. The first strategy, used by Carey and Siavelis and by Taylor-Robinson, is to generate hypotheses about behavioral patterns that are consistent *only* with the existence of a particular informal institution, and then test empirically for the existence of those patterns. Thus, Carey and Siavelis hypothesize that if the informal norm of electoral insurance exists, high-quality losing candidates are more likely to be rewarded with government posts. Using statistical analysis, they find empirical evidence of such a pattern. Similarly, Taylor-Robinson hypothesizes that if norms of clientelism (as opposed to electoral rules) are driving legislative behavior, then legislators from poor rural districts are more likely than other legislators to sponsor locally oriented pork-barrel projects. She, too, finds statistical evidence to support this hypothesis.

A second strategy is to focus directly on actors' expectations about the informal rules of the game. By examining actors' mutual understanding of the rules, one can distinguish more carefully between informal behavior patterns and informal institutions. Ethnography is an important research tool in this task.[43] Several analyses in this volume (including those by Brinks, Desposato, Freidenberg and Levitsky, Mejía Acosta, Samuels, Siavelis, and Van Cott) draw heavily on ethnographic research, identifying shared expectations about informal rules through extensive interviews with (and observation of) the actors who are affected by those rules. Such case expertise is invaluable for understanding how the actors themselves understand the informal constraints they face. Yet other methods may also be employed to get at actors' expectations. Stokes's chapter, for example, offers a novel use of survey research techniques to establish shared expectations. Rather than merely gauging citizens' attitudes and values, she designs survey questions to investigate whether citizens in different localities in Argentina hold different expectations about whether fellow voters will punish politicians who behave dishonestly.

A third approach to identifying informal institutions is to focus on mechanisms of enforcement. If informal behavior is rule-bound, then violations of the rule must trigger some kind of external sanction. Unlike formal sanctioning mechanisms (i.e., legal systems), informal sanctioning mechanisms are often subtle, hidden, and even illegal. They range from different forms of social disapproval (hostile remarks, gossip, ostracism), to the loss of employment, to the use of hired thugs and other means of extrajudicial violence.

As Brinks and Samuels note in their chapters, a problem with identifying informal institutions through incidents of enforcement is that when they are functioning well, enforcement is rarely necessary.[44] Still, even rare instances of deviation and punishment can be telling. For example, Samuels shows how Brazilian politicians who fail to deliver government contracts to their financial supporters have difficulty raising money in future elections, and how politicians are able to delay or block government contracts to firms that provide insufficient financial support. He shows how the Collor government blacklisted entrepreneurs who had previously financed Collor's presidential bid but balked at another round of donations after his inauguration. Later, when Collor broke the rules and began to investigate corruption outside his inner circle, many of the same politicians and entrepreneurs responded by supporting his impeachment. Similarly, Mejía Acosta demonstrates how "going public" about illicit vote-buying activities serves as a mechanism of enforcing ghost coalitions in Ecuador's legislature. He shows that when the Durán Ballen government deemed that the Social Christian Party's (PSC) demands had escalated beyond the terms of the original "ghost coalition" pact, Vice President Alberto Dahik publicly accused PSC leaders of corruption. In response, the PSC launched an impeachment drive that forced Dahik into exile. Likewise, Langston shows how PRI executives used their control over state resources and electoral institutions to ensure that defectors would lose elections and pay an enormous cost in terms of their political careers. After defectors failed on three successive occasions during the 1940s and 1950s, the threat of sanction became sufficiently credible that no major PRI politician broke the rules for nearly three decades.

In a slightly different vein, Brinks's chapter focuses on "permissive" rules, or informal institutions that *allow*, but do not require, certain behavior. Under these rules, sanctioning operates in a somewhat different manner. Actors may avoid the permitted behavior without fear of sanction. Instead, punishment is meted out to those who seek to enforce the formal rules that prohibit the behavior in question (i.e., "whistleblowers"). Thus, Brinks finds that judges, prosecutors, and police investigators who seek to enforce laws prohibiting extrajudicial killing by police face harassment by superiors, noncooperation by the police, and even death threats.

The above discussion suggests that efforts to identify and measure informal institutions require substantial knowledge of the communities within which those rules are embedded. Although this is certainly true, it would be a mistake to identify informal institutional analysis only with case study research. In fact, the chapters in this volume engage in a variety of innovative methods. For example, many of our contributors use subnational comparisons to increase the number of observations or cases while holding a variety of national-level variables constant.[45] Thus, Desposato pairs two Brazilian states with similar formal legislative and electoral institutions but different levels of clientelism, thereby setting up a "natural experiment" that allows him to isolate the independent effects of clientelism on legislative behavior.[46] Brinks engages in both subnational and controlled cross-national comparisons. His study of five urban areas in Argentina, Brazil, and Uruguay produced evidence of informal norms of police violence in Salvador (Brazil), São Paulo (Brazil), and Buenos Aires (Argentina) but not in Córdoba (Argentina) and Montevideo (Uruguay). Stokes uses subnational-level survey data to compare localities in which informal institutions are presumably strong with those in which they are not.

Other chapters increase the number of observations by comparing single cases across time. For example, Langston examines evolution of the *dedazo* across several presidencies, from its establishment under Lázaro Cárdenas in the 1930s to its collapse under Ernesto Zedillo in the 1990s. Through this comparison, Langston is able to show how increased electoral competition helped erode the foundations of the *dedazo.* Similarly, Eisenstadt examines the use of *concertacesiones* across four time periods, which allows him to show how changing political conditions (particularly the increased credibility of formal electoral institutions and the rise to power of the PAN) led to the demise of informal bargaining tables.

Finally, as the chapters by Carey and Siavelis, Stokes, and Taylor-Robinson demonstrate, large-n statistical analysis may be employed both to identify informal institutions and to test propositions about their effects.

ORGANIZATION OF THE BOOK

This introduction has sought to provide an initial framework for studying how informal institutions shape democratic politics. The chapters that follow build on this framework. Drawing on diverse methodological tools, the contributors explore how informal rules shape and constrain political actors, how they interact with formal democratic institutions, and what they mean for the quality and stability of democracy.

Part I focuses on executive-legislative relations. Chapter 1, by Siavelis, examines informal power-sharing norms in post-Pinochet Chile. Chile's formal democratic institutions are among the least conducive in Latin America to effective governance. Yet Chile is widely viewed as one of the most successful third-wave democracies. Siavelis contends that three sets of accommodating informal institutions contributed to democratic governability by facilitating cooperation within the governing Concertación: the *cuoteo* (a formula to distribute candidacies and government posts), the *partido transversal* (a supra-party core of elites within the governing coalition), and a pattern of informal settlements known as *democracia de los acuerdos* (democracy by informal agreement). Chapter 2, by Desposato, examines the impact of clientelism on legislative organization and behavior. Comparing two Brazilian states with virtually identical formal institutions but significant differences in the level of clientelism, he shows how the presence of clientelism can dramatically shape how legislative parties and individual legislators operate, even reversing the incentives provided by formal institutions. Chapter 3, by Mejía Acosta, examines how legislative "ghost coalitions" facilitated democratic governance and economic reform in Ecuador. He argues that even though severe party fragmentation made Ecuador a "least likely" case for successful democratic reform, ghost coalitions—an informal institution in which opposition parties exchanged support for patronage and pork but did not publicly align with the government—enabled presidents to pass major legislation while protecting legislative allies' reputations from charges of collaborating with an unpopular government.

Part II focuses on informal institutions and electoral politics. Chapter 4, by Samuels, examines informal campaign finance contracts in Brazil. He argues that the familiar elements of the logic of "credible commitments"—reputation, iteration, and the possibility of punishment—can support informal campaign finance contracts, but that these conditions are most likely to be sustained within particularistic relationships, such as personal and family networks. Chapter 5, by Taylor-Robinson, explores how incentives created by clientelism affect the behavior of elected officials in Honduras. She argues that entrenched norms of clientelism may induce politicians to behave in ways that are at odds with their interests as defined by formal electoral institutions. Using data about the propensity of Honduran legislators to initiate locally targeted bills, Taylor-Robinson finds that clientelism creates incentives for legislators to initiate local pork-barrel legislation even where electoral institutions create no incentive to attend to local needs. Chapter 6, by Stokes, examines informal norms of electoral accountability in Argentina. Although accountability in national-level Argentine politics is usually seen as low, Stokes finds substantial within-country variation. In some cities, such as Mar del Plata, shared expectations around a rule on retrospective voting decisions—whereby voters weigh politicians' past performance more heavily than personalities or particularistic favors—have enhanced both accountability and the overall performance of democratic institutions. Stokes then offers some thoughts about the origins of such norms.

Part III focuses on party politics. Chapter 7, by Langston, examines the origins, institutionalization, and eventual collapse of the Mexican *dedazo*, in which the exiting president personally chose his successor for the top executive office. She shows how sitting PRI executives devised rules to deter ambitious PRI politicians from independently seeking the presidency, and how they used the resources afforded by hegemonic politics to impose steep costs on those who broke the rules. As electoral competition grew in the 1980s and 1990s, however, the ability of PRI presidents to enforce the *dedazo* eroded and the institution collapsed. Chapter 8, by Carey and Siavelis, looks at "electoral insurance" in Chile. Due to the country's $M=2$ electoral system, Chilean parties and coalitions must put their strongest candidates in the most precarious electoral list positions in order to secure legislative majorities, which generates a divergence of interests between coalitions and politicians. During the 1990s, the governing Concertación resolved this dilemma through the informal practice of providing appointed posts for candidates who accept personal risk on the coalition's behalf and run good—but just not good enough—campaigns for congress. Although this insurance system helped hold the coalition together for more than a decade, changes in the post-2000 electoral environment may threaten the Concertación's control over the appointed posts required to "pay for" the informal institution, which may hamper its prospects for survival. Chapter 9, by Freidenberg and Levitsky, examines informal party organization in Latin America. Because many Latin American parties lack effective formal structures, party organizations in the region are widely viewed as weak. Yet such a view obscures the vast informal structures—from clientelistic networks to soccer fan clubs—that sustain many parties. Drawing on an analysis of Argentine Peronism and the Ecuadorian Roldosista Party, Freidenberg and Levitsky develop indicators of formality and informality in nine different areas of party life.

Part IV focuses on judicial politics and the rule of law. Chapter 10, by Brinks, examines informal norms sustaining police violence in the Southern Cone. The police in Brazil and Argentina continue to kill with impunity, long after the establishment of democratic regimes and laws that purport to protect civil rights. To examine whether this behavior pattern can be attributed to an informal institution that grants the police discretion to use lethal force at will, Brinks develops a set of tests for the presence of informal institutions. In Salvador da Bahia, São Paulo, and Buenos Aires, he finds both direct evidence of an informal institution, such as the presence of enforcement behavior, and indirect evidence, such as behavior that seems to anticipate the existence of the hypothesized rule. Chapter 11, by Eisenstadt, outlines the evolution of *concertacesiones* as an alterative form of electoral dispute resolution in Mexico. After explaining how these bargaining tables resolved otherwise intractable postelectoral conflicts, to the benefit of Mexico's ruling PRI and its conservative opposition, Eisenstadt traces the rise and demise of *concertacesiones* from the late 1980s until 2000. He concludes that although bargaining tables helped to delegitimize electoral courts and other formal authorities established to resolve postelectoral conflicts, the opposition's decision to simultaneously use them and work to strengthen formal electoral institutions meant that these substitutive informal institutions could ultimately be replaced by genuinely autonomous formal ones. Chapter 12, by Van Cott, examines three forms of informal community justice administration that emerged in the vacuum created by the weakness of the rule of law in Latin America: indigenous law, *rondas campesinas* in rural Peru, and *juntas vecinales* in urban Bolivia. She explains how and why these informal legal institutions emerged, how they have evolved, and their relationship to the state. She also examines recent efforts to legally recognize informal justice institutions—and the challenges associated with those efforts.

The volume concludes with a chapter by Helmke and Levitsky that reflects on how lessons from this book may be applied beyond Latin America and charts out areas for future research on informal institutions and democracy in the developing world. An afterword by Guillermo O'Donnell offers some critical reflections on—and several new insights into—the themes raised in this book.

PART I

The Informal Politics of Executive-Legislative Relations

CHAPTER ONE

Accommodating Informal Institutions and Chilean Democracy

PETER SIAVELIS

Chile's formal political institutions are regularly categorized as among the least conducive to effective democracy in Latin America. The country has an exaggerated presidential system, a weak legislature, a majoritarian electoral system, a partially appointed senate, and high quorums for constitutional reform. In addition, despite the efforts of military reformers, Chile remains a multiparty system. The comparative theoretical literature suggests that this undesirable institutional combination should create disincentives for cooperation, coalition formation, and political accommodation. Presidents should have trouble legislating, particularly given Chile's multiparty system, and we should expect presidents to strong-arm or step outside the legislature to advance their agendas. Theory also suggests that such an institutional framework should ultimately lead, at best, to some type of delegative democracy, and at worst to deadlock and possible democratic breakdown (Mainwaring 1993; Linz 1994; O'Donnell 1994; A. Valenzuela 1994; Jones 1995; Mainwaring and Shugart 1997).

Nonetheless, Chile's democratic transition is recognized by scholars as among the most successful in Latin America, and in regional perspective the country has one of the best records of democratic governability. Following Chile's return to democracy in 1990, a stable pattern of two-coalition competition quickly emerged between an alliance of the center-left (the Concertación) and an alliance of the right (the Alianza por Chile). The Concertación alliance, which has governed since the return of democracy, initially was cobbled together from more than a dozen parties and has been the most stable coalition in the country's history. Presidents have successfully legislated despite lacking majorities in congress and have not wielded the wide-ranging powers granted them by the constitution. Rather, they have worked with congress and the opposition to constructively negotiate their legislative programs (Siavelis 2002b). Instead of the deadlock and difficulty scholars would predict, Chile embodies the best of representative democracy and consensus politics in Latin America. Formal institutional analysis sheds little light on the reasons for this success, making for quite a puzzle in explaining Chile's democratic success from this perspective.

Part of the solution to the puzzle lies in understanding informal institutions. A complex network of informal institutions helped attenuate the problems that might otherwise have developed as a result of Chile's awkward institutional arrangements, and also helped moderate the actions of presidents who have the formal powers to be quite authoritarian. In particular, Chile's democratic performance has been enhanced by what Helmke and Levitsky (in their introduction to this volume) call *accommodating informal institutions*. Elites had strong incentives to create accommodating informal institutions to allow them to achieve goals within an institutional framework that creates an uncomfortable fit and militates against many of their fundamental interests.

In theoretical terms, evidence from Chile supports Helmke and Levitsky's contention that accommodating informal institutions are most likely to emerge where strong effective formal institutions exist. However, it also underscores additional conditions that facilitate the emergence of accommodating informal institutions. Informal institutions are most likely to be found where political actors face difficulty operating within formal institutions, or where there is a lack of congruence between political reality and formal institutional arrangements. Informal institutions are more likely where all actors gain equally from their creation, where there are shared expectations about potentially negative and positive outcomes, and where the shadow of the future makes their maintenance worthwhile for the long term. Finally, the notion of "informality" has a long trajectory in the literature on Latin American politics and is most often expressed in terms of the negative consequences of nepotism, patron-client relations, corporatism, and patrimonialism (e.g., Hagopian 1993; Hillman 1994; Wiarda and Kline 1996). Less critical and normative treatments of the importance of informal institutions are not as prevalent. This dim view of informal institutions finds its roots in a general tendency to view politics in the developing world as somehow dysfunctional if it does not conform to the norms of political processes in developed countries. Evidence from Chile shows the very positive role that informal institutions can play.

THE PUZZLE: SUCCESSFUL DEMOCRACY WITH
AN AWKWARD INSTITUTIONAL FRAMEWORK

Chile returned to democracy in 1990 with a weak congress and an extremely strong executive. Presidents, who are universally recognized as "colegislators," have wide latitude to control the legislative process, broad emergency powers, a monopoly on the presentation of legislation on social policy or expenditures, and effective decree power in budgetary affairs (Siavelis 2000, 11–31). The comparative literature suggests that this constellation of executive powers is problematic in terms of democratic governability and may provide disincentives for interbranch cooperation (Shugart and Carey 1992). This is the case because very powerful executives are tempted either to abuse their privileges and simply compel congress to cooperate when they lack majorities, or to ignore congress and impose their own agendas when they can rely on majorities (Cox and Morgenstern 2002b). In short, Chilean presidents have all the formal tools to dominate politics in the same fashion so often seen among Latin American presidents.

The electoral and party systems also complicate the workability of presidentialism in Chile. At the core of the military's project of social transformation was an attempt to reduce the number of political parties through electoral engineering and the adoption of a majoritarian, two-member district parliamentary electoral system (known as the *binomial* system). Carey and Siavelis (this volume) describe and analyze the system in detail. For the interests of this chapter, it is crucial to highlight the system's majoritarian characteristics, which, in theory, should have tempered the historically fractionalized party system. However, rather than reducing the number of parties, the electoral system has encouraged the development of an extensive array of accommodating informal institutions, like those described by Carey and Siavelis, to underwrite the continued existence of a multiparty system in the face of the electoral system's powerful integrative tendencies. Therefore, Chile continues to be a multiparty system composed of four or five major parties and a number of minor parties (Siavelis 1997a; J. Valenzuela and Scully 1997). This "difficult combination" of exaggerated presidentialism and multipartism has been repeatedly analyzed as a recipe for deadlock, executive-legislative conflict, and decree-prone presidents (Shugart and Carey 1992; Mainwaring 1993).

This institutional constellation created a central dilemma for Chilean political elites who were committed to making democracy work after the transition. They faced a complex game in which the future of democracy depended on the ability to legislate and govern, the ability to govern relied on coalition maintenance, and coalition maintenance was contingent upon the capacity of political elites to construct mechanisms for the widespread and fair representation of parties in government and policymaking. The formal institutional structure militates against all of these goals. In addition, the very high constitutional thresholds for changing the system eliminated reform as an option for elites to make the institutional structure better fit their needs. How did Chilean elites solve this dilemma? In essence, this chapter argues that informal institutions made this "difficult combination" much less difficult.

THE PUZZLE'S MISSING PIECES: INFORMAL INSTITUTIONS

In their introduction, Helmke and Levitsky define informal institutions as "*socially shared rules, usually unwritten, that are created, communicated, and enforced outside officially sanctioned channels.*" They identify four types of informal institutions: complementary, competing, accommodating and substitutive. The four types are differentiated along two dimensions, ordering informal institutions on the basis of whether the outcomes produced by following informal rules converge with or diverge from those produced by adhering to the formal rules, and whether formal institutions are effective or ineffective. In Chile, accommodating informal institutions have been the most prevalent and important, primarily because the country's formal institutions have historically been strong and effective. Because the current institutional framework was imposed by the military, the goals of democratic actors are clearly at odds with the outcomes the military intended to produce through its constitutional engineering. If democratic elites had strictly adhered to formal rules, the outcomes would have been much less desirable from their perspective. Thus, elites had incentives to build accommodating informal institutions to allow them to achieve their goals in an awkward and inflexible formal institutional context, generating outcomes that diverged substantially from those one would expect the formal institutional framework to produce.

This chapter argues that Chile's governing Concertación coalition built several sets of accommodating informal institutions that reinforced each other and allowed the coalition to effectively solve the problems associated with Chile's extreme presidentialism. I focus on three of these informal institutions: the *cuoteo* (a formula to allot government positions and parliamentary candidacies), the *partido transversal* (a supra-party core of elites within the governing Concertación), and a pattern of informal settlements known as *democracia de los acuerdos* (democracy by informal agreement).[1] These institutions, in turn, have facilitated the functioning of other formal and informal institutions, underwritten the stability of Chile's coalitional configuration, mitigated the most negative characteristics of exaggerated presidentialism, and contributed to the success of Chilean democracy.

The chapter analyzes each of these informal institutions, identifying the actors, incentives, and sanctions involved in their formulation and maintenance, and underscoring how they successfully underwrote the pattern of coalition formation that has been crucial to the stability of Chilean democracy. It then presents a discussion of the theoretical insights Chile provides regarding the conditions under which accommodating informal institutions are likely to emerge, and concludes with a tentative discussion of the future of informal institutions in Chile.

INFORMAL INSTITUTIONS AND THE TWIN CHALLENGES OF CHILEAN PRESIDENTIALISM

While the challenges of maintaining a majority in a parliamentary system can lead to cooperation among many parties, there are far fewer incentives for coalition formation in a multiparty presidential system. Legislating is also much more difficult for presidents in multiparty systems, given the lower likelihood that presidents will be able to rely on working majorities. Indeed, as table 1.1 shows, postauthoritarian Chilean presidents have been able to rely on a majority only in the lower chamber. These realities created two challenges for Chilean presidents: (1) to maintain a minimum governing alliance among the multiple allied parties of the Concertación, and (2) to cull a few votes from the opposition in order to legislate. The stakes of these challenges were even higher in Chile than elsewhere in Latin America, given the delicacy of the democratic transition and the reality that the failure to form and maintain a workable legislative coalition could mean the end of the democratic regime.

A confidential internal memo written by the first General Secretary of Government, Edgardo Boeninger, and circulated among high-level members of the Concertación alliance, explicitly recognized this reality. He wrote, "The fear of a military regression, and the understanding of the risk of such an event occurring, will be directly determined by the level of conflict that exists between political parties" (1989, 1). Political actors across the spectrum recognized the need to avoid conflict by constructing mechanisms of accommodation within the inflexible formal institutions they inherited.[2] To ensure stability and party unity, some integration of diverse parties into the executive branch was necessary. However, the very nature of presidentialism (exacerbated by the concentration of power in Chile's exaggeratedly strong presidency) made this type of integration difficult. Informal institutions pro-

TABLE 1.1
Chamber of Deputies and Senate Elections, Chile, 1989–2001

Party	1989 No. of seats	1989 % seats	1993 No. of seats	1993 % seats	1997 No. of seats	1997 % seats	2001 No. of seats	2001 % seats
CHAMBER OF DEPUTIES								
PDC	38	31.7	37	30.8	38	31.7	23	19.2
PPD	16	13.3	15	12.5	16	13.3	20	16.7
PS	—	—	15	12.5	11	9.2	10	8.3
PRSD	5	4.2	2	1.7	4	3.3	6	5.0
Others	10	8.3	1	0.8	0	0.0	3	2.5
Concertación total	69	57.5	70	58.3	69	57.5	62	51.7
RN	29	24.2	29	24.2	23	19.2	18	15.0
UDI	11	9.2	15	12.5	17	14.2	31	25.8
Others	8	6.7	6	5.0	6	5.0	8	6.7
Alianza total	48	40.0	50	1.7	46	38.3	57	47.5
Others	3	2.5	—	—	5	4.2	1	0.8
Total	120	100	120	100	120	100	120	100
SENATE[a]								
PDC	13	27.7	14	29.8	14	29.2	12	24.5
PPD	1	2.1	2	4.2	4	8.3	3	6.1
PS	—	—	4	8.5	2	4.2	5	10.2
PRSD	3	6.4	1	2.1	—	—	—	—
Others	5	10.6	—	—	—	—	—	—
Appointed[b]	—	—	—	—	—	—	4	8.2
Concertación total	22	46.8	21	44.7	20	41.7	24	49.0
RN	13	27.7	11	23.4	7	14.6	7	14.3
UDI	2	4.2	3	6.4	5	10.4	9	18.4
Others	1	2.1	3	6.4	6	12.5	2	4.1
Appointed[b]	9	19.1	9	19.1	10	20.8	7	14.3
Alianza total	25	53.2	26	55.3	28	58.3	25	51
Others	—	—	—	—	—	—	—	—
Total	47	100	47	100	48	100	49	100

Source: Author's calculations with data from www.elecciones.gov.cl.

Notes: PDC, Christian Democratic Party (Partido Demócrata Cristiano); PPD, Party for Democracy (Partido Por La Democracia); PRSD, Radical Social Democratic Party (Partido Radical Socialdemócrata); PS, Socialist Party (Partido Socialista); RN, National Renewal (Renovación Nacional); UDI, Independent Democratic Union (Unión Demócrata Independiente).

[a] All elective senate seats were filled in the 1989 elections. However, only one-half of the senate is elected every four years. For 1993, 1997, and 2001, data reflect final membership of the senate.

[b] While appointed senators have no obligation to support the right, they are listed with this sector until 2001 because they were appointed from the ranks of the military or institutions influenced by it. Voting records show they sided with the right, providing effective veto power on especially controversial legislation. Beginning in 2001, some of the designated senators were appointed from the ranks of the governing parties and are listed with them. Two former presidents with constitutionally mandated "life seats," are counted along with their respective ideological sectors (Concertación President Eduardo Frei and former General Augusto Pinochet—though he does not actively serve in the senate).

vided presidents with the tools to solve these twin problems. What is more, each of the institutions built upon and relied upon the others. For example, *democracia de los acuerdos* would have been impossible without the *partido transversal*, which would in turn have been impossible without the *cuoteo*.

One might contend that there is a functionalist tone to the arguments set out here, which would suggest that informal institutions simply "emerged" because they were "necessary." Coalition maintenance was, obviously, a collective good. However, the individual good of parties, it would seem, should at times trump this collective good, creating incentives for parties to go it alone as collective-action problems emerge. Nonetheless, this type of stark, rational choice analysis of the problem overlooks the complexity of the multilayered game of postauthoritarian Chilean politics, which provided sufficient incentives for actors to purposefully and simultaneously act to resolve multiple collective-action problems. Informal institutions did not "emerge" in a functional manner; they were built by political elites with the goals of coalition maintenance and effective government in mind.

First, regime maintenance was a systemic collective good with very costly collective *and* individual sanctions. Going it alone and noncooperation were an extraordinarily high-risk strategy, given that players very clearly knew the consequences of interparty wrangling, coalition dissolution, and the governing incoherence and instability they would produce. Regime crisis would mean the end of the democratic game for everyone. Though in hindsight this may seem absurd, at the time it was a very real possibility. The military was put on a state of alert at several key moments in the transition, and on very high alert as late as 1993.

Second, one could contend that elites faced a similar threat of regime dissolution in all of Latin America's third-wave transitions, yet failed to resolve collective-action problems as successfully as in Chile. However, echoing Helmke and Levitsky's contention about the importance of effective formal institutions in facilitating the functioning of informal ones, Chile's strong formal institutions provided a more fertile ground for the growth of informal institutions than did those that existed in other countries. Also, the unusual (in Latin American terms) structural characteristics of Chilean groups and social organizations further facilitated the building of accommodating informal institutions. Weyland shows that, in general, Chilean parties, unions, business associations, and other "encompassing organizations" are significantly more cohesive than those in neighboring countries, giving them more capacity to punish free riders and effectively solve collective-action problems (1997, 39).

Third, postauthoritarian cooperation was an iterated game in which repeated interactions among elites built trust and underscored the benefits of coalition maintenance. Parties received individual benefits from participation in the collective game, and these benefits underwrote continued participation. The tremendous success of Concertación governments further contributed to this self-reinforcing dynamic.

Finally, the postauthoritarian Chilean political system was not a zero-sum game, in which gains for parties represented proportional losses for the coalition. Large and small parties had different goals, which amounted to a win-win situation that enhanced the incentives for coalition formation and maintenance and, hence, for the purposeful creation of informal institutions to achieve these goals. Large parties needed small parties on board to maintain a semblance of unity and ensure unified presidential candidacies, and small parties simply wanted to participate in the governmental game. In this sense, the informal institutions to which this analysis now turns were successful primarily because they reconciled the collective *and* individual goals of politicians, parties, and the governing coalition.

THE *CUOTEO*

During Chile's first postauthoritarian government, elites made a concrete, though informal, pact to counteract both the negative characteristics of the concentration of presidential power and the exclusionary characteristics of the electoral system: the *cuoteo*. The term roughly translates as "quota," though the English term fails to completely capture the essence of its meaning in Chilean Spanish.[3] It refers to two things: the distribution of executive-appointed positions based on partisan colors, and the quota of parliamentary candidacies allotted to each individual party within the Concertación. Both types of *cuoteo*, which still operate today, are informal institutions that are crucial to the maintenance of the governing coalition, the legislative success of presidents, and, in turn, Chilean democracy.

The significance of the distribution of ministerial portfolios for the performance of governments has been extensively analyzed in the literature on parliamentary democracies (Austen-Smith and Banks 1990; Laver and Shepsle 1990). Less has been written on the significance of portfolio distribution in presidential systems.[4] This is, of course, because generally, parliamentary governments, more often than presidential governments, must rely on coalitions to function.

As an informal rule, the Concertación's presidents have distributed cabinet portfolios among its constituent parties. Vice-ministers have generally been of a different party (and usually of a different ideological sector) than the minister. While there is no formal agreement for such an arrangement, the informal institution of widespread party input into ministerial decision-making has provided an incentive for coalition maintenance. What is more, throughout the ministries, and particularly in the "political" ministries,[5] each postauthoritarian administration has sought to provide representation for the complete constellation of the Concertación's parties in upper-level staffs.

Presidents have had to maintain a balance of party forces in determining the appointment not only of ministers and vice-ministers. Different party factions within the coalition's parties also appeal to the president to place a range of officials from each of the factions in positions of power throughout the executive branch and in other areas where presidents make appointments (*El Mercurio* 2000; *La Tercera* 2000). This form of portfolio distribution has reinforced trust, by ensuring widespread party input into governmental decision-making and equalized access to information. The dispersion of cabinet authority throughout the ministries also prevents the verticalization of particular ministries into patronage-dispensing institutions for a single party. Patronage and influence have been dispersed throughout the coalition, spreading the spoils of electoral success and transforming the presidential system into much more of a positive-sum game (Rehren 1992, 7).

The *cuoteo* in the distribution of executive-appointed positions is very clearly an informal institution. Agreements are not written down, though it is unmistakably understood by the actors involved that a fair distribution of positions will be devised by the president and his representatives through negotiations. The players involved in this informal institution are high-level party leaders in the inner core of the Concertación (and members of the *partido transversal*, discussed below). Presidents who fail to provide a "fair" distribution of seats will face sanctions for violating the *cuoteo*. Parties react vociferously to any perceived violation in the balance of party forces, often threatening to withdraw from the coalition. Debates in the national media and between parties also point to sanctions for violating the *cuoteo*. For example, the press and the public at times refer derisively to the politics of the *cuoteo*, with partisan colors purportedly mattering more than the talent and experience of ministerial candidates. Ironically, however, when the rules of the *cuoteo* are broken, the press and elites cast aspersions on the honor of violators. When President Eduardo Frei was perceived to have violated the informal *cuoteo* with the appointment of Christian Democrat Carlos Figueroa to replace Socialist Interior Minister Germán Correa in 1994, he was accused of creating a *círculo de hierro* (an iron circle) in the cabinet that was at odds with the multiparty tradition of the alliance. Threats of coalition disintegration followed, suggesting that despite its negative image, party leaders and even the public recognize the *cuoteo* as a necessary evil.[6]

Elites adopted a similar *cuoteo* in the electoral arena in response to the inflexibility of the electoral system. The deeper reasons for the electoral *cuoteo* are similar to those set out for the *cuoteo* in the executive branch—the abiding necessity to provide widespread representation of all political parties within a formal institutional system that discourages it. Chile's political parties faced a dilemma at the onset of democracy. Four or five major and many small parties existed, yet the majoritarian electoral system ensured, given district magnitudes of two, that the highest number of parties that could achieve representation in each district was two (and in practice one, given that the Alianza was expected to garner a seat in each district). Thus, leaders recognized that just as the concentration of power within the executive could divide the governing coalition, so too could perceived unfair representation in parliament, because important party players in the coalition would be shut out. Carey and Siavelis (this volume) analyze the elaborate postelectoral reward system that provided coalitional glue, showing a sophisticated network of accommodating informal institutions. However, they do not analyze the very root of that coalitional dilemma—the exclusionary characteristics of the election system and the rational fear that without widespread representation of all parties, the governing coalition and, in turn, democracy would be threatened.

Chile's preauthoritarian, multimember district proportional representation system did not force parties to form multiparty electoral slates. Smaller parties could simply field a list of candidates, and the proportionality of the system permitted a wider array of party representation. However, Chile's current, posttransition binomial electoral system is at odds with the country's strong tradition of multipartism, since smaller parties are far less likely to be represented. To respond to this inflexibility, the various parties and coalition players agreed on a *cuoteo* to provide a wider range of party representation.

Each of Chile's major parties has formalized rules for candidate selection. In addition, each party belongs to a "subpact" that unifies parties with common ideological orientations. Each coalition contains two subpacts (the center and left in the Concertación, and the center-right and hard right in the Alianza), and each subpact also acts as a negotiating unit. Given the exigencies of negotiation among so many actors, and the give-and-take inherent in cobbling together two member lists from multiparty coalitions, informal processes take over where formalized processes fail. These informal rules respond to the well-understood incentives created by the electoral system. Though formal institutions govern some of the rules of candidate placement, ultimately it is informal agreements between the highest-level party officials that determine which candidate will run where and with which party partner (i.e., which other candidate from the same coalition on the ballot in the district). Once again, the informal party *cuoteo* within and between parties and subpacts trumps formalized candidate selection procedures.

The *cuoteo* as an informal institution of the Concertación goes further than just the simple splitting of candidacies. There is a consistent set of informal rules and norms that govern candidate placement and respond to the constraints of the formal electoral system. It would seem quite easy to simply divide candidacies between the Concertación's two subpacts, which have been relatively equal in levels of support since the return of democracy. Indeed, the informal *cuoteo* begins with the assumption that candidacies are shared equally between the subpacts of the left and the center, and negotiation and tinkering proceeds from this assumption of parity.

However, the shared understandings of this informal institution do not end there. Minor parties are crucial for coalitions to rally enough support to pass thresholds nationally and to ensure the ability to maintain single coalitional presidential candidacies. But small parties cannot win by running alone. Further, as Carey and Siavelis note (this volume), it is crucial for candidates not only to be placed on lists, but to be placed on lists with a partner they can potentially beat. With district magnitudes of two, a minor-party candidate paired with a coalition colleague from a major party stands to lose, as each coalition is likely to win only one of the two seats in the district. Small parties want not just candidacies, but seats they can win. In fact, summing up the logic that prevails for small parties paired with larger ones, one small-party negotiator who was locked in a struggle with a larger-party partner replied to a very generous offer of candidate slates (in all of which the smaller party was likely to lose!), "Don't give me slates, I am asking for seats."[7] Therefore, the *cuoteo* also provides that small-party candidates be paired with other small-party candidates, or weak major-party candidates, to allow for some victories for minor parties (and probably an overall lower district vote total than two major-party candidates would garner). This is a counterintuitive logic from the perspective of coalition victory. It means that the candidate capable of garnering the highest number of votes in a district may be replaced by a weaker candidate in the interests of coalition unity.[8]

How do major parties distribute this cost of ensuring unity? After beginning with an assumption of evenly dividing candidacies between subpacts, parties understand that the share of the seats they must cede to smaller-party partners depends on how well they have performed in previous elections and where they stand according to public opinion data. If a major party has a drop in support, it is understood that this party will be the one within its subpact to cede seats to smaller partners, assuming the costs of including small parties in the coalition.

These dynamics are well understood by adherents to the informal institution and, in turn, lead to the type of enforcement mechanisms that are typically employed. The main enforcement mechanism is withdrawal or threatened withdrawal from the coalition or, for small parties, switching subpacts. Throughout the 1990s the Union of the Center-Center (UCC) flirted with both coalitions in an attempt to extract seats and, indeed, in 2001 the Radical Social Democratic Party (PRSD) switched from the center-left subpact to the left subpact in order to cut a better deal. Debates play out both in closed meetings and in the press, where parties contend that they will definitively cede no more seats, or that if they are pressured to surrender additional seats it will mean the end of the coalition.[9] Still, each of the players needs the other, and the consequences of failure to reach an agreement are high and well understood by negotiators.

Enforcement is also more complex, however, because it takes place on more than one electoral level. It is not a simple question of wrangling over the quota of candidacies for each subpact and party. Short of coalition dissolution, parties also threaten sanctions regarding the placement of candidates, withdrawing previous concessions if they lose a particular candidacy to a competitor. They also engage in horse-trading that involves multiple and multilevel sanctions. Indeed, leaders sanction doubters in their own parties who question whether the leadership has reached optimal seat-share agreements. In the final hours of negotiation before the 1993 elections, one party leader slammed his fist on the table and threatened the resignation of the entire party executive council if party loyalists failed to approve the pact that he admitted was "not the best," and indeed might be "bad," but was better than "committing suicide" (*La Segunda* 1993). The use of the word *suicide* is common in the lead-up to every election, as parties play chicken to see who will give in first. Indeed, one analyst sums up both the difficulty of negotiations and the stakes for parties in not reaching an agreement, arguing that the binomial system is a "time bomb treacherously placed under negotiating tables of the two alliances every four years" (Otano 2001). The statement also suggests the centrality of informal institutions in defusing this bomb.

Thus, in response to the inflexibility and lack of representativeness of the formal electoral system, elites adopted commonly understood and enforceable informal rules for the distribution of seats among the Concertación's parties. The enforcement mechanisms are internal and external. Internally, the "election insurance" solution (Carey and Siavelis, this volume) provides rewards for risk takers, while the externally generated threat of coalition dissolution provides incentives to reach agreements. By losing coalition membership, individual parties surrender both their ability to compete successfully in elections and their access to executive branch appointments.

The formal electoral system provides a concrete logic related to the relative party strength and the placement of candidates that is well understood, and to which parties have adapted through the use of informal rules of candidate placement.

These rules have, in turn, shaped and affected the nature of the elaborate informal strategies designed to simultaneously balance the goals of promoting party interests, ensuring coalition survival, and winning political office. Rather than simply merging as the military expected, political parties have used candidate selection processes as just one of many sets of informal institutions constructed to ensure their survival. Elites devised informal institutions to deal with the complexity of successfully reconciling the goals of candidates, individual parties, and the coalition.

THE *PARTIDO TRANSVERSAL*

The *partido transversal* is another informal institution that has been critical to governing and the success of the Concertación coalition. The term *partido transversal* refers to a shifting but consistent informal group of leaders, with crucial roles in the first democratic governments, who define themselves more as "leaders of the Concertación" than as leaders of their respective parties. Members of the *partido transversal* are centered around presidents and hold key jobs in the most important so-called political ministries. Though there is no formal organization or formalized meeting of the *partido*, the actors themselves know who they are, and they structure informal relationships among themselves, between their parties and the coalition, and, as discussed later, with social actors whose input is crucial to *democracia de los acuerdos*. Ignacio Walker, who served in the Ministry of the General Presidency (SEGPRES) under the first postauthoritarian president, Patricio Aylwin, notes that the *partido's* members "correspond to informal networks that have . . . exercised a strong influence under the three administrations of the Concertación, both in terms of strategic design and the set of public policies that have been pursued" (2003, 5).

The *partido transversal* traces its origins to a troika of leaders who were Aylwin's most important advisors: Edgardo Boeninger (Christian Democratic Party [PDC]–SEGPRES), Enrique Correa (Socialist Party [PS]–Secretaria General de Gobierno [SEGGOB]), and Enrique Krauss (PDC–Interior). The *partido* was originally centered in SEGPRES, an office Aylwin charged with structuring relationships between the executive branch and congress, among the various ministries, and between the government and social groups. As Boeninger's earlier-cited memo (1989) suggests, coordination among parties was recognized as crucial to the coalition's success and, in turn, the maintenance of democracy. Initial conversations structured within SEGPRES evolved into more consistent communications outside SEGPRES, among what Walker has termed a number of "complicit" like-minded leaders from several parties engaged in a series of ongoing "conversations."[10] The informal membership of the *partido transversal* quickly extended throughout the ministries (Fuentes 1999, 204). The success of the initial *partido transversal* translated into the maintenance of a "supra-party" core that consistently looked out for the interests of the coalition during the first three Concertación governments. Thus, though SEGPRES may have been its incubator, the *partido* as an informal institution took on a life of its own.

What is more, the key actors in the *partido transversal* provided the communication networks that allowed SEGPRES to structure relations between political parties and powerful social and political actors. The formal consultative mechanisms of SEGPRES and informal mechanisms of the *partido transversal* interact to ensure that legislation receives widespread input from the constituent parties of the Concertación in both branches of government, making it more likely to pass. Formal meetings between the representatives of the executive branch—many of them members of the *partido*—and legislators have been the norm. Legislators of governing parties meet with ministers, subsecretaries, and high-level officials within the ministries working in the same substantive area to discuss what type of legislation is necessary and should be incorporated into the executives' program.[11] This consultation continues throughout the legislative process and informally through the channels of the *partido transversal*.

The *partido transversal* thus facilitates cross-party communication among actors in different branches of government and distinct ministries. However, it plays an equally important role in building consensus among parties in the Concertación. Walker notes how informal agreements are struck among members of the *partido*, who share a "common view in terms of public policies and at the same time are rooted in their own parties."[12] In this sense, the *partido* is not a one-way street where the voices of constituent parties are heard on the level of the coalition. The members of the *partido* influence the policies of their own traditional parties, effectively serving as advocates and "salespeople" for the coalition, further facilitating coalition unity (Walker 2003). Not only do they do the selling, but as preferred interlocutors of the president they have the capacity to discipline their parties, because of their power and influence and because of their access to the decision-making structures that determine appointments in the executive branch. Still, the *partido transversal* is not just a new "super party." Indeed, members continue to serve as party agents and must demonstrate party loyalty to ensure their viability as party representatives. Individual party organizations remain the central organizational unit of Chilean politics, and the *partido* has not engaged in activities that are within the traditional domain of parties, such as cultivating clientelistic networks or nominating its own candidates for office (Walker 2003, 5).

Finally, the *partido transversal* allows the disparate parties of the Concertación to negotiate as a unit (rather than as a squabbling multiparty committee) with other social actors to ensure the passage of legislation and facilitating *democracia de los acuerdos*.[13]

The roots and the incentives surrounding the operation of the *partido transversal* as an informal institution are similar to those of the *cuoteo*. The clear recognition of the threat of an authoritarian regression, combined with the reality that regime maintenance was a shared goal of the coalition and individual parties, provided sufficient incentive to solve what potentially could have been numerous collective-action problems. However, while the threat of a military incursion may have provided the impetus for the creation of the *partido transversal*, the continued benefits it provides to both parties and the coalition are the incentives for its maintenance. Parties benefit from an influential voice in government and legislation, while the coalition and the president are better able to pass legislation. Parties gain effective agents to manage their relationship with the coalition, while the coalition can rely on members to sell the coalition's product to a sometimes skeptical clientele.

These relationships shed light on the incentive structures that gave birth to and maintain the *partido transversal* as a crucial accommodating informal institution. For the core of the *partido*, rewards and appointments grow out of service to the coalition, not to the party. While the president is certainly a member of a party, since the return of democracy the president's primary job has been to maintain the coalition to achieve other goals. Therefore, presidents reward service to the coalition, making members of the *partido transversal* especially valued and more likely to enjoy the beneficence of presidents in the distribution of ministerial seats within the *cuoteo*.

Chile's awkward formal democratic institutions also combined to provide incentives for the creation and maintenance of the *partido transversal* and condition some of the external sanctions for its violation. Former Aylwin spokesman Enrique Correa noted that "as long as there is multipartism and presidentialism, the norm will have to be supra-partism."[14] He suggests that members of the *partido* recognize the damaging consequences of the model of coparty government, in which different parties negotiate with each other to maximize their own individual utility and are less likely to solve collective-action problems. This was the model of Chilean coalition government in the past, and particularly during the chaotic years of Salvador Allende's Popular Unity government. The point of departure for members of the *partido transversal* is a desire to control the damaging consequences of the emergence of coparty government.

DEMOCRACIA DE LOS ACUERDOS

Multiparty presidentialism creates many negative incentives for coalition formation and for building legislative majorities. Legislation was even more complicated for postauthoritarian presidents in Chile, given the initial intransigence of conservative social forces that reacted negatively to the Concertación's electoral success. With the return of democracy, powerful conservative social groups expressed concern that a Concertación government would upset the positive record of Chilean economic performance and threaten private property (Boylan 1996; Weyland 1997). One of the right's common campaign themes throughout the early years of the transition was that a Concertación victory would amount to a return to the "bad old days" of Salvador Allende. Thus, in addition to legislating and making good on their promises of redressing inequality, presidents sought to put to rest the idea that the right, and the powerful groups backing it, should have something to fear from Concertación governments.

To overcome this threat to legislative success, presidents, backed by the *partido transversal*, consistently engaged in a pattern of informal negotiations that have come to be known as *democracia de los acuerdos*. The model of *democracia de los acuerdos* allowed presidents to advance their legislative agendas while consistently assuaging the fears of a potentially reactionary right. These negotiations have consistently been carried out with the congressional opposition and with powerful social groups outside congress.

Examples of the pattern of informal negotiations and the reaching of *acuerdos* abound. The tax reform of 1990 is perhaps the most cited, but it is simply one example of what was a regularized and normalized pattern of informal pact-making. Key members of the executive branch (including members of the *partido transversal*) sought links with the business community and producer groups in order to neutralize any potential opposition to the tax reform, which passed with very limited congressional input. Boylan shows how the tax reform itself was designed to assuage "powerful business interests in an environment of uncertainty." However, more importantly in terms of the argument advanced here, she shows that the "reform was characterized by a series of extra-parliamentary negotiations in which the government clinched the support of the chief opposition party, thus defusing any potential opposition to the reform and ensuring its rapid passage" (1996, 15, 23). Indeed, President Aylwin's behavior led many to contend that he had "gone over the heads" of his own congressional contingent to precook a deal that powerful interest groups and thus rightist members of congress would support (Siavelis 2000, 57). Officials in the executive branch also have met and consistently negotiated with members of the opposition in relation to legislation on tax reform, labor standards, and the minimum wage.

That said, contrary to what one would expect given the extent of presidential powers in Chile, all three postauthoritarian presidents have been circumspect in the use of *democracia de los acuerdos*. This is intriguing in an age when delegative democracy is the norm in countries with formally far weaker presidencies than Chile's. As noted, Chilean presidents have almost complete control over the budgetary process. The president presents the national budget every year, and if congress fails to approve it, the president's budget enters into force (Constitution of the Republic of Chile, art. 64). However, scholars of budgetary politics have noted that although deputies are barred from formal consultation on the budget, in reality members have a good deal of informal input in its formulation stage (Baldez and Carey 1996, 18). Their influence continues during negotiations in legislative conference committees of the two houses and in negotiations outside formal congressional institutions. Presidents routinely consult with legislators of their own parties and members of the coalition to reinforce coalition unity and ensure that the budget is acceptable to coalition partners.

More importantly, informal negotiation has also been central to securing the votes of the *opposition* to pass budgets, even though presidents do not necessarily need these votes. During negotiations on most budgets, the Concertación's various ministers of finance have met and negotiated with opposition leaders. Formally, presidents have the capacity to simply implement their budget, but it makes little sense to do so given the consequences this would have for the long-term capacity of presidents to legislate. Because budget negotiations are only one piece of presidents' legislative agendas, in order to continue to be able to legislate they must avoid completely alienating the opposition (Siavelis 2002a). Hence, despite their impressive formal budgetary powers, presidents consistently choose informal avenues of negotiation and consultation to come to budget agreements that are acceptable both to members of the presidents' coalition and to the opposition. This is a stark departure from the familiar model of "delegative democracy" and the image of Latin American legislatures as compliant rubber stamps.

Chile's three postauthoritarian executives also have engaged in a series of regular, yet informal, consultations with the business community, producer groups, and members of the conservative media.[15] Silva is correct in noting that capitalists were granted privileged access to the executive branch in order to stem the fears of business elites that the neoliberal model would be abandoned; he goes as far as to characterize this influence as "institutional veto power" (1992, 103). He notes that business elites lobbied directly with the executive branch on crucial legislation that affected business, and that Chile's main business lobby, the CPC (Confederación de Producción y Comercio), was particularly influential in derailing initiatives that were perceived to be antibusiness. While Silva characterizes this relationship as one that sacrificed potentially progressive economic reform in exchange for political democratization, these relationships also granted executives the power to persuade conservative forces in congress that business interests had been taken into account in elaborating budgets and controversial economic legislation.

Democracia de los acuerdos, then, helped stave off potentially destabilizing conflicts both within the coalition and between the coalition and the opposition. By ensuring that the fundamental interests of allied parties, the opposition, and key social groups were not threatened, Concertación presidents have succeeded in governing and in passing legislation in what is, in formal institutional terms, a very infertile environment for consensus politics.

While one could contend that this pattern of conflict resolution is simply a creative legislative strategy for presidents, the roots of *democracia de los acuerdos* as an informal institution run deeper. First, there is a shared understanding among the legislative right, powerful social groups, and Concertación governments on the rules of the game. Concertación governments have informally acknowledged that social groups have veto power over important legislation, and the government has responded with informal strategies to preempt potentially destabilizing opposition. Now, important social groups expect to be informally consulted on controversial legislation, resulting in an informal rule that for such legislation, reaching a prelegislative *acuerdo* is an integral part of the Chilean informal political game, with consequences for violation.

Second, the rules of the game and the sanctions are clear. Entrepreneurs, the conservative media, and active and retired members of the armed forces have pressured the parties of the right on controversial legislation, and these powerful social groups have important influence on the right's parliamentary contingent. The transitional political system was a high-stakes game, in which presidential failure has serious consequences. If presidents wanted to legislate, they would have to marshal the support of at least some of the right, and failure to do so would have serious consequences for presidents' legislative agendas and, ultimately, for democracy. At several stages in the democratic transition, rightist parties and interest groups made clear that they feared the entire Pinochet economic model was in danger and that this was unacceptable to them (Boylan 1996). By systematically engaging in a game of *democracia de los acuerdos*, presidents assured business elites and the parties of the right that their fundamental interests were taken into account.

Finally, *democracia de los acuerdos* has become a concrete, well-recognized, and repeated strategy. Not only is it a phenomenon that has been named, but a similar dynamic of negotiation and accommodation has been repeated for numerous pieces of legislation related to tax policy, the budget, human rights, and the labor code, among many others (Fuentes 1999, 205).

The potentially positive role of informal institutions is a guiding precept of this chapter. However, the elitist and often extra-institutional and antidemocratic nature of *democracia de los acuerdos* is certainly a problem for the longer-term consolidation of democracy. Nonetheless, in terms of defense of democracy in the first fragile years after the dictatorship, the informal institution of *democracia de los acuerdos* was central to the governability of Chile and to the democratic transition.

EXPLAINING INFORMAL INSTITUTIONS: WHY AND HOW DO THEY EMERGE?

Informal institutions, then, explain a good deal of the success of Chilean elites in solving the problems of exaggerated presidentialism in a multiparty system. Contrary to what one would expect, elites formed coalitions, presidents legislated, and the scope of presidential power was circumscribed. Still, this fails to answer the deeper question of why and how Chilean elites built informal institutions.

What does Chile tell us about the conditions under which accommodating informal institutions are created? Helmke and Levitsky argue in their introduction that these types of informal institutions are more likely to emerge where effective formal institutions already exist. Empirical evidence presented here both confirms this assertion and sheds some additional light on the determinants of the emergence of accommodating informal institutions. These, in turn, suggest several broader theoretical implications.

In many cases the creation of accommodating informal institutions is tied to the inability of political actors to solve problems or effect change within the context of formal institutions. It is certainly costly to create and maintain informal institutions. However, it is often more costly to change existing formal ones. Thus, most informal institutions emerge when the cost of changing formal institutions exceeds the cost of creating informal ones. Within the bounds of these general contexts, there are several reasons why formal institutions can become less than optimal mechanisms for solving problems, and informal ones are created.

The Chilean case shows that elites create accommodating informal institutions where there is a lack of congruence between political reality and formal institutional arrangements—that is to say, where political contexts make it difficult for elites to work within established institutional structures. Actors universally attempt to adopt institutions that serve their own interests: small parties call for proportional representation, while large parties are loath to abandon majoritarian electoral systems. One should expect that elites create rules that allow them to achieve their goals (whether electoral or policy-related). In theory, if elites design institutions, these institutions should be perfectly responsive to their needs, but this is not always the case: as political circumstances change, institutions (which may be difficult to reform) may reflect earlier elite preferences. In addition, rules and institutions can outlive their usefulness.

Accommodating informal institutions may be used both to make up for these disconnects between political institutions and elite preferences and, indeed, to build coalitions to reform formal institutions. Further, where alteration of rules is difficult or unlikely because of inflexible institutional arrangements (rules—including constitutions—that cannot be easily changed), accommodating institutions may add flexibility. Where constitutions and institutions are imposed, elites are forced to tinker informally with institutions to better fit their interests. In essence, through informal tailoring, an ill-fitting suit can be made to better fit an owner for whom it was not made. This reality is particularly important for analyzing institutional change in Latin America. As Chull Shin notes, "anti-democratic provisions in new constitutions . . . protect the privileges of the most affluent and powerful . . . The inability to undertake . . . substantive reforms is one of the most serious problems facing new democracies in the current wave of democratization" (1994, 168).

Mershon (1994) contends that politicians create informal rules to change formal institutions that do not work to their benefit. The cost of a formal change in institutions is extremely high. While the possibility for such change exists, informal and/or piecemeal institutional change may prove less costly. March and Olsen note that institutional change often occurs by way of "incremental adaptation to changing problems," rather than "intentions, plans or consistent decisions" (1989, 94). The costs of pursuing "incremental adaptations" are often likely to be lower in the informal sphere. In this vein, Mershon adds that politicians are "wary of fastening themselves to new institutions that will be difficult to overthrow, and so they experiment with informal rules" (1994, 75). Indeed, because strong formal institutions are also more likely to be difficult to change, we should find additional impetus for informal institutions in these contexts.

Still, these explanations of why informal institutions emerge fail to answer the, perhaps more important, *how* question. A central question for those interested in the potential for informal institutions to play a positive role in enhancing governability across contexts is that of how Chilean elites were able to overcome problems of collective action to formulate accommodating informal institutions, when this endeavor has clearly failed in other contexts. The Chilean case is illuminating and provides important tentative theoretical propositions about how the need for informal institutions translates into their concrete creation.

First, the formation and maintenance of informal institutions in Chile was an elite project. It was the highest-level party leaders, presidents, presidential candidates, and legislators who created the informal institutions and communicated the rules of the game. We know from other chapters in this volume that many informal institutions are society-wide and characterized by diffuse enforcement mechanisms. Nonetheless, evidence from Chile suggests that accommodating informal institutions that temper already strong formal institutions may be more likely to develop and endure when a small number of actors is charged with creating them and communicating their rules and sanctions for violations. Many of the more diffuse informal institutions emerge spontaneously. Accommodating institutions, on the other hand, are more purposefully created to correct for failures in often complex formal institutional frameworks and are less rooted in long-standing, routinized forms of behavior. Elite-created informal institutions may also be successful for other reasons. Weyland (1997) notes how a pattern of elite political learning contributed to the success of the Chilean transition because both the left and the right had learned from painful past experiences during and after the military regime, and understood the consequences of failure in this high-stakes environment.

Second, elites are more likely to create informal institutions when there are shared expectations about potentially negative and positive outcomes. In terms of regime crisis and military intervention, Chilean elites understood clearly that a political crisis produced by partisan wrangling would bring a quick military intervention. Thus, proactive efforts to stem conflict were essential, and the best way to do so was to form coalitions that would decrease uncertainty. Because the formal institutional structure created disincentives for accommodation, elites sought to improve the incentive structure to better underwrite coalition formation and maintenance. We might even go as far as to say that a shared external threat can provide incentives for the creation of accommodating informal institutions as protective mechanisms. As time passed, party elites also understood the consequences of failing to maintain the coalition and, in turn, failing to put together joint electoral lists. There was widespread understanding of the new constraints created by the electoral system, which provided a powerful mechanism of enforcement for maintaining informal institutions. This information was constantly communicated not only by political elites, but also by think tanks and partisan study groups that consistently provided electoral simulations and other evidence to demonstrate the catastrophic electoral consequences of failing to maintain coalitions.

Third, the Chilean case also suggests, however, that simple elite recognition of threat may not be enough to solve collective-action problems related to regime maintenance. Evidence from Chile suggests that informal institution-building by elites may better succeed where social organizations are highly cohesive and better able to sanction free riders. These types of organizations may have a greater capacity to solve collective-action problems in the negotiation of posttransition settlements.

Fourth, informal institutions are more likely to form when all actors stand to benefit more or less equally from their creation, and where there are few veto players. The informal institutions that helped sustain Chilean coalitions benefited presidents, party leaders, and legislators alike. Presidents and presidential candidates benefited from the knowledge that they would not face intracoalitional competition. Large political parties benefited from the knowledge that the addition of small parties would help them cross crucial electoral thresholds. Small parties benefited from the knowledge that they would receive a certain number of electoral slates and some degree of representation in the ministries. The potential for veto players to undermine coalition unity was minimized. Indeed, as the Carey and Siavelis chapter in this volume shows, a reward system even developed for those actors who faced sacrifice on the altar of coalition unity, but who otherwise might have upset the delicate balance of agreements that sustained the coalition.

Finally, evidence from the Chilean case suggests that the "shadow of the future" and iterated interactions can help encourage the formation and maintenance of informal institutions (Axelrod 1984, 174). For example, the subpact of the left knew and expected that it would be awarded a presidential candidacy following the administrations of two Christian Democrat presidents from the center-left subpact. This encouraged the left subpact to continue to respect the rules of the coalition game, with the expectation that it would benefit from continued cooperation. At a lower level, sitting ministers are hesitant to upset the partisan balance within ministries, to ensure that there are places for them in future governments whose presidents might be from other parties in the coalition.

CONCLUSION

Chile inherited an institutional structure that in formal terms is among the least conducive to cooperation, consensus, and the legislative success of presidents, and that seems to be a recipe for delegative democracy and exaggerated majoritarianism.

And yet, surprisingly, Chile is arguably the most successful of the third-wave Latin American democracies. The analysis here has shown that this outcome cannot be explained without reference to a series of accommodating informal institutions that allowed elites to successfully achieve their individual and collective goals within what is an unquestionably awkward and inflexible formal institutional arrangement. Power-sharing in the form of the *cuoteo*, widespread consultation by way of the *partido transversal*, and the adoption of an informal yet regularized pattern of *democracia de los acuerdos* provided Chilean elites with the tools to solve the many collective-action problems created by multiparty presidentialism and to meet the challenge of coalition maintenance in a multiparty presidential system.

There is little doubt that informal institutions will change where shared expectations change, and where the benefits to be gained by informal institutions begin to be distributed unevenly. Indeed, talk of coalition dissolution has increased in Chile. We know from the Carey and Siavelis chapter that Chile's informal reward structure is likely to change should the president not be from the Concertación or should the relative power of parties change radically. Similarly, as the threat of the military recedes we would expect a diminished incentive to adhere to some of the informal rules that govern the operation of informal institutions, because the collective threat that was so important in spawning them will recede. Relations within the Concertación are already more raucous than at any time in the past. It is difficult to say whether this is the result of the age of the coalition or the charges of corruption within it, or is a reflection of the changing fortunes of the country's parties. However, while the military threat may have provided the initial impetus for the creation of informal institutions, a constant threat is not necessary to maintain them. If informal institutions continue to meet the other conditions for the maintenance of informal institutions, as set out here, their pure workability and demonstrated success may induce the increased formalization of the accommodating informal institutions that have been so central to Chile's democratic success.

CHAPTER TWO

How Informal Electoral Institutions Shape the Brazilian Legislative Arena

SCOTT W. DESPOSATO

Informal institutions pervade political systems and far exceed formal institutions in their age, number, and scope. Evolving work has made a compelling case for their impact on the behavior of political actors, complementing formal institutions and shaping equilibria where formal institutions are absent. But how much importance should we ascribe to informal institutions? Do they just "fill in the gaps" where formal institutions are absent? Do they disappear in the presence of strong formal institutions? Or can informal institutions trump formal rules in shaping actors' incentives?

In this chapter, I explore these questions by examining the effects of informal electoral institutions on legislative politics in the case of Brazil. Recent scholarship on that country has emphasized the importance of formal institutions in shaping legislative politics, but mostly ignores the role of informal institutions in politics. Through a comparative analysis of state assemblies, I show how informal electoral institutions have important effects on legislative behavior, countering and even reversing the impact of formal electoral institutions. In particular, I show how the nature of informal electoral institutions—whether clientelistic or programmatic—shapes the nature and structure of legislative behavior across states.

FORMAL AND INFORMAL INSTITUTIONS IN BRAZILIAN POLITICS

Previous work on Brazilian legislative politics focuses on the role that two formal institutions play in shaping the legislative arena: federalism and electoral rules. On the first of these, scholars have argued that the decentralization of resources in Brazil has fragmented national power. In particular, federalism gives state-level actors substantial influence over the behavior of national legislators. Brazilian federalism grants subnational actors control over resources that are valuable for advancing political careers. In particular, state governors control "pork," campaign resources, and even state ministerial jobs, all of which are coveted by national legislators. State parties control nominations for all state and national legislative positions. Consequently, national legislators should be responsive to pressure from state-level actors that control career-enhancing and -advancing resources. The implication is that national political parties are fragmented by state interests, and presidents must compete with these interests to advance a national policy agenda (Mainwaring 1997, 1999; Selcher 1998; Souza 1998; Ames 2001; Samuels 2002; Desposato 2004).

The second institution, open-list proportional representation, is said to promote personalism and weaken political parties. Under electoral rules of this type, citizens cast a single vote, either for an individual candidate or for a party list (in Brazil, most vote for an individual). After election results are tallied, seats are distributed in two steps: first, to parties, in proportion to the share of the votes received by all their candidates; second, within the parties to the top vote-getters. The easiest way to achieve office under these rules is almost always to be one of the best vote-getters in a party, and the easiest way to be at the top in a party is to run a campaign that attacks others within one's own party. Within-party competition for votes should be fierce, and this competition, the argument goes, weakens national parties' cohesiveness (Mainwaring 1991, 1999; Pinheiro 1998; Graeff 2000; Ames 2001).

Informal institutions are largely excluded from the theory and empirical analysis of both federalism and electoral systems. But evidence from other democracies suggests that these formal institutional rules are not nearly a complete explanation for politicians' behavior. For example, both Chile and Finland use similar electoral systems, but neither has been characterized as an "antiparty system," as has Brazil. At least one explanation for the difference could lie in informal institutions; for example, the nature of partisan cleavages. This is not sufficient evidence that informal institutions matter, however. In each case, one might also attribute these differences to differences in formal rules. For example, Brazil has a federal system of government, but Chile's is unitary; Finland uses a parliamentary form of government, but Brazil uses presidentialism. So cross-country differences might be the result of informal institutions or of other institutional features. Because there are many institutional differences across all countries, it is difficult to isolate whether informal institutions help explain cross-country differences.

Ultimately, any cross-country comparison of institutions makes inferences about

the effects of informal institutions difficult. When faced with differences in outcomes across two countries with very similar formal institutions, those skeptical of
the explanatory power of informal institutions may suggest that subtler formal institutional rules may explain the disparities. Two countries may share presidentialism and single-member districts, but their nomination procedures or internal legislative rules may differ substantially. This is why a within-country comparison of
Brazilian states is so useful. The states share nearly identical formal institutional
rules, including the same electoral rules, terms of office, nomination procedures,
basic form of government, and separation of powers. Differing dramatically across
states, however, are the informal electoral institutions. In some states, clientelism is
an important part of electoral politics; in others, it has been replaced by largely
programmatic electoral markets.

The Brazilian state legislatures provide a nearly ideal laboratory for testing the
impact of informal institutions. The states vary greatly in their informal institutions,
but share virtually identical institutional environments, most of which were imposed
by the national constitution. In this project, I chose two Brazilian states that capture
the extreme regional diversity of that country: Piauí and São Paulo. The first, Piauí, is
extremely poor, is less-developed, and has very clientelistic politics. São Paulo is
wealthier, has a more diverse and vibrant economy, and is generally accepted as
having a much smaller private goods component to elections than Piauí. Therefore,
if only formal institutions shape legislative behavior, there should be no differences
in legislative politics across states. But if societal variables—specifically, the presence
or absence of the informal institution of clientelism—matter as well, we should find
obvious differences across states.

This topic is of importance for several reasons. First, it provides a strong test of the
relative effects of informal and formal institutions. Most work on legislative politics
focuses on formal institutions as explanatory variables, including electoral systems,
procedural rules, and constitutions. Implicitly, these studies assume that all electoral
markets are alike or that voters and their characteristics do not matter. Consequently,
legislative institutional rules should have the same effects in any electoral context.
Relaxing and testing these assumptions is an important next step for political science. Do legislatures work the same way regardless of the presence or absence of
informal electoral institutions? If not, we should be explicit and systematic in adjust-
ing institutional theories to fit different realities.

In addition, the chapter tests the idea that informal institutional effects can spill
over into multiple political arenas. Previous work has focused on the impact of
informal institutions in insular settings. For example, political scientists study informal institutions within legislatures, or vote-buying within electoral markets, but

we have not studied their spillover into other and broader political arenas, policy-making, or democratic consolidation. This chapter shows how the effects of informal institutions are not limited to local contexts, but these institutions can also directly affect other political arenas.

ELECTORAL MARKETS AS INFORMAL INSTITUTIONS

I use the term *electoral markets* to define the mechanisms and patterns whereby voters and candidates exchange votes and policy promises. The market is created by formal institutions that endow citizens with votes and election winners with power to direct government. Two idealized extremes of electoral markets are *clientelistic* and *programmatic*. In clientelistic systems, candidates cannot enforce the behavior of "bought" votes. In programmatic systems, voters cannot enforce the provision of policy goods. In each case (and in those in between), informal institutions help make these markets function.

At one extreme, electoral markets may be cleared by the exchange of cash or other private goods for votes—effectively, vote-buying or clientelism. This exchange is enforced by either informal norms or illegal campaign activities. Payments are typically made *before* the election and ballots are usually secret, so candidates cannot enforce exchanges. Citizens may agree to vote for a candidate in exchange for a cash payment, but a candidate cannot enforce delivery of the promised vote. However, informal norms and mechanisms have evolved to overcome the otherwise missing incentives for compliance. Creative candidates have found quasi-enforcement mechanisms. For example, candidates might buy votes with new shoes, delivering one shoe before and the other after the election. In other cases, voters simply have developed norms of moral obligation to vote-buyers. Observers of, and participants in, vote-buying schemes have effectively described a sense of gratitude and obligation to the vote-buyers. In any event, with the secret ballot, vote-buying would disappear without informal institutions that effectively enforce market mechanisms. Voters could easily take payments and not vote for candidates—certainly some proportion of voters do this. Ultimately, such an outcome could be seen as inefficient for voters and politicians. Poor, risk-averse voters may well prefer private goods rather than policy promises, and noncompliance would, over time, destroy the market for such exchanges.

Where clientelism predominates in elections, politicians' career survival depends on obtaining and delivering private goods. In some countries, political parties control access to clientelistic goods. But in many presidential systems, including Brazil, executives are the best source for valuable campaign goods. Presidents typically dominate spending, as do governors at the state level. They make initial budget proposals, often have exclusive bill-initiation powers for fiscal legislation, and control the disbursement of appropriations (Schneider 2001). Government funds are not the only sources for vote-buying, as candidates may use their own resources or donors' funds. But, especially in poor areas, state coffers are the easiest and most abundant source of campaign financing, direct or indirect.[1]

At the other extreme, electoral markets may be driven by the exchange of votes for broad policy promises. Candidates offer policy positions and voters support those candidates whose proposals are closest to voters' own. In programmatic environments, voters commit to candidates first and have no enforcement mechanism to guarantee that candidates will deliver their promised policies. Typical understandings of representation rely on enforcement through repeated and frequent elections —politicians who do not deliver will soon lose reelection bids. In programmatic systems, however, evaluating the performance of individual candidates is very difficult, certainly much more difficult than in clientelistic environments. Politicians' work cannot be measured simply in terms of whether the environment has been noticeably improved, corruption eliminated, or the International Monetary Fund's model of development defeated, because everyone knows that a single legislator rarely can do all these things in a single term. So measuring and evaluating effort requires observing credible policy moves toward that ultimate policy goal. Such effort has many facets, including roll-call votes, committee work, and legislative proposals. By contrast, with vote-buying, voters know immediately whether or not candidates have complied with their promises. But how does one evaluate efforts to fight globalization or work to implement the death penalty?

Ultimately, the challenges that legislators face—delivering goods or representing policy positions—create very different challenges for strategic politicians. Clientelistic informal institutions will increase pressure for the short-term delivery of private or local public goods. Consequently, where electoral markets work through the informal institution of clientelism, legislators will focus on obtaining state resources for distribution to voters and donors. In the case of Brazil, with strong executives, this means that legislators should trade legislative power for access to resources. Executives should have solid and sizeable majority coalitions in legislatures, opposition parties should effectively collapse as members begin to support the governor's position, and executive-legislative conflict should be minimized—all the result of incentives created by informal institutions.

Programmatic informal electoral institutions will increase incentives for policy efforts and aggressive credit-claiming. Legislators should work hard to advance platforms, through legislation, committee work, and floor debates, and also to advertise their efforts and positions as credible to constituents. Increased incentives for policy work and advertising have a number of behavioral implications. Unlike in clientelistic systems, close relationships with the executive are not necessary to satisfy constituents, so executives cannot dominate legislative politics, and executive-legislative conflict is much more likely. Furthermore, although political parties are not important for career advancement in clientelistic Brazil, they are important in programmatic systems, in at least two ways.[2] First, meaningful party labels are advertisements to voters—effectively, information shortcuts that convey credible policy positions. These labels overcome the information challenges posed for representation in programmatic electoral markets. Second, collective effort by parties facilitates the defense and advancement of a policy agenda. In other words, cohesive parties make it possible for legislators to better advance the agenda preferred by voters *and* to claim credit for their efforts (Desposato 2001).

Note that governors play little role in legislative career advancement in this case. Governors control pork, but they have effectively no impact on legislators' ability to "fight the good fight" to advance policy. Further, ideology is commonly viewed as spatial, while pork is not. Governors can negotiate over pork with legislators of any ideological alignment, but can please only part of the ideological spectrum when it comes to policy. Consequently, legislative-executive conflict and legislative independence should be much more frequent in programmatic electoral markets than in clientelistic electoral markets.

CLIENTELISM AND LEGISLATIVE POLITICS IN TWO BRAZILIAN STATES: THE CASES OF SÃO PAULO AND PIAUÍ

São Paulo and Piauí, as noted earlier, represent polar extremes in Brazilian politics. Piauí is one of Brazil's poorest and most rural regions. This northeastern state ranks among the most backward in Brazil on many indicators. In contrast, São Paulo is Brazil's economic engine, the center of modern industrial and financial activity.

Table 2.1 provides a basic demographic profile of the two states on three dimensions: percentage of residents with less than one year of education; percentage earning less than the minimum wage; and percentage with running water plumbed into their homes. There are stark differences between the two states on each dimension. The great majority of Paulistas have more than one year of education (87%), while a majority of Piauíenses have less (53%). A small percentage of Paulistas live in poverty (12%), but nearly two-thirds of Piauíenses live on less than the minimum wage (about US$100 in 1998). Finally, almost all Paulista homes have running water (96%), but only a third (34%) of Piauíenses enjoy the same.

TABLE 2.1
Demographic Profiles of São Paulo and Piauí, Brazil
(percentage of residents in state), 1990 Census

	São Paulo	Piauí
No/low (< 1 year) education	13	53
Poverty (less than minimum wage)	12	65
Running water (plumbing) in home	96	34

For many reasons, clientelistic electoral markets tend to appear in poor, less-developed environments, while programmatic systems are more common in more developed areas. Piauí and São Paulo are not exceptions to these trends. In Piauí, clientelism has been an important part of elections, while in São Paulo, electoral markets are much more programmatic. Note that neither state represents the idealized extreme described above, where elections are completely determined either by vote-buying or by highly charged and informed ideological voters. There are ideological voters in Piauí, and there are vote-buyers and -sellers in São Paulo. But overall, the two states occupy very different positions on the scale from one extreme to the other. That is, although Piauí and São Paulo may not be idealized extremes of pure clientelistic electoral markets or pure ideological electoral markets, they clearly fall at different ends of that spectrum.

A few examples illustrate the differences between the two states. In Piauí, all deputies that I interviewed confirmed that vote-buying is common, and all described electoral relations based on the provision of local public or private goods. One interviewee told me that many deputies were directly purchasing votes: "he [the impoverished voter] wants a guardian angel so that when he is hungry, when the rain is weak, the boss gives food and medicine. The boss resolves his principal problem: dying of hunger, or a child dying from disease."[3] He also noted that while ten or so of the thirty state deputies would directly purchase votes with payments, *all* deputies provided services to constituents—access to public health clinics, say, or a chance to enroll their child in a public school. One deputy's major accomplishment was getting a road built, but he noted that this was not enough to get himself reelected. He also had to provide transportation for voters, medical care, and other private goods. That is, local public goods such as roads were not sufficient for election; voters demanded private goods.

Other interviews in Piauí produced similar results. Deputies emphasized the importance of providing goods to voters or groups of voters. A politician might finance a graduation party, or pay for a musical group to perform for the community, or pay for a medical exam, x-rays, or other kinds of health care. These sorts of exchanges were obvious and institutionalized. During one interview, a constituent burst in to ask for funds for medicine. The state assembly had several doctors on staff, and deputies could refer voters for medical care. Private goods, and local public goods, politics were clearly central to politics in Piauí.

These examples seem to be part of an enduring pattern. Regarding the 1978 gubernatorial campaign in Piauí, Teixeira (1985) notes that the government's candidate bought votes in low-income neighborhoods through direct payments to voters, jobs, and deals with local leaders. He also lists several threats made by the candidate to encourage voters: "Whoever does not vote for our candidate will not drink from my well during the four years of my term. Whoever doesn't vote for our candidate will be fired. If you don't vote for my candidate we'll shut off the water and light to this city. If you doubt me just try it" (1985, 128).

São Paulo is quite different. Brazil's largest and most diverse state has a sizeable middle class and large labor movement, but also a significant lower class in São Paulo's growing *favelas*. This societal diversity explains why São Paulo's electoral market is similarly diverse, with both very ideological and very particularistic voters.

Interviews with deputies and other political actors in São Paulo reflected different kinds of electoral markets within a single state.[4] All agreed that direct vote-buying was very rare or nonexistent. Interviewees did note that some candidates, especially those with lots of financial resources, seek votes in the *favelas*, distributing "immediate" goods, such as *cestas básicas* ("baskets of basic foods"), shirts, or other such items. But many other deputies spoke of a very different kind of electoral connection. The leader of the Brazilian Democratic Movement Party (PMDB) noted that the more informed sectors do pay attention to roll-call votes and hold deputies accountable for their behavior. Others told me that their most important accomplishments in office were bills to limit child labor and simplify income tax—in contrast to the stories of roads and scholarships that I heard in Piauí. One deputy even told me that he lost his reelection bid largely because of opposition to a single roll-call vote he had cast.

While Piauí and São Paulo may not be extreme ideal types of electoral markets, they certainly do fall at opposite ends of the spectrum. Clientelism, vote-buying, and particularistic politics are common and essential to electoral success in Piauí, while programmatic considerations matter much more in São Paulo. These differences in informal institutions imply that Piauíense legislators should focus their efforts on negotiating with the governor for deliverable goods, and legislators in São Paulo should dedicate themselves more to advancing policy agendas and advertising their credible policy efforts. But the formal institutional settings are virtually identical across states and have been linked to weak parties, dominant governors, and personalistic politics. So if informal institutions "matter," we should observe distinctly different patterns of party cohesion, gubernatorial influence, and position-taking across states.

RESULTS: PARTY COHESION AND POSITION-TAKING

A comparison of legislative roll-call behavior across Piauí and São Paulo reveals substantial differences in the two states (table 2.2). First, political parties in São Paulo are, on average, much more cohesive than those in Piauí: overall cohesion scores of .86 versus .69. Both states use open-list proportional representation electoral rules, which are highly personalistic and should cause intraparty conflict and low party cohesion scores. But São Paulo's score is much higher than Piauí's. This difference is consistent with an informal institutional explanation of legislative behavior. São Paulo's electoral markets are more programmatic than Piauí's, increasing pressure for, and payoffs from, cohesive political parties.

Second, in addition to open-list proportional representation, both states have powerful governors. Given the combination of personal vote-seeking and budget-controlling governors, party organizations should be trumped by state governors. Opposition parties should have difficulty maintaining cohesion, as their members support governors' proposals in exchange for access to the state budget. The evidence, however, again shows differences across states. In Piauí, all is as expected. The governor's coalition members have very high discipline (cohesion score .94) due to the alignment of partisan and gubernatorial preferences. But the opposition parties have virtually collapsed, with cohesion levels below .50. As expected, alignment with the governor is much more important than party consistency where clientelism is common. But the pattern reverses in São Paulo—opposition parties are slightly more cohesive than government parties. Again, the difference between Piauí and São Paulo reflects the incentives provided by informal institutions. In São Paulo, increasing emphasis on programmatic goods in elections means that legislators focus more on delivering policy, not pork. This informal institutional difference means that governors have much less influence over roll-call votes in São Paulo than in Piauí.

Finally, just comparing the frequency of roll-call votes across states shows how informal institutions can dramatically change legislators' behavioral incentives. São Paulo had a fair number of roll-call votes: 1,042 over the period studied. Piauí had only 20 such votes. The difference can again be ascribed to informal electoral institutions. In Piauí, there are no payoffs for taking public positions on policy issues

TABLE 2.2
Legislative Behavior in São Paulo and Piauí, 1991–98: Roll-Call Cohesion

State	Cohesion score				
	Overall	Government	Opposition	Difference	No. of votes
São Paulo	.86	.84	.87	−.03[a]	1,042
Piauí	.69	.94	.48	.46[a]	20

[a] Difference (government minus opposition) significant at the .1 level.

through roll-calls. Voters' emphasis was on personal attention and particularistic goods. In São Paulo, there were approximately fifty-two times as many roll-call votes.

The programmatic component of electoral markets in São Paulo created incentives and payoffs for public position-taking and participation in legislative procedure, through at least two mechanisms. First, roll-call votes can be useful demonstrations of effort and position-taking or part of a legislative strategy. Deputies can use roll-call votes to demonstrate their effort on behalf of a public goods agenda—support for a new environmental law, say, or opposition to tax hikes, or working for a raise for public employees. Such votes can similarly be used against their opponents in future elections. Opposition deputies might seek recorded roll-call votes so they can criticize their opponents who supported any policy initiatives that failed or proved unpopular. Second, roll-call votes can be part of a legislative strategy to obstruct or otherwise prolong a legislative session. During a polemical debate on the budget, privatization, or administrative reform, in which hundreds of amendments are considered, calling for roll-call votes (instead of symbolic votes) can turn an afternoon's work into weeks of legislative sessions that last all day and well into the early morning hours.

My qualitative observations and interviews in each state confirmed that the quantitative evidence reflected informal institutional differences across states. In Piauí, after the 1998 elections, the governor had only a minority coalition in the assembly—fourteen of thirty deputies. I discussed this with the leader of the opposition parties, Deputy Leal Junior of the Liberal Front Party (PFL). I asked him why the opposition—with a majority in the state assembly—did not challenge the governor's legislative agenda more aggressively. He simply answered: "We negotiate." Although he was the majority leader, he went on to note that "being in the opposition in the northeast is tough" and that his party "can't get anything [from the government]." His comments were a bit more forthcoming in a newspaper interview a year later, in March 2000. When asked about the opposition's decision to vote in favor of the governor's proposals, he noted: "Certainly there will be an opposition.

We will continue just as firm as before, but we will be able to vote in favor of the government's proposals."[5] It turned out that deputies in his own party were publicly siding with the governor, and that others had simply switched to one of the governmental parties in exchange for "benefits." The PFL leadership had tried to strengthen their party's opposition to Governor Santo—but failed as its members sided with the governor.

I asked opposition deputies in Piauí why they did not use verifications to obstruct the government's agenda. Some deputies simply made reference to "negotiation" with the governor and the majority, with no additional comment. I interpreted these comments as indicators of legislative-executive negotiations, trading roll-call votes for particularistic state resources.

I also spoke with opposition deputies from parties with reputations for disciplined and ideological behavior (the Worker's Party [PT] for example). The few deputies in Piauí from these parties claimed that *they did not know they could request verifications.* Some seemed to like the idea—one said it was a way to "give names to the cattle," and others claimed they would begin to use this strategy in the legislature. This may generate roll-call votes for use by scholars in the future; or the deputies' responses might simply have been dishonest. Either way, the lack of roll-call votes suggests that public position-taking or moving forward with a legislative agenda have had little to do with legislators' career strategies in Piauí.

Politics in São Paulo were distinctly different. Political parties in São Paulo were relatively cohesive. Observers told me that most deputies follow their party leader's orientation for roll-call votes. The differences between Piauí and São Paulo were reflected in the way São Paulo dealt with controversial legislation. I observed the opposition using quorum calls, roll-call votes, and its allotted discussion time to prolong both the 1999 budget and the privatization of Comgas (Gas Company of São Paulo) processes as long as possible, with many sessions extending well past midnight.

But just as the São Paulo electorate is diverse, so are that state's deputies. As discussed above, some have attentive sectoral constituencies, but others have more private-goods-oriented voting bases. Abrúcio (1998) noted how Governor Covas was elected with a minority in the assembly, but quickly and easily assembled a coalition —from deputies whose electoral strategy required private and local public goods. One of the governmental party's chief analysts acknowledged the emotional debates in the state legislature, but qualified this by noting that none of the governor's key policy proposals had been defeated—all passed eventually.

While cohesion was relatively high in São Paulo, there is no conclusive evidence that it reflects party discipline. Cohesion indicates that deputies from a party are voting together, but discipline means that such voting is encouraged by the party and that significant costs are imposed on deputies who refuse to conform. Party leaders from the "catch-all" PMDB and Brazilian Progressive Party (PPB) both complained to me about the lack of party discipline.[6] Deputy Tonin (leader of the PMDB) noted that he had formal powers to discipline members, including control over their committee memberships, but suggested that these powers were of little value. He did recount party meetings to discuss polemical roll-calls, where he would expound the need to "stay together on this one." Members of several parties told me they could vote against their party if they chose to. Only members of the PT mentioned that party cohesion was mandatory and that there were costs to voting against the party. Finally, other interviews suggested that roll-call votes had nothing to do with discipline or ideological cohesion. One observer, when discussing the legislative battle over Comgas privatization, simply said: "The price must be very high," referring to the cost of deputies' bargaining for state resources in exchange for support for that bill.

My interviews in São Paulo left the impression that two mechanisms were at work there. First, there was a relatively disciplined opposition that did not need to seek private goods from the governor. These deputies, like those in the PT, had public goods constituencies and did not need to bargain with the executive. Second, deputies in the government's coalition included both ideological supporters of the governor's agenda and goods-seeking bargainers. Further, because fewer deputies needed private goods, the governor's market for votes on controversial legislation was smaller. As a result, the price of votes may have been higher, and prolonged negotiations were sometimes necessary. In contrast to Piauí, where the governor dominated the legislature, the São Paulo executive, though clearly influential, had to engage in substantial negotiation to advance his agenda.

Of course, clientelistic politics are still important in São Paulo. Not all deputies used roll-call votes in campaigns or speeches, or faced criticism of their voting records on the campaign trail. But the fact that roll-call votes are frequent in São Paulo and not in Piauí, and that deputies in São Paulo *did* use roll-call votes as part of their career strategy whereas deputies in Piauí did not, is evidence of the impact of informal institutions.

CONCLUSION

This chapter offers several contributions to the study of legislative politics and informal institutions, both in Brazil and more broadly. First, by controlling for the many confounding variables that can plague cross-country studies, it provides strong evidence for the importance of informal institutions. In the two cases examined, informal institutions led to very different outcomes even in the context of identical formal institutions. The implication is that explanations of political phenomena that rest only on considerations of formal institutions will often be incomplete and lack generalizability. Second, this chapter shows how the effects of informal institutions can spill over beyond their local context. Previous research on informal institutions in legislative politics has focused on the evolving rules and norms within the institution and their effects on legislation. This chapter, however, shows how informal institutions *outside* the legislature can be just as important, shaping legislators' basic behavioral incentives. In particular, it shows that where the informal institution of clientelism is present, politicians focus less on credit-claiming and more on delivery. Where electoral markets are not constrained by the institutions of clientelism, politicians' priorities shift toward policy formation and credit-claiming.

In addition, this project suggests some revisions to purely institutional explanations for political behavior. In particular, Brazil's electoral system has been heavily blamed for producing an "inchoate" party system. My analysis, however, suggests that this particular set of institutional rules need not deterministically lead to feckless democracy. The differences observed across states point to an important role for noninstitutional variables.

More broadly, these results offer a challenge to any study that focuses exclusively on formal institutions to explain political phenomena. The institutional arrangements in Piauí and São Paulo are as close to a natural experiment as we could observe anywhere, and were mostly exogenously imposed. The diverse outcomes observed—some attributable to voting behavior and campaign styles, others to historical paths—present an important challenge to institutional studies. The outcomes show that institutional theories are clearly incomplete unless we incorporate electorate and societal variables, and that these variables can have very powerful effects on the political arena. Such societal variables may prove even more influential than formal rules.

CHAPTER THREE

Crafting Legislative Ghost Coalitions in Ecuador

Informal Institutions and Economic Reform in an Unlikely Case

ANDRÉS MEJÍA ACOSTA

From an institutional standpoint, Ecuador represents a typical candidate for legislative gridlock and policy failure. Since the country's transition to democracy in 1979, the presence of a strong ethnic and regional cleavage, combined with highly permissive electoral institutions, has meant that no Ecuadorian president has had even close to a majority in Congress. Strong presidentialism in the context of a highly fragmented party system tends to result in the notoriously "difficult combination" lamented by scholars of Latin American politics. Moreover, for most of the period of this study, the electoral calendar has imposed term limits on all legislators, with midterm elections scheduled every two years. Thus, according to institutional theories of coalition formation and policy change, Ecuadorian presidents should rarely, if ever, succeed in enacting sweeping policy change.

Yet, despite the continuing presence of multiple—and often myopic—veto players, Ecuador's experiences do not entirely conform to the standard stalemate prediction yielded by most institutional theories, particularly in the area of market-oriented reforms during the 1980s and 1990s.[1] For, although most scholars focus on the pervasive political conflict in Ecuador, evidence suggests that presidents were often able to "muddle through" important fiscal, financial, and banking reforms during the 1990s (Grindle and Thoumi 1993; Hey and Klak 1999). In contrast to conventional wisdom, moreover, such successes did not come exclusively from increased use of presidential decree authority (Mejía Acosta 2004, 99–101). Rather, presidents could rely on less formal means to accomplish their objectives. Here, I focus in particular on presidents' capacity to craft what I call "ghost coalitions," or clandestine legislative agreements with party leaders who passed economic reforms in exchange for policy concessions, patronage, and "pork."

At the most general level, this chapter shows that informal institutions can play an important role in explaining the gap between the outcomes predicted by standard institutional theories and the observed patterns of policy change and economic reform. More specifically, the chapter illustrates how ghost coalitions helped to promote interbranch cooperation and to surmount the institutional rigidities imposed by formal (electoral and legislative) rules. Although presidential coalition building has helped solve problems of multiparty presidentialism in several Latin American countries, including Chile, Bolivia, and Brazil, Ecuadorian coalitions differ in one important respect: they tend to be hidden from public view. Publicly visible cross-party coalitions are unpopular among Ecuadorian voters, who have become suspicious of the nature of political deals. Thus party leaders view public coalitions as nonviable politically, and negotiations between opposition parties and the government must be clandestine. Here, the absence of roll-call voting mechanisms in the legislature is crucial, for it allows vote-trading while protecting the electoral reputation of coalition partners who vote for unpopular economic reforms. At the same time, threats of "going public" with such arrangements provide an especially powerful enforcement mechanism to deter noncompliance.

The first section of this chapter describes in more detail the puzzling approval of economic reforms despite rigid political institutions and public disbelief. I then explore the informal nature of ghost coalitions, highlighting various incentives and sanctions. The third section illustrates the crafting of ghost coalitions by focusing on the adoption of modernization reforms during the administration of President Sixto Durán Ballén (1992–96). I conclude with a discussion of implications for the study of informal institutions and coalition making in comparative perspective.

THE FORMAL INSTITUTIONAL CONTEXT FOR REFORM

Like many other Latin American countries in the 1980s, Ecuador confronted the challenge of replacing the state-led import-substitution industrialization model with tight fiscal discipline aimed at servicing lofty debt commitments and promoting economic liberalization. For more than two decades, Ecuadorian presidents battled a highly fragmented Congress and a skeptical public to enact adjustment policies and structural reforms recommended by international financial institutions, in order to become eligible for fresh international credits. Such policies, largely shaped by the so-called Washington consensus, prescribed the adoption of financial and trade liberalization, fiscal discipline, reduction of the public sector (including privatizations), and flexible labor reforms (Williamson 1990, 402; Hey and Klak 1999, 67). During this period, Ecuador's reform attempts were also affected by a series of powerful exogenous shocks, including fluctuations in international oil prices, armed conflicts, and natural disasters.[2] In the face of low growth, widespread unemployment, galloping inflation, a rapidly depreciating currency, and a severe financial crisis, the economy teetered on the brink of collapse.

From the standpoint of existing institutional analyses, several aspects of Ecuador's formal institutional framework should have made successful policy reform unlikely. First, the use of a closed-list proportional representation system to elect legislators between 1979 and 1996 and the absence of effective barriers for obtaining congressional representation increased the effective number of parties and prevented presidents from obtaining partisan majorities in the legislature. Second, the peculiar combination of term limits with midterm elections seemed to remove incentives among legislators to make long-term agreements.[3] Third, partly to confront such congressional opposition, Ecuadorian presidents are endowed with some of the strongest constitutional powers in the region, including strong legislative powers to decree and veto legislation. In this context, there seemed to be few political incentives to ensure the political cooperation and power-sharing necessary to pass reform legislation.[4]

The media and public opinion exacerbated the problem of making coalitions for reform. As in other Latin American countries, government efforts to enforce fiscal discipline and promote economic liberalization were often confronted by public discontent and mobilization. Voters felt betrayed by parties and politicians who attempted market reforms despite campaign promises, and their discontent was reflected in surveys (Stokes 2001). Job approval ratings between July 1988 and March 2002 (figure 3.1) show that Ecuadorian presidents reached (net) negative ratings before six months in office, and by the end of their first year in office, they had lost well over 40 percentage points in popularity (Araujo 1998).[5]

Widespread popular discontent with government performance thus should have hindered the president's ability to recruit coalition partners for passing economic reforms. Indeed, political parties often publicly adopted an *anti-gobiernista* (anti-government) discourse to dismiss any association with the government and to assert their independence from presidential initiatives, especially in the vicinity of new elections. In this context, collaborating with a generally unpopular president acquired a pejorative connotation. According to Congressman Wilfrido Lucero, when his Democratic Left (ID) party attempted to negotiate a tax reform with President Jamil Mahuad in 1999: "We were disqualified, accused of being *gobiernistas*, by other parties and our own. This has been a political prejudice (*complejo político*),

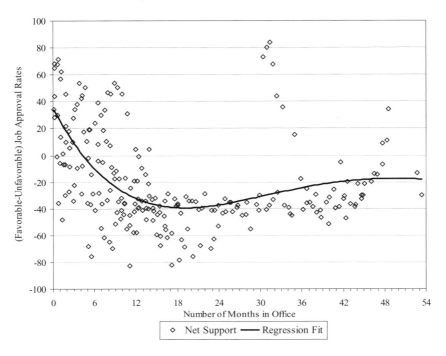

Figure 3.1. Presidential Net Job Approval Ratings (percent): Quito and Guayaquil (July 1988–March 2001). *Source:* Informe Confidencial, Quito.

some kind of bad word in the political arena when it comes to negotiating with the executive."[6] As former President Mahuad himself put it: "The worst insult you can tell an Ecuadorian congressperson is to be a *gobiernista.*"[7]

The media contributed to raising the costs of government cooperation by associating incidents of interbranch bargaining with illegal or corrupt practices. When asked about the role of the media in the formation of government alliances, eleven of twelve legislators interviewed in 1999 claimed that the media made government cooperation less likely, since media had a tendency to demonize political alliances by focusing on corruption scandals rather than positive actions of Congress.[8] Over the years, popular slang embedded this *anti-gobiernista* discourse in the Ecuadorian political culture.[9] In this sense, public mistrust and the media's role in disclosing political alliances severely increased the politicians' costs—and electoral liabilities—associated with crafting public cooperation agreements with the government.

Notwithstanding this difficult environment, Ecuadorian governments managed to avoid the hyperinflation crises and control the spiraling fiscal deficits that plagued other Latin American economies in the 1980s and early 1990s. Presidents obtained the approval of legislation to improve tax collection and limit government spending during the 1980s (Grindle and Thoumi 1993). Under the generic label of "modernization reforms," the government passed significant financial, trade, and banking liberalization laws in the early 1990s, despite having little or no formal party support in Congress (Hey and Klak 1999; De la Torre et al. 2001). In 2000, a coalition of opposition parties in Congress passed the government-proposed Monetary Stability and Economic Recovery Law (Trole I) to adopt the U.S. dollar as the national currency.[10] Other important reforms such as the Fiscal Responsibility, Stabilization and Transparency Law (approved in March 2002), as well as financial, banking, and labor legislation required to implement dollarization reforms, were passed despite a minority presence of the government party in Congress.

From a comparative perspective, the institutional barriers to successful policy reform seem to have proven far less daunting in Ecuador than one might predict. Most notably, Ecuador's General Index of Structural Reform through 1995 (.801) was only slightly below the regional average (.821).[11] Indeed, Ecuador liberalized to a greater degree than countries with far less party fragmentation, including Mexico (before 1997) and Venezuela (before 1993).

The question, then, is why, given the country's fragmented institutions and adverse public opinion, were Ecuadorian governments consistently able to "muddle through"? The next section develops one set of answers: ghost coalitions, an informal institution adopted by Ecuadorian presidents and party leaders to overcome the constraints imposed by a multiparty presidential system and enable the approval of economic reforms.

THE RULES OF FORMATION OF GHOST COALITIONS

Students of Latin American politics are well aware of the instrumental role played by clientelistic practices in cementing political agreements between different agents, whether politicians seeking the support of potential voters, or party leaders trading favors. At the same time, most accounts stress the inefficient and transient nature of clientelistic practices for achieving determined outcomes, claiming that they solely favor opportunistic and expensive instances of cooperation over finite issues.[12]

The Ecuadorian experience of ghost coalition formation suggests an alternative view. Treating the informal system of patronage associated with such coalitions as a specific form of clientelism (Mainwaring 1999, 176),[13] I argue that it provides actors with the incentives and punishments to sustain cooperation games over time, thus enabling them to achieve legislative outcomes that would not be possible through formal institutions alone. Such clientelistic exchanges are based on mutually shared expectations in which political elites believe that the failure to comply carries some kind of external sanction, or at least the exclusion of certain agents from the benefits of the political trade. Ghost coalitions may be viewed as complementary informal institutions (Lauth 2000; Helmke and Levitsky, introduction to this volume), for they enhanced governability by "filling in the gaps" and improving the efficiency of the legislative process.

Despite the clandestine character of ghost coalitions, observers of Ecuadorian politics have been aware of them since the return to democratic rule. As any newly elected Ecuadorian president soon comes to realize, vote-buying (trading legislative votes for political favors) is "the name of the game" for crafting policy coalitions in Congress.[14] As in many other Latin American democracies, Ecuadorian presidents have discretion over the distribution of a wide range of public "goodies," including appointments and particularistic concessions to potential political allies, such as cabinet positions, subnational authorities, granting of licenses and contracts, allocation of government resources, and other payments.[15] What is distinctive about the Ecuadorian case is that the favored parties often need to protect themselves from the public censure of being called *gobiernistas*. Thus, the specific mutual understanding underlying ghost coalitions between presidents and congress can be expressed as follows: (1) presidents are expected to distribute clientelistic payoffs in exchange for legislative cooperation, and (2) maintaining the secrecy of an agreement is a precondition for effective legislative cooperation. The first premise refers to the accepted *currency* for enabling coalition formation; the second refers to the *nature* of the transaction itself.

Concealing political agreements from the public sphere allows politicians to benefit from the gains of the trade while protecting parties from electoral liability for collaborating with the government. During the Hurtado administration (1981–84), for example, Gary Esparza was elected vice president of Congress in 1982 and president in 1983 with the support of the Christian Democrats (Popular Democracy; DP), the Democrats (PD), and his own Roldosista Group (GR). Although the alliance had been in place for nearly two years, "no party dared to call this relationship a 'pact' much less a government pact" (Mills 1984, 87).[16] Indeed, Esparza—himself a GR legislator—consistently denied being the candidate of the official alliance in 1983, and when reporters asked about his decisive collaboration in passing past key government proposals, Esparza replied that his "only interest was the preservation of democracy [from a military reversal] and not any government cooperation."[17] During the Mahuad administration (1998-2000), the media reported on the workings of a "legislative steamroller," or *aplanadora*, to describe a perceived association between the governing DP party and the Social Christian Party (PSC). Party leaders on both sides deny the existence of a political alliance between the two, but this "coincidence of interests"—as they prefer to call it—facilitated the joint appointment of the attorney general, the ombudsman, and the directory board of the Electoral Tribunal (with the PSC in the presidency and DP in the vice presidency). In Congress, both parties supported the approval of a peace treaty with Peru, the approval of a major fiscal reform package (including the creation of new taxes) to finance the deficit, and the 1999 budget. President Gustavo Noboa (2000–2003) helped cement a ghost coalition with the appointment of "independent" politician Patricio Jamriska to the Health Ministry in January 2001.[18] Although all sides denied any formal collaboration, Jamriska's ties to the National Integration Movement (MIN) help explain that party's crucial involvement in supporting subsequent government initiatives, including key fiscal reform packages, in 2001 and 2002.

A crucial element for making ghost coalitions work in Ecuador is that there is no public record of legislative votes. Roll calls are rarely taken in Congress and, over time, legislators have consistently blocked the implementation of electronic vote-counting mechanisms on the floor.[19] As one legislator put it, secret voting gave legislators more flexibility for crafting alliances: "this way they claim to oppose something but vote in favor of it."[20] I further explore the logic of ghost coalitions by focusing, first, on the trade-offs posed by various types of patronage and, second, on the mechanisms used to monitor and enforce compliance with such agreements.

The Cement of Ghost Coalitions: Patronage and Legislative Vote-Buying

In cases of persistently divided government, such as in Ecuador, presidents' capacity to implement policy reform depends on their ability to use the resources of the executive branch to build and sustain legislative coalitions. In Ecuador, coalition incentives include—in addition to public policy concessions—cabinet and subcabinet appointments, executive appointments of governors and heads of state-owned enterprises, government licenses and contracts, diplomatic appointments, pacts to elect individuals to electoral, judicial, and other control authorities, resource transfers to local governments, special "off-budget" allocations, and—until 1995—direct payments from discretionary spending funds.

In crafting coalitions, Ecuadorian party leaders confronted a trade-off between the value of government rewards and the electoral liability for cooperation. Cabinet posts provide political parties with substantial policymaking influence in strategic areas, as well as access to a rich source of pork and patronage for their constituencies.[21] Because they are so publicly visible, however, cabinet posts leave Ecuadorian parties vulnerable to charges of being government partners, or *gobiernistas*, which, as noted above, is generally expected to bring adverse electoral consequences. Smaller and more particularistic forms of payment (pork and patronage) are less subject to public scrutiny, but they provide scarcer resources to reward the rank and file.

Between 1979 and 1998, executive-legislative coalition-building efforts often centered on the annual election of legislative authorities.[22] The outcome of these elections determined who would control the policymaking agenda, committee allocation, political impeachment processes, and the nomination processes of other government authorities.[23] The election of legislative authorities thus provided the president with a crucial opportunity to form a pro-government coalition and to secure control over key bargaining resources. Despite the adverse political-institutional environment, pro-government majority coalitions were formed in fifteen of twenty-three congressional elections (65%) between 1979 and 2002 (Mejía Acosta 2004).[24]

As in parliamentary systems, cabinet appointments are often seen as the primary bargaining chip for cementing presidential coalitions.[25] Consistent with the logic of ghost coalitions, however, parties backing the executive were less likely to acknowledge the acceptance of cabinet positions, preferring to disguise or deny any government cooperation or settling for policy-influential, but less visible, subcabinet-level positions.[26] Between 1979 and 1994, Ecuadorian presidents had the lowest percentage of partisan cabinets in Latin America, as most cabinet members were not identified with any political party (Amorim Neto 1998, 67). A classic example comes from the administration of Rodrigo Borja (1988–92), when the president offered the DP cabinet positions to formalize a political alliance. The offer provoked a severe split between the party hard-liners—led by Osvaldo Hurtado, who called this alliance a "historic mistake" (1990, 220)—and the *gobiernistas*, who decided to leave the party and take the cabinet positions.

Less visible, but extremely important, were dozens of appointments to direct state-owned enterprises in the oil sector, electricity, telecommunications, social security, the modernization council (Conam), the customs authority, and national development banks. Governors were also appointed by the president to represent the executive in the provinces, and they influenced important public works appointments at the subprovincial level. Presidents were also able to appoint up to 25 percent of diplomatic mission chiefs (with the remaining percentage being filled by career diplomats), and had discretionary authority to appoint other diplomatic officials of lower ranking. When negotiating with the president, party leaders were often interested in bulk entitlements (also known as "collective contracts") to sectors of the government or "asked for [control of] entire provinces" that they considered their strongholds.[27] Leaders, in turn, used these "baskets of goodies" to discipline and reward their party members.[28]

Budgetary allocations to specific districts or provinces were also offered to benefit the constituencies of political parties in exchange for legislative cooperation. Even though budgetary spending was heavily restricted, Araujo shows that Congress increased the proposed government spending by 45 percent, on average (1998, 145).[29] Other useful side payments included the issuing of operating licenses, government contracts, the speedy approval of public works, the fast-track approval and channeling of foreign development loans, and judicial pardons.

Presidents have filled out their legislative coalitions with the support of small parties and party switchers, or individuals who were willing to abandon party loyalties to support the government's initiatives in exchange for particularistic payments for themselves and/or public works, government transfers, and personal favors for their constituents. Most of these individuals came from marginal and overrepresented rural districts, belonged to center or populist parties, and were amateur legislators with short political careers (Mejía Acosta 2004, 164).[30] The use of selective payments to break party loyalties was particularly widespread in the case of governments with very weak partisan representation in Congress, such as that of interim President Gustavo Noboa (2000–2003).[31]

Responding to public and media concern over party switching, Congress adopted an ethics code in 1998 that included the revocation of party switchers' mandates. However, some party leaders adopted an alternative informal rule of "impunity by consent" to protect the political survival of legislators defecting to the government camp.[32] The first beneficiaries of this new norm were Felix Garcia and Mario Moreira, who abandoned the Ecuadorian Roldosista Party (PRE) in August 1998. When the PRE initiated a recall motion, the governing DP intervened to stall the process, and soon thereafter the two legislators continued voting along government lines.

Crafting coalitions around individual legislators entails greater uncertainty for both presidents and the legislators themselves. Although pivotal legislators are in a position to extract significant rents for their votes at any given point, legislators have learned that in a fragmented environment, they gain bargaining leverage by clustering around a political leader rather than acting alone.[33] Governments, in turn, prefer to promote and reward the formation of "proto-parties," or clusters of independent legislators and party switchers, as a way to reduce transaction costs and make wholesale agreements with legislative leaders (Mejía Acosta 2004, 154). For example, President Hurtado courted the support of the GR faction (composed of disaffected Concentration of Popular Forces [CFP] members) with government perks in exchange for legislative support. Similarly, the Noboa government compensated for its lack of partisan support by offering coalition rewards to the "independent" MIN, mostly composed of disgruntled DP members. This pattern of making informal coalitions with proto-parties composed of independent legislators challenges the conventional view that Ecuador's so-called independent legislators are "loose" or "floating" (Conaghan 1995).

Monitoring and Sanctioning

Because ghost coalitions are clandestine rather than public, monitoring and sanctioning are critical issues for ensuring effective cooperation between presidents and party leaders. Acting in an institutional environment that offers few formal incentives for alliance formation, and often cementing alliances through unsavory and even illicit deals, coalition partners cannot turn to officially sanctioned channels to enforce compliance. However, political actors employ a wide range of levers and strategies, ranging from judicial investigations and impeachment threats to party-sponsored street protests and other regional and municipal conflicts,[34] to try to enforce compliance with legislative agreements.

For presidents, the most important sanctioning mechanism lies in discretionary power to dismiss appointed officials affiliated with parties that break the terms of the alliance. The use of this authority to reward or punish congressional coalition partners is clearly seen in the case of governors, who in Ecuador are appointed rather than elected. Available data on the duration of mandates of provincial governors indicate an extremely high turnover rate: governors lasted an average of 1.2 years, and only 28 percent of those who left the office did so due to "natural" causes (completion of mandate or death). Leaving aside those governors who were "promoted" or transferred to another posting, it can be inferred that more than 53 percent of governors were directly dismissed by the president or were asked to resign.[35] As in cabinet dismissals, presidents removed (or threatened to remove) appointed governors to ensure compliance with agreements made with congressional partners or to accommodate new coalition partners. Reshuffling of provincial authorities is also associated with periods of successful policy change.

Political parties use a variety of sanctioning mechanisms to ensure presidential compliance with the terms of ghost coalitions. For one, legislators may punish presidents by requesting impeachment proceedings against cabinet members and censuring them with a simple majority of votes.[36] It is often argued that the congressional opposition in Ecuador consistently dismantled cabinets through

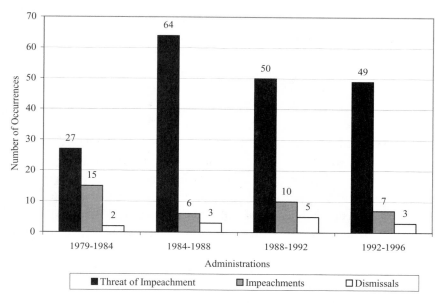

Figure 3.2. Threats versus Actual Impeachment Proceedings across Four Administrations (1979–96). *Source:* Sánchez-Parga (1998, 85, 203).

impeachment procedures. From the perspective of the ghost coalitions framework, however, the same dataset reveals a more complex pattern of cabinet reshuffling.[37]

First, the congressional *threats* to impeach cabinet ministers played a far more prominent role than the impeachment procedures themselves. Second, most cabinet dismissals came from the executive itself, *not* from the congressional opposition. The data from four administrations (figure 3.2) reveal an impressive gap between the number of cabinet impeachment threats made by legislators and the actual "conviction rates" or dismissals of ministers: an average ratio of 14.6 to 1 across all periods and more than 20 to 1 during the Febres Cordero administration (1984–88). Given the costly and uncertain nature of assembling impeachment coalitions in a fragmented congress, the trend suggests that legislators instead issued threats as a cheap way to remind presidents of existing legislative commitments, while earning a public reputation of being devoted opposition parties.[38]

Government and party officials have at times attempted to secure compliance by "formalizing" ghost coalitions through secret written agreements. In 1993, for example, officials of the Durán Ballén administration and a group of independent legislators known as the National Concentration Legislative Bloc signed a secret "letter of commitment" in which the government agreed to promote legislators' career paths, provide government jobs, and allocate "off-budget" transfers in exchange for support for its candidates for the legislative leadership and help in passing elements of its modernization reforms.[39] Writing down secret agreements does not ensure they will be binding, however. In the midst of a tightly disputed congressional election, PRE congressman Jorge Montero surprised fellow legislators and the media by going public with the contents of the agreement just before he switched sides and voted for the leading opposition candidate. The public disclosure nullified the government alliance, and the whistleblower was, in turn, expelled from his party.[40] Montero's motivation for defection became clear when he gained a seat on the Budget Committee during the subsequent legislative period, probably a more lucrative payoff for cooperation than the one originally signed in the government's collective contract.[41]

Perhaps the most effective means of enforcing ghost coalitions is the threat of "going public," or revealing publicly the (often illicit) deals underlying the original pact. As José Sánchez-Parga has observed, political scandal in Ecuador offers a "remarkable laboratory to study the process of political construction in a society" (1998, 119). Indeed, the threat or the actual triggering of scandals is a crucial political instrument to maintain or renew clandestine alliances in congress. Both governments and their legislative allies stand to lose from such scandals, so the threat to go public may be used effectively by both sides. Indeed, if such threats usually are effective, easily observable cases of enforcement through public disclosure should be relatively uncommon (in other words, when an informal institution is working, players know the rules and the costs of breaking them, so acts of enforcement should be rare). Nevertheless, as the following section suggests, cases of public disclosure are often quite spectacular—and instructive.

GHOST COALITIONS AT WORK: THE DURÁN BALLÉN GOVERNMENT AND THE MODERNIZATION REFORMS (1992–95)

Perhaps the clearest example of monitoring and sanctioning of a ghost coalition is found in the administration of Sixto Durán Ballén (1992–96), in which the government formed a secret alliance with the opposition Social Christian Party to pass a significant set of market-oriented reforms, jointly labeled Modernization Laws. On his inauguration, the conservative Durán Ballén laid out a plan "to end the shameful structure of privilege of the inefficient public sector, that absorbs state resources, provides poor services and stifles national development."[42] The key agent behind the "modernization reforms" was Vice President Alberto Dahik, a Princeton-trained economist and hard-line proponent of fiscal austerity and economic restructuring

(Hey and Klak 1999). Durán Ballén inherited a moderately growing economy (3.6% annual GDP increase) with a relatively small fiscal deficit of 1.2 percent of gross domestic product.

Durán Ballén's administration was marked by a dramatic lack of partisan support in congress. Before the 1992 presidential election, Durán Ballén had abandoned the PSC to form his own party, the Republican Union Party (PUR). Although the move helped him win the presidency in 2002, the PUR gained only twelve of seventy-seven seats in the legislature, which, combined with the six seats of his Conservative Party (PCE) allies, gave the government control over less than a quarter of the congress. Confronted with this scenario, the new president opted to seek a legislative agreement with the PSC, the largest party in Congress (with twenty-one seats). Notwithstanding Durán Ballén's defection in 1991, the PSC was a natural coalition partner, since it shared a center-right ideology and a similar commitment to market-oriented reforms. An alliance with the governing party created a political dilemma for the PSC: on the one hand, party leader Jaime Nebot had been a runner up in that year's presidential election, and he did not want to be seen collaborating with the government he was planning to run against in 1996. On the other hand, the PSC sought access to state resources, and party leaders were interested in passing economic reforms that would facilitate their own policy goals in the future.

Government officials, including Vice President Dahik and Chief of Staff Marcelo Santos, held a clandestine meeting with PSC leaders León Febres Cordero and Jaime Nebot, at a private Guayaquil residence, to craft a legislative agreement. The context and contents of the agreement were only revealed three years later, when Vice President Dahik made it public during his congressional impeachment hearings (Congreso Nacional del Ecuador 1995). The "broad political agreement" with the PSC required the government to make budgetary allocations for PSC-controlled electoral strongholds in the coastal provinces of Guayas, Manabí, Los Rios, and Esmeraldas, totaling more than 200,000 million sucres (approximately US$100 million). It also included direct cash transfers—from the government's discretionary spending fund (*gastos reservados*)—to purchase individual legislators for as much as US$500,000 each to approve laws on the privatization of telecommunications or electricity, government jobs for PSC cronies in the state-owned oil (*Petroecuador*) and energy (*INECEL*) companies, and, most importantly, the PSC's control of the Supreme Court and the Electoral Tribunal.[43]

The government also used particularistic payments (usually from discretionary funds) to purchase the support of smaller parties and independent legislators to secure the required legislative majorities.[44] These negotiations included the ill-fated written pact (mentioned above) with the National Concentration Legislative Bloc, in which the government offered a number of public appointments, off-budget transfers, and support for the passage of constitutional reforms to eliminate mid-term elections and permit immediate reelection for all legislators (which would allow sitting deputies to extend their mandate for at least two more years)—all in exchange for the bloc's commitment *not* to oppose key elements of the modernization reforms.[45]

The ghost coalition helped Durán Ballén approve an ambitious program of market-oriented reforms between 1992 and 1994. The most significant reforms included the Public Sector Budgets Law, tax reform, administrative reform (State Modernization Law), deregulation of intellectual property rights and foreign investment regimes, reform of the financial system, a Capital Markets Law, a Hydrocarbons Law, and an Agrarian Reform Law that commercialized many rural lands (Araujo 1998, 85–86; Hey and Klak 1999; De la Torre et al. 2001).

Maintaining these ghost alliances was a costly endeavor. Legislative cooperation was difficult to enforce, and the terms of the informal bargain were frequently contested and modified. Dahik later revealed that PSC legislators demanded additional government transfers for their provinces and "their family members would be contractors. It was an absurd situation because their leaders were in opposition, but meanwhile some of the deputies were constantly sitting down with us, demanding money. It was like collective bargaining and the whole process was very expensive."[46]

In 1995, the government-PSC coalition collapsed. When the government deemed that PSC demands had escalated beyond the original pact, Dahik tried to enforce the agreement by threatening to "go public." During an interview with journalist Jorge Vivanco in July 1995, Dahik suggested that some Supreme Court justices—linked to the PSC—had sought bribes from the executive to determine the constitutionality of certain Modernization Laws that were being challenged by the opposition. The accusation put the PSC in the spotlight, because it had played a key role in appointing the Supreme Court judges in 1992. According to Congressman Castello, the government and PSC leaders met once more after the controversial interview, but failed to reconcile positions when the government refused to give more government transfers to the PSC (1995). An angry Febres Cordero (then mayor of Guayaquil) launched accusations of corruption against Alberto Dahik, ironically for buying votes in Congress, and warned him: "The fox has tried to play smart again but his time has come . . . the people will capture and sentence him."[47] The PSC and other opposition parties from the left initiated impeachment proceedings against the vice president. After a three-day trial, Dahik was acquitted by a 39 to 19 majority in Congress (with 14 abstentions), but he resigned from office in October 1995. Shortly after, he fled into exile to Costa Rica when a Supreme Court justice issued a warrant for his arrest (Sánchez-Parga 1998, 121; Saltos Galarza 1999, 209).

In the aftermath of the vote-buying scandal, several constitutional reforms were passed to curb the discretionary spending funds of the executive and to limit the abilities of legislators to negotiate resource allocation for their provinces. The PSC did not escape unharmed from the corruption scandal, and its presidential candidate, Jaime Nebot, lost the 1996 presidential election for a second time.

CONCLUSION

Crafting ghost alliances with the opposition has been an informal but systematic practice employed by political leaders to surmount the institutional rigidities of the Ecuadorian system and obtain significant policy reforms in the legislature. According to an informal set of rules for coalition formation, policymakers shared the common expectation that legislative votes could be traded for particularistic payments and policy concessions. But making policy agreements with usually unpopular presidents imposed high liability costs for potential partners, especially before electoral events. Thus, the secrecy of such agreements was an important part of the informal rules of coalition formation, protecting politicians from the electoral implications of backing unpopular economic reforms by the government. Yet, the threat to break the "secrecy clause" and eventually go public with a clandestine agreement was also an instrument for monitoring compliance: disgruntled politicians issued different kinds of warnings to promote compliance with existing agreements.

The construction of informal elite power-sharing agreements, of course, has been common among Latin American democracies (Siavelis, this volume). What makes the Ecuadorian case distinctive is the fact that political currencies for coalition making have been curtailed or demonized by the media. In this context, party leaders forged clandestine coalitions with the government while at the same time publicly denying any association with it—and even actively proclaiming their opposition in order to maintain an image of "political chastity." The absence of roll-call voting and legislative watchdogs allowed the survival of this informal institution.

This chapter offers two contributions to the study of political institutions in Latin America. First, it goes beyond the description of the formal institutional framework and its predictions for policy change. By analyzing the informal rules of coalition making, I explore the value and nature of different coalition incentives and the effective use of threats and sanctions to enforce legislative cooperation. In other words, this study avoids focusing on the purely written rules in favor of exploring the "actual rules" guiding coalition building in Ecuador. In so doing, it opens the door for future comparative research. One potential area of research, for example, lies in comparing informal coalition dynamics in Latin American presidential democracies and in parliamentary minority governments in Europe.

A second contribution has been to outline how the interaction of formal and informal institutions can shape the prospects for democratic governance. I have argued that ghost coalitions played a complementary role by helping to improve the (poor) policymaking capacity of a fragmented legislature. By enabling executives to build functioning legislative majorities through the distribution of pork, patronage, and policy concessions, ghost coalitions facilitated governability, which helped Ecuador's fragile democracy survive some of the worst economic crises in its history. From the perspective of accountability, however, such patterns of clandestine cooperation also hindered the development of a policy-oriented or programmatic connection between parties and voters at the national level. Thus, from a normative perspective, informal institutions have "double-edged" effects, playing both positive and negative roles simultaneously (Helmke and Levitsky, introduction to this volume).

This analysis thus reveals the inherent tension in institutional reforms designed to "clean up" Ecuadorian politics.[48] Recent efforts to reform the political system have focused on curbing the available currencies that entice legislative cooperation, such as doing away with the executive's use of discretionary spending accounts, eliminating legislators' ability to negotiate budgetary allocations for their provinces, or punishing with mandate recall those legislators who defect from their parties or bargain for government jobs.[49] Though beneficial from the standpoint of transparency and accountability, such reforms could well have the (largely unintended) effect of undermining Ecuador's fragile governability.[50] As one party leader put it, eliminating those bargaining chips is like "tying our hands and feet" when it comes to making alliances.[51] Understanding the informal rules and dynamics of existing vote-buying practices, in a context in which the "difficult combination" of multiparty presidentialism prevails, may well be a starting point to improve the notoriously fragile bases of Ecuador's governability.

PART II

Informal Institutions and Electoral Politics

CHAPTER FOUR

Informal Institutions
When Formal Contracting Is Prohibited

Campaign Finance in Brazil

DAVID SAMUELS

In most countries, private campaign finance contributions are highly restricted or even prohibited, and the government funds political parties and campaigns. This is also the norm in Latin America (Ferreira Rubio 1997; Castillo and Zovatto 1998). In contrast, in countries such as the United States, Japan, and Brazil, most campaign finance comes from private sources. Regardless of whether campaign finance is publicly or privately provided, the explicit exchange of money for political influence remains illegal: a lobbyist who promises to provide a "donation" in exchange for a legislator changing sides on an issue is engaged in bribery, and a politician who suggests that a corporation provide a "donation" if it wants to avoid becoming victim to a regulation that would put it out of business is engaged in extortion. The legal prohibition on explicit contracting between politicians and potential campaign financiers means that formal campaign finance contracts cannot exist.

In addition, because such formal contracting between donors and recipients is illegal, neither "buyers" nor "sellers" of campaign finance can credibly commit to completing the letter of an agreement, for the state cannot and will not enforce any *informal* campaign finance commitments that do occur. Thus, contributors and recipients should have a difficult time developing strong expectations about each other's behavior, which means that actors are less likely to commit to the contract in the first place. Nevertheless, informal institutions do tend to emerge in campaign finance markets. Helmke and Levitsky (introduction to this volume) define informal institutions as "*socially shared rules, usually unwritten, that are created, communicated, and enforced outside officially sanctioned channels.*" Informal institutions are rooted in shared expectations about other actors' behavior. My definition of a campaign finance contract follows from Helmke and Levitsky's definition of informal institutions: it is an informal deal by which a donor agrees to provide money to a politician in exchange for services at some later time. Who initiates the deal is unimportant at this point. What is important is that violation of such arrangements by either partner should generate punishment.

These sorts of deals are the "string theory" of politics: they may comprise the very fabric of the political universe, but they are probably impossible to see. After all, politicians never write such deals down and are typically unwilling to even discuss them. Given that such institutions must by necessity be informal, we are left with a puzzle: what supports the credibility of informal campaign funds exchanges? The literature on credible commitments provides guidelines as to the roots of secure contracting: when transaction costs are high and actors cannot turn to a third party for contract enforcement, both "buyers" and "sellers" of campaign funds have incentives to develop institutions or, at the least, quasi-institutional mechanisms to counteract the effects of uncertainty and enhance the possibility of successful contracting. The campaign finance market, like many political markets and in contrast to many economic markets, is a realm of informal institutions.

What kind of informal institution are campaign finance contracts? Where do campaign finance "contracts" fit on the typology Helmke and Levitsky provide? Helmke and Levitsky's typology has two dimensions. The first dimension is the formal institutions' effectiveness. Whereas some informal institutions operate in a context of effective formal institutions in which the rules are routinely enforced and complied with, others exist in a context of weak or ineffective formal institutions in which noncompliance routinely goes unsanctioned. The difficulty with classifying informal campaign finance contracts is the reference point—the relative effectiveness of the formal institutions. As noted, by definition formal contracting in campaign finance *cannot* exist, so it is unclear whether any such reference point exists.[1] I will consider the relevant formal institutions to be the legal sanctions against "formalizing" the relationships of exchange that characterize campaign finance contracts.

Perhaps paradoxically, the fact that politicians never write down "you gave me $100,000 and I will insert your interests into a bill this year" indicates that we can classify the relevant formal institutions in campaign finance as *effective and stable* (and thus that actors' expectations of the likelihood of punishment exist) even in countries prone to corruption, such as Brazil. After all, if the relevant formal institutions were wholly ineffective, we would expect (even, or perhaps especially, honest) politicians to flout the formal rules and begin writing down their campaign finance contracts!

The second dimension of the Helmke-Levitsky typology is the degree of convergence between formal and informal institutional outcomes. Politicians who enter into campaign finance contracts certainly undermine the letter of the law regarding bribery or extortion, and thus we may assume that campaign finance contracts are "accommodating" informal institutions, because politicians seek to avoid having their exchanges characterized as breaking the law. However, politicians are also uninterested in overturning the laws on bribery or extortion. Following Helmke and Levitsky's definition of accommodating informal institutions, campaign finance contracts do violate the spirit, if not the letter of laws against bribery or extortion and "help reconcile . . . actors' interests with the existing formal institutional arrangements."

How do campaign finance contracts, as informal institutions, emerge? Such arrangements are predicated on (1) the formal prohibition of bribery, extortion, and other forms of corruption; and (2) the relative importance of money in politics, which is in turn a function of several other factors, which I describe below. But as Helmke and Levitsky note, to avoid functionalism, we need to account for the mechanism by which informal institutions emerge. We thus need to identify "the who and the how" of informal institutional emergence, a task I attempt to accomplish through an exploration of the Brazilian case.

In this chapter I employ a methodologically individualist approach to study the emergence and impact of informal institutions. Rational choice approaches are most informative when we can identify the relevant political actors, plausibly assume their motivations, intuit the range of their actions, and understand the potential payoffs. Campaign finance is usually (and unfortunately) one of the most opaque areas in the study of politics, because good data are hard to find. When campaign finance data do exist, a rational choice approach to the study of the "brown areas" of clientelism and particularism gains plausibility and utility, for several reasons: we can identify the actors and make assumptions about their interests, we possess an empirical referent (amounts of money) that cleanly operationalizes political exchanges, and, most importantly for the present study, we can derive expectations about actors' strategies, even in the absence of formal rules governing political exchanges. As I will show, campaign finance data can provide insight into the existence of informal political market mechanisms.

I begin by exploring the question of whether a campaign finance "market" can actually be said to exist. I then present hypotheses about the existence of campaign funds markets, deriving expectations about when we would expect a supply of and demand for campaign funds, and when credible contracting commitments can emerge to support that market. I then describe how the campaign finance market in Brazil seems to fit with the hypothetical expectations. I conclude by placing the Brazilian experience in perspective and suggest how the theoretical framework might be more broadly applied.

WHAT DRIVES INFORMAL CONTRACTING IN CAMPAIGN FINANCE?

Formal or informal contracting between principals and agents will be difficult when a (political or economic) market is poorly institutionalized. Institutional fluidity makes contract enforcement problematic. Neither buyers nor sellers can credibly commit to completing the letter of an agreement, and so are less likely to commit to the contract in the first place. Fluid political markets—characterized by electoral personalism, the rapid emergence and disappearance of parties, and/or high voter volatility—characterize many emerging democracies. Can campaign finance "contracts" exist in such systems?

In terms of campaign funds, a poorly institutionalized political market might limit the credibility of implicit political contracts that exchange government services for money. Not all campaign finance is "service-induced" in this way; some may be "policy-induced" and designed to sway a politician toward a nonparticularistic political position, such as pro— or anti—gun control in the United States. However, in countries such as Brazil—where most parties' identities are relatively weak, politicians change political allegiances frequently, and obtaining government contracts (i.e., pork-barrel politics) is critical for political survival—it is likely that campaign funds will be largely service-induced. When this is the case, a politician seeks and a donor agrees to provide money in exchange for expected services at some undetermined time later.[2] The key point for the study of informal institutions is that because formal contracting is legally proscribed, potential donors may lack confidence that politicians will hold up their end of the deal. Following standard economic theory, if buyers lack good information, then the existence of sellers in the market who offer inferior goods can even drive the market out of existence (Akerlof 1970). In no democracy are campaign finance contracts actually legal, so informal institutions are the only way to generate confident expectations between contracting parties.

UNDERSTANDING CAMPAIGN FINANCE MARKETS

To begin to understand why informal campaign finance contracts emerge, we need to develop clearer theoretical expectations about the dynamics of the campaign finance "market." Three fundamental issues need to be addressed to explain why informal contracting occurs: the presence of supply, of demand, and of credible commitments to support market exchange. Without supply, demand, and informally institutionalized market exchange mechanisms, we can be sure that no market will emerge and thus that no informal institutions need emerge either. On the other hand, if these conditions are met, we ought to see substantial market exchange and thus expect informal institutions to develop. I propose the following five hypotheses about the campaign finance market:

- H1: The overall supply of campaign funds is a function of the incentives that potential financiers have to influence the distribution of government services.
- H2: The overall demand for campaign funds is a function of the degree of inter- and intraparty competition.
- H3a: Market exchange will proceed to the degree that politicians desire to establish collective and/or individual reputations.
- H3b: Market exchange will proceed to the degree that politicians and donors expect to engage in repeated interactions.
- H3c: Market exchange will proceed to the degree that politicians and donors have established quasi-institutional sanctioning mechanisms.

These hypotheses are general, permitting cross-national comparative research. They are also cumulative; that is, each hypothesis is a necessary but insufficient condition. Only if all five conditions are met will a campaign funds contract emerge. I explore here the reasoning behind each hypothesis.

H1: Expectations Regarding the Supply of Campaign Funds

The first hypothesis addresses the question of whether individuals, businesses, and/or interest groups have reason to supply campaign funds by investing in candidates or parties. This question is important: regardless of the demand, if there is no supply of money, then there will be no contracting. We have good theoretical reasons to suppose that political actors in new democracies will invest in politics. This claim requires the following assumptions: that a supply of government services exists, that elected officials exert at least minimal control over that supply, and that interest groups, corporations, and individuals want access to that supply and have money to distribute. These assumptions are reasonable: in a democracy, political actors will attempt to influence areas that affect their interests. Unless we are willing to assume that all those who possess money are uninterested in "purchasing" government services, we have substantial a priori reason to believe that contributors will potentially be willing to supply campaign funds. Even in such highly oligopolistic systems as Brazil, some competition is more than no competition, and when competition exists, actors have incentives to provide a supply of campaign funds in an attempt to shift resources in their direction.[3] I therefore hypothesize that if private interests desire access to government services, and elected officials exert some control over the distribution of such resources, then we ought to see these same interests providing a supply of campaign funds to candidates for office.

H2: Expectations Regarding the Demand for Campaign Funds

Under certain conditions, demand for campaign funds may be low. For example, campaigns may be wholly or partly publicly funded, eliminating or reducing candidates' ability or need to raise funds. When campaigns are publicly funded, even informal campaign finance contracts should not exist, because (at least in principle) private sources of money are not relevant to the electoral process.[4]

When campaigns are privately funded, under what conditions will demand exist? The main factor is the degree of electoral competition. On the one hand, demand may be low because campaigns are cheap, because they are not competitive. If one candidate or party has scared off viable rivals, there would be little need to raise money because there would be no need to spend money to win votes. On the other hand, as the competitiveness of elections increases, so do their costs, and so does politicians' demand for money (Crain 1977). Such demand is also a function of the particular electoral rules. For example, in countries with rules such as Brazil's open-list system, the demand for campaign funds is a function not only of interparty competition but also of the degree of intraparty competition in each constituency (Cox and Thies 1998). That is, if candidates must compete against one other for votes in each district, then they have strong incentives to spend money in an attempt to differentiate themselves from their copartisans as well as from candidates of other parties.[5] Whether intraparty competition matters depends on the electoral system.

Thus, when candidates face competition, we need only assume that they desire to win to conclude that a demand for campaign funds exists. The degree of demand depends on intra- and interparty competition and other costs of running a campaign, which will vary widely based on contextual factors.[6] However, other elements are required to ensure credible commitments and thus the generation of informal campaign finance institutions.

H3a–c: Expectations Regarding the Existence of Credible Commitments

Supply and demand are necessary but insufficient reasons for market exchange to proceed and thus insufficient for informal institutions to emerge. Market exchange also requires contracting between those who produce the supply and those who generate the demand. Contracting is problematic, because both buyers and sellers have few guarantees that the terms of the deal will be fulfilled. For example, potential campaign financiers may be reluctant to invest because they lack confidence that they will get what they paid for. This issue boils down to whether suppliers of campaign funds expect politicians to provide an adequate return on money "invested." If they do not, then campaign funds should be undersupplied. Even if investors are interested in obtaining government services and politicians demand money, we may see underinvestment because of contracting problems—that is, because informal institutions have failed to emerge. By contrast, if investors are confident they will obtain a good return on their investment, then we have good reason to suppose that campaign funds will be supplied.

What guarantees do potential contributors have that politicians will come through with their end of the bargain? Unfortunately, campaign financiers can never obtain a rock-solid guarantee. The reason is quite straightforward: in any country, campaign funds contracts are legally unenforceable (McCarty and Rothenberg 1996; Kroszner and Stratmann 1998). Contributors cannot take their case to a higher authority if a politician "reneges on a deal," nor can a politician sue contributors for failing to provide "promised" campaign funds. Consequently, credible commitments in campaign finance contracts anywhere cannot rest on institutionalized punishment mechanisms.

Given the absence of credible sanctioning mechanisms, contributors' investments may be subject to *ex post* expropriation without compensation. In this situation, we might see underinvestment even where supply and demand are high. That is, even if we assume that politicians do not actually "expropriate" contributions *ex post*, the absence of formal contractual obligations to provide service in exchange for money means investing in campaigns is at a minimum a highly risky proposition.

What, then, maintains the credibility of campaign funds contracts? The literature on credible commitments provides clear guidelines as to the roots of secure contracting: when transaction costs are high, political actors (both "buyers" and "sellers" of campaign funds) have incentives to develop institutions or quasi-institutional mechanisms to counteract the effects of uncertainty and enhance the possibility of successful contracting. Political actors can develop three kinds of mechanisms to enhance the credibility of their commitments: reputation, repetition, and sanctions.

Consider reputation first. To enhance their credibility, politicians have incentives to develop a "brand name." A successfully developed brand name indicates quality to potential voters, and also provides voters with a target against which to retaliate if quality does not meet expectations (Akerlof 1970, 500). Candidates could attempt to develop either a collective or an individual brand name. A politician could develop a collective brand name by committing to a party that espouses an ideology and that possesses a collective identity. By committing to a party, a politician admits that he or she is at least partly substitutable by another candidate who also carries that brand name. In this way, committing to a collective reputation limits politicians' ability to "renege" on contracts.

However, developing a collective reputation reduces politicians' autonomy in ways that development of a personal reputation may not (Crain 1977, 829). Politicians could also invest in a personal brand name, often referred to as the "personal vote" (Cain et al. 1987). Particularly if the electoral system allows or encourages individualistic campaign tactics, politicians have incentives to develop a reputation as private-goods providers (including geographically targeted "pork") and to develop a core constituency of voters who know them, trust them, and consistently vote for them. More importantly, delivery of pork not only might solidify a reputation with voters, but it also could help politicians develop a reputation with potential campaign contributors, such as the construction firms that will build the roads, dams, bridges, post offices, and so forth, that the politicians successfully obtain.

Yet success in reputational development is insufficient to reduce contract uncertainty; repeat play is a second necessary ingredient. In the absence of formal sanctions, politicians face only one potential cost from reneging on a contract: the loss of the present value of potential gains from future dealings with the donor or from others who learn about the defection. That is, reputation matters little if the investor believes that the politician will renege anyway because he or she has a short time horizon. The more the politician plans to deal with the donor over time, however, the greater are the costs of his or her defaulting. When politicians expect a long-term relationship with donors, fewer resources need to be spent on contract enforcement.

If elected officials are mainly amateurs and do not intend to pursue a career in politics, then iterated play is less likely. However, if politicians plan to stick around, then the credibility of their commitments increases, and they have fewer incentives to defect from campaign finance contracts. For example, the relatively long careers of members of the House of Representatives support the credibility of campaign funds contracts in the United States (Kroszner and Stratmann 1998). Interpreting the likelihood of credible contracting in new democracies therefore requires an understanding of the nature of political careers. Where politicians have relatively short political careers, contract credibility is damaged. Where political careers are longer, politicians have more and better opportunities to develop their reputation and ensure greater contributions (Kroszner and Stratmann 1998, 1166n). Thus, where contributors expect to repeatedly interact with politicians over a relatively long period, iteration can help establish credible commitments.

Still, even if we assume that politicians want to build their reputations and have long-term career goals, North and Weingast (1989) have argued that reputation and iteration are insufficient to support institutionalized political markets. Thus we cannot yet conclude that we have "enough" to generate informal campaign finance institutions. This is because neither reputation nor iteration can fully restrict politicians' *ex post* behavior or prohibit them from manipulating the market in their favor once they are in office. This occurs only when threats to punish defection are made credible, through the creation of sanctioning mechanisms. However, as noted above, such institutions are precluded in all campaign funds markets, at least formally, because the state will not enforce implicit campaign finance deals.

We might therefore conclude that because campaign finance contracts are unenforceable, a campaign finance market does not exist, anywhere, and thus informal institutions in campaign finance markets are chimerical. Or we could hypothesize that sanctioning mechanisms can also emerge informally. Because both contributors and politicians have strong interests in maintaining exchange in the campaign finance market, they could endogenously develop enforcement mechanisms or behavioral norms to enhance credible commitments. Scholars have demonstrated that such mechanisms have emerged in the United States: politicians have deliberately crafted quasi-institutional contractual safeguards such as seniority rules and committee specialization as ways to enhance their reputation and the likelihood of repeat play (Kroszner and Stratmann 1998, 1183).

Campaign funds contracts cannot rest on formal institutional safeguards. Instead, exchange must rely on informal institutions of reputation, iteration, and sanctions. To illustrate these hypotheses more clearly, I now turn to the case of Brazil.

INFORMAL CAMPAIGN FINANCE INSTITUTIONS IN BRAZIL

Until 1994 we lacked any hard information about the cost of Brazilian campaigns, because only in that year did candidates have to start submitting records of all contributions (e.g., Samuels 2001a, 2001b, 2001c, 2002). We now possess data confirming that elections at all levels in Brazil are very costly, and that money matters a great deal.[7] Tables 4.1 and 4.2 provide information on the amounts of money candidates raised for campaigns in Brazil.[8]

Brazilian elections are expensive, across the board. To put these costs in perspective, we can first note that in August 2002 the U.S. dollar was worth about R$2.50.

TABLE 4.1
Declared Contributions, Presidential Races, Brazil

Year	Candidate	Contributions (R$, Aug. 2002)	Vote %
1994	F. H. Cardoso (PSDB)	77,259,290	54.3
	Lula (PT)	3,125,494	27.0
	Quércia (PMDB)	23,052,571	4.4
	Amin (PPR)	470,937	2.7
1998	F. H. Cardoso (PSDB)	66,363,204	53.1
	Lula (PT)	3,572,438	31.7
	Ciro (PPS)	1,622,729	11.0
2002	Serra (PSDB)	18,177,712	23.2
	Lula (PT)	26,589,234	46.4
	Ciro (PPS)	13,028,981	12.0
	Garotinho (PSB)	1,411,265	17.9

Note: PSBD, Brazilian Social Democratic Party; PT, Workers' Party; PMDB, Brazilian Democratic Movement Party; PPR, Progressive Renewal Party; PPS, Popular Socialist Party; PSB, Brazilian Socialist Party.

TABLE 4.2
Average Declared Contributions by Office

Year	Position (no.)	Contribution (R$, Aug. 2002)		
		Winners	Losers	All
1994	Governor (82)	5,929,190 (87.5%)	1,523,653 (62.8%)	2,680,107 (67.8%)
	Senator (127)	857,311 (91.2%)	316,739 (53.8%)	485,268 (62.7%)
	Deputy (1,542)	252,401 (90.9%)	65,139 (53.4%)	114,808 (59.9%)
1998	Governor (81)	3,263,717 (62.9%)	1,094,682	1,549,912
	Senator (90)	1,392,398	106,475	477,964
	Deputy (1,849)	—	—	101,884 (54.1%)
2002	Governor (145)	2,762,693 (96.3%)	899,862 (71.3%)	1,223,270 (74.7%)
	Senator (242)	814,926 (98.1%)	149,223 (72.5%)	295,018 (77.3%)
	Deputy (2,554)	224,433 (100%)	36,254 (55.0%)	74,034 (60.5%)

Note: Percentages in parentheses are percentage of candidates in each cell who provided data.

Thus, for example, even though a winning congressional candidate in Brazil does not spend nearly as much as a winning U.S. House candidate does ($530,000 on average in 1994), candidates in Brazil are legally prohibited from purchasing television or radio advertising,[9] and a dollar goes a lot further in Brazil, where annual per capita income is less than US$5,000.

Why Provide a Supply?

Clearly, a market for campaign funds thrives in Brazil. Why is this so, and what supports informal campaign finance institutions? Why do potential contributors provide money? Potential contributors in Brazil are very willing to open their wallets because elected officials control the distribution of valuable resources—for example, export subsidies, banking regulations, exchange rate controls, and pork-barrel funds (Ames 1987, 1995a, 1995b; Abrúcio 1998; Bezerra 1999). Let me focus briefly on the exchange of campaign funds for government public works contracts. Brazilian legislators can influence the geographic distribution of pork-barrel projects, and spend a good deal of their time attempting to do just that (Ames 1995b). Construction companies desire government contracts for such projects, and they have two reasons to provide a supply of campaign funds to politicians. First, they want the funds directed to where their firm operates, as opposed to where other firms do. They invest in candidates who, so they believe, will successfully "bring home the bacon" (Bezerra 1999, 242). Second, politicians not only influence the distribution of projects and authorize their initiation, but can also influence when and even whether the firm will actually get paid for an existing project (Bezerra 1999, 245). Because funds for pork-barrel projects are scarce, potential donors have strong incentives to invest heavily, so that they are not excluded from the division of the spoils.

What Generates Demand?

An exploration of the demand side of the equation also explains why Brazilian campaigns are so costly. Demand is a function of inter- and intraparty competition, and both forms of competition in Brazil have grown increasingly fierce since the return to competitive elections. The number of effective parties in legislative elections rose from 2.4 in 1982 to 8.2 by 1994 and has stayed fairly high since then (Nicolau 1997, 316). Candidates in all parties now face more intense interparty competition. Because party organizations are generally weak and do not help individual candidates on the campaign trail, candidates must raise their own funds to survive the electoral battle—and must raise as much as they can.

In legislative elections, intraparty competition also drives up campaign costs. For congressional elections, Brazil uses open-list proportional representation electoral rules in at-large districts that conform to state boundaries (there are twenty-six states and a federal district). The number of seats per state/district ranges from eight to seventy (the total number of seats is 513). Parties can nominate up to 1.5 candidates per seat in each district, and multiparty alliances can nominate up to 2 candidates per seat in each district. In the largest district in 2002 (São Paulo), this meant that 705 candidates competed for seventy seats, while 60 candidates competed for eight spots in the smallest district with the least competition (Tocantins).

This electoral system generates tremendous incentives for individualistic campaign tactics (Carey and Shugart 1995). Candidates must compete for votes against their list-mates—as well as opposing parties' candidates—and cannot appeal to voters solely on a partisan (i.e., programmatic) basis. Instead, to win votes they must build up a "personal vote" base. This requires raising and spending money on favors, gifts, or other particularistic goods. Because of this need, electoral systems like Brazil's promote relatively high individual campaign spending, and as the degree of competition in such systems increases, so does the level of spending (Cox and Thies 1998). Like interparty competition, intraparty competition has also increased in Brazil following redemocratization. The number of candidates per seat in federal deputy elections increased from 3.3 in 1982 to 8.2 in 2002 (Santos 1994, 60; Brazil Tribunal Superior Eleitoral 2002a, 2002b). When candidates under open-list proportional representation face increased intraparty competition, they must raise and spend more money in order to stand out from the crowd.

Reputation and Iteration I

We know that campaigns are expensive in Brazil partly because of the considerable incentives to provide supply and generate demand. However, these are insufficient for market exchange to occur and thus insufficient to explain the emergence of informal campaign finance institutions. We still must discover whether reputation, iteration, and sanctions exist to support such institutions. Scholars concur that Brazilian politicians—even those on the left, though to a lesser degree—strive to construct a strong personal reputation for delivering particularistic goods (Ames 1995a, 1995b; Mainwaring 1998). Politicians seek recognition for generating public works project for their region, and for providing individualized favors such as jobs, food, or small loans. Such a reputation is the key to most Brazilian politicians' career success, and few politicians survive in the system merely as advocates of programmatic policy positions. A Brazilian politician who turned away from the provision of particularistic goods would be subject to retaliation. A reputation as one who "brings home the bacon" not only helps solidify a reputation with voters, but also helps the politician develop a reputation with potential campaign contributors, who might also shy away from a purely "programmatic" politician.

One might question whether firms and congressional politicians in Brazil can develop long-term relationships, because turnover in the Chamber of Deputies with each successive election exceeds 50 percent. In contrast, turnover in the U.S. House is less than 10 percent with each election. Do Brazilian deputies not "stay bought"? In fact, Brazilian politicians do have long-term *political* careers, even though they may not have long-term *congressional* careers. Most deputies arrive in the Chamber after spending some years serving in a state legislature, on municipal councils, or even as mayor. Typically they spend one or two terms in the Chamber and then continue their careers outside the national legislature, returning to state or local politics. For example, they seek to serve again as mayor or to move to a more powerful position in state government (Samuels 2003). In Brazil, executive positions in subnational governments wield significantly more power to hire and fire and to implement public works projects than do positions in the national legislature.

As in the United States or Japan, the structure of political careers in Brazil solidifies politicians' reputations and establishes that they will engage in repeat play with potential campaign financiers, but in a particular way. Brazilian politicians never stray far from their local or state origins, even while serving in the national legislature; they begin cultivating relationships with campaign financiers early in their careers. When they reach the Chamber of Deputies, they continue to develop these relationships and seek to deliver more substantial government contracts. Subsequently, their career path both leads them to positions with greater capacity to dip into the pork barrel and returns them to where the projects will actually be implemented. Firms with budget interests take a long-term view and seek to invest in enduring relationships with politicians who will exert long-term influence over government resources (Bezerra 1999, 245).

Brazilian politicians have long-term political careers that require constant sources of funding, and thus they have strong incentives to develop long-term relationships with potential campaign financiers. Likewise, potential financiers want to support politicians who will enrich their coffers through delivery of government contracts over the long term. The structure of political careers in Brazil thus serves as an analogue to the seniority system in the U.S. House and lends credence to the notion that reputation and iteration support informal contracting mechanisms in Brazil (Kroszner and Stratmann 1998, 1183).

Reputation and Iteration II: The Importance of Friends and Family

Another factor supports this notion. If credibility is a function of reputation and iteration, then familiarity breeds confidence. In Brazil, although the campaign funds market is well capitalized, it is dominated by relatively few actors. Only about ten individuals, on average, contribute to each congressional campaign, in contrast to the dozens or even hundreds of contributors to congressional campaigns in the United States. Moreover, many of those who do contribute are candidates' immediate family, close friends, or business associates. Nepotism and family political "dynasties" are facts of Brazilian political life (e.g., Lewin 1987). This very narrow contributor base makes any implicit "contract" more credible and visible, because candidates and contributors are highly likely to be personally close to each other in a social network.

The "neighborliness" of the market for campaign funds in Brazil contrasts with the more open system of campaign funds in the United States. For example, Sorauf (1988, 43) estimated that as much as 10 percent of the U.S. voting-age population contributed money to some campaign in 1984. Even a significantly more conservative estimate exposes an extraordinarily wide difference between Brazil and the United States: if we assume that only 1 *percent* of the U.S. voting-age population contributed money, that is still more than a million people. In Brazil, fewer than seventy-five thousand individuals give to *all* campaigns in each cycle. This is about 0.075 percent of Brazil's voting-age population of about a hundred million, less than a tenth of the conservative estimate for the United States.

Unfortunately, we lack data on the number of corporate contributors to political campaigns in the United States, because direct corporate contributions are prohibited and because political action committees may represent one or hundreds of corporations. Thus, we cannot directly compare Brazil and the United States along these lines. Still, we can note how relatively few firms in Brazil contribute to political campaigns: less than three corporations, on average, provided campaign funds to each congressional candidate, even though firms provide about two-thirds of all contributions, on average, in each congressional election (Brazil, Tribunal Superior Eleitoral 2002). As with individual contributions, we often see dozens of PAC contributions to each U.S. congressional campaign.

The relatively "closed" nature of the campaign finance market in Brazil means that candidates are likely to be personally familiar with their campaign financiers, which facilitates construction of the politician's reputation and increases the likelihood of iteration. In addition, familiarity—the high probability that contributors are members of the candidate's family or are the candidate's business partners, as well as the high probability that the politician plans to return to local politics later on—serves to strengthen "sanctioning" norms. Specific examples from two states illustrate the situation.

In the state of Rio Grande do Norte, known for its patrimonial and insular politics (not unlike many of Brazil's other states), nine of the twenty-nine donors to one winning deputy candidate in 1994 had his family's name. These donors were responsible for providing 85 percent of the candidate's funds. Three of the seven individual donors to another winning candidate from the same state were family members, and these donors accounted for 53 percent of his campaign funds (Brazil, Tribunal Superior Eleitoral 2002).[10] This familiarity is not only a characteristic of Brazil's smaller, more backward states. São Paulo, Brazil's largest and most economically advanced state, has a population of about thirty million (about the size of Argentina), and accounts for about 40 percent of Brazil's gross domestic product, which is the tenth-largest in the world (perhaps). Still, the state's industrial base is highly concentrated, and despite its large population and relatively complex economic base, relatively few people and companies enter the campaign finance market. Several of the candidates best known for their business connections received contributions from relatively few firms. Deputy Antônio Delfim Neto, who previously held the positions of Minister of Finance, of Agriculture, and of Planning, received contributions from a grand total of seventeen firms and three people. The firms provided 85 percent of his total of approximately R$700,000 in contributions in 2002 (Brazil, Tribunal Superior Eleitoral 2002).

Politicians in Brazil seek to establish iterated, long-term relationships with potential campaign financiers to develop their reputations. They want to establish themselves as competent providers of pork, both to voters and to the firms that thrive on government contracts. Given that most campaign contributions come from family members and a small number of firms, Brazilian politicians are much more likely to have a tight personal relationship with their financiers. This familiarity helps solidify a reputation, enhances the long-term prospects for the relationship, and reduces the likelihood that the politician (or the contributors) will "defect."

Sanctioning Mechanisms

Campaign finance relationships in Brazil seem quite "cozy." Not only does familiarity breed confidence, but the limited number of contributors to each campaign serves as an informal oversight and sanctioning mechanism. It is likely that those who give to a campaign know who else has given (the data are available on the internet soon after the election), and given their small numbers and the possibility that kinship connections exist between them, donors can observe and share information about the politician's behavior. We therefore ought not to see many politicians reneging on their deals, because information about their behavior is relatively good among their financial supporters. Still, despite the apparent coziness of campaign funds relationships, the possibility exists that politicians and/or financiers could renege on implicit campaign funds contracts. A family feud could erupt, or competition for government contracts could emerge between firms in a politician's bailiwick, which would allow a politician to break a contract with one firm if another offered a greater payoff.

However, the threat of punishment for reneging does exist. For example, a firm that fails to receive preferential treatment in exchange for a contribution can refuse to supply additional funds for the politician's next election. Elsewhere, I have found a strong statistical relationship between deputies' ability to obtain pork from the executive branch and their ability to obtain campaign finance (Samuels 2002). This provides (indirect, at least) support for the notion that informal contracts exist. Politicians who fail to "bring home the bacon" will subsequently fail to reap substantial campaign finance contributions.

Officeholders can also play hardball. Politicians control substantial government resources that potential campaign financiers desire. If a politician directs a government contract to a firm with an implicit understanding that campaign funds will be forthcoming in exchange, but then receives none, the politician can retaliate in at least two ways. As noted above, he or she could refuse to direct any other projects that firm's way or could attempt to delay payment on the firm's existing contract. A delay of several months or a year could substantially affect a firm's cash flow.

Sanctioning should not occur very often; we should observe it only in extraordinary circumstances. Detecting such instances of defection will be extremely difficult for an academic observer, but a good example does exist: the impeachment of President Fernando Collor de Mello in 1992. In 1989, Collor won Brazil's first democratic presidential election since 1960, but by early 1992 his administration was embroiled in a scandal that had at its center his campaign funds "bag man," Paulo César Farias. In 1989, Farias had requested and obtained massive infusions of cash to win the election against the leftist Workers' Party candidate Lula, who led early in the polls. However, after the election, Farias made the rounds once again and demanded more cash, this time in exchange for "access" to the newly elected president. "Going to the well" a second time violates the spirit of the campaign finance contract, since it seems that donors gained nothing from their initial contribution before Farias reappeared and demanded additional funds. Because the requests for money now openly stank of extortion, many firms refused to provide additional contributions. As punishment, Collor and Farias then "had [these firms'] disbursements for goods and services already performed through 1989 halted, and they were blacklisted from any new contracts." Some of the more vulnerable firms were bankrupted (Fleischer 1997, 302).

This attitude violated accepted practice. "Normal" campaign finance contracts carry implicit understandings that money buys at least access, if not influence. In contrast, Collor's scheme implied that money buys nothing, and failure to contribute would result in government interference in your business. Moreover, Collor apparently did not let sleeping dogs lie—he actively attempted to "undermine established political forces and power centers" that opposed his scheme (Weyland 1993, 13). These forces were not just opposition parties, which lacked broad representation in Congress, but members of the traditional political class and the business community.

Collor's corrupt practices paralleled his attitude toward Brazil's party system. He sought to govern without Brazil's established political parties and regional leaders and their congressional representatives, refusing to engage in the pork-barrel "wheeling and dealing" that had long characterized Brazilian politics. Thus Collor not only failed to share the wealth through his corruption schemes, he alienated potential political allies through his unilateral governing style. This also deviated from expected norms.

Collor's presidency failed because the enormous scale of his corruption schemes attracted substantial press attention, and because his corruption and his governing style alienated the dominant, established political class. It remains unclear whether these politicians wanted a piece of the action or wanted an end to the corruption. Regardless, the point remains that Collor had violated expected norms of behavior. (My view does imply that if Collor had "shared the wealth" a bit earlier, he could have saved his presidency.) As his administration came under increasing press scrutiny, Congress opened an investigatory commission. By that time the business community and those politicians whom Collor had excluded or punished returned the favor by refusing to support the president when he attempted to negotiate for their support. In the end, Collor's scheme came crashing down and he was impeached by a Congress unwilling to let him rewrite the rules of political bargaining in Brazil. Collor's impeachment demonstrated not only that Brazil's political institutions can work as expected, but also that politicians will punish those who clearly divert from long-established expected behavioral norms.

Even a relatively chaotic and fragmented political market like Brazil's can support the ingredients necessary for credible campaign finance contracts to emerge.

Politicians may have strong incentives to construct solid reputations that will endure over time and that can develop sanctioning mechanisms. Politicians' desire to develop a "personal vote" characterizes many systems. Although Brazil's particular career path may be unique, politicians elsewhere are likely to have established signaling devices or ways to provide contributors with the information that they are in politics for the long haul. Likewise, the importance of family is not unique to Brazil, nor is the highly elitist nature of politics. In short, in many countries, similar dynamics may ensure that market exchange in campaign finance can occur and thus informal campaign finance institutions may emerge that are accommodative to the formal prohibition of bribery and extortion, yet reflect donors' desire to influence government and politicians' desire for money to continue their careers.

CONCLUSION

In this chapter I have outlined five hypotheses that permit a cross-national exploration of the emergence of informal campaign finance institutions. First, the supply of money in elections is a function of the incentives that potential contributors have to influence the distribution of government services. Second, the demand for campaign funds is a function of the degree of inter-and intraparty competition. Third, market exchange and thus informal contracting will occur to the degree that (a) politicians seek to establish a reputation, (b) politicians seek to engage in repeated interactions with donors, and (c) politicians and donors have established quasi-institutional sanctioning mechanisms. Additional research is obviously necessary to further assess these hypotheses and to further explore the importance of campaign finance for politics.

These hypotheses may not hold everywhere. Potential contributors' incentives to provide a supply of money will vary based on elected officials' (as opposed to unelected bureaucrats') ability to influence the distribution of government services and funds. The focus of contributors' largesse may also vary, based on the executive-legislative balance of power. In addition, politicians' incentives to develop a reputation, play an iterated game, and develop secure contracting mechanisms will also vary, depending on the nature of political career structures both internal and external to political parties. As implied in this analysis of Brazil, we may have to look to the state or even local level to detect sanctioning and reputation-enhancing mechanisms.

In broad perspective, the "democratic problem" in Brazil and similar countries is not the absence of credible commitments, or their relatively weak institutionalization, but their excess. Informal institutions are the glue that holds clientelistic relationships together. Credible commitments are the roots of personalism, patrimo-nialism, and nepotism, all of which are based on trust, familiarity, the strength of reputations, and the high likelihood of repeat interactions, possibly over numerous generations. The problem is whether these are the "right" kind of credible commitments for democratic consolidation. A discussion of that important issue is beyond the scope of this chapter. Nevertheless, I have argued that by adopting a methodologically individualist "soft" rational choice approach to the study of campaign finance, scholars can obtain a more precise and thus more informative view of the dynamics of these often opaque yet critical dynamics of democratic politics.

CHAPTER FIVE

The Difficult Road from *Caudillismo* to Democracy

The Impact of Clientelism in Honduras

MICHELLE M. TAYLOR-ROBINSON

In democratic theory, the legislative branch of government is supposed to be the representative branch, representing the views of the people in policy debates.[1] But despite the legislature's intended function of representing the people's interests in government, electoral institutions do not necessarily create an incentive for legislators to represent the interests of the people of their district (Cox 1987; Taylor 1996). They may instead create an incentive for deputies to represent their party or the party elites who control their political future (Carey and Shugart 1995). If so, the legislature will be ineffective at fulfilling its representative function.

Part of what makes this theory elegant is its transportability to any democratic setting, but whether context and preexisting informal institutions affect how legislatures function is a question of growing interest (Desposato 2001, and this volume). Theory about formal institutional design predicts the ways in which electoral institutions and party nomination procedures create incentives for legislators to seek a personal or a partisan vote and to deliver pork-barrel projects to their district (Mayhew 1974; Lancaster 1986; Cain et al. 1987; Carey and Shugart 1995). Yet the incentives that formal electoral institutions create are often not sufficient to explain the behavior of legislators in Latin America (Taylor 1992; Carey 1996).

Instead, informal institutions may fill, or partly fill, the representation gap left by the ineffective representation provided by formal institutions. For example, in Costa Rica, parties have developed informal incentives for their deputies to represent local interests (Taylor 1992; Carey 1996). Parties view the representation of local interests as necessary for winning the next presidential election. Thus, party leaders monitor whether deputies attend to local community and constituent needs, and indicate to deputies that performing such service is an important part of their job and their contribution to the party's next campaign effort. Because Costa Rican deputies cannot be immediately reelected, the only way they can continue their political careers is if their party wins the presidency, in which case they can be appointed to a post in the executive branch. Thus, if they do not help their party to maintain strong local support, they may be unable to continue their political career.

In many Latin American countries, it is assumed that because deputies serve their party and its leaders, local interests are not represented in the national policy debate (Shugart 2001). Informal institutions may help fill this local representation gap. Parties may be able to use the informal institution of patron-client relations, particularly clientelistic networks attached to parties, to "represent" (some) local interests. Informal institutions—such as clientelism—that have long helped people get things done may enhance, or substitute for, the performance of formal institutions installed as part of a new democratic regime (Whitehead 2002; Helmke and Levitsky, introduction to this volume). For example, parties that developed in a patron-client environment may expect deputies to maintain the support of their clients so that the party will retain its mass support in the next election.[2] If so, clientelism is a "substitutive" informal institution (Helmke and Levitsky, introduction). Clientelism is obviously not a perfect substitute, as clients of opposition parties are excluded from representation, and programmatic representation is minimal. However, particularly for poor people, for whom state patronage and local public goods are likely to be of greater value than representation on national policy issues (Desposato 2001), clientelism creates a chance that their legislative patron will represent their interests when their party is in power. This substitutive role of clientelism may help explain why an apparently anachronistic informal institution persists even as procedural democracy consolidates. To explore these questions, this chapter examines the legislative record of members of the Honduran Congress.

A TALE OF TWO LITERATURES:
ELECTORAL SYSTEMS AND CLIENTELISM

The electoral systems and clientelism literatures rarely speak to each other. The former is firmly grounded in the rational choice school, and thus intent on showing how electoral institutions create incentives for certain types of behaviors by rational actors ranging from voters to parties to politicians. The latter literature is based in sociology and anthropology, and it focuses on explaining social relationships in traditional societies; political scientists studying machine politics have adopted it

(Banfield and Wilson 1965; Scott 1969). The two literatures have in common the assumption that actors pursue the strategy that they think will best enable them to achieve their goals.

The electoral institution literature assumes that rational reelection-seeking politicians will work to please the party elites and constituents who control their renomination and reelection chances (Fenno 1978; Cain et al. 1987). The rational patron will provide enough services to clients to keep them from looking elsewhere for help, but will not squander scarce resources that could be used to acquire more clients (Graham 1990).

Electoral institutions create incentives for politicians to seek a personal or a partisan vote.[3] As the party becomes increasingly important for winning elections, politicians have an incentive to build the party's reputation—to make the party label a meaningful brand name for voters. Where a responsible party model applies, the voter can choose the party whose platform is closest to her ideal point. Where parties do not present competing packages of policies, but compete for voter loyalty at an emotional level, the party label still frees the voter from having to know each candidate as an individual. In either case, the voter votes for a party, not for the candidate as an individual. By contrast, where parties have less influence on how people vote, candidates have an incentive to seek a personal vote by creating an individual image, through advertising, credit-claiming, and position-taking (Mayhew 1974). Closed-list proportional representation (PR) electoral rules, particularly where national party leaders control ballot access and list position, produce a strong incentive to build a partisan reputation. Politicians have an incentive to build a personal reputation in open-list PR and preference voting systems, and where competitive primaries determine nominations.

Electoral strategy also varies with district magnitude (DM). In closed-list PR elections, the incentive to seek a partisan vote should rise as DM increases. The larger the number of candidates on a party's list, the harder it is to distinguish oneself from copartisans, since the voter has to vote for a party's entire list even if he would like to vote for a particular politician. However, when DM is small, politicians can seek a personal vote along with a partisan vote, because an individual candidate can stand out to voters (Shugart et al. 2005). In open-list PR elections, the incentive to seek a personal vote should increase as DM rises, as it becomes more important for a candidate to distinguish herself from copartisans and from candidates of other parties (Ames 2001).

Carey cautions that "when legislators cannot be reelected, they have no direct electoral incentives to build personal support among voters through particularism, regardless of how the electoral system is organized" (1996, 103–4). This logic should also apply when reelection is permitted but is unlikely.

In the U.S. Congress, members who experience a close election are expected to perform more constituency service than those who win by a large margin (Fenno 1978; Johannes 1984). In PR systems, a similar incentive should exist for deputies elected from a marginal position on their party's list. They should perform more constituency service as part of their effort to move up the list to a safe position to protect themselves from a possible vote swing against their party.

In sum, the electoral institution literature points to several hypotheses about when politicians would be expected to engage in constituency service work:

- H1: Politicians will be more likely to perform constituency service when they are elected by open-list PR than when elected by closed-list PR electoral rules.
- H2: Politicians elected by closed-list PR electoral rules will be more likely to perform constituency service as DM approaches 1.
- H3: Politicians will be more likely to perform constituency service as the chance of reelection increases.
- H4: Politicians elected from a marginal position on their party's list will be more likely to perform constituency service than those elected from a safe list position.

The clientelism and machine politics literature also has implications for the behavior of elected officials. Clientelism can be defined as a mode of social stratification in which clients and patrons are tied to one another in a mutually beneficial but unequal exchange relationship (Lemarchand 1981). A political machine is a party organization in which local political bosses are patrons who offer inducements to clients in exchange for political support and votes (Banfield and Wilson 1965). Two specific circumstances are conducive to political machines. (1) A candidate needs to win votes to obtain office, but can win votes by delivering favors and tangible rewards to people, rather than promises about policy. (2) Traditional deference patterns have broken down, so that parties maintain the support of their voters by providing "concrete, short-run, material inducements" (Scott 1969, 1146). As new loyalties emerge (e.g., class, occupational ties) and the state provides universal social welfare programs to attend to basic needs, people become more concerned about policy or ideology, and the machine is no longer feasible (Banfield and Wilson 1965).

When these propitious circumstances exist, the machine specializes in the "political distribution of public works through pork-barrel legislation and in the dispensation of jobs and favors through more informal channels" (Scott 1969, 1147–48). This type of community and personalistic service-providing machine is likely to occur where electoral politics exists in a context in which much of the population is poor and has little education (Banfield and Wilson 1965; Scott 1969, 1149). Poverty forces voters to care more about personal inducements or projects they can see in their community than about policy platforms that may not produce real benefits for a voter in the near future. Yet, clients should have power under certain circumstances. If the patron is a monopoly provider of services, clients cannot expect much service in exchange for their political loyalty and votes. When patrons are competing for a community's support, they must pay higher dividends to their followers in exchange for their votes (Scott 1969; Auyero 2000a).

Thus, the clientelism and machine politics literatures also point to hypotheses about when politicians would be expected to engage in constituency service work:

- H5: Politicians should engage in more constituency service work in poor districts than in districts with more middle-class voters.
- H6: Politicians should provide more services in competitive districts, where voters have the option of transferring their loyalty to another politician (power broker) or party that seems more likely to deliver concrete services.

WHY HONDURAS?

The Honduran Congress offers a likely case for finding that long-standing informal institutions affect the performance of newer formal democratic institutions. Two traditional political parties with clientelistic connections to voters dominate Honduran politics. The country's limited economic resources and poverty mean that the state faces demands for services that exceed its capacity to respond. Formulaic, needs-based criteria for state aid to communities and individuals would bankrupt the state and break tight budgets imposed by international lending agencies. Clientelistic connections provide a mechanism for allocating state resources, and allow the party in government to use time-honored methods to reward supporters.[4] For example, a person may need a deputy's help to get a doctor's appointment at a state hospital, or a scholarship for schoolbooks. When a new government (party) takes office, throngs of party supporters (clients) line up for government jobs. On the opposite side, a community organization affiliated with the out-of-power party will be passed over for state resources.

The Liberal (PLH) and National (PNH) parties have dominated Honduran politics since the beginning of the twentieth century.[5] They were established as tools in the competition between the international banana companies operating in the country, but became autonomous entities after the banana companies merged in 1929. The parties continue to compete for power and the access to state resources that power provides. During their periods in office, both parties have been accused of corruption and political favoritism, as state resources (such as jobs, contracts, infrastructure projects) have been distributed to supporters, and opposition supporters have been excluded from the spoils.

Clientelism (among other factors such as lack of raw materials and isolation) is often blamed for the lack of economic development in Honduras (Posas and del Cid 1983; Euraque 2000; Mahoney 2001). During the many brief civil wars in the nineteenth century, and the period of competition between the banana companies in the early twentieth century, it was not rational for villages to invest in economic development, as battles often destroyed their efforts. It was easier to support the winning side in a conflict and obtain a share of the state spoils (Munro 1967, 126–32). A patron was a necessity in this poor country made up of isolated communities, as the government had no capacity to take care of the vast range of people's needs. Economic and political elites took on the role of providers and, in return, their clients supported them in elections and civil wars.

This expectation that political *caudillos* would share state resources with their supporters has continued in the current democratic regime. Honduran presidents have difficulty pursuing policy initiatives, despite their strong partisan powers (Mainwaring and Shugart 1997), because they are busy attending to the promises of "pork" and patronage they made to get elected (Taylor 1996). Deputies also feel pressure to attend to the needs of communities and individual supporters. As one deputy remarked when explaining why it is difficult to focus on legislating: "Honduran voters do not understand that a deputy's job is to legislate, and they do not value legislation because you cannot eat a law."[6] Local party activists work to promote the electoral fortunes of their faction leader. In return, they expect jobs, personal favors, and pork-barrel projects for their communities. As elsewhere, however, clientelism in Honduras is an unequal relationship, for it is very costly for a client to defect from her patron. The client can switch allegiance to another party, but will receive benefits from doing so only if the party wins the presidency, and if there are not many more people with stronger connections to the patron/party who precede her in the line for benefits.

The current democratic regime in Honduras was installed in 1982 after a decade of military rule, but, in many respects, democracy brought little real change. The traditional parties continue to dominate elections, control all branches of government, and dole out state resources to their supporters. The Christian Democratic Party (PDCH) and the Innovation and National Unity Party (PINU) won a few seats in Congress beginning in 1982, and Democratic Unification (PUD) won representation beginning in 1997. The small parties have campaigned on ending corruption and substituting a policy-oriented platform for patronage politics, but they have not been electorally successful, as voters continue to support the traditional parties.[7] The clearest indicator of popular frustration with the status quo is decreasing voter turnout. One reason for the decline in turnout is that Honduran voters with clientelistic attachments to traditional parties do not want to vote for the opposition, even if they are displeased with the policies and performance of the government. Thus, clients of the incumbent party show their frustration by staying home on election day, rather than by voting for the opposition.

Honduras holds closed-list PR elections (DM ranges from 1 to 23), and national party elites control party lists. The president, three vice presidents, and a unicameral Congress are elected concurrently for a four-year term. Until 1997, elections for the president and Congress were "fused," giving the president long coattails and ensuring his position as the leader of his party's clientelistic network (Rosenberg 1995; Taylor 1996).[8] Under such conditions, theory predicts strong party loyalty by elected officials and an emphasis on building the party label rather than a personal reputation.

National-level party leaders, who are the leaders of the party's main factions, control ballot access and determine list positions. During the 1990s, both traditional parties began holding primaries to select their presidential candidate, but deputy slates are still the result of backroom dealing. Presidential precandidates run with a slate of deputy aspirants in the primary, but results are not binding. Some deputies claim that their list position improved after local party activists insisted that the listings were too low for deputies who were valuable to the party and would win local votes,[9] but party leaders, especially the presidential candidate, still have the final say over party lists.

DATA AND OPERATIONALIZATION OF VARIABLES

To examine how electoral rules and clientelism affect the behavior of elected officials, I analyze whether deputies initiate bills with a local target.[10] These projects, if passed into law, represent concrete benefits for a community. A school, a road, or electricity is a project for which the deputy can credibly claim credit, which can further his political career, or enhance his reputation as a patron.[11]

Initiating local legislation is only one of many activities for deputies. They have other legislative activities, such as initiating other types of bills, committee work, and debates; party duties, such as campaigning and training local party activists; and constituency-oriented activities, such as trips to the district and helping individuals with problems. However, examining deputies' legislative records has some advantages for the investigation of the behavior of deputies. First, initiating bills is public behavior. It is work that the deputy can easily advertise to party leaders and constituents, so it is a type of electoral currency deputies can use to further their political careers. Second, both governing party and opposition deputies can initiate bills. While opposition deputies' bills are less likely to become law, they provide examples of the type of work the deputy would do if his party were in power. By comparison, contacting a minister or agency head to obtain a benefit for a community or individual is almost completely infeasible for an opposition deputy.[12]

Bills are not the only way a deputy can produce services for constituents, and electoral or clientelism benefits for herself. Deputies from the governing party can work through the executive branch to add items to a ministry's budget (e.g., for the Ministry of Health to build a clinic in a village). They can help constituents obtain government jobs, and provide other services (e.g., transporting a sick person to the doctor, interceding to get a constituent out of jail). Opposition deputies can work with nongovernmental organizations to obtain aid for their district, and use personal resources to help constituents. These activities are part of the patron-client relationship (Graham 1990; Auyero 2000a),[13] and deputies mentioned them in interviews as an expected part of their job, though we lack systematic data to measure them in Honduras. However, providing pork-barrel services to communities is another way that a deputy can build her reputation as a strong local patron, foster a personal reputation in politics, and represent at least some of the interests of poor communities. Entrepreneurial deputies (patrons trying to expand their client base, or politicians seeking a personal vote) can use pork projects as part of their strategy to achieve their goals. If a deputy obtains a project for a community (e.g., an electricity generator or a school), she can establish herself as a patron for the community. Pork-barrel projects are also an efficient way in poor areas for a deputy or her party to win the support of the beneficiary community in the next election.

I analyze the legislative records of 256 deputies from the 1990–93 and 1994–97 congresses. During the 1990–93 term, the PNH held the presidency and 71 of the 128 seats in Congress. From 1994 to 1997, the president was from the PLH, and the Liberals held 71 of the 128 Congress seats. In both terms, the major opposition party held 55 seats, and the PINU held 2 seats. Only *propietarios* (elected representatives) are included in the analysis because *suplentes* (substitutes) can propose bills only when called to fill in for a *propietario*. While some *suplentes* do initiate bills, most do not, and it is not possible to determine whether that is due to a lack of interest in legislating or a lack of opportunity.

Dependent Variable. As the indicator of deputy behavior, I use a binary variable, coded 1 if the deputy initiated at least one locally targeted bill (mean = .33, SD = .47). This indicator focuses on the differences between deputies who initiate local bills and those who do not (67% of deputies initiated no local bills). For the 84 deputies who initiated locally targeted bills, the number initiated ranged from one bill each by 39 deputies to nineteen local bills initiated by 1 deputy.[14] Twenty-three deputies initiated two locally targeted bills, 11 deputies initiated three, and 6 deputies initiated four local bills. Thus, of the 84 deputies who initiated locally targeted bills, 79 initiated four or fewer, so it was most interesting to explore the differences between deputies who initiated at least some locally targeted legislation and those deputies for whom local bills were not a part of their legislative agenda.

Independent Variables. The following independent variables are constructed to measure electoral and clientelism incentives. The closer district magnitude is to 1, the greater the incentive to seek a personal vote. Honduras's 18 departments are the country's electoral districts, and *district magnitude*, the number of *propietarios* elected from a department, ranges from 1 to 23 (mean = 11.7, SD = 7.33).

Electoral incentives are expected to influence politicians' behavior only if they can be reelected. Reelection is possible in Honduras, but reelection rates vary across departments. The variable *average percentage of deputies reelected in department* is the percentage of deputies elected as *propietarios* or *suplentes* for term t_1 who were also elected as *propietarios* in term t_2 (range = 0%–64%, mean = 39, SD = 11.5).[15] This percentage was calculated for the 1982–85/1986–89 term pair, the 1986–89/ 1990–93 term pair, and the 1990–93/1994–97 term pair. The average of the first two term pairs was used as *average percentage of deputies reelected in department* for the deputies serving in the 1990–93 Congress, and the average of all three term pairs was used for the deputies serving in the 1994–97 Congress.

Whether a deputy's list position is marginal or safe can also create an incentive to seek a personal vote. A party can develop expectations about the number of seats it is likely to win in a district based on its past performance, and can place the most important or valued candidates in safe positions near the top of the slate. *Marginal list position* is coded 1 if the deputy's list position was marginal (mean = .41, SD = .49).

The level of education in a department, specifically *percentage of department population with no education* (no formal schooling), is used as the proxy indicator for demand for clientelistic services.[16] The clientelism literature expects people with little or no education to have both the highest need for a patron to intercede to help them and their community with problems and the most difficulty in obtaining and evaluating information about abstract policy proposals (Banfield and Wilson 1965;

Scott 1969). Desposato (2001) also used this indicator to compare incentives faced by politicians across Brazilian states to trade votes on executive bills for pork. While poor people can have preferences about national policy issues, the difficulty of monitoring and enforcing such policies and the delay before a benefit is received should cause poor constituents or clients to place a higher value on local public goods than on national politics. The variable *percentage of department population with no education* ranges from 11.6 to 55.1 percent (mean = 32.6, SD = 10).

Clients are expected to be able to demand a higher payment for their vote where patrons are competing for clients. Party competition is a proxy indicator for competition among patrons. Beginning in 1993, municipal governments were elected on a separate ballot, allowing voters to split their vote and giving parties new information about their support in different localities. *Department dominance* ranges from 0 for a department where the two major parties won an equal number of municipal elections to 50 for a department where one party won all municipal elections (mean = 30.4, SD = 15.5).[17] This measure is available only for the 1994–97 Congress, since before 1993 municipal elections were part of the fused ballot that elected Congress and the president.

Models also include a binary variable coded 1 if the deputy is from the president's party and 0 otherwise. *Number of terms in Congress* ranges from 1 to 4 (mean = 1.6, SD = 0.8), and 1 indicates a deputy's first term.

FINDINGS

Various models assess the impact of electoral and clientelism incentives on the propensity of deputies to initiate local legislation. Colinearity between *district magnitude* and *percentage of department population with no education* necessitates separate models (partial correlation of −.72). The strong negative relationship between DM and poverty measures is not surprising. When a government has very limited budgets, it is logical to invest resources where the population density is highest, to produce the greatest popular impact. Citizens often "vote with their feet," moving where resources and opportunities are greatest, so the wealthiest departments have the highest populations. Since representation in the Honduran Congress is not intentionally malapportioned, the most populous departments have the largest DM.[18] Other measures of electoral incentives (e.g., reelection rates, marginal list position) can be used in the same model with measures of clientelistic incentives.

Model 1 contains the DM variable as one measure of how electoral incentives affect the propensity of deputies to initiate local bills, but does not include the poverty variable (table 5.1).[19] The model provides strong support for hypothesis 2—

TABLE 5.1
Impact of Electoral and Clientelistic Incentives on the Propensity of
Honduran Deputies to Initiate Locally Targeted Bills, One Congress Term (1994–97)

	Model 1		Model 2		Model 3	
	b (SE)	OR	*b* (SE)	OR	*b* (SE)	OR
Percentage of department population with no education	—	—	0.08** (0.02)	1.08	0.08** (0.02)	1.08
District magnitude	−0.10** (0.03)	0.90	—	—	—	—
Marginal list position	—	—	—	—	−.33 (0.48)	.72
Deputy is member of president's party	2.52*** (0.57)	12.41	2.60*** (0.56)	13.56	2.63*** (0.56)	13.84
Average percentage of deputies reelected in department	1.28 (2.29)	3.58	0.70 (2.64)	2.02	0.77 (2.76)	2.15
Department dominance	0.02 (0.01)	1.02	0.03* (0.01)	1.03	0.03* (0.02)	1.03
Number of terms in Congress	0.47*	1.60	0.45*	1.56	0.40†	1.50
	(0.23)		(0.22)		(0.24)	
Constant	−2.95* (1.21)		−6.74*** (1.87)		−6.62** (1.92)	
n	128		128		128	
χ^2	25.23**		28.33***		29.64***	
Log likelihood	−63.72		−63.57		−63.31	

Note: Table reports logit coefficients (*b*) and standard errors (SE) along with odds ratios (OR) calculated with Stata 7.0.
  †$p < .1$, *$p < .05$, **$p < .01$, ***$p < .001$

deputies will be more likely to initiate local bills as DM approaches 1. Hypothesis 3—politicians will be more likely to perform constituency service as the chance of reelection increases—lacks support. The sign is in the expected direction, but the variable is not significant. Deputies from the president's party are significantly more likely than opposition deputies to initiate local bills, and being a member of the governing party has a substantively large impact on the likelihood of initiating local pork. Finally, deputies with more experience are more likely than new members to initiate local bills.

Table 5.2 presents simulations conducted using Clarify with Stata to provide a sense of the magnitude of the impact of the significant variables (King et al. 2000; Tomz et al. 2003). Simulations based on model 1 show that when DM is set at its maximum there is a 32 percent probability that a deputy from the governing party will initiate locally targeted bills, and only a 4 percent chance that an opposition deputy will initiate local pork. As DM decreases, the likelihood that a deputy will initiate local pork increases. When DM is 1, a deputy from the president's party has an 80 percent probability of initiating local legislation, and there is a 26 percent probability that an opposition deputy will initiate a local bill.

Deputies with more experience in Congress are more likely to initiate locally targeted bills. Even when DM is set at its maximum, a deputy from the president's party who has been in Congress for four terms has a 57 percent probability of initiating local pork. However, those deputies are likely to be party and Congress leaders,[20] and they may be sponsoring bills for backbenchers that think the pork has a greater likelihood of being delivered to their district if a party leader initiates the bill. Of more interest is that senior deputies have a high likelihood of initiating local pork bills when elected from districts where DM is small. When DM is 1, senior governing party deputies have a 91 percent probability of initiating local pork, and opposition deputies with four terms of experience in Congress have a 50 percent probability of initiating a locally targeted bill.

Model 2 (table 5.1) contains the poverty variable to measure how clientelism incentives affect the propensity of deputies to initiate locally targeted bills, but does not include the DM variable. The model shows strong support for hypothesis 5— deputies are more likely to initiate local bills as the percentage of the population in their department with no education increases. Hypothesis 6, however, is not supported. Deputies' propensity to initiate locally targeted bills was expected to increase with competition for client support. The *department dominance* variable is significant, but the sign indicates that deputies are instead more likely to initiate local pork when one party dominates a department.[21]

Model 3 uses *marginal list position* as a measure of electoral incentives. Since *marginal list position* is not correlated with the poverty indicator, it can be included in the same model as *percentage of department population with no education*. While *marginal list position* does not test the theory about how electoral systems affect the incentive to seek a personal vote, it does model an incentive for a reelection-seeking politician to move to a more secure position on the list. The results are interesting because, while the department education variable is again significant and positive, contrary to hypothesis 4, deputies in marginal list positions are *less* likely than their colleagues with safe positions to initiate locally targeted bills.[22] Results for all other variables are similar to those in models 1 and 2.

These results provide strong support for the view that clientelism induces politicians to initiate locally targeted bills. Regardless of whether a deputy was elected from a safe or a marginal position on his party's list, and whether the reelection prospects in the department are high or low, deputies from poor departments are more likely to initiate locally targeted legislation than are their colleagues from

TABLE 5.2
The Probability of a Deputy Initiating a Locally Targeted Bill

SIMULATIONS BASED ON MODEL 1

	If the deputy is a member of:	
	the President's Party	the Opposition
If DM of the department is set at the:		
Minimum (DM = 1)	.80	.26
	(.63–.91)	(.12–.46)
Mean (DM = 11.7)	.58	.11
	(.46–.71)	(.05–.22)
Maximum (DM = 23)	.32	.04
	(.17–.51)	(.01–.12)

	If the deputy is a member of:			
	the President's Party and no. of terms served is set at:		the Opposition and no. of terms served is set at:	
	Min (= 1)	Max (= 4)	Min (= 1)	Max (= 4)
If DM of the department is set at the:				
Minimum (DM = 1)	.74	.91	.21	.50
	(.55–.88)	(.72–.98)	(.09–.39)	(.21–.78)
Mean (DM = 11.7)	.51	.79	.08	.27
	(.37–.65)	(.56–.93)	(.03–.18)	(.10–.52)
Maximum (DM = 23)	.26	.57	.03	.12
	(.11–.46)	(.29–.82)	(.01–.11)	(.03–.33)

better-off departments where the population has a higher educational level. However, contrary to expectations in the clientelism literature that patrons will deliver more services to clients where they face competition for client support, in Honduras deputies are most likely to initiate locally targeted bills if they are elected from a department that is dominated by one party. This indicates that when parties and government face severely constrained resources, they target state resources to reward and retain existing supporters, not to seek out new clients.

Hypotheses derived from the electoral institutions literature find less support. DM has the expected effect on deputies' propensity to initiate locally targeted bills, but it cannot be tested directly against the poverty variable. Other variables measuring an electoral incentive to initiate local bills did not perform as predicted. Election from a marginal position on the party's list does not increase the probability that a deputy will initiate local legislation. The reelection rate in a department also did not have a significant effect on the propensity to initiate local bills. Thus it seems that more than a decade after the installation of democracy, clientelism is influencing deputy behavior.

TABLE 5.2
Continued

SIMULATIONS BASED ON MODEL 3

	If the deputy is a member of:	
	the President's Party	the Opposition
If percentage of the department's population with no education is set at the:		
Minimum (11.6%)	.23	.03
	(.09–.44)	(.00–.09)
Mean (32.5%)	.59	.11
	(.48–.70)	(.04–.23)
Maximum (55.1%)	.88	.40
	(.72–.97)	(.17–.69)

	If the deputy is a member of:			
	the President's Party and no. of terms served is set at:		the Opposition and no. of terms served is set at:	
	Min (= 1)	Max (= 4)	Min (= 1)	Max (= 4)
If percentage of the department's population with no education is set at the:				
Minimum (11.6%)	.19	.43	.02	.07
	(.07–.40)	(.15–.73)	(.00–.08)	(.01–.23)
Mean (32.5%)	.53	.77	.09	.22
	(.39–.66)	(.51–.93)	(.03–.20)	(.07–.49)
Maximum (55.1%)	.86	.94	.34	.61
	(.66–.96)	(.78–.99)	(.13–.64)	(.26–.89)

	If the deputy is a member of:			
	the President's Party and dept. dominance is set at:		the Opposition and dept. dominance is set at:	
	Min (= 0)	Max (= 50)	Min (= 0)	Max (= 50)
If percentage of the department's population with no education is set at the:				
Minimum (11.6%)	.12	.35	.01	.05
	(.02–.33)	(.15–.60)	(.00–.05)	(.01–.17)
Mean (32.5%)	.37	.73	.05	.18
	(.16–.62)	(.58–.85)	(.01–.16)	(.07–.36)
Maximum (55.1%)	.75	.93	.22	.54
	(.44–.94)	(.81–.98)	(.05–.55)	(.24–.81)

Note: Probabilities were computed holding other variables at their mean; 95% confidence intervals in parentheses. DM = district magnitude.

Simulations based on model 3 (table 5.2) show that there is an 88 percent probability that a deputy from the president's party will initiate a locally targeted bill if she represents one of the poorest departments. When the educational level of the department is comparatively high, there is only a 23 percent probability that a governing party deputy will initiate a local bill.[23] While opposition deputies are overall less likely than deputies from the governing party to initiate locally targeted bills, they are most likely to initiate a local bill if they represent a department with an extremely low level of education. This would seem to indicate that when deputies represent districts that fit the conditions where patron-client relations should still be the norm, politicians are likely to act like patrons who deliver services to their district, using their position as deputy to enhance their reputation as a patron.

The number of terms the deputy has served in Congress enhances this relationship. A senior deputy from the president's party who represents a department with very low educational levels has a 94 percent probability of initiating a local pork bill. Senior opposition deputies are also quite likely to initiate local pork. There is a 61 percent probability that an opposition deputy with four terms of experience in Congress representing a department where a high percentage of the population has no education will initiate a local bill. Politicians who have been in Congress since the beginning of the democratic regime seem to view delivering pork to their district as part of their job. Newer deputies are still likely to initiate local bills if they represent very poor districts, but they are less likely to do so.[24] This may indicate a generational change, or that deputies from poor districts who deliver pork are more likely to be reelected.

Deputies are more likely to initiate local pork bills in departments dominated by one party, which is contrary to the expectation that patrons will pay a higher price for votes in competitive areas. Simulations (not shown in table 5.2) show that when dominance is at a minimum (i.e., both parties won an equal number of municipal elections in the department), there is a 16 percent probability that a deputy will initiate local legislation, but if one party dominates a department, the probability increases to 46 percent. If the percentage of a department's population with no education is set at its maximum value and no party dominates the department, there is a 75 percent probability that a deputy from the president's party will initiate a local pork bill. However, if one party dominates that same department, the probability that a governing party deputy will initiate local legislation increases to 93 percent (table 5.2).

The findings of the logistic regressions in models 1 through 3 are robust to an analysis that examines two terms of legislation (1990–93 and 1994–97), dropping the *department dominance* variable that was not available for the 1990–93 term.[25] Simulations based on models with two terms of legislation data (not presented) yield results similar to those from models 1 through 3. However, the probability that a deputy from the governing party will initiate a local pork bill is somewhat lower. When DM is set at the minimum, simulations based on model 1 show that a governing party deputy has an 80 percent probability of initiating a local bill (table 5.2), while simulations based on a model using two terms of legislation data predict a 59 percent probability (not shown). When the percentage of a department's population with no education is set at the maximum, simulations based on model 3 show that a governing party deputy has an 88 percent probability of initiating a local bill (table 5.2), while simulations based on a model using two terms of legislation data predict a 62 percent probability (not shown). This decrease could be due to the greater access to the executive branch that deputies from the PNH had during the presidency of Rafael Callejas (PNH, 1990–94), compared with the access PLH deputies had to the president, ministers, and agency heads during the presidency of Carlos Roberto Reina (PLH, 1994–98). PLH deputies complained during interviews that President Reina did not meet regularly with his party's caucus in Congress, and deputies had difficulty getting appointments with ministers and agency directors. Instead, the executive branch began dealing directly with municipal governments, and the deputy was no longer an essential facilitator for getting the national government to attend to local government and community needs. Only more data from later administrations will reveal whether this is a permanent change in executive-legislative relations.

DISCUSSION

This chapter examines the incentives that electoral institutions and clientelism create for legislators to attend to the needs of local communities. Electoral institutions prompt deputies to represent local interests when these institutions create incentives to seek a personal vote. Clientelism creates different incentives for a deputy to attend to the needs of communities and individuals. If the deputy wants to maintain or expand his status as a patron who can be counted on to solve community problems and to help individuals with their needs, he must deliver services. These two incentive structures can be reinforcing—a politician who wants to maximize his personal vote can work to address the needs of clients as part of his personal vote-seeking strategy. However, even if electoral rules do not give politicians an incentive to seek a personal vote (e.g., a closed-list PR electoral system with large district magnitude), legislators can still respond to the incentives created by the informal institution of clientelism. Deputies who view their role in Congress as acting as a patron for residents of their district, or who sought a seat in Congress to expand their resource base for attending to clients, can use the opportunities their position provides to attend to client needs, even if seeking a personal vote is not necessary for their reelection. This resource base includes the ability to initiate legislation to target state resources toward the deputy's client communities (the behavior examined here), connections to the executive branch that facilitate lobbying for community development projects, and helping clients get jobs, scholarships, and licenses.

The analysis finds that deputies are more likely to initiate locally targeted bills when elected from small-magnitude districts—in other words, when there is some electoral incentive to seek a personal vote. However, other measures of the incentive generated by the formal electoral institutions (i.e., marginal list position, reelection rates in the deputy's district) did not affect attention to the district. Clientelistic incentives to attend to local needs, as measured by the poverty of the district, increased the probability that a deputy would initiate locally targeted legislation. This result held regardless of reelection rates in the district or whether the deputy's list position was marginal or safe (i.e., whether electoral incentives were present or absent). Thus, the incentive for attention to local communities created by clientelism can help explain behavior that seems odd if only electoral incentives are considered.

In Honduras, electoral incentives for deputies to represent local interests are weak. The electoral system (closed-list PR with a high average DM and, until 1997, fused elections for Congress and the president) creates a strong incentive to seek a partisan vote. Still, some deputies take it upon themselves to initiate locally targeted legislation, though most do not (84 of the 256 deputies in the dataset initiated local bills). Many Honduran deputies initiate no bills during a term in Congress (96 deputies in the dataset initiated no bills of any type), which makes the initiatives of those deputies who did target bills at local communities even more interesting. Incentives created by clientelism help explain this behavior.

Backbench deputies in Honduras have an incentive to be seen and not heard. National party leaders control nominations and list position, and they seem to reward quiescent backbenchers. For example, deputies who initiate no national-level bills have a greater chance of reelection to Congress (Heath and Taylor-Robinson 2003). Yet, some deputies use their time in Congress to target state resources at specific communities. This is rational behavior for a patron-deputy, even if it is not necessarily useful for the deputy's political career. The rationality of this behavior is enhanced because deputies have some ability to select the type of district they represent. An aspiring deputy may self-select to represent a small, rural, traditional department if she wants to play a patron role, while a an aspiring deputy who wants to make national policy or represent sectoral interests may seek to run for office in a large and urban department.

The electoral law allows a deputy to represent the department where she was born or where she currently resides. Of course, the aspiring deputy still needs to obtain an "electable" place on her party's list, and national party leaders make those decisions. But the reality of Honduran politics is that many deputies who represent the departments that include the country's major urban areas are not natives of those departments, while many deputies who represent provincial departments were born in the department but now live in the capital. Since patronage networks in Honduras work through political parties, seeking election to Congress to enhance or expand one's client network is a risky strategy for patrons, because they will obtain few resources if their party is in the opposition—only the ability to initiate bills and only a low probability that those bills will become law. Being a deputy, however, increases a politician's or patron's profile in her community, and if the deputy's party wins the presidency, she will be able to take part in the distribution of the spoils of victory.

It makes sense that Honduras's traditional political parties would support clientelistic behavior by their deputies. The electoral system creates little incentive for elected officials to represent local interests (Shugart and Carey 1992; Taylor 1996). Lack of attention to local needs is criticized as one of the failings of democracy in some PR systems in which national party elites control nominations (e.g., Venezuela) (Shugart 2001). In Honduras, however, voters continue to give overwhelming support to the traditional parties.[26] If the traditional parties want to maintain their popular support base, they need to maintain their links to their clientelistic networks.

This raises an important point about the sources of informal institutional stability in Honduras. Clientelism has been part of the Honduran cultural landscape for so long that its persistence is more frequently taken for granted than explained. Any explanation of the stability of clientelism in Honduras must begin with the fact that the dominant parties benefit from it. Clientelism is an important asset for the traditional parties as they work to maintain their political dominance within the constraints imposed by free and fair, competitive, democratic elections. To continue to win control of the executive branch, the Liberal and National parties must obtain the support of voters. Delivering clientelistic benefits is a cheap way to do so that has the added benefit of not threatening traditional elite interests. Honduras's traditional parties were created as clientelistic networks competing for access to state resources, not over policy or ideology, and they continue to function in the same manner today. In the context of an overwhelmingly poor electorate, providing clientelistic services is a logical way for parties to compete for voter support. If parties do not provide the expected level of service to their clients when they win the presidency, party supporters/clients have shown that they will stay home rather than support the party in the next election.[27] Hence, it is beneficial to the traditional parties if their back-benchers use their time in Congress to build their local client base, because those clients will support their patron's party in the next election.

In sum, clientelism seems to be a "substitutive" informal institution in Honduras, providing at least some representation of local interests in the legislature even when the formal electoral rules do not provide an incentive for elected officials to repre-sent local needs. In other words, clientelism seems to help Congress perform the representative function it is charged with in democratic theory.

CHAPTER SIX

Do Informal Rules Make Democracy Work?
Accounting for Accountability in Argentina

SUSAN C. STOKES

VOTERS' INFORMAL DECISION-RULES AND DEMOCRACY

Political rules may be written down, or they may not be. And the punishment triggered when rules are violated may happen in officially sanctioned channels, or it may not. This is the essence of the distinction between formal and informal institutions that Helmke and Levitsky make in their introduction to this volume. But there are other dimensions on which rules vary. They may, for instance, be explicitly understood by those who follow them, or they may be only implicitly understood. When rules are implicit, even people following them quite closely are frequently unable to render a formalized account of them. Consider the difference between the rules of a game and the rules of a language. The rules of chess are explicit; to be able to play, one has to know the rules. If I do not know, say, that the rook may move an unlimited number of spaces in horizontal or vertical straight lines, whereas the king may move only one space but in any direction, I cannot play the game. But if I do know these rules, I can both make them explicit and play by them.

The rules governing the speaking of a language are quite different. We learn to follow these rules well before we learn what the rules are—if indeed we ever learn what they are. A quite average five-year-old will utter many sentences of his or her "native" (first, early-acquired) language in ways that conform to the formalized grammatical rules of that language, whereas even a highly intelligent adult speaker of the same language will have great difficulty explaining these rules unless trained to do so.[1]

I call rules that can be rendered explicit by those following them *game rules*. I call rules that are implicit and difficult to formalize by those using them *grammatical rules*.

Two central premises of this chapter are (1) that the way people vote in elections is rule-governed—that the phrase *voters' decision-rules* is to be taken seriously—and (2) that voters' decision-rules are grammatical. They are rules, and not simple responses to physiological or material incentives; they are diffused through social mechanisms, not merely thought up by individuals; they are not normally rendered explicit, at least not in a formalized version, by people who use them; and, to varying degrees depending on the rule, they are violated at the risk of social—and even, sometimes, physical and material—sanction.

Much is at stake for democracies in the informal and grammatical decision-rules that voters adopt. Consider eight rules, each of which has a large political science literature behind it, claiming that it is *the* rule that voters use.

1. If the economy grows by at least *x* percent on an incumbent's watch, vote for the incumbent; otherwise, vote for an opposition party (*retrospective sociotropic rule*).

2. If my salary grows by at least *x* percent on the incumbent's watch, vote for the incumbent; otherwise, vote for an opposition party (*retrospective egocentric rule*).

3. Vote for the political party that my father voted for (*socialization rule*).

4. Compare the distance between all parties' programs and my own ideal point, and vote for the one that minimizes this distance (*spatial rule*).

5. If the candidate who minimizes this distance has no chance of winning, vote for the next best one who has a chance of beating the candidate that I most want to keep out of office (*strategic rule*).

6. Consider the extreme statements of competing parties in order to identify the one on my side, and vote for that party (*directional rule*).

7. Count the number of people from my ethnic group on parties' lists, and vote for the party with the largest number (*ethnic rule*).

8. Compare the value of the private goods proffered to me during the campaign, and vote for the candidate whose gifts have the highest value (*clientelistic rule*).

These decision-rules, when adopted by large numbers of voters, have major and varying implications for how well democracy works. At least in theory, retrospective voting can induce accountability if it is sociotropic, but not if it is egocentric (Ferejohn 1986). Spatial, strategic, and directional decision-rules hold out some hope for responsiveness.[2] In turn, egocentric and socialization voting cut governments loose from both responsiveness and accountability. Clientelistic decision-rules allow voters to hold politicians accountable (Kitschelt 2000)—although in a paltry way—but they also allow politicians to hold voters accountable (Stokes 2005).[3]

Skepticism that voters' decision-rules are in fact informal rules or institutions, in the sense used in this volume, may arise from doubt that violation of voting rules provokes social disapproval or sanctions. In one image, voting is carried out by lonely voters who make up their minds in isolation, with no communication (let alone sanctions) among voters. Assuming the ballot is secret, furthermore, people's actual votes are (presumably) opaque; hence they cannot be punished for voting for one party and not another. If one's vote cannot be known, presumably nor can one's method of deciding how to vote. To the extent that they are voluntary and unenforceable, voters' decision "rules" are not informal rules or institutions, as the concept is used in this volume.

But the image of the lonely voter is overdrawn. Parents talk about politics and elections to children and with one another in the presence of children; in these ways, people's party sympathies and ways of thinking about politics are nurtured in childhood and early adulthood. During campaigns, people deliberate informally about the quality of candidates, the performance of incumbents, and the strategies posed by alternatives. Especially when decision-rules clash, informal deliberations over the rules can become frequent and heated. An acquaintance of mine recounted numerous conversations with fellow members of her dog-walking group about whether to support an ideologically proximate (to them) candidate in a Democratic primary or switch strategically to a less sympathetic Democrat in order to keep a particularly odious Republican out of the Massachusetts governors' office. According to some theories, voters choose which party to vote for as a means of expressing their political identities: "expressions" have to be *expressed*—communicated to other people: to family members, coworkers, and other acquaintances (Schuessler 2000).

Whether they are expressing themselves or working out problems of strategy, voters who engage in such informal deliberations also try to persuade one another. And when they fail, they aim "social sanctions" at one another—they get angry and indignant and, in extreme cases, cut off social intercourse with those whom they have failed to persuade, if only temporarily.

Sanctions for violating an electoral decision-rule can go beyond unpleasant interactions. It is worth noting in this connection that the secret ballot is not an absolute impediment to knowing, or forming good inferences about, how individuals vote. Clientelistic parties insert themselves deeply into the social networks of neighborhoods and civic associations, and garner extensive information about the likely votes of individual members and neighbors. It is difficult for many voters to dissimulate their voting decisions. In Argentina, a Peronist party operative reported in an interview that he could tell how his neighbors had voted by whether, the day after the election, "they can't look me in the eye."[4] When parties can make good inferences about individuals' votes, then client-voters who break the rule "vote for the party that gave out the most valuable gifts" run the risk of sanctions, especially the loss of future "favors" and "gifts." Suggesting what is known in game theory as a grim-trigger strategy in response to defections, another Peronist explained how she dealt with people in her neighborhood to whom she had given bags of food or clothing but who then voted for another party: "They're dead. They died forever."[5]

In Helmke and Levitsky's usage, informal institutions generate (or encapsulate) expected, patterned actions. Regarding democratic responsiveness and accountability, *expectations* are crucial. If informal institutions and informal rules are to help achieve responsive government, they must accurately describe not just what people do but what they expect others to do. Without these expectations the rules are eviscerated. Consider the retrospective sociotropic rule. If a voter uses this rule as a method of enforcing accountability, she must have certain expectations about the motives and actions of officeholders. If she does not think that anticipation of the next election will discipline an officeholder, then she may interpret anything good that happens on his watch as fortuitous and owing to circumstances that the voter cannot observe (e.g., a favorable international economic climate). She should then pay no attention to the incumbent's apparent performance in office and focus entirely, perhaps, on whatever she can learn about politicians' characters or preferred policies during the campaign (or choose by some other criterion).

As is true of languages, the grammatical decision-rules of voting are variable over even fairly compact geographic spaces. Political accents, dialects, even distinct "languages" can emerge within a single national territory. In this chapter I offer evidence of cross-regional variation in electoral decision-rules in contemporary Argentina.

Argentina is a new democracy in which formalized political institutions—understood either as rules or, more traditionally, as political parties and bureaucracies and elections—are, to put it mildly, enfeebled (Levitsky 2003a, 2003b). Popular protest and economic distress, not constitutional rules, frequently determine the length of Argentine presidents' terms. In the last few years, primary elections have been canceled when they threaten to produce a result opposed by those who have the power to cancel them, whether that power comes from a command over party machinery or from physical force. And political parties have failed in one of their key functions: allocating the scarce resource of candidacies among their members. It is not my claim here that informal institutions can save Argentine democracy or that they can prop up that country's formal institutions of democracy when the latter really collapse. Rather, my claim is that democracy functions better there (and probably in most democracies, new and old) when informal rules enforce accountability.

I begin by noting substantial differences in the quality of democracy across towns, cities, and provinces in Argentina. I then pose the question, do these differences correspond to systematic differences in the electoral decision-rules that voters employ across regions? Are there distinct dialects, if you will, in the grammatical rules underlying voters' choices? I draw on survey research indicating that the answer is yes. People in regions where democracy works relatively well display a heightened appreciation for mechanisms of accountability and, more than people from other regions, expect others—their neighbors and officeholders—to follow decision-rules that make accountability possible. People in regions where democracy has worked less well expect their neighbors to follow voting rules that are supportive of clientelism. I do not offer here a full account of the origin of these expectations and rules, but I do eliminate some explanations that the literature on the transition and consolidation of democracy suggests, and speculate about a better answer. Neither the income levels of individuals nor social capital explain regional differences in the prominence of rules of accountability. What may matter more are traits not of individuals but of communities: their levels of social equality. I conclude by returning to the general question of the importance of informal institutions to democracy.

ACCOUNTABILITY AND EXPECTATIONS OF ACCOUNTABILITY IN ARGENTINA

Local democracy works better in some parts of Argentina than in others.[6] Some provinces are good at maintaining balanced budgets; others are profligate spenders. Some provinces strive to implement good public policy; in others, public assistance is glossed as personal charity by the governor. Experts deem the Argentine federal budget and the process by which it is written to be far more opaque than in other Latin American countries; yet a handful of mayors have tried to bring community organizations and individuals into the process, at least at the local level. In some cities, powerful political and economic actors impose their will on the citizenry; in others, the political leadership has experimented with relatively novel forms, such as the referendum, to give residents a voice in crucial collective decisions. These comparisons allow Cleary and Stokes (forthcoming) to posit a ranking for a set of four regions in which we conducted sample surveys. Among these four regions, we ranked the city of Mar del Plata and the surrounding district of General Pueyrredón the highest on measures of democracy, followed by the rest of the provinces of

TABLE 6.1
Responses to Questions about Institutional Trust and
Trust in Politicians by Region, Argentina

	Mar del Plata	Buenos Aires	Córdoba	Misiones	Total
Services: When governments provide good services to the people, is this because					
—they are under the watch of the courts, Congress, or the press?	65% (311)	56% (268)	48% (232)	40% (192)	52% (1,003)
—they are good, committed people?	30% (142)	40% (192)	40% (194)	53% (256)	41% (784)
No answer	6% (27)	4% (20)	11% (54)	7% (32)	7% (133)
Efficient: When governments function efficiently, is this because					
—they know if they don't, people won't vote for them in the next election?	71% (340)	75% (362)	68% (326)	67% (321)	70% (1,349)
—the people governing are good, committed people?	24% (116)	22% (106)	26% (125)	29% (140)	25% (487)
No answer	5% (24)	3% (12)	6% (29)	4% (19)	4% (84)
Attention: When politicians really pay attention to people like you, is this because					
—they want to be reelected?	85% (410)	80% (386)	78% (375)	78% (375)	81% (1,546)
—they really care?	11% (55)	17% (83)	16% (76)	18% (87)	16% (301)
No answer	3% (15)	2% (11)	6% (29)	4% (18)	4% (73)

Buenos Aires, Córdoba, and, finally, the province of Misiones, where case studies of local politics find an extensive clientelism, personalism, and extreme domination of political life by powerful economic actors.[7]

Do people in Mar del Plata perceive the motivations for politicians' actions and the constraints they are under differently than people in, say, Misiones? In the three survey questions listed in table 6.1, we asserted that politicians sometimes behave well—provide good public services (*services*), are efficient (*efficient*), pay attention to the opinions of constituents like the respondent (*attention*)—and then asked respondents to choose among several alternative explanations for this good behavior. In each case one option attributed good behavior to the personal qualities of politicians ("they are committed people," "they really care about constituents' opinions"), whereas the other attributed it to mechanisms of accountability ("they are under the watch of the courts," "people won't vote for them in the next election"). Among respondents across all three provinces, the "accountability" answer was in all cases the one respondents chose more frequently.

Responses to these questions differed systematically by region. The number of respondents offering "accountability" responses to the questions in table 6.1 is highest in the most democratic region and then trends downward. For example, 65 percent of respondents from Mar del Plata attributed good services to institutional monitoring, while only 40 percent of respondents from Misiones made such an attribution. In many cases, institutional trust declines monotonically as the level of democracy declines.

To probe systematic differences across regions, we coded answers to *services*, *efficient*, and *attention* as dummy variables for an "accountability" answer. Thus for a person who chose the answer "when municipal governments are efficient, this is because otherwise people won't vote for them in the next election," the score is 1 on the dummy variable *efficient*; otherwise the score is 0. We then estimated logit regression models of these accountability answers. The results (table 6.2) show that older people were more skeptical of the characters of politicians and more likely to ascribe good behavior to mechanisms of accountability. Women were more likely to ascribe good government to the characters of politicians; men, to politicians' fear of losing votes. Most important for our purposes, respondents in Buenos Aires, Córdoba, and Misiones were generally less likely to offer "accountability" responses than were respondents in Mar del Plata.[8] They were significantly less likely than were people from Mar del Plata to say that governments provide services when they are under the watch of the courts, the congress, and the press; somewhat less likely to say that efficient governments are ones that fear losing office; and significantly more likely to say that politicians who pay attention want to be reelected.

The regional effect on expectations of accountability was sometimes quite strong. To give a sense of how much of a difference region makes in institutional trust, consider a typical respondent in our sample, one with an average household income, educational level, and quality of housing, and living in a city of average size. Simulations show that if she lived in Mar del Plata, this typical respondent had a 68 percent chance of saying that governments provide good services "because they're monitored." But if she lived in Misiones, the chance dropped to 41 percent.[9]

Expectations of accountability, when they do occur in Argentina, focus both on formal institutions and on informal rules and behaviors. In some settings people believed that politicians performed well when under the watchful eye of the courts or other branches of government. But they also believed in informal rules of accountability. In more democratic regions, the belief was more widespread that anticipation of the "future retrospective judgment of voters" (Manin 1997) or anticipation of "the moment when their power is to cease, when their exercise of it is to be reviewed" (Madison et al. 2000 [1788]) could induce governments to be efficient. The electoral connection involves several informal rules and the expectation that other people will follow these rules. For the connection to hold, voters must expect other voters to use appropriate criteria in deciding how to vote. Consider again the question "when

TABLE 6.2
Logit Models of "Accountability" Responses to Questions about Politicians

	Model 1 Services	Model 2 Efficient	Model 3 Attention
Income	−0.057	0.005	−0.105
	(0.043)	(0.038)	(0.054)
Education	0.041	−0.073	−0.060
	(0.037)	(0.038)	(0.043)
Housing	−0.006	−0.065	0.018
	(0.076)	(0.089)	(0.094)
Gender	**−0.318**	−0.014	−0.062
	(0.102)	(0.103)	(0.119)
Age	**−0.013**	**−0.017**	−0.006
	(0.004)	(0.004)	(0.004)
Peronist supporter	**−0.230**	0.049	**−0.420**
	(0.116)	(0.127)	(0.150)
Radical supporter	−0.058	−0.036	0.045
	(0.144)	(0.142)	(0.226)
Log population	0.006	0.040	0.031
	(0.037)	(0.046)	(0.046)
Buenos Aires	**−0.408**	0.081	**−0.438**
	(0.184)	(0.190)	(0.214)
Córdoba	**−0.618**	−0.115	−0.313
	(0.187)	(0.224)	(0.255)
Misiones	**−1.080**	−0.384	**−0.517**
	(0.229)	(0.222)	(0.247)
Constant	**1.605**	**1.881**	**2.664**
	(0.528)	(0.697)	(0.742)

Note: The models reported were estimates that drew on five datasets with imputed values for missing data. To generate the imputed datasets, I used the Amelia program described in King et al. (2001) and implemented in Honaker et al. (2001). Bold type indicates coefficients significant at the >.05 level.

Dependent variables: Model 1: *services*, dummy for response, "Governments provide good services when they're under the watch of the courts, congress, and the press." Model 2: *efficient*, dummy for response, "When municipal governments are efficient, this is because they know otherwise people won't vote for them." Model 3: *attention*, dummy for response, "When politicians pay attention to people like me, this is because they want to be reelected." Independent variables: *income*, self-reported by respondent, 9-level scale of family income; *education*, 9-level scale, from no formal education to university; *housing*, assessed by interviewer, 5-level scale (1 = poorest quality, 5 = highest quality), based on assessment of building materials, flooring, and presence or absence of consumer durables; *gender*, male = 0, female = 1; *Peronist*, coded 1 for respondents who said, independent of how they voted, they liked the Peronist Party more than others, 0 otherwise; *radical*, coded 1 for respondents who said, independent of how they voted, they liked the Radical Party more than others, 0 otherwise; *log population*, natural log of the number of inhabitants, according to 2001 census, residing in the municipality where the respondent lived; *Buenos Aires*, *Córdoba*, and *Misiones*, dummy variables for interviewees living in each of these regions; the base region is therefore Mar del Plata.

municipal governments work efficiently, is this because they are staffed by good, committed people, or because they know that if they don't work well people won't vote for them later?" To answer "because they know that if they don't work well people won't vote for them later," respondents have to believe that other voters do consider the incumbent government's efficiency when they decide how to vote. They must expect other voters to use retrospective criteria and not to be bought off by the small, individualized inducements of clientelism, which tend to come at the cost of efficiency and the provision of public goods (Estévez et al. 2003; Medina and Stokes 2003).

TABLE 6.3
Responses to Questions about Voters' Decision Rules

Question	Variable	Accountability response	Non-accountability response	No answer
Do people sympathize with [most important party in neighborhood] because it has a better program, or because it gave out things during the campaign?	*Handout*	Better program: 53%	Gave out things: 28%	19%
Do people sympathize with [this party] because they believe it is concerned about everyone, or because it has given out a favor?	*Favor*	Concerned about everyone: 45%	Gave out favors: 33%	22%
In the last campaign, did you receive any good from a party operative?	*Gift*	Yes: 7%	No: 92%	1%
Do people sympathize with [this party] because it managed things well or because it has a good program?	*Past*	Managed well: 32%	Good program: 43%	24%

The survey provides more direct evidence that the expectation that one's neighbors would follow retrospective and not clientelistic decision-rules in deciding how to vote was more widespread in Argentina's higher-performing democratic regions than in its lower-performing regions. We asked survey respondents questions about how they vote and how they expected other people in their neighborhood to vote (table 6.3). Table 6.4 reports logit regression estimations. In the first two models, the dependent variables are dummies for people who said that their neighbors used clientelistic decision-rules, rules that would *not* support accountability: that they responded to handouts (*handout*) or favors (*favor*), not a party's program or its concern for everyone, when deciding how to vote. The negative coefficient on dummies for Mar del Plata (*Mar del Plata*) indicates that respondents from that city perceived their neighbors as less clientelistic than did respondents from other cities and towns. People from Mar del Plata were also less likely to be the targets of clientelistic mobilization. The dependent variable in the third model (*gift*) is a dummy for people who reported that they had received a handout from a party operative in the last campaign. The negative sign on the *Mar del Plata* coefficient shows that people there were less likely to have received such handouts, leaving them freer, presumably, to take performance into account.

In one way, Mar del Plata residents were less prone to accountability than people from elsewhere. We asked whether people in the respondent's neighborhood paid attention to how well a party performed in the past versus how good its proposal was for the future (*past*). People in Mar del Plata viewed their neighbors as more prospective than did people elsewhere (as indicated by the negative sign on the

TABLE 6.4
Logit Models of Clientelistic (Non-Accountability) Responses to Questions about Voting

	Model 1 Handout	Model 2 Favor	Model 3 Gift	Model 4 Past
Income	−0.067	−0.038	−0.217	0.027
	(0.042)	(0.034)	(0.078)	(0.034)
Education	0.034	0.048	−0.221	**0.095**
	(0.034)	(0.031)	(0.080)	(0.031)
Housing	−0.034	0.099	−0.311	−0.087
	(0.079)	(0.068)	(0.131)	(0.068)
Gender	0.021	0.005	−0.184	0.007
	(0.105)	(0.095)	(0.195)	(0.095)
Age	−0.003	−0.010	−0.014	0.009
	(0.004)	(0.003)	(0.006)	(0.003)
Peronist	**−0.453**	**−0.848**	**0.718**	**−0.253**
	(0.137)	(0.117)	(0.221)	(0.118)
Radical	**−0.661**	**−0.329**	−0.321	−0.203
	(0.176)	(0.145)	(0.385)	(0.148)
Log population	0.028	**0.081**	−0.096	**−0.167**
	(0.033)	(0.032)	(0.051)	(0.033)
Poverty rate	**−0.048**	0.003		0.012
	(0.018)	(0.016)		(0.016)
Mar del Plata	**−1.635**	**−0.705**	**−0.886**	**−0.437**
	(0.183)	(0.136)	(0.398)	(0.133)
Constant	0.056	−0.191	1.368	**1.771**
	(0.426)	(0.419)	(0.758)	(0.434)
No. of observations	1,920	1,920	1,920	1,920

Note: The models reported drew on five datasets with imputed values for missing data. To generate the imputed datasets I used the Amelia program described in King et al. (2001) and implemented in Honaker et al. (2001). Bold type indicates coefficients significant at the >.05 level.

Dependent variables: Model 1: *handout*, dummy for response, "People support [most important local party] because it gave things out in the campaign [not because it has a better program]." Model 2: *favor*, dummy for response, "People support this party because it has done them a favor [not because it is concerned for everyone]." Model 3: *gift*, dummy for people who said they had received a campaign handout from a party operative during the previous (October 2001 national legislative) campaign; the modal handout was some food. Model 4: *past*, dummy for response, "People support this party because it has performed well in the past [not because it has a good proposal for the future.]" Independent variables: As defined in table 6.2, and *poverty rate*, proportion of residents living in substandard housing, from the 1991 census.

coefficient relating the *Mar del Plata* dummy to *past* in model 4; table 6.4). As Fearon (1999) explains, retrospective and prospective considerations can interfere with one another when voters attempt to use their vote to induce politicians to be responsive.

Yet the central finding thus far is that people who live in regions where democracy functions fairly well, in a national context where democracy more often performs badly, differ from people from other cities and towns in that they are more likely to abide by informal rules of politics that support accountability, and they are more likely to expect their neighbors also to abide by these rules. They also show a stronger appreciation of formal institutions that support democratic accountability.

WHAT'S TRUST GOT TO DO WITH IT?
EXPECTATIONS OF ACCOUNTABILITY IN MAR DEL PLATA

Social scientists have emphasized in recent years the importance of *trust*, and of the institutions that promote trust, in making social relations work smoothly, both market relations (see esp. North 1990) and relations between citizens and representatives (Putnam 1993; Levi 1997; Ferejohn 1999). Are people from more democratic regions of Argentina particularly trusting?

We asked a series of questions designed to measure levels of interpersonal trust. By *trust* I mean A's belief that B will act in A's interest, even though B would stand to gain in some way by not so acting and even though A cannot directly monitor B's relevant actions (Cleary and Stokes, forthcoming). Table 6.5 lists questions that explore levels of interpersonal trust: whether respondents trust their neighbors, and whether they view other people in the abstract as trustworthy. Respondents across the three provinces were quite trusting of their neighbors, saying by a margin of three to one that they would trust a neighbor to care for their home while they were away. But they displayed widespread distrust of abstract others, with majorities agreeing that most people will take advantage of you when they can, and that a minority of people are trustworthy. Several studies indicate that Argentines came to trust each other less and less over the first two decades of renewed democracy. The percentage responding in the World Values Survey that one could trust other people fell from 26 percent in 1984 to 18 percent in 1995 (Mussetta 2002, 66).

If democracy worked unusually well in some regions of Argentina, this was not because people there were more trusting in a generalized sense than were people in other regions. Consider the question "thinking about the locality or *barrio* where you live, if you were to go on a trip, do you have any neighbors whom you could trust to care for your house while you were away?" (variable *neighbor*). To discern the factors influencing people's answers, we estimated logit regression models (not shown) in which the dependent variable was a dummy that took the value of 1 when a person said she would leave her house in the care of a neighbor, 0 when she said she would not. Information about individuals' income and the quality of their housing, and about the size of the city or town they live in, would help us predict their answer to this question. (People with relatively high incomes, who lived in high-quality housing, and who were from smaller towns and cities were more likely to trust their neighbors.) But knowing the region where the person lived would not help us predict the answer.

Expectations of accountability among residents of regions where democracy

TABLE 6.5
Responses to Questions about Personal Trust, by Region, Argentina

	Mar del Plata	Buenos Aires	Córdoba	Misiones	Total
Neighbor: If you go away on a trip, do you have a neighbor whom you could trust to care for your house?					
Yes	75%	80%	75%	68%	75%
	(360)	(383)	(359)	(328)	(1,430)
No	25%	20%	24%	30%	25%
	(113)	(97)	(117)	(146)	(473)
No answer	2%	0%	1%	1%	1%
	(7)	(0)	(4)	(6)	(17)
Advantage: Do you believe most people would take advantage of you if they had the chance?					
Yes	55%	53%	50%	57%	54%
	(263)	(254)	(241)	(272)	(1,034)
No	42%	45%	45%	37%	42%
	(203)	(215)	(214)	(178)	(810)
No answer	3%	2%	5%	6%	4%
	(14)	(11)	(25)	(30)	(80)
Trust: Which is closest to your way of thinking?					
You can trust a majority of people.	20%	26%	23%	18%	22%
	(96)	(123)	(111)	(84)	(414)
You can only trust a minority.	61%	61%	56%	59%	59%
	(294)	(291)	(271)	(284)	(1,140)
I don't trust anyone.	18%	13%	20%	22%	18%
	(87)	(64)	(95)	(105)	(351)
No answer	1%	0.4%	1%	2%	1%
	(3)	(2)	(3)	(7)	(15)

worked unusually well focused on politics, and did not extend to commercial relations. Our survey asked: "Considering now merchants who act honestly, is this because (1) they are honest people, (2) if they weren't, they know they could be fined, or (3) they could lose clients?" Among all respondents, 45 percent answered "because they are honest"; 8 percent, "because they know they could be fined," and 45 percent, "because they could lose clients." One can think of people who answered "they know they could be fined" as believing in formal, legal institutions of commercial accountability, and those who answered "they could lose clients" as believing in informal rules—there is no law that says customers must abandon merchants whom they discover to be dishonest, and no sanction for failing to abandon them, but we would expect many customers to do just this. Such beliefs (as well as formal legal institutions) help reduce transaction costs and smooth the functioning of market economies (North 1990). But what is important for our purposes is that residents of Buenos Aires (including Mar del Plata) were significantly *less* likely to believe in either a formal or an informal institution of market accountability than were people in Córdoba and Misiones.

In sum, neither greater interpersonal trust, nor a generalized belief in rules enforcing accountability, but a belief specific to political relations is what distinguished the expectations of people in more democratic regions from those of people in less democratic regions.

SOME PRELIMINARY THOUGHTS ON
THE ROOTS OF ACCOUNTABILITY

The question that immediately suggests itself is, do these informal (and formal) rules, and the expectations that others will follow them, in fact *cause* democracy to function better? Or, instead, is the causal sequence reversed, and relatively lively local democracy causes beliefs in these informal rules? *Why* does democracy function relatively well in some settings, and are informal rules of accountability really the cause? Although I will not attempt here a full answer to these questions in the Argentine case, I offer some preliminary thoughts.

Notice first some explanations that we can reject. One line of thinking, proposed most prominently by Robert Putnam (1993), focuses on a political culture of trust. Some regions in a country may develop a relatively rich associational life, a greater reservoir of personal trust, and hence larger supplies of social capital. According to Putnam, democracy works better in the north than in the south of Italy because "the civic community" in the north "is marked by an active, public-spirited citizenry, by egalitarian political relations, by *a social fabric of trust and cooperation*," whereas the south is "cursed with vertically structured politics, a social life of fragmentation and isolation, and *a culture of distrust*" (1993, 15; emphasis mine). Social trust in the polity acts like market trust in the economy, allowing people to achieve higher levels of efficiency. A trusting society secretes a well-functioning democracy.

In Argentina, as we have seen, people in places where democracy worked relatively well did *not* trust people in general, or their neighbors, or merchants, or politicians, more than did people in regions where democracy worked less well. They were not particularly prone to entrust their homes to their neighbors, but they did trust their fellow voters to punish politicians who underperformed, and they trusted their fellow voters not to be bought off by handouts. And they did not trust politicians except in the convoluted sense of trusting them to follow their own interest in staying in office and out of jail. A final piece of evidence that social capital is not the key to our story is that people in more democratic regions do not seem to have created more social capital than people elsewhere. We asked a range of questions about respondents' involvement in organizations and about whether and how frequently they attended meetings. These measures of social capital failed to predict adherence to rules of accountability; nor were people from more democratic regions more involved in associational life than people from less democratic ones.

Another venerable line of research links the emergence and consolidation of democracy with economic development. Higher incomes are supposed to imbue people with longer time horizons and make them less conflict-prone and more tolerant of others' opinions—all of which are in turn supposed to promote democracy (see esp. Lipset 1958, 1960). Among people who answered our surveys, we observed no straightforward effect of income, education, or quality of housing on beliefs that might promote democracy. Just as important, whatever effects people's household incomes or educational levels or quality of housing might have had, they did not reduce the effect of region on expectations of accountability. If we compare a resident of Mar del Plata with a resident of a Misiones city or town of the same size as Mar del Plata, both with the same level of income, we find the Mar del Plata resident is considerably more likely to abide by, and expect others to abide by, informal rules that support accountability.

In contrast, income and development, not as traits of individuals but as structural traits of communities, may help explain differences in the quality of local democracy in Argentina. Regions and cities vary in their levels of development and in their class structures. Scholars in comparative politics have contended that equality promotes democracy (see esp. Boix 2003; Acemoglu and Robinson 2005; this idea also appears in places in Lipset 1958). When the gap between rich and poor is relatively narrow, the rich may view the poor as less "beyond the pale" (Lipset 1958, 83) and hence more readily incorporated into civic life; and social equality may make the poor look less threatening to the wealthy, because they are less prone to pursue strongly redistributive measures (Boix 2003). Applied to our context, one could imagine that a community that is not socially polarized would also be one in which people would be relatively ready to expect others to follow courses of action appropriate to sustaining democratic accountability. It is tantalizing to note, along these lines, that a higher percentage of self-reported incomes in Mar del Plata than in any of our other three regions were concentrated in the middle of the range (300–700 pesos per month; 44% reported this as their household income in Mar del Plata, whereas only 33% did in Misiones, with the other two sampling regions falling in between). It is also tantalizing to note that when asked to place themselves in the lower, middle, or upper class, a larger percentage of people in Mar del Plata chose "middle class" than in any of the other regions. Yet these comparisons could be misleading: they involve comparing income distribution in a single city with income distribution across whole provinces.[10]

My hunch is that beliefs in accountability are both a cause and a consequence of well-functioning democracy, and that both structural factors and good luck are often at play. Imagine that a city happens, for no structural reason, to generate a set of judges and lawyers who aggressively prosecute corruption and waste in city government. Citizens who observed politicians being held accountable should display a growing belief that politicians can be held accountable. Because they hold this belief, they are gradually willing to concede more power and resources to city government. Local government does more for people, and its own structures are strengthened, including those that strengthen accountability. A virtuous cycle is underway. At the same time, structural factors, such as development and equality, are likely to further strengthen both the reality of, and expectations of, local democracy.

CONCLUSION

When democracy works well, when it achieves the effects that make it better than other systems of government, this is because formal institutions, informal institutions, and informal rules of behavior interact in felicitous ways. The new institutionalism in comparative politics may have underestimated the importance of informal institutions and informal rules—whether they are more like the rules of a game or the rules of grammar—for democratic outcomes. Comparativists have tended to conceive of institutions as creating incentives that map straightforwardly onto outcomes. A better way to think about the mapping of formal institutions on outcomes is that their effect is often conditional on informal institutions and rules, and these informal institutions and rules are variables that need to be unpacked empirically. As Helmke and Levitsky note in their introduction, the role of informal rules in democracy goes beyond one of filling the gaps left by formal institutions. In fact, formal institutions in some instances will not work in the way they were meant to unless the appropriate informal rules are in place.

We have seen a lot of evidence from Argentina that certain informal rules covary, at least, with good democratic outcomes. What seems to have mattered for a relatively lively local democracy is not that people trust politicians or other people in the simple sense of expecting them to promote one's interests if unconstrained. Expectations of accountability, rather than trust, were the informal rules that helped support local democracy in Argentina.

PART III

Informal Institutions and Party Politics

CHAPTER SEVEN

The Birth and Transformation of the *Dedazo* in Mexico

JOY LANGSTON

One of the central informal political institutions of Mexico's authoritarian regime was the *dedazo*, or the imposition of the next president by the outgoing executive. In most modern authoritarian regimes, the turnover of executive power is a highly destabilizing political juncture. Yet Mexico's remarkable hegemonic party regime, which lasted from 1929 to 2000, was in part predicated on a set of stable informal rules to transfer presidential power every six years. These institutionalized (though nondemocratic) rules of executive succession kept intraregime conflict to a minimum while permitting an energetic reshuffling of different groups and factions within the governing coalition.

Under the Party of the Institutional Revolution (PRI),[1] the Mexican political system was widely known as an exceptional party-based authoritarian regime in which informal rules determined important political outcomes, while many constitutional provisions were ignored (González Casanova 1981; Garrido 1982). Important formal institutions, including elections, were subverted by political elites that, using fraud, special access to state resources, and other informal mechanisms, fixed outcomes in a highly ritualized fashion outside constitutional or statutory channels (Craig and Cornelius 1995, 251; Cornelius 1996, 51). Informal rules were used not only to undermine the political opposition but also to maintain cohesion among the PRI's own wide-flung and ambitious political elite.

There were few informal institutions more critical to the stability of the PRI regime than the *dedazo*. The *dedazo* allowed the sitting president to single-handedly (or in consultation with his closest political allies) determine who would succeed him as the PRI's presidential candidate, and to impose that choice on the party's political elite. The PRI candidate would then go on to win a noncompetitive general election. Related informal rules later grew up to support this informal prerogative, including a restriction of the universe of possible successors to the president's cabinet and a prohibition against openly seeking the nomination or criticizing other potential nominees. These rules of the game were institutionalized during the 1940s and 1950s and remained intact into the mid-1990s.

The *dedazo* resolved some important dilemmas for the post-revolutionary elite. Neither formal party statutes nor the competitive elections prescribed by the Constitution could achieve this elite's two main goals: maintaining PRI dominance while avoiding an internal rupture. By ensuring regular leadership turnover while at the same time creating mechanisms to limit internal conflict, the *dedazo* helped put an end to the military rebellions and political defections that had threatened the regime since the 1920s. Once institutionalized, informal rules drove up the costs of disobeying regime leaders and made disloyalty by a member of the PRI a losing proposition. Thus, party politicians chose to remain within the governing coalition, helping to make the PRI practically invincible for seven decades.

In this chapter, I examine the origins and evolution of the *dedazo*. Whereas much research has gone into questions of formal institutional creation and change, little has been written on the origins, evolution, and collapse of informal rules. The chapter shows how, beginning in the administration of Lázaro Cárdenas (1934–40), PRI elites devised a set of informal rules and procedures that minimized the possibilities of rupture. Regime leaders used a series of instruments available to them because of their hegemonic control over the state, including electoral fraud, changes to the electoral laws, and a variety of selective political benefits, to reward PRIistas who played by the rules and punish those who broke them. The process of learning and adapting to the informal rules of presidential succession was slow and evolutionary. But once top leaders accepted the rules and it became clear that underlings lacked the power to contest them, a stable equilibrium emerged that endured for decades.

I also examine the collapse of the *dedazo*. Like formal institutional change, informal institutional change occurs for a variety of reasons. In Mexico, important changes in the external environment—particularly the rise of electoral competition, which created opportunities for politicians inside the PRI—led to a change in formal rules, which in turn allowed ambitious party politicians to dismantle the underlying informal power arrangements. After the onset of electoral competition, the conditions were set for a new bargaining game between presidents and ambitious PRI politicians. Presidents had power over ballot access and key financial and patronage resources, but emerging subnational politicians possessed a resource that was critical in a context of competitive elections: public support. These politicians could use the now credible threat to leave the PRI and run under another party label to leverage concessions from the PRI leadership. The resulting bargaining process produced both formal and informal rules change, as ambitious politicians used party statutes to weaken the informal prerogatives that PRI leaders had previously enjoyed in imposing candidacies.

The Mexican story goes against much of what we have learned about the relationship between formal and informal institutions. First, contra distinctions between formal and informal rules that center on external (state) versus self-enforcement, the *dedazo* was a *state-enforced* informal institution. Although it maintained the fiction that the Constitution and the PRI's statutory rules determined electoral outcomes, the Mexican state systematically enforced these informal arrangements. The consequences for breaking the informal rules were clear and known: government officials would block political advancement, engineer attacks in the state-controlled press, or manipulate the judicial system to take legal action, in some cases leading to imprisonment. Although this enforcement took place outside officially sanctioned channels, it was clearly backed by the power of the state. Second, whereas informal institutions are frequently viewed as endogenous to formal institutional arrangements, in the sense that actors create them in response to certain formal rules, the Mexican case suggests that the relationship may also be reversed. The PRI's formal statutes were written (and, in some cases, rewritten) to support the informal rules of the game. For example, statutory rules were couched in a highly ambiguous manner so as to lower the costs of utilizing the informal rules. Finally, whereas most of the existing literature on informal institutions portrays them as changing very slowly, the *dedazo*—though it took decades to become fully operational—collapsed relatively quickly.

THE *DEDAZO* AS AN INFORMAL INSTITUTION

The *dedazo* was one of the few institutionalized nondemocratic mechanisms of executive succession in the modern world (Johnson 1971; Butler and Bustamante 1991; Cordova 1992; Castañeda 1999). Yet, it was a thoroughly informal institution. Under the Mexican Constitution, voters elected the chief executive from among the candidates of several parties. And according to PRI statutes, the party's presidential candidate was to be nominated in a convention, by representatives of the PRI's three corporatist sectors (labor, peasant, and "popular") and other groups.

In practice, however, the president (who was also the de facto leader of the PRI) imposed his choice of successor. He communicated his decision to his secretary of the home office (*gobernación*) and the leader of the sector that would announce the designee at the convention. Then a party nominating convention was convened, whose delegates could vote on only one option. It was important for the president to maintain the fiction that he had nothing to do with the succession choice and to keep the identity of his chosen successor a mystery as long as possible. An informal shadow play developed around the succession process that included underground attacks among presidential hopefuls (*los posibles*), the utter denial of one's presidential ambitions, and a humorous bandwagoning effect after the announcement of the official candidate. It was understood by all actors that the president's handpicked choice would go on to win the general election, in part because of the weakness of opposition parties, in part because of the enormous resource advantage held by PRI candidates, and in part because the PRI thoroughly controlled—and, when necessary, manipulated—the electoral process. Once the president decided on his favorite and communicated this decision through one of the PRI's three sectors, the end result of the electoral process was a foregone conclusion. Neither the voters nor losers in the succession battle could overturn the president's choice.[2] Aside from his successor, the president unilaterally selected the president of the PRI and almost single-handedly decided the PRI's nominees for governor and senator (Smith 1979; Camp 1980; Bailey 1988; Philip 1992; Nacif 1995).

Related informal rules later grew up to support the president's important prerogatives. After three successive splits from the ruling party, the universe of possible successors was restricted to the cabinet, entry to which was strictly controlled by the president. Ambitious cabinet members were not permitted to openly admit their presidential aspirations, nor were they allowed to publicly criticize other potential rivals in the cabinet or campaign outside the regime coalition until the president had made his choice. Openly mobilizing a group within the coalition (or society) to contest the presidential nomination was tantamount to defeat in the nominating contest, and any attempts to win the nomination had to be done in the most discrete fashion so as not to create momentum for a candidacy not of the president's choosing. Once the nominee was chosen, losing candidates and their supporters were expected to publicly display their support for the winner and declare their willingness to work for him.

The *dedazo* solved important collective-action problems for the regime's elite. All ambitious politicians wanted to be nominated for public office, but internal battles over candidacies would have made the party vulnerable to ruptures and opposition challenges. The president's informal right to choose candidates solved this problem: members did not leave the party, given the lack of external opportunities, and loyalty could be rewarded in the medium and long run. This informal prerogative to select lower-level candidates reinforced each president's ability to maintain control over the enormous PRI political elite, which was often divided into different ideological wings and personalized factions.

THE CREATION OF THE *DEDAZO*

When and how was the *dedazo* born? The origins of the *dedazo* lie in the reactions of coalition leaders to the harsh reality of political anarchy prevalent in Mexico during and after the Revolution. Post-revolutionary elites faced an important collective dilemma. If they all cooperated and none rebelled against or challenged the new regime, then they all would be better off, because a unified governing party would be able to exclude other groups from power. However, some actors (i.e., those who won the presidency) benefited far more than others, so there were strong incentives to attempt an exit and capture of the presidency either by military rebellion or, in later decades, by competing against the PRI incumbents in the general election. In other words, competition for the presidency generated severe internal conflicts that threatened to divide the governing party and possibly undermine its grip on power.

Between the end of the Revolution (roughly 1917) and the first clear-cut *dedazo* of 1939–40, presidential succession was anything but institutionalized. Presidents emerged out of armed conflict, elite negotiation, and the imposition of nonelected strongmen. The initial post-revolutionary period was characterized by instability and violent conflict. Assassinations and armed rebellions marked the turnover of power from General Venustiano Carranza's defeat of Francisco Villa in 1915, to Carranza's assassination in 1920, to Adolfo De la Huerta's rebellion in 1923-24 to protest the imposition of Plutarco Elías Calles as presidential candidate (Meyer 1985). This continued in the failed revolt of 1927 (and the shooting of approximately fifty generals in its aftermath), to General José Gonzalo Escobar's challenge to Calles's authority in 1929. Alan Knight writes that these episodes were "all examples of a Darwinian (or Hobbesian) competition within the revolution itself" (1992, 131). There were no clear rules of succession aside from the "survival of the fittest" and most savage, which played out in an unending series of violent conflicts to decide the right to govern Mexico.

During the 1920s, two leading generals, Álvaro Obregón and Plutarco Elías Calles, worked out a power-sharing plan in which they alternated in the presidency. When Obregón was assassinated in 1928, Calles became the *jefe máximo* of the entire nation. During a short period between 1928 and 1934 (known as the Maximato), General Calles was able to place his handpicked allies as presidents of the nation and, in one case, force the president's ouster. Most politicians considered Calles the true leader of the nation, and would often travel to his compound, close to Mexico City, before conducting business with the elected president. Calles imposed a former governor of the state of Michoacán and former cabinet minister, Lázaro Cárdenas, as the presidential candidate in 1934 and expected he would be able to control this president as he had the last three. However, Cárdenas used his executive power to exile the strongman Calles and to remove the former president's allies from government and elective positions (González Casanova 1965; Lerner de Sheinbaum and Ralsky 1976; Medina 1977; A. Knight 1990).

The struggles within the governing coalition threatened the very foundation of the fledgling regime. If the post-revolutionary elite continued to split apart during each presidential turnover, they would be unlikely to consolidate power. One possible mechanism of succession was, of course, that prescribed by the Constitution: competitive elections. Yet such a system would threaten the revolutionary elite's hegemonic grip on power. Another option would have been to permit presidential reelection and thus follow the Soviet or Taiwanese solution of allowing a strong leader to stay in office until his death. Yet Mexico's recent experience with the thirty-year dictatorship of Porfirio Diaz (in which political mobility was blocked and succession was ultimately achieved only through large-scale violence) created an incentive for post-revolutionary leaders not to allow executives to legally succeed themselves, and reelection was prohibited in the 1917 Constitution. Although this clause was not as well institutionalized as is often believed,[3] the fact that several revolutionary generals with access to arms were contending for the presidency suggested that reelection would invite violent turnovers in power.

Cárdenas's solution was to impose his favored successor on the political class and the nation at large, while not retaining executive authority for himself. When Cárdenas named Manuel Ávila Camacho to succeed him, a tradition of presidents imposing their successors and then turning over power to them was born. The regime's leaders decided that the best way to avoid overt conflict was for the sitting president to decide the succession (and allow future presidents the right to do the same). The new *dedazo* rule would eventually lower levels of conflict over the succession, because only one man—the current president—would decide the issue. This also made the president the ground zero of loyalty until very late in his single six-year term, because other politicians' political futures depended on him up until he had made his decision.

Why did PRI elites choose not to enshrine the *dedazo* in the Constitution or the party statutes? There are several reasons why they opted for an informal institutional solution. For one, they sought to uphold the image that Mexico was an emerging democracy, and the formally democratic 1917 Constitution was far better suited to this purpose than was the authoritarian *dedazo*. Informality also helped the PRI leadership maintain a greater degree of flexibility and discretion vis-à-vis opposition parties and members of the PRI coalition. It was less costly to create and enforce informal institutions of intraparty governance than to work through formal rules and procedures. If the openly authoritarian practices had been written down in the party statutes, they would have been exposed to public scrutiny and debate, and PRI politicians could have focused on changing them. Unwritten rules were a much more difficult and ambiguous target.

INSTITUTIONALIZING THE *DEDAZO*

Simply because President Cárdenas in 1939 unilaterally imposed his favored candidate on the political elite did not mean that its members immediately or automatically accepted this new method of deciding who would govern. The other two informal rules that supported the basic succession arrangement stemmed from the three regime ruptures of 1940, 1946, and 1952, in which leading politicians who had been passed over in the nomination decision attacked the right of the president to decide his successor, organized groups to support their candidacy, and finally left the PRI to run against its candidate in the presidential elections. Many PRI politicians may not have wanted truly fair elections to decide among different parties' candidates, but there could have been many different ways of choosing *within* the PRI regime other than the *dedazo*. These challengers came close to dislodging the regime's official candidate, because they were able to mobilize supporters both within and outside the regime. By exercising voice and complaining of the unfair method of choosing a PRI candidate, they won fame; and by criticizing the president's social and economic policies, they won support for their electoral challenges from both PRI members and important allies in society.

Both the 1940 and 1952 challengers had been members of the cabinet in prior presidential administrations, which meant they had been close political allies of former presidents but not of the current leader, who would make the decision.[4] Although they were excluded from the current president's circle, they or their allies considered themselves potential candidates for the highest post in the land. As mentioned above, it was imperative to stop these internal challenges to presidential authority. One way of achieving this goal was to give only those politicians in a restricted universe the right to be considered. It became a firm but unofficial rule by the 1958 succession that only those politicians who were serving in the current president's cabinet were even eligible to compete for the presidential nomination

(Reyna 1985, 108). This move eliminated all PRI governors, former cabinet ministers (and therefore allies of former presidents), and all federal legislators from consideration. Now those who could aspire to win the nomination had to belong to the president's closest circle and thus depend on the good will of the current leader. The president literally controlled the universe of potential candidates, because he placed and removed them from cabinet positions and, in doing so, could manage the conflict over the succession, which now took place within the executive bureaucracy. This, the second informal rule, also made cabinet appointments and shuffles hugely important.[5]

A third informal rule that formed the base of the succession process was the prohibition against openly stating one's presidential ambitions or too actively engaging in political mobilization within the regime's highest reaches before the president had made his decision and communicated it (Reyna 1985). In the 1940, 1946, and 1952 ruptures, groups within the regime had formed openly to support both the official nominee and the challenger before and after the sitting president had made his choice known (Garrido 1982, 279, 287; Meyer 1985, 93; Paoli Bolio 1985, 142). This open mobilization within the regime's confines had to be stopped, or at least dampened, if the sitting president were to control his succession process. Thus, an informal rule was created to block "pre-candidate" mobilization within the regime and executive bureaucracy. This made it more difficult to openly promote one's own candidacy, which had in earlier successions created "momentum" for potential candidates (both within and outside the PRI) and thus created problems for the president when he attempted to impose his favorite. As Fidel Velasquez (former long-lived leader of the PRI's most important workers' peak-level association, the Mexican Workers Confederation [CTM]) once stated: "He who moves won't come out in the picture," meaning that if one mobilizes political support openly, this will be held against him and he will not be chosen.

In each rupture attempt, the learning process of both regime members and leaders advanced toward the equilibrium of regime stability and discipline in the face of nomination defeat. In the early years of the PRI regime, from roughly 1934 to 1958, although none of the regime's leaders may have thought that the specific changes or adjustments they made to the succession process would eventually end up creating a regime that would remain in power for more than seventy years, the sum of their actions did help lead to this outcome. The historical record leads one to conclude that Cárdenas (1934–40), Manuel Ávila Camacho (1940–46), Miguel Alemán (1946–52), and Adolfo Ruíz Cortines (1952–58) all aimed to ease the conflicts inherent in the turnover of executive power, and, on taking office, each incoming president during this period made further incremental changes that also helped create a less troubled road to the following succession. In all three ruptured successions, the regime's leaders used a mixture of positive incentives and credible threats to keep those supporters of the challengers who were poised to leave firmly within the ranks of the coalition. As early as the 1940s, the Mexican state had control of substantial amounts of resources, graft, and public posts (including lower-level elected positions) that could be selectively doled out. Once politicians had left the party to back a challenger's bid, and had seen him lose at the ballot box, they were welcomed back into the regime and allowed to remake their careers. Simply put, after the failure of three successive bids (by leaving the coalition) to break the president's informal prerogative to choose his successor, PRI politicians did not believe an electoral challenge would succeed, especially after the 1946 electoral reforms that centralized the organization, management, and outcomes of the elections in the hands of the secretary of *gobernación.*

Another important rule of this period was that no seated bureaucrat or elected official who had held a position in the six months before the election could run for the highest office of the land. This forced ambitious presidential hopefuls and their supporters to make a crucial decision long before they could gauge whether a split from the hegemonic party would be successful, and gave the regime's leaders more time to immobilize the challenger. By the 1952 rupture, there were indications that an exit would not be successful and, as a consequence, supporters of General Miguel Henríquez were determined to win the official nomination rather than leave the party for an external run at the presidency (Rodríguez Araujo 1974, 108). Because most politicians, even if they were not close allies of the next presidential candidate, would eventually find a post within the regime, the potential gains to be had from remaining disciplined were far higher than the potential gains of a most likely unsuccessful bid to unseat the hegemonic party at the ballot box. There were few incentives to challenge the president's informal right to designate his successor, and no important PRI politician would do so until the 1987 rupture, which took place after several years of economic crisis and a profound shift in economic development model (Garrido 1993; Bruhn 1997).

Regime leaders also created new formal electoral rules to dampen the temptation to leave the coalition during the presidential succession process. Molinar (1991) has shown that the 1946 electoral reforms to centralize the electoral process under the aegis of the secretary of *gobernación* were an important step in corralling losers within the coalition, because they substantially raised the costs of forming a new party. Because party registration was now controlled by Gobernación, it became far more difficult for politicians to leave the PRI and run under another party's banner. Thus, both formal and informal rules were created to permit each outgoing president to single-handedly select his successor.

THE COLLAPSE OF THE *DEDAZO* IN THE 1990S

The *dedazo* was highly resistant to change; from 1952 until 1987, there were no serious challenges to the president's prerogative of choosing his successor. It took a combined punch of both a disastrous economic crisis (1980s) and growing electoral competition (1990s) to finally allow ambitious politicians within the party to rework the tradition of the *dedazo*. In this section, I examine changes to the *dedazo* in the late 1990s that were due to a split in 1987 and to rising levels of electoral competition and shocks at the ballot box, changes that encouraged PRI members and activists to use the *formal* statutory rules to strengthen their position against the informal presidential imposition of his successor.

Informal rules are usually understood to be an instrument for playing an end run around inefficient or undesirable formal institutions: in the former case—following Helmke and Levistky's terminology in the introduction to this volume—informal institutions are substitutive; in the latter, they are competing. Yet, because the informal rules played such an important role in political outcomes in Mexico and were undergirded by executive power and noncompetitive electoral conditions, party actors who were dissatisfied with arbitrary impositions in the presidential succession could do little except wait for a future opening. This began to change with electoral competition. PRI politicians were empowered by electoral competition, because it gave them an exit option that had been nonexistent under hegemonic conditions. PRI politicians would end up using the formal party rules to shore up their weak position and force the president to allow more participation in the final nomination decision. So, while most scholars of Mexico have ignored the interplay between informal and formal institutions, believing that only the former matter, the formal statutory rules of the game in fact empowered weaker party actors to dilute the informal prerogatives of party leaders.

The 1987–88 presidential succession was undermined by a rupture caused by a small number of left-leaning PRI politicians who protested both the method of selecting the next president and the economic model that the group in power had adopted. The decade of the 1980s was marked by two extraordinary economic crises that finally convinced President Miguel de la Madrid (1982–88)—with the support of his economic team, led by the secretary of planning and budget, Carlos Salinas de

Gortari—to take initial steps toward liberalizing the Mexican economy. The leaders of an antineoliberal faction within the PRI, the Democratic Current (Corriente Democrática; CD) publicly protested de la Madrid's right to unilaterally impose his successor, in part because they were (rightly) convinced that the president would choose the neoliberal Salinas to succeed him.

The regime leadership was quick to use old-fashioned methods of suffocating the proto-rebellion, and offered many of those who had been present at the first meetings selective incentives to leave the CD. Others left when they realized the course the CD's leaders were taking—a rupture with the regime. The regime's other reaction to the threat of a rupture was to organize a "beauty contest" among several possible candidates, who gave speeches to several groups within the PRI and executive bureaucracy. However, the *pasarela* ("charade") fooled no one: President de la Madrid would make his decision regardless of the opinions of his fellow PRI politicians. A seemingly innocuous change in the electoral rules, however, now allowed multiparty coalitions to back a single presidential candidate, and this allowed the now ex-PRIistas to run against official PRI candidate Carlos Salinas in the 1988 election.[6] The 1987–88 presidential succession constituted the first serious breakdown in the *dedazo* tradition since 1952. However, it was the electoral competition of the 1990s that dealt the final death blow to presidential impositions.

Competition at the ballot box began to threaten the PRI's hegemony in the mid-1980s and grew sharply in the 1990s. This process changed the incentives of politicians in the almost seventy-year-old governing coalition by making them less likely to accept their defeats in nomination contests. When they had no exit option because of the weakness of opposition parties and the government's control over the apparatus of elections, disgruntled PRI politicians had little choice but to accept the will of the president (or governor, for local electoral posts such as mayors and state deputies) and await a better political moment. With the growth of the electoral popularity of party options other than the PRI, its politicians were strengthened: they could again leave the coalition and run under another party's banner and hope to win the election. At the same time, as opposition parties battled to reduce the use of fraud to change election results, there was a greater likelihood that electoral outcomes would be respected. Electoral competition, which made party ruptures more likely, helped end the *dedazo*.

In the 1993 succession process for the 1994 presidential election, then-president Carlos Salinas Gortari played a traditional game in imposing his successor. After the 1987–88 rupture from the party ranks, it was of utmost importance that Salinas control the succession, meaning that no disgruntled losing pre-candidate should leave the ranks of the PRI, form a new party, and run against the official candidate. In late 1993, the PRI's candidate was announced, and all losers accepted the presidential decision (in one case, grudgingly). However, once the armed rebellion in Chiapas began on January 1, 1994, the succession began to unravel. One of the losing contenders, Manuel Camacho Solís, left the government to head up the negotiations with the Zapatista rebels. Because he gave up his position more than six months before the general election, Camacho was still legally able to participate as a candidate. It was debated publicly whether Salinas second-guessed his initial decision by allowing Camacho to continue in the public eye without staying in his government post. In March 1994, in a crime that still has not been fully solved, the PRI's presidential candidate was assassinated while campaigning. Salinas remained strong enough to impose another close ally, the former secretary of planning and budget Ernesto Zedillo, but the succession process was sullied: it was the first time since 1928 that a presidential candidate had been murdered. The 2000 transfer of power would end the *dedazo* forever. Unlike the presidents of the 1940s and 1950s, there was little the PRI presidents could do in a fundamentally more evolved electoral context to dampen the ambitions of its politicians and control their behavior. The *dedazo* had been created under conditions of weak electoral institutions and weak political parties in a largely rural nation. This situation had changed radically by the 1990s.

In the 1990s, PRI politicians operating under newly competitive conditions began to use the *formal* statutory rules to revoke the president's control over the presidential succession. There were two steps in the process to remove power from the hands of the president. The first step was new statutory rules that stripped President Zedillo (1994–2000) of his control over the universe of choice by forcing presidential candidates to have prior electoral experience. This rule opened up the ranks of possible PRI presidential candidates to many outside the cabinet, while disqualifying several secretaries inside it. This rule not only remained on the books but was also respected. The second step was a radical change in the procedure to choose the presidential nominee; instead of a party assembly that simply ratified the president's nominee, President Zedillo was obligated in 1999 to devolve the nomination decision to all registered voters in an open presidential primary.[7]

The Zedillo era would see fundamental changes in relations between the presidency and the PRI. Ever-rising levels of electoral competition, a severe economic crisis in 1994–95, and Zedillo's desire to negotiate reforms with both opposition parties weakened the traditional ties between president and party. These new circumstances not only allowed statutory rule changes that favored lower-level party actors, but also made it too costly for President Zedillo to revoke the changes that directly harmed his interests in the presidential succession.

The Seventeenth National Assembly of the PRI, September 1996

The Seventeenth National Assembly of the PRI was called after the shocking electoral losses at the gubernatorial level in 1995 (and the resulting fall of the leader of the party) and the dramatic economic crisis of 1994–95. The party assembly constituted a confrontation between the president, on the one hand, and the governors and members of the party bureaucracy on the other. The challenge to limit the president's choice of his successor and strengthen the autonomy the National Executive Committee (CEN) and party bureaucracy came in the form of the requisites for becoming a PRI candidate for president and governor. These requisites were crucial, because no president since President Gustavo Diaz Ordaz (1964–70) had held elective office before winning the nomination for the presidency. Zedillo's favored candidate was typical for the 1970–95 period: an economist who had never held office but had risen politically through various posts in the executive bureaucracy.[8] For the governors (and other PRI politicians) to become potential candidates, they had to revoke the *informal* rule that disbarred them from the internal competition. With the 2000 presidential elections on the horizon, these actors used the National Assembly to rework the formal statutes to their political advantage.

The fight over limiting the president's prerogatives came in the form of a carefully worded change in the statute to increase the requisites that politicians would have to meet to be a presidential (and gubernatorial) candidate. Originally, the reform proposal that was to be presented in the National Assembly in September 1996 stated that presidential hopefuls should have been *either* a party leader *or* an elected official. This would have made it more difficult, but certainly not impossible, for the "technocrats" serving in the president's cabinet, who tend not to have experience in elected posts, to meet the standards.[9] However, after an uproar in the statutory working session of the assembly, the final wording of the document to come out of the National Assembly was changed to specify prior experience as a "militant, *and* party leader *and* elected official." This left only a few of the president's cabinet secretaries eligible and created many more eligible candidates *outside* the cabinet, including several governors who obviously met the electoral requirements. Thus, the ability of the president to handpick his successor was considerably diminished, as most of his cabinet members were disqualified because they did not have elected experience. This forced President Zedillo to prepare his allies' way by sending them to the Senate in 1997, by bringing already eligible politicians into leading cabinet positions (which he eventually did), or by calling for another National Assembly to remove the offending requirements.

During this period, rising electoral competition at the ballot box at the municipal and state levels gave the PRI governors far more political weight. First, they were responsible for winning the federal deputy elections in their states under far more competitive circumstances. Second, ambitious PRI politicians who wished to become governors now had an exit option if they were passed over in the nomination battle. And finally, the governors were now in a position to argue that they were the best possible candidates to defeat popular opposition candidates in the presidential elections.

The president and his party leadership traditionally had veto power over the PRI governors' choices of their local deputies and municipal president candidacies, and the PRI governors also had to negotiate with the center over what percentage of federal deputy nominations they could place. As we saw above, the rule that only cabinet members could be considered presidential candidates meant that sitting governors were necessarily excluded. To remedy this situation, the governors and party bureaucrats used the *formal* candidate selection rules to weaken the president's informal right to impose his successor. In abstract terms, a PRI governor would prefer to end five decades of exclusion from the PRI presidential succession game and win the informal right to be considered a candidate. To achieve these goals, he would have to either modify the formal rules of the presidential nomination process or pressure the president to give up his informal prerogative to name his successor, a very unlikely scenario. Actors such as governors could attempt to reduce the universe of presidential possibilities to exclude the president's closest technocratic allies or change the nomination method so the president could no longer simply impose his successor.

The 1999 PRI Presidential Primary

President Zedillo was thus unable to simply overturn the formal statutory rules—an astonishing change in "politics as usual" in Mexico. Zedillo's institutional position, which obliged him to negotiate with the opposition in Congress, and the economic difficulties during his presidential term were some fundamental causes of his weakness relative to the PRI and the PRI governors. Most importantly, the ever-rising levels of electoral competition forced him to concede a radical change in the presidential nomination process and, thus, an end to his traditional succession prerogatives. It was better for him to attempt to win the nomination struggle within his own party even under the new, more restrictive requisites than to risk an internal split, such as those seen in the 1940s and in 1987. The changes made in the reform assembly of 1996 and Zedillo's failure to overturn these rules demonstrate two fundamental points: first, the growing importance of both the governors and the party bureaucrats within the PRI; and second, the use of formal party rules as instruments by weaker members of the coalition to shore up their position vis-à-vis the informal prerogatives of the president.

Because the president could no longer guarantee electoral victories for his party members, the collective good of assured victory was no longer provided in exchange for loyalty and obedience. Thus, if an individual politician refused to remain loyal when he was passed over for the nomination, then he could leave and run for another party option, and there was no guarantee that the PRI would win the general election. This raised the costs of staying loyal to the president, while at the same time lowering the gains from remaining disciplined to the president's mandates. Loyalty and obedience to presidential impositions made sense when there was no chance the PRI would lose in the present or future; now there were no guarantees.

The creation of formal requisites for presidential nominees was not the only shocking change in the reigning balance between the formal and informal rules. In 1999 the covert imposition of the candidate ended when the president chose to organize a primary of all registered voters to nominate the PRI's presidential candidate.[10] This process took the selection out of his hands and gave it to the general electorate, the rank and file (who were more likely to vote in the primary) and other powerful actors within the party who helped organize support for the four candidates at the state level.[11] Looking carefully at the statutes for choosing presidential candidates, one finds that in 1999 there were no clear indications that an open primary was included in the nomination methods (which included selection by the National Assembly, made up of sectors and other groups within the party, or through a vote of the National Political Council). The statutes were not changed in 1999 to explicitly include a primary, because Zedillo did not wish to call another assembly (the party body charged with statute reform). In yet another example of statutory ambiguity, a primary was held under the "other method in special circumstances that the leadership [read president] decides" clause of the article covering nominations (Party of the Institutional Revolution 1993, art. 159).

On November 7, 1999, with ten million voters reportedly participating, the PRI overturned seventy years of top-down decision-making within the party. Electoral competition made the threat of a rupture of the PRI by one of the losing candidates real and credible. This forced Zedillo and his advisors to find a procedure that would be accepted as fair by all those competing for the nomination. None of the presidential hopefuls would have accepted a party nominating convention or a vote of the members of the National Political Council, because of the ease of predetermining the outcome via the selection of delegates.[12] The open primary, despite the dangers it represented in terms of fairness, was considered the best method available.

Due to the changes in levels of competition and the power this gave to other PRI actors, several informal practices surrounding the presidential succession changed in 1999. The president could no longer unilaterally impose his candidate without risking a regime split, and this gave PRI leaders the power to change formal rules in an explicit attempt to disqualify some of his favorites. Because the sitting president no longer had complete control over the succession process, and because of the exclusionary requisites, many prominent members of the PRI who were not members of the cabinet were considered (or at least considered themselves) serious contenders for the nomination. It became rational to openly state one's presidential ambitions and to mobilize support within the coalition for a run at the presidential nomination. Powerful members of the PRI, such as Roberto Madrazo (then governor of Tabasco), Manuel Bartlett (then governor of Puebla), Francisco Labastida (then secretary of *gobernación* and Zedillo's favorite), and Humberto Roque Villanueva (a former leader of the PRI and congressional majority leader), declared that they would compete, and warned Zedillo to avoid a regime rupture through more open and democratic selection mechanisms. As a result, Madrazo, the strongest runner-up to the eventual winner—Zedillo's favorite—accepted his defeat and stayed within the confines of the coalition.

CONCLUSION

In examining the creation of some of the most important informal institutions in Mexico's party-based authoritarian regime, we find that they were constructed by PRI presidents working to serve their political interests in a strategic game to end intracoalition ruptures, which had proved so dangerous to nascent PRI dominance over the electoral and governmental arenas. The most fundamental informal institution—that the president single-handedly designated his chosen successor—was born of a conflict in the mid-1930s between the sitting president and the *jefe máximo*, Elías Calles. When President Cárdenas decided who would follow him in the presidency, several powerful coalition members refused to accept the president's informal prerogatives and continued to challenge him (and subsequent presidents) over the nomination. The supporting informal practices (as well as several important formal electoral rules put in place by the government beginning in 1946) made it far more difficult for disgruntled losers in the succession process to mobilize support within and outside the coalition, or to create an electoral vehicle to challenge the PRI's official candidate at the ballot box.

These developments seem to show that the informal rules were competing with some of the most important constitutional provisions that allowed for democratic elections and party provisions that allowed for rank-and-file participation in choosing candidates. However, this is too simplistic a representation. First of all, PRI regime leaders had such utter control over the nation that they could have changed the Constitution if they had chosen to. Informal rules were not so much competing with the formal institutions as underlying them. Second, many formal rules, both electoral and statutory, were in fact written to support the more basic informal prerogatives. The 1946 electoral reforms, and all of those until the early 1960s, concentrated the organization and management of elections in the hands of the regime's executive bureaucracy and made party registration increasingly difficult. All candidates had to represent a registered party, and independent candidates were barred from competing. And once the elections had taken place, the sitting Congress determined the validity of the processes, and so could always approve any fraudulent behavior on the part of the PRI's electoral machine. Far from being a residual category, informal institutions were ultimately the basis for political outcomes.

These informal rules were transformed half a century later, in large part because of an external shock in the form of heightened electoral competition. The series of electoral victories that began in the 1980s changed actors' incentives and resource base, which eventually led many of them to use the formal party rules to improve their chances of winning candidacies or of curtailing the president's ability to unilaterally impose his successor. The threat of rupture became far more credible in a context of heightened competition—a paradoxical outcome, because opposition parties had fought to rewrite offending electoral rules to ensure fairer electoral processes, not to empower PRI party politicians. Once the electoral balance of power had shifted, party actors used seemingly insignificant formal rules to quickly transform informal practices that had endured for decades.

CHAPTER EIGHT

Election Insurance and Coalition Survival

Formal and Informal Institutions in Chile

JOHN M. CAREY AND PETER SIAVELIS

One of the most striking elements of Chilean politics in the years since the return to democratic government in 1990 is the stability of the governing Concertación coalition. Originally founded in the 1980s as a broad amalgamation of parties and civic groups in opposition to the perpetuation of General Augusto Pinochet's military regime, the Concertación evolved into an electoral and governing alliance composed of four major parties—the Christian Democrats, the Socialists, the Party for Democracy, and the Radical Social Democrats—along with a handful of independents, that has endured through three presidential elections, four legislative cycles, and four cycles of municipal contests. This stability stands in striking contrast to the coalitional fluidity that characterized Chile's long pre-Pinochet democratic experience (A. Valenzuela 1994, 120–25). Chile's current governing alliance bears resemblance to governing coalitions in parliamentary systems, which are frequently characterized as more durable than legislative coalitions in multiparty presidential systems, the latter frequently characterized as improvisational, circumstantial, and devoid of recognizable policy content (Mainwaring 1993; Linz 1994). As a result, Chile's coalition ought to be immune from the ills frequently attributed to loose presidential coalitions, in particular that they undermine accountability by making it difficult for voters to identify which parties share in responsibility for government performance.

The formal institutions handed down by the Pinochet regime during Chile's transition to democracy have, by some accounts, contributed to coalition stability (Rabkin 1996; Carey 2002; Agüero 2003). In particular, the unique rule by which all elected legislative seats are contested in two-member (M=2) districts encourages coalitions in that, in any given district, only candidates from the top two lists can win representation. At the same time, however, the M=2 rule implies that to secure legislative majorities, coalitions must nominate their strongest candidates in the most precarious electoral list positions. This conundrum can generate substantial tension within coalitions, particularly one as broad as the Concertación, in which nominations must be divided among many actors (Siavelis 2002b).

In this chapter, we argue that the Concertación has responded to the challenge implied by the M=2 formal institution by creating and sustaining an informal institution of insuring strong candidates who incur risk on behalf of the coalition against the vagaries of the electoral marketplace. Specifically, there is an informal system of rewarding good also-rans with appointed government posts. The mutual expectations generated by this arrangement, on the part of politicians and party leaders, have helped to recruit strong candidates and sustain the Concertación. At the same time, recent changes in the Chilean electoral landscape threaten Concertación control over the pool of resources that indemnify its best candidates against electoral risk, and these changes may therefore threaten the viability of the coalition itself.

"THE REPORTS OF MY DEATH ARE GREATLY EXAGGERATED"

The Concertación's demise has been predicted often over the decade and a half during which it has governed. Even the coalition's leaders have issued premature announcements of its death (*Latin America Adviser* 2002; *El Mercurio* 2003a). Some observers of Chilean politics, therefore, might regard the dissolution of the Concertación as both a foregone conclusion and an overdetermined event—that is, as the product of so many factors, all working toward the same end, that it is impossible to assign responsibility among them. We share the opinion that the Concertación may not endure much beyond Chile's 2005 election, but not for the reasons commonly cited. Our argument is based, instead, on the structure of Chilean political careers, which in turn is connected inextricably with Chile's unusual electoral rules.

Those foreseeing the Concertación's demise point out that the Chilean economy slowed in the early years of the twenty-first century, after the coalition's first years in government during the 1990s. Moreover, the coalition itself was initially galvanized around opposition to the Pinochet regime of the 1970s and 1980s, so as time passes, the compelling force of that initial motivation might naturally weaken. In addition, the Concertación, and even its component parties—most notably the Christian Democrats—are internally divided over social issues, such as the legal status of divorce and access to birth control. Finally, by the 2005 elections, the Concertación will have held the presidency and a majority in the Chamber of Deputies (the

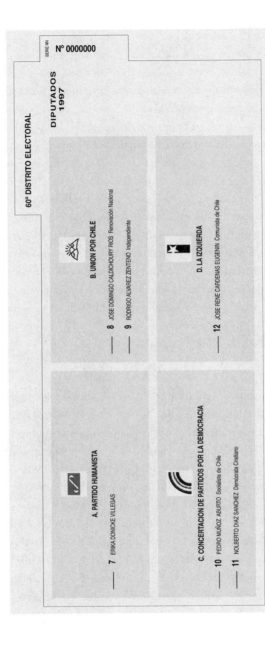

Figure 8.1. Sample Ballot from 1997 Election for Chamber of Deputies

legislative house elected by popular vote) for sixteen years. By the standards of multiparty coalitions anywhere, much less among Latin America's presidential systems, the Concertación is geriatric, bearing the scars of miscellaneous corruption charges against members—including the stripping of parliamentary rights from five of the coalition's deputies in 2002—and the general disillusionment that goes with holding the reins of power for so long. One might conclude, then, that the coalition is simply ready to expire.

Any of these forces, or some combination of them, could indeed undermine the Concertación, but we do not regard these factors as necessarily devastating to the coalition's survival, for a number of reasons. In the first place, the Chilean economy came through the lean years at the turn of the century in far better shape than that of any of its Southern Cone neighbors, and employment and growth figures rebounded in 2003-4, providing the coalition with a plausible claim to good economic stewardship. Next, while internal differences on social issues plague the coalition, this has been the case since it began to govern, and similar divisions bedevil its main opponents on the right (here designated the Right). Finally, who is to say how old is too old for a coalition? Based on Chile's historical experience, the Concertación had already far exceeded the life expectancy of any multiparty coalition as early as the 1997 legislative elections, yet it prevailed in that instance, and in the 1999–2000 presidential election, and yet again in the 2001 legislative elections (Carey 2002).

To sum up, many of the conditions widely regarded as threatening to the Concertación's survival are not new. They have been present during much of its lifetime, and so represent constants in the electoral environment. Moreover, as many observers have noted, Chile's electoral system presents substantial risk for parties that abandon coalitions and run on their own. Indeed, the explanation we advance here regarding the Concertación's potential demise rests on the unique nature of Chile's electoral law and how this interacts with recent changes in the electoral environment.

TWO-MEMBER DISTRICT ELECTIONS AND COALITION STRATEGIES

The most noteworthy characteristic of Chile's legislative election system is that all districts elect two representatives to Congress.[1] Each list on the ballot, therefore, can include up to two candidates. The lists are "open," in that voters indicate a preference for one candidate or the other within their preferred list. An example of a Chilean Chamber of Deputies ballot is shown in figure 8.1.

Despite the candidate-centered nature of the preference vote, the total votes for both candidates on any list are first pooled together for the purposes of distributing

TABLE 8.1
Summaries of District-Level Coalition Competition in Chilean Congressional Elections,
1989–97

	Right doubles	Concertación doubles Right	Concertación wins neither seat	Concertación wins one seat, plus non-Right winner	Concertación runners-up
Chamber					
1989[a]	0	11	2	1	40
1993	1	11	1	0	48
1997	0	9	0	4	47
Senate					
1989[b]	0	3	0	0	16
1993	0	0	0	0	9
1997	0	1	0	0	9

[a] In six districts in 1989, the Concertación ran only a single candidate for the Chamber of Deputies, leaving no runner-up. Thus the row does not add up to sixty, the total number of districts.

[b] In 1989, all thirty-eight elected Senate seats (nineteen districts) were up for grabs. In subsequent elections, alternately nine or ten districts are contested every four years.

seats to lists, then seats are awarded to individual candidates in the order of their rank within their list. Seats are allocated by the D'hondt method, such that the first-place list in a district can win both seats only if it more than doubles the vote total of the second-place list; otherwise, each of the top two lists wins one seat.[2]

Though the electoral rule is procedurally straightforward, its combination with the contemporary party system generates substantial strategic complexity for candidates, parties, and coalition leaders. Electoral politics in postauthoritarian Chile has been dominated by two major coalitions: the Concertación on the left and the Alianza por Chile on the right—each of which in turn is composed of two subpacts. For most of this period, the Concertación has been composed of four significant parties (PDC, PRSD, PPD, PS) and the Alianza por Chile has consistently included two major players (RN, UDI), along with some minor regional parties.[3] Independents associated with particular ideological sectors play an important role and have also had to negotiate themselves onto major lists.

The constituent parties of each coalition must negotiate sixty two-seat electoral slates for the Chamber of Deputies and either nine or ten two-seat slates for the Senate, depending on the cycle of turnover in the upper house. The pattern in past elections has been for each of the coalitions to allocate one seat to each of its two subpacts in each district, and then to tinker with list formation around the edges to attract small parties that can lend a helping hand in bolstering national coalition vote totals for presidential elections.

Two stark realities shape negotiations. First, most lists can expect one defeat in each district, because the threshold for two-seat victories is so high. Table 8.1 summarizes the number of two-seat victories in recent elections for each major coalition. Second, and more important for our purposes, the pairing of candidates is crucial. The key to victory is for subpacts and parties to place their candidates on the same list either with an extremely strong candidate, who will help them more than double the vote total of the second-place list, or a relatively weak candidate, who will not outpoll their own candidate while the list pulls enough votes to win one seat. This delicate balance creates a tension between the preference of candidates and coalitions. Coalitions would like sixty pairings that maximize votes, whereas candidates may often prefer a weak list partner.[4] Those who are outpolled by their list partner in these two-seat pairings we refer to as "runners-up." We explore their fate below.

COALITIONS, MAJORITIES, AND THE RISK OF DOUBLING

Chile's $M=2$ system presents a complex problem of distributing risk in situations where the collective goals of an electoral coalition conflict with the career goals of individual candidates. Consider the following: coalition leaders want to maximize the number of seats they control in Congress—and, in particular, they prefer to control the legislative majority. A coalition cannot win a majority without doubling the vote total of the second-place list in at least one district. Given the uncertainties associated with electoral politics and, of course, the desire to capture the most seats possible, an ambitious coalition should seek to "double" as often as its electoral strength will allow. Thus, coalition leaders that aspire to majority status face the challenge of identifying districts where doubling is possible and targeting sufficient resources at such districts to cross the critical threshold.

One of the most important resources that coalition leaders can allocate among districts is candidates. During the first decade after the democratic transition, a Concertación list that turned in a particularly strong performance could reasonably expect to double the list of the Right, whereas the Right faced prospects of doubling only under extremely rare and propitious circumstances.[5] Doubling, then, has been a strategic issue primarily for the Concertación, and its prospects for doing so depend on putting up candidates who can turn in outstanding performances on behalf of the list, providing the necessary boost to cross the magic threshold. The problem is that the coalition's collective goal under such circumstances runs directly counter to the most immediate political goal of most candidates for elective office—political survival.

Candidates want to win elections, whether they are motivated only by base ambition or by the loftier desire to make good public policy, or by some combination of these. If they lose, their ability to realize either type of goal suffers. Moreover, it is precisely the strongest candidates—the ones whose personal qualities and popularity among voters make them best able to win elections—that coalitions need to put in the riskiest positions in order to pursue the collective goal of doubling and win legislative majorities.

A strong candidate has every reason to prefer to be paired on a list with a relatively weak partner in a district where her coalition is willing to settle for the one-one split between first- and second-place lists most common in Chilean elections. To be the strong candidate on such a list is, effectively, a guarantee of personal victory. To be nominated in a district where one's coalition aspires to "double," on the other hand, means facing not only competition from other lists but also competition from one's list partner. The very imperative that leads coalitions to run strong pairs of candidates in districts where they seek to double threatens the electoral security of their best politicians.

THE INFORMAL INSTITUTION:
INSURANCE AGAINST ELECTORAL RISK

How has the Concertación resolved this conundrum? We suggest that to induce strong candidates to embrace the risk inherent in a doubling campaign, the coalition has offered insurance. In the language of political economy, for over a decade the Concertación has reaped substantial profits from its ability to act collectively, and the currency of those profits is control of the government—both of the leadership positions in Congress, due to the Concertación's success in doubling its opponents in key districts, and of the executive, due to the coalition's ability to nominate presidential candidates and support them in a unified manner. For strong legislative candidates who take risks on the coalition's behalf by attempting to double, insurance takes the form of a promise of attractive appointed positions in the government if one should fall short in the electoral competition.

The participants in this informal institution are potential candidates for nomination to legislative lists, and the coalition leaders who recruit candidates and negotiate the allocation of nominations among parties participating in the coalition. Coalition leaders, in this case, are the leaders of the Concertación's component parties—who may not necessarily hold elected office—in conjunction with the parties' top legislative leaders, aides of the president of the Republic, representatives of the Ministry of the General Secretary of the Presidency, and members of the *partido transversal*. The *partido transversal* is an informal, though well-recognized, cadre of supra-party elites whose loyalty lies as much with the Concertación coalition as with their individual parties. The *partido* has been crucial in generating the many agreements that hold the coalition together (Fuentes 1999; Walker 2003; Siavelis, this volume). These sets of actors strike deals in informal and multilevel negotiations. In the most basic terms, the deal with respect to legislative candidates is: "You put yourself at risk in this election for the good of the coalition. If we win both seats, terrific. If we fail to double and you lose out despite having done your best on behalf of the coalition, you will be compensated with a ministry or some other attractive executive appointment." The deal, of course, is not a written contract but an informal agreement on which the mutual expectations of candidates and coalition leaders are based. In conversations with legislators from both inside and outside the Concertación, we have confirmed that such an expectation exists among politicians.[6]

Our goal here is to identify the conditions under which runner-up candidates on Concertación lists that failed to double are appointed to top government posts during the four-year period in which, had they won, they would have served in Congress. Our hypothesis is that "good losers"—those that competed valiantly in defeat—are the most likely to receive appointments, and in a manner consistent with the informal institution of insurance for candidates that incur risk for the good of the coalition. The dependent variable, then, is whether the runner-up received an appointment as a minister, vice-minister, or ambassador during that time. We posit that the factors that should affect the probability of appointment are: for which chamber the runner-up ran, how narrowly his or her list failed to double the next closest list, and how evenly the personal votes for candidates were split within the Concertación list.

Senate races are more important than Chamber of Deputies races because, although the chambers have analogous powers, there are fewer seats in the upper chamber, rendering each seat more precious. The Senate is also perceived as the launching pad for presidential candidacies. Because the stakes are higher, electoral competition for the Senate is fiercer, so strong performance is more impressive. Also, the candidates recruited for Senate races are more prominent. This has two implications. First, their experience and qualifications mean these candidates are often "ministerial caliber." Second, high-credential Senate candidates have attractive outside options, and to induce such individuals to undertake a risky campaign, the insurance for runners-up must be more generous than that for Chamber candidates. For all these reasons, we expect senatorial good losers to be more likely to receive appointments than Chamber good losers.

The closer the Concertación came to doubling the Right,[7] the more impressive was the collective performance of the list in its attempt to double. Our expectation is that runners-up from such lists should be increasingly likely to be rewarded for their contribution to the collective effort.

How evenly matched the two candidates on the Concertación list are in terms of personal votes is a more subtle issue. If a strong list performance is largely the product of the vote-attracting capacity of one candidate, then the runner-up may be regarded as not instrumental to the list's overall performance, and therefore not as deserving of postelection reward as when the list's two candidates ran neck and neck. By this logic, runners-up from "lopsided" lists should be less likely to receive appointments. Yet it is not necessarily in the coalition's collective interest to foster intra-list competition. That is, a coalition benefits from having strong candidates who attract votes, in a generic sense, to the list, but it does not profit from a competition by which list-mates seek to take votes from each other. Indeed, too much internecine competition could prove damaging to a list's overall status and depress its overall votes, much as parties in the United States worry about the effects of a tough primary campaign on the party's eventual candidate. In order to mitigate incentives for "cannibalistic" intra-list competition, then, the coalition may want to emphasize collective list performance in providing insurance to runners-up.

In short, we expect a higher probability of the Concertación runners-up getting an appointment (1) in Senate, rather than Chamber, races; (2) when the Concertación list beats the Right more severely (approaching a doubling); and (3) (with less confidence here) when the two Concertación candidates contribute more equally to the list's overall vote total. We would interpret such results as evidence that the "insurance policy" of appointments by the executive was wielded systematically as a way of attracting strong candidates to fight tough races and rewarding those that did so valiantly in a losing cause.

At this point, it is worthwhile to emphasize what we regard as the relevance, and the limitations, of our statistical analysis. Our model measures whether, among runners-up, stronger candidates are more likely than weaker candidates to receive appointments. Our measure of candidate strength is based entirely on electoral outcomes, which reflect combinations of two types of characteristics: (1) inherent quality (charisma, qualifications, personal prominence) and (2) effort on behalf of the campaign. The logic by which these two types of qualities contribute to the probability of appointment differs. We expect that a potential candidate's inherent strength raises the opportunity costs of accepting a risky electoral list position, because the same qualities that make candidates inherently strong also increase the odds that they have career options more attractive than placing themselves at electoral risk. For these types of candidates, a promise of insurance is critical to entice them to accept a spot on a high-risk (attempting-to-double) list. With respect to a candidate's effort, the logic is more straightforward. All else being equal, the president should be more inclined to reward those who worked hard on behalf of the coalition and thus fell just short of doubling than those who campaigned less effectively and so fell further short of the mark. Although there are two distinct logics at work here, both generate the same expectations with respect to the parameter estimates in our model.

Ideally, we could know inherent candidate quality separate from candidate effort, and thus separate out the independent effects of each characteristic. If we could do this, then a relevant comparison would be between Concertación winners from lists that elect only one candidate (i.e., those that do not double) and Concertación runners-up in districts that the coalition targeted to attempt to double. If we are correct, then good losers from attempting-to-double districts should be of even higher inherent quality than winners from the full set of districts in which only one candidate from the Concertación was elected. Unfortunately, we do not have a way of measuring inherent candidate quality distinct from electoral outcomes. In the end, then, we acknowledge that our analysis does not allow us to disentangle the "inherent quality/opportunity costs" story about insurance from the "reward for effort" story. In fact, of course, these two stories are mutually consistent, and we think there is truth to both of them.

EVIDENCE

Information about electoral results—with returns broken down by candidate, party, and coalition list—is publicly available and reasonably easy to collect at the Chilean Ministry of Interior website.[8] Data on appointments, on the other hand, are more labor-intensive to collect and more difficult to measure comprehensively. We pursued two strategies in collecting data on appointments. First, we identified runners-up who received appointed posts, following three steps:

1. We identified the potential Concertación good losers, who are the coalition's runner-up candidates in districts *except* where the following conditions apply:
   - the Concertación doubled the Right, thus electing both candidates on its list to Congress (i.e., no losers);
   - the Concertación list included only one candidate, who won a seat;
   - the Concertación won neither seat, thus suffering electoral humiliation in the district; or
   - the Concertación won the first seat, but the second was won by a candidate from a list other than the Right, such that the Concertación failed to double even against a divided opposition—the conditions that ought to be most propitious for doubling. (Table 8.1 shows the frequency of each of

these scenarios, as well as the remaining number of races from each election (in the column "Concertación runners-up")—races that produced potential good losers and so comprise our data set.)

2. We collected the names of those appointed to a set of political posts during the period 1990–2001—the legislative periods following the three elections we analyze.

3. We matched the names of our runners-up with those who received a plum appointment during the legislative period following their electoral defeat.

Table 8.2 categorizes the positions for which we searched and our sources. The Chilean president has wide powers of appointment, naming approximately thirty-five hundred government officials (*El Mercurio* 2003b). We focus only on high-profile posts. Lower-level positions are less attractive to ambitious politicians and are less likely to be used as rewards. We certainly do not include all important appointments. There are other posts with which presidents might reasonably reward politicians who served valiantly in their coalition's electoral battles for which we were unable to obtain systematic data (e.g., boards of state-run corporations, regional governorships). Beyond these, there are still other positions (e.g., judicial appointments, party offices, future nominations to congressional or municipal council slates of candidates) that are not direct presidential appointments but over which presidents could exercise considerable influence on behalf of their allies. In short, our search for appointees almost certainly includes some Type II error, but not Type I error. That is, we almost certainly miss identifying some good losers who received appointments from the executive, or at the behest of the executive, but we are certain that all those we identify as having received appointments are correctly classified.

Our second strategy for collecting data on appointments complements the first by minimizing Type II error (failing to detect appointments that *were* made) through intensive efforts to map the career trajectories of runners-up following their electoral losses. Because we could not conduct such exhaustive efforts for all candidates in the study, we limited this strategy to those Concertación good losers who were *most* and *least* likely candidates for appointment, according to our hypotheses. We identified "most likelies" as those runners-up on lists in which the Concertación-to-Right vote ratio was greater than 1.8—that is, the list won more than 90 percent of the necessary share of the vote to be able to "double" the Right, falling just short. There were twenty such good losers: fourteen candidates from the Chamber of Deputies and six from the Senate. We identified "least likelies" ("bad losers"?) as runners-up on lists that received *fewer* votes than the coalition of the Right (Concertación-to-Right ratio between 0.5 and 1.0). This yielded nineteen Chamber runners-up and only one from

TABLE 8.2
Available Positions Included in Appointment *Variable, Data for 1990–2001*

Position	Number of available posts	Sources of data
Minister	21	*Keesings Record of World Events,* various dates
Vice minister	30	Ministerio Secretario General de la Presidencia, División Coordinación Interministerial
Ambassador	82[a]	Ministerio de Relaciones Exteriores

[a] This is the number of positions to which presidents appointed ambassadors from 1990 to 2001, according to data provided by the Ministerio de Relaciones Exteriores (Ministry of Foreign Relations).

the Senate. So as not to exclude the Senate among "least likelies," we added the next four least successful Concertación Senate runners-up (with ratios up to 1.13).[9]

For our set of "most and least likelies," we supplemented the data included in our systematic search for appointments with standard internet searches; "manual" searches of Chilean government, party, newspaper, and nongovernmental organization websites and archives; and email correspondence with Chilean academics and government officials, inquiring about the postelectoral careers of specific runners-up. This approach yielded information on some executive-level appointments to positions for which we do not have comprehensive data, as well as information on some appointments to other posts, but for which presidential support may have been instrumental.[10]

As a first cut at the question of whether Concertación good losers were systematically rewarded with appointments, consider the results of the exhaustive search approach for appointments to "most and least likelies" (summarized in table 8.3). We identify desirable postelectoral appointments for 70 percent of our "most likelies," but for only 25 percent of our "least likelies." These include presidential appointments during the immediate post-good-loser period for three of our six "most likely" Senate good losers, plus prominent public posts not directly appointed by the president for two others, and nomination to a (successful) senatorial bid for the sixth. Thus, all six "most likely" Senate runners-up prospered. Among the five "least likely" Senate runners-up, we identified a presidential appointment during the subsequent period for one, during the second subsequent period for another, and nothing for the other three. There are more Chamber runners-up, but the pattern is the same: we identify subsequent posts for most of the "most likelies," but nothing for the "least likelies."

The manner in which we selected cases for exhaustive career-trajectory searches, of course, should be expected to generate a bias toward such stark results. What we can conclude at this point is that those runners-up we have posited to have the most promising post-electoral-loss prospects do, in fact, have good odds of receiving plum appointments (perhaps even better odds than the table shows, given that we may still

TABLE 8.3

Postelectoral Career Trajectories for Runners-up Deemed Most and Least Likely to Receive Appointments, According to Their Lists' Concertación-to-Right Vote Ratios

Post-runner-up appointment	Most likelies	Least likelies
Presidential appointment during period after electoral loss	*Jara Wolff* *Lagos Escobar* *Rebolledo González* Saavedra Cortés Aylwin Oyarzún Pérez Lobos Molina Valdivieso	*Estévez Valencia* Auth Stewart
Presidential appointment during period subsequent to that after electoral loss	Yunge Bustamante Santelices Altamirano	*Correa Díaz*
Nomination for election to Congress next period	*Zaldívar Larraín*	Girardi Lavín Romero Fuentes
Political post not appointed by president	*Sule Candia*[a] *Navarrete Betanzo*[c] Arenas Escudero[d] Dintrans Schafer[e]	Torres Gutiérrez[b]
Unknown	Gajardo Chacón Morales Abarzúa Del Valle De La Cruz Sepúlveda Gutiérrez Vargas Vega Leblanc Valenzuela	*Vodanovic Schnake* *Sáenz Rojas* *Carmine Zúñiga* Campos Leal Esquivel Santander Alvarez Pinto García Villarroel Arancibia Silva Gustavo Núñez Witker Velásquez Fuentes Araya Calquín Monardes Alarcón Rojas Rossetti Gallardo Molina Sepúlveda Ibáñez Vergara Apara Álamo Makluf Campos

Note: Information based on exhaustive searches. Senate runners-up in *italic.*
[a] President of the Radical Social Democratic Party after good loser election; deceased.
[b] Nominated by party to run (and was elected) as municipal council member in 2002.
[c] President of the Chilean Olympic Committee.
[d] Secretary General of the Party for Democracy as of 2000.
[e] Barrister before the Appeals Court of Rancagua—a status accorded by judicial, not presidential, appointment.

have missed some appointments), whereas for those whose prospects we posited as least promising, the odds were a lot worse.

In other work (Carey and Siavelis 2005), we test a logistic regression model of the conditions under which second-place candidates receive appointments, drawing on all Concertación lists during the first three electoral cycles since Chile's transition to democracy in 1990. Here, we briefly describe the analysis and its results.

The likelihood of an appointment depends considerably on which chamber the candidate ran for, and on list performance, although not on the relative parity of candidates within a given Concertación list. The effects of all three independent variables on the probability of an appointment are in the expected direction—positive for Senate candidates relative to Chamber candidates, positive for those on lists that come closer to doubling, and negative for runners-up who captured smaller shares of the personal votes cast for their lists. The first two effects are statistically significant at conventional levels, whereas the latter falls short, suggesting that individual good losers within Concertación lists are rewarded according to the collective performance of the ticket rather than their individual vote totals. Other things being equal, the odds of receiving a postelection presidential appointment are 15 percent higher for Senate than for Chamber good losers. Similarly, holding Chamber constant, the odds of an appointment are substantially (6%–10%) higher for runners-up from lists that performed well than those from lists that performed poorly. Given that the raw probability of an appointment is only 9 percent among all our good losers, the difference between being on a Concertación list that almost doubles and being on a list that runs even with the Right translates roughly into doubling the runner-up's odds of an appointment.

Of course, documentary evidence of an electoral insurance policy is scarce, precisely because it is an *informal* institution. Moreover, the beneficiaries of such an arrangement naturally tend to regard themselves as worthy of their current posts and are not inclined to attribute any postcampaign appointments to their own electoral defeat. However, in addition to the data presented here, there is considerable anecdotal evidence for the existence of electoral insurance. Interviews with deputies from both the Concertación and the opposition, as well as with party officials, confirm that although not explicit, there is a tacit understanding that losers will be rewarded for loyalty. Consider the following exchange from an interview with an Independent Democratic Union deputy:

> *Interviewer:* Is there an agreement, for example, where if you lose this election, then you get a post?
>
> *UDI Deputy:* Certainly, yes. In practice, everyone—above all, in the government, which has more resources to give positions than the opposition . . . in the opposition, it's less—receives a post within the party or some compensation. But it's not very centralized—for example, some businessman has a job . . . In the government, there are a lot more resources to provide positions, either in the government itself, in foreign relations, embassies, which are very attractive.
>
> *Interviewer:* Are there agreements ahead of time?

UDI Deputy: I don't know if it's so explicit, but certainly I believe that there is an understanding. The Concertación has been pretty efficient—probably too efficient—
in keeping its leading politicians inside the system, you know? They haven't lost
important leaders. And they've been able to keep them in the government, in Congress, in party positions, in public corporations or foreign relations posts.[11]

Another UDI deputy elaborated further, suggesting that insurance in the form of
appointments to government posts has been more important for the governing coalition than it would be for the Alianza, because candidates of the center-left parties
have fewer personal resources and so rely more heavily on public sector employment.[12] Finally, we note that the public reaction to an early version of the argument
in this chapter, published in Chile in 2003, suggests widespread acknowledgment
of the insurance system by politicians and political observers (*El Mercurio* 2003c;
El Sur 2003).

The Chilean electoral system generates a tension between the incentives for
coalitions and those for individual candidates. To align politicians' incentives with
those of the broader coalition, the Concertación has provided insurance for its good
losers. The bottom line from our analysis is that those who were recruited for the
most prominent (i.e., Senate) races and those whose efforts most nearly bore fruit
(i.e., whose lists nearly doubled those of the Right, thus contributing to Concertación legislative majorities) were the primary beneficiaries of the insurance-through-
appointments. This evidence suggests, then, that the Concertación has used political appointments to reconcile the interests of individual politicians with those of the
coalition as a whole—to reward politicians who accepted personal risk on behalf of
the coalition and who contributed toward the collective performance of their lists—
and thus to overcome the divergence of incentives generated by Chile's unique
electoral system.

THE NEW CHILEAN ELECTORAL LANDSCAPE

This insurance system has worked well for the Concertación, and for its candidates, in each of the four elections since the transition to democracy in Chile. Why
might it fail now? We suggest that the insurance claim fund is no longer as secure,
because it depends on control of the executive branch. The danger, from the perspective of would-be doubling candidates, is that the Concertación may not control
the executive branch after the 2005 election. The possibility began to crystallize in
1999–2000, in the form of Joaquín Lavín's stronger-than-anticipated challenge to
Ricardo Lagos for the presidency. After that initial campaign, Lavín positioned

himself to run again in 2005. According to a Centro de Estudios Públicos poll conducted in December 2002, 40 percent of respondents named Lavín when presented with the open-ended question: "Whom would you want to be the next president?" The next highest figure at that stage, foreign minister in the current Concertación government, Soledad Alvear, was named by only 9 percent of respondents. Fifty-six percent of respondents thought Lavín would be the next president, and 53 percent expressed a willingness to vote for him (Centro de Estudios Públicos 2003). As of late 2005, Lavín remains a strong contender, although the electoral prognosis has grown increasingly complex. On the one hand, outstanding economic performance and the emergence of another strong candidate within the Concertación, former defense secretary Michelle Bachelet, have revived the prospects for the incumbent coalition. On the other hand, prominent businessman and president of National Renewal, Sebastián Piñera, announced his candidacy in May 2005, positioning himself as a more moderate alternative to Lavín, appealing to centrist voters tired of the Concertación as well as voters on the right who regard a centrist candidate as electorally viable against the incumbent coalition.

However the 2005 election plays out, the situation is fundamentally different from that which has preceded every posttransition congressional election so far. In each of the previous cases, the Concertación's control over the executive branch, and all the appointed posts it commands, has been in no doubt:

- In 1989, the victory of Patricio Aylwin was virtually unquestionable, following on his leadership of the unified "no" forces in the 1988 plebiscite and his stewardship of the opposition to Pinochet's government during the subsequent transition.
- In 1993, once agreement was reached within the Concertación on Eduardo Frei's candidacy (*before* the selection of candidate lists for the legislative races), the outcome of the presidential election was never in doubt.
- The establishment of a six-year presidential term meant that the 1997 legislative elections occurred when Frei had two years remaining in his term—sufficient time to provide substantial compensation to good losers in terms of appointed posts.
- The next set of legislative elections occurred in 2001, two years after the Lavín threat to the presidency became apparent, but when President Lagos still had four years remaining in his term—and thus ample time to compensate Concertación good losers with appointments.

In 2005, the situation will be different. Viable presidential challengers from the Right (unlike in 1989 or 1993) mean that the coalition's ability to pay insurance to "doubling losers" will be less than certain. In 2005, moreover, legislative and presidential elections will be concurrent for the first time since 1993. The 1997 and 2001 legislative elections were held in the middle of presidential terms. The existence of a concurrent presidential election in 2005 adds an additional dimension of uncertainty for coalition leaders and for prospective legislative candidates, because bargaining over the composition of lists for the legislative election will take place before the Concertación's presidential candidate is determined by a primary election. Facing uncertainty about compensation in the event of an unhappy outcome, the question is whether strong candidates, and their associated parties, will remain committed to maintaining the coalition.

INSTITUTIONAL CHANGE: FORMAL AND INFORMAL

In the terms set out by Helmke and Levitsky in their introduction to this volume, the insurance system for good losers in Chile's Concertación is a complementary informal institution in that it serves to compensate for a dilemma generated by a formal institution that might otherwise undermine political cooperation. The dilemma is the incentive in Chile's two-member district elections for coalitions to place their strongest candidates in their most electorally vulnerable races. Insurance, as an informal institution, compensates candidates for the risk they take on, and thereby helps maintain the coalition. Helmke and Levitsky argue persuasively that among informal institutions, complementary ones ought to be particularly responsive to changes in formal institutions, on the grounds that if the complementary institution took shape to compensate for some characteristic of the formal institutional environment, we might reasonably expect it to wither, or adapt, if the formal institution it complements is altered. We find Helmke and Levitsky's logic compelling here, but in the case of insurance for good losers, we suggest a potential wrinkle—that change in the *informal* institution may encourage reform of its *formal* complement.

We have argued that the two-member district electoral system and insurance for good losers are mutually reinforcing in Chile, but also that the latter is sustained by the Concertación's electoral dominance and may be threatened if such dominance is in jeopardy. It follows that if the system of insurance is undermined, the strategic dilemma inherent in two-member district elections reasserts itself. Of course, the dilemma is always present for those outside the dominant coalition, but in a political environment where *all* actors face uncertainty about who will control future appointments, such that even the majority coalition can no longer be indemnified, lawmakers may find the two-member district electoral rule itself increasingly distasteful.[13] A more even electoral competition between Chile's two major coalitions, then, may increase support among legislators for a return to large-magnitude proportional electoral rules more closely resembling those of Chile's mid-twentieth-century democracy. In this case, we would suggest that not only might changes in formal institutions foster changes in complementary informal institutions, but the reverse may be true as well.

Our findings also have cross-national theoretical applications, especially as political systems around the world increasingly adopt complex electoral systems in an attempt to balance representation and stability. We think it plausible that in other systems, compensation mechanisms could exist for losing candidates who bore risk on behalf of their coalitions. Insurance systems may be less critical to coalition maintenance elsewhere, because, under all other electoral systems with which we are familiar, electoral economies of scale are more straightforward than under Chile's M=2 system. That is, the efficiency with which votes are converted into seats under higher-magnitude systems means that the need to put strong candidates in the most marginal list positions is mitigated. Still, findings from Chile suggest that compensation systems of the sort resulting from the two-member system are likely to develop in other strategically complex electoral systems. In terms of future theorizing about both electoral systems and informal institutions, it is crucial to analyze the extent to which strategic complexity in electoral systems can lead to the creation of informal institutions to compensate for uncertainty.

We want to emphasize two last points in closing. First, we do not suggest that the good-loser system is the only, or even the most important, source of unity for the Concertación. Our point is that the system provides an important coalitional adhesive overlooked by analysts of Chilean politics, and the demise of this reward system, along with other tensions emerging in the coalition, can significantly hasten the dissolution of the Concertación. Second, we are not advocating the demise of the Concertación, nor are we prepared to applaud this result, if it should come to pass. In our estimation, the Concertación governments and legislative majorities have, since 1990, provided Chile with some of the most enlightened and temperate political leadership in the country's history. Rather, our guarded opinion about its prospects is based entirely on what we see as a fundamental change in the Chilean electoral landscape since 2000, and what we understand to be the effects of this change on the strategic nature of coalition formation and maintenance.

CHAPTER NINE

Informal Institutions and Party Organization in Latin America

FLAVIA FREIDENBERG AND STEVEN LEVITSKY

In much of Latin America, formal party organizations are strikingly underdeveloped. Party bureaucracies lack resources and professional staff, party congresses and other organs are treated as little more than window dressing, and statutes are widely circumvented or ignored. Consequently, scholars often view Latin American party organizations as weak and ineffective, and electoral politics in the region are frequently characterized as highly personalistic and media-based (Perelli 1995; Weyland 1996).

Yet the weakness of formal party structures in Latin America should not obscure the vast *informal* organizations that often lie behind them. Major parties in Argentina, Brazil, Colombia, the Dominican Republic, Ecuador, El Salvador, Honduras, Mexico, Nicaragua, Paraguay, and Uruguay possess vast, deeply rooted, but predominantly informal, grassroots organizations. These organizations, which range from patronage and clientelistic networks to soup kitchens and soccer fan clubs, are frequently hidden from public view: they do not appear in party statutes and are rarely registered with party or state authorities. Nevertheless, they constitute the "meat" of many Latin American party organizations: they recruit activists, select candidates, raise money, maintain societal linkages, and, most importantly, deliver votes.

The contemporary literature on political parties pays insufficient attention to informal organization.[1] Because this literature draws heavily on studies of western European parties,[2] many of which are highly formalized, it often assumes a tight fit between formal structure and actual organization. Such assumptions do not travel

well to Latin America. Although many Latin American parties are formally structured along the lines of their European counterparts, there is often a vast gap between how those parties are organized on paper and how they function in practice.
In many cases, decision-making power lies not in formal leadership bodies but in
individual leaders or office-holding party bosses; career paths are determined not by
bureaucracies but by personal and patronage networks; local organizations do not
take the form of branch offices but rather are informal networks that operate out of
state agencies or activists' homes; and legal party finance is dwarfed by informal (and
usually illicit) forms of finance, such as patronage, kickbacks, illegal donations, and
embezzled state resources.

These differences have important implications for how we study parties. If the
bulk of a party's organization lies at the margins of its formal bureaucracy, or if party
work is carried out by members of a soccer fan club rather than official members,
then measurements of party organization that examine only official branches or
membership data will seriously understate the size or density of the organization.
Similarly, if decisions, resources, and career paths pass through informal networks
rather than a party bureaucracy, then analyses that focus only on formal structures
will produce a flawed understanding of how that party functions. Indeed, there is
growing evidence that informally organized parties behave differently from their
more formal counterparts in areas such as electoral and legislative behavior, candidate selection, and adaptation to environmental change.[3]

Drawing on ethnographic research on party organizations in Argentina and Ecuador, particularly the Argentine (Peronist) Jusicialista Party (PJ) and the Ecuadorian Roldosista Party (PRE), this chapter takes an initial step toward conceptualiz-
ing and measuring informal party organization. The chapter develops indicators of
formality and informality in nine areas of party life: internal rules and procedures,
decision-making bodies, central bureaucracies, grassroots infrastructure, organizational boundaries, career paths, party membership, ancillary organizations, and finance. These areas cover both institutions as defined in Helmke and Levitsky's
introduction to this volume (e.g., rules regarding membership, leadership selection,
and finance) *and* entities that are generally treated as organizations (e.g., local
branches and ancillary organizations).

Most of the informal party structures discussed in this chapter fall into one of two
types. Some (charismatic decision-making norms, illicit channels of finance) are
competing institutions, in that they run directly counter to party statutes and/or state
law; others, such as informal branches that perform such party work as activist
recruitment and voter mobilization, are best characterized as substitutive. Informal

structures thus thrive where formal party organizations are weak—where the guide-lines laid out in party statutes are not fully implemented or enforced.

FORMAL VERSUS INFORMAL PARTY ORGANIZATION

Formal party organizations are those that are officially sanctioned. They are created through established party channels, usually according to guidelines estab-lished by party statutes, and are recognized by official party (and often state) authori-ties. This includes official headquarters, bureaucracies, and local branches or cells. Informal party organizations, by contrast, are those that carry out partisan functions without official sponsorship. Examples include personal, clientelistic, and patronage networks, as well as civic and social organizations that are not affiliated to parties but nevertheless engage in partisan work. Informal structures are not found in party statutes and may not be recognized by party or state authorities. However, if we define political party as "any political group that presents at elections, and is capable of placing through elections, candidates for higher office" (Sartori 1976, 64), then informal structures must be considered elements of party organization.

Informal party organizations should be distinguished from *weakly institutional-ized* organizations. Party institutionalization, which may be defined as a "process by which a practice or organization becomes well established and widely known, if not universally accepted" (Mainwaring and Scully 1995, 4), is often conflated with for-mal institutionalization. For example, Panebianco equates institutionalization with an increasing "correspondence between a party's statutory norms" and its "actual power structure" (1988, 58–60). According to this conceptualization, all organiza-tional patterns that depart from the "statutory norms" are noninstitutionalized. Yet, as this volume makes clear, informal organizational activity may also be institu-tionalized. For example, clientelistic or machine parties are often based on estab-lished patron-client networks that operate with widely known and accepted norms and procedures. Indeed, many of the most highly institutionalized parties in Latin American history, including the Mexican PRI (Party of the Institutional Revolution), the Colorados in Paraguay, and traditionally dominant parties in Colombia and Honduras, are predominantly informal.

Distinguishing between formalization and institutionalization allows us to cap-ture three distinct party types: (1) *formally institutionalized* parties, in which rules and organizational structures are institutionalized in line with party statutes; (2) *in-formally institutionalized* parties, in which formal structures are weak but informal structures are well established; and (3) *weakly institutionalized* parties, in which neither formal nor informal structures are well-established. Although both informally institutionalized parties (e.g., patronage-based machines) and weakly institutionalized parties (e.g., personalistic or charismatic parties) are informal, in that their formal structures are largely decoupled from the real organization, the two types are very different and should not be conflated.

MEASURING INFORMAL PARTY ORGANIZATION

All parties contain elements of both formal and informal organization. Personal networks and informal factions exist even in the most bureaucratic of parties. The difference lies in the relative weight of formal and informal structures. In formally organized parties, bureaucratic structures predominate. Decision-making, resource allocation, and career advancement take place largely through official channels. Informal networks operate within the parameters of the bureaucracy and do not seriously compromise its effectiveness. By contrast, in informally organized parties, decision-making, resources, and careers pass through informal structures at the margins of the bureaucracy—often rendering it ineffective.

As an initial step toward more rigorous measurement and comparison, this section develops a set of indicators of formality and informality in nine areas of party life: (1) internal rules and procedures, (2) locus of authority/decision-making bodies, (3) central bureaucracies, (4) local organization, (5) organizational boundaries, (6) party hierarchy/career paths, (7) membership, (8) ancillary organizations, and (9) finance.

Internal Rules and Procedures

A basic indicator of formal institutionalization is the degree of correspondence between the rules and procedures outlined in party statutes and actual intraparty behavior. Where party institutions are formalized, there exists a relatively tight fit between the formal rules and actual behavior. Party statutes are broadly accepted, routinely complied with, and consistently enforced. In formally institutionalized parties such as the Brazilian Workers Party (PT), the Chilean Communist Party (PCCh), the Mexican National Action Party (PAN), and—in its heyday—Democratic Action (AD) in Venezuela, violations of party rules routinely trigger sanctions, including suspension or expulsion. In such a context, leaders and activists take party rules and rule-making processes seriously, often investing substantial time and energy into attempts to modify or defend them.

Where party organization is informal, behavior conforms less closely to the rules laid out in the statutes. Formal rules are routinely violated or ignored (often by party leaders themselves), and, due to a lack of effective enforcement, rule infractions are rarely punished. As a result, the formal rules—and rule-making processes—are taken less seriously. Some informal party organizations are characterized by the absence of any (formal or informal) set of stable or binding rules. Thus, in charismatic parties, "no accepted procedures exist, and improvisation is the only real organizational 'rule'" (Panebianco 1988, 146). In other cases, such as patronage-based or machine parties, behavior may be guided by informal rules that, while diverging from party statutes, are nevertheless widely known, accepted, and complied with. For example, in the Mexican PRI before the 1990s, a variety of informal rules and procedures— including the *dedazo* system of candidate selection—were highly institutionalized (Langston, this volume).

The Locus of Authority: Formal versus Informal Decision-Making

In formally organized parties, authoritative and binding decisions are made by officially designated organs such as congresses and executive councils. These bodies serve as the primary arena for decision-making, and they possess authority that is independent of particular leaders, factions, or governments. Consequently, members take formal leadership bodies seriously, investing heavily in efforts to control or influence them.

In informally organized parties, the power to make and enforce binding decisions lies outside the formal party structure. Formal party leadership organs lack autonomy from de facto power-holders and, as a result, are often viewed as mere window dressing by party members. In personalistic parties such as Argentina's original Peronist Party or Alberto Fujimori's Change 90/New Majority in Peru, power is concentrated in the hands of the founding leader—even when that leader holds no formal post. In machine parties such as the Mexican PRI or the Paraguayan Colorados, the locus of decision-making authority lies within the state. Because power is rooted in patronage, mayors, governors, and presidents become de facto party bosses—whether or not they hold positions in the formal leadership.

The Centrality of the Party Bureaucracy

Where party organization is formal, the central bureaucracy is important. It often serves as a nerve center, controlling access to critical resources and information and overseeing, if not coordinating, the activities of party subunits. Party headquarters tend to be major hubs of activity. In many northern European parties, for example, headquarters are well staffed (by paid professional bureaucrats), well equipped, and endowed with substantial resources. The party treasury controls the bulk of finance, and party bureaucrats maintain reliable records of finances, membership, and local organization.

Where party organization is informal, central bureaucracies exist only on paper. Official headquarters are often dormant. They generally lack resources and professional staff, possess little information about finance, membership, or local organization, and play virtually no role in directing or overseeing lower-level party activities. Fundraising, resource allocation, record-keeping, the coordination of local organizations, and other key party activities are carried out at the margins of the central bureaucracy—usually within patronage networks or other informal organizations.

Local Organization: Integrated versus Autonomous Subunits

A party's grassroots infrastructure is the collection of organizations that carry out on-the-ground operations such as recruitment and campaigning. Where party organization is formal, these activities are carried out by official subunits—such as branches, committees, or cells—that are integrated into the central bureaucracy. Subunits are created by (or under the supervision of) the party bureaucracy and operate in locations that are known to (and often dictated by) higher-level authorities. Their form and operating procedures are standardized in accordance with party statutes, and they must ultimately answer to higher-level authorities. They are also linked financially to the party bureaucracy. In some cases, the central bureaucracy finances local branches; in others, local branches channel membership dues upward into the bureaucracy.

Where grassroots infrastructures are informal, subunits are neither created by, nor integrated into, the central bureaucracy. Rather, they emerge at the margins of the party bureaucracy, often without the permission (or even knowledge) of higher-level authorities. Subunits are often self-created, self-operated, and self-financed. They frequently take forms that are not prescribed by party statutes or recognized by party authorities. Often they are not easily visible to the public. Instead of officially designed offices, informal subunits often operate within neighborhood clubs, civic associations, government offices, or activists' homes or businesses. Less dependent on the central bureaucracy than are formal cells or branches, informal subunits generally operate with substantial autonomy from the party leadership.

Organizational Boundaries: Clear versus Ambiguous Borders

Formalized party organizations are characterized by clearly defined external boundaries and effective barriers to entry. Explicit criteria for affiliation, reliable membership records, and effective enforcement make it relatively easy to determine which individuals and groups belong—or do not belong—to the party. There are also few "gray areas" between the party and other organizations, and cases of ambiguous or contested affiliation are rare and short-lived. In such cases, schisms or expulsions tend to be clear-cut and permanent.

Where party organization is informal, the boundaries between the party and other organizations are ambiguous and fluid. Few, if any, effective barriers to entry exist. Membership rules are often ill-defined or unenforced, and the absence of reliable records and effective bureaucracies makes verification and enforcement difficult. As a result, individuals and groups may simply declare themselves members, participating in party activities in the absence of formal affiliation or authorization. This leads to frequent disputes over whether particular individuals or groups actually belong to the party. In the absence of clear membership criteria or enforcement, individuals and groups may float in and out of the party, working within it during one electoral cycle and outside it (often with another party) in a subsequent election. Although parties may expel temporary defectors, they often lack the capacity to enforce such expulsions, and, in many cases, defectors later return to the fold.

The Party Hierarchy: Formal versus Informal Career Paths

Where party structures are formal, actors seeking to advance their careers in the organization must follow certain specified—and generally written down—rules and procedures. Leadership posts are filled through formal, publicly known procedures, such as congresses or primaries. Often, procedures exist to filter out newcomers. For example, the statutes of many mass bureaucratic parties stipulate that members must belong to the party for a specific number of years before holding leadership posts, or that leaders ascend through the hierarchy by means of sequential election to local, midlevel, and then national leadership bodies. In many cases, party members cannot be elected to a national leadership position without first being elected to a lower-level body.

Where party organization is informal, career paths do not conform to formal rules. Bureaucratic procedures either do not exist or are not enforced. In charismatic parties, career advancement takes place through personal ties. Politicians' careers hinge on their personal relationship with the leader (Panebianco 1988, 145). Leadership bodies may be reorganized at the leader's discretion, and individuals without careers in the party—often family members and cronies—may gain top positions. In machine parties, career advancement takes place through patronage networks. Activists are recruited into networks led by sitting or aspiring public officeholders and ascend through the ranks when those politicians are elected to higher office.

Membership: Formal versus Informal Obligations

Where party organization is formal, membership obligations are explicit and enforced, and, due to reliable records and effective enforcement, party authorities are able to ensure that these obligations are met. Although parties vary with respect to the level of commitment demanded of their members, these commitments are generally higher than in informally organized parties. In many European parties (and a few Latin American ones, such as the Brazilian PT) members pay regular dues. Prospective members of the Mexican PAN must be sponsored by an active member, take a course on party doctrine, and then be subject to approval by a municipal party committee—a process that can take six months (Mizrahi 2003, 56–57).

Informally organized parties may have large memberships and activist bases, but the character of rank-and-file participation differs markedly. Although strict membership criteria and obligations may exist on paper, given the absence of effective bureaucracies they are rarely enforced. As a result, formal membership commitments are often limited to filling out a form. Nevertheless, substantial informal obligations may exist. In clientelistic parties, for example, members often must engage in party work—participating in rallies and voting for their patrons in primary or general elections—in exchange for desired selective material benefits.

Ancillary Organizations: Formal versus Informal Linkage

Formal and informally organized parties differ with respect to their linkages to social and civic organizations, such as labor confederations or business associations. Where party organization is formal, these linkages are explicit and, in most cases, written into party statutes. Formal linkages may take the form of party-sponsored labor confederations, corporatist organs of representation within party leaderships (such as the PRI's labor and peasant sectors in Mexico, or the Labor Bureau in Venezuela's AD), or statutory women's or youth wings. These linkages may be reinforced by formal rules such as quotas for candidacies and leadership posts, bloc votes in party congresses, and collective peasant or union membership.

Where party organization is informal, societal linkages are not explicitly recognized. Parties and social groups may routinely exchange human, financial, and organizational resources, but these relationships are not institutionalized in formal statutes or organizations. Rather, they take the form of loosely structured—often patronage-based—alliances. These alliances may be with traditional social actors such as unions or business associations, but they may also be with soccer fan clubs, ethnic or religious groups, neighborhood associations, or nominally nonpartisan civic organizations.

Finance: Formal versus Informal Channels

Finally, formal and informally organized parties differ in terms of finance. Where party organization is formal, fundraising is done through legal and transparent channels. Both private and public contributions are regulated by the state. Private finance is often subject to limits on contributions and rules requiring disclosure of all contributions. Public finance is legal and transparent, often in the form of state subventions and free media time. In most formally organized parties, private and public finance passes through the central bureaucracy (i.e., the party treasury), as opposed to particular factions or politicians.

Where party organization is informal, finance is nontransparent, unregulated, and often illicit. Parties do not keep reliable records of private contributions, and rules of transparency and public disclosure either do not exist or are not enforced. Private contributions routinely exceed legal limits, and they may include payments from illicit sources, such as mafias, drug cartels, or foreign actors. Informally organized parties also make widespread use of unregulated—and often illicit—forms of public finance. These include the widespread appropriation of public sector jobs for patronage use, the use of kickbacks on government contracts to fill party coffers, and the embezzlement of money and other resources (food, transportation) from state agencies. In these cases, finance rarely passes through the central bureaucracy. Rather, it is channeled through individual candidates and patronage networks.

These nine dimensions are summarized in table 9.1. Latin American party organizations are highly diverse (Alcántara Sáez and Freidenberg 2001; Alcántara Saez 2004) and may thus be found throughout the formal-informal spectrum. Some, including the Brazilian PT, Mexican PAN, Venezuelan AD, and Chilean PCCh, score fairly consistently on the formal end of these dimensions and thus can be characterized as formally organized parties. Others, including the traditional clientelistic parties in Brazil, Colombia, Ecuador, Honduras, and Paraguay and personalistic parties in contemporary Peru, are predominantly *informal*. Many other parties, including the Argentine Radical Civic Union, Peru's Aprista Party, and Mexico's PRI, exhibit a mix of formal and informal characteristics.

TWO CASES OF INFORMAL PARTY ORGANIZATION

To highlight how informal party structures work, this section examines two informally organized parties: the Argentine PJ and the Ecuadorian PRE. Although the two parties differ in important ways (the PJ is patronage-based, whereas the PRE mixes elements of personalism and charisma), in both cases, informal organization predominates over the formal bureaucracy, producing behavior that deviates substantially from party statutes.

The Argentine Justicialista Party

The Justicialista Party is one of the best-organized parties in Latin America. It possesses a powerful grassroots organization and a membership in excess of three million. Yet the Peronist party structure is thoroughly informal. Born as a charismatic party during the 1940s, Peronism has long been characterized by a vast gap between formal rules and actual behavior (Levitsky 2003b). PJ statutes are neither widely known nor taken seriously, and as a result, party rules are "openly violated all the time."[4] Peronist leaders describe their statutes as being in a "state of permanent infraction."[5] To the extent that party rules are complied with, they are employed selectively and instrumentally. As one activist put it: "We use the party statutes when they are useful. When they are not useful, we don't use them."[6]

The locus of decision-making in the PJ lies outside the party's formal structure. During the first presidency of party founder Juan Perón, decision-making authority was concentrated in Perón's hands. Even during his long exile after 1955, Perón remained the undisputed decision-maker, and formal leadership bodies such as the Superior Council were widely viewed as window dressing. During the 1980s and 1990s, the PJ became an increasingly patronage-based party, with decision-making power concentrated in the hands of public officeholders. Formal leadership bodies such as the party congress and the National Council lacked independent authority vis-à-vis Peronist officeholders, particularly presidents and governors. Under President Carlos Menem during the 1990s, party decisions were "made in the government house."[7] The National Council was largely ignored, and PJ president Roberto García complained of having to "read about the party's communiqués in the newspapers."[8] Under President Néstor Kirchner in 2004, when the National Council's

TABLE 9.1
Indicators of Formal versus Informal Party Organization

	Formal organization	Informal organization
Internal rules and procedures	Intraparty behavior corresponds to formal statutes; formal rules enforced and taken seriously	Intraparty behavior diverges from formal rules; formal statutes not effectively enforced · Charismatic parties: no stable rules · Machine parties: informally institutionalized rules
Locus of authority	Official party organs (party congress; executive board), as stipulated by statutes	De facto authorities, which often do not correspond to formal leadership · Founding leader (charismatic party) · Public officeholders (machines)
Central bureaucracy	Well-staffed and well-equipped; controls flows of finance and information; coordinates most party activities	Central bureaucracy an "empty shell"; lacks professional staff, equipment; does not control flows of finance or information, or coordinate activities
Local organization	Subunits formally structured, homogeneous, and integrated into central bureaucracy · Examples: official party branches, committees, or cells	Subunits not integrated into central bureaucracy · Self-organized and operated; often do not take form outlined in statutes · Often "hidden" in civic associations, clubs, government offices, or homes
Organizational boundaries	Clearly defined · Rules for membership clear · Reliable records and effective enforcement limit ambiguity	Ambiguous, fluid, and often contested · Ill-defined membership rules · Lack of reliable records or enforcement allows for ambiguity · "Self-proclaimed" affiliation
Party hierarchy / career paths	Career paths correspond to formal structure; career advancement requires adherence to formal prescribed rules (i.e., sequential election from lower- to higher-level bodies)	Career advancement via informal networks · Charismatic party: personal ties to leader · Machine party: patronage networks

TABLE 9.1
Continued

	Formal organization	Informal organization
Membership	Formal obligations (e.g., payment of dues) enforced and routinely complied with · Commitments vary, but may be relatively high	Formal obligations rarely enforced or complied with · Members recruited as clients, with few formal obligations · Informal obligations (such as voting in primaries) may be enforced
Ancillary organizations	Explicit ties to social organizations; linkage written into party statutes · Examples: official ancillary organizations, collective membership, candidate quotas, bloc votes in the party congress	Linkages are de facto, but not formally recognized or written down
Finance	Regulated and transparent; channeled through formal bureaucracy · Public finance subject to limits and rules of disclosure · Public subsidies via legal channels	Unregulated, nontransparent, and often illicit; channeled through individuals and patronage networks, not party bureaucracy · Private finance unregulated and sometimes illicit · Alternative/illicit sources of public finance (patronage, public sector embezzlement, kickbacks)

mandate expired and the party congress failed to elect a new council, the body was left vacant, leaving Peronism without any formal leadership whatsoever.

The PJ's central bureaucracy is strikingly underdeveloped. The party lacks a professional staff and has virtually no record of membership, finances, or activities. Beyond custodial personnel, its headquarters are often empty. When Roberto García became party president in 1990, the PJ headquarters were located "in a small office that didn't even have a sign outside."[9] Local party offices are equally underdeveloped. In 1997, the PJ's Buenos Aires headquarters had no paid staff and was open only twice a week, and the Tucumán headquarters lacked funds, phone service, or a functioning bathroom for much of the year (Levitsky 2003b, 73). The bulk of Peronist party activities are channeled through informal patronage networks, or *agrupaciones*. These networks are not mentioned in the party statutes, and local party offices generally keep no record of them. Yet they function as the de facto PJ organization, financing and coordinating local party activities, selecting candidates, and organizing campaigns. As one local leader put it: "The party bureaucracy just maintains the headquarters, which is nothing more than an office and the ten employees who run and clean the place. The rest of the organization is financed and coordinated by the various *agrupaciones*. The party's real infrastructure . . . is in the hands of the *agrupaciones*."[10]

Peronism's grassroots infrastructure is almost entirely informal. On paper, the PJ's base-level organization takes the form of base units (UBs), or neighborhood-level offices that fall under the jurisdiction of the local party council. In practice, however, UBs are autonomous of the party bureaucracy. They are created and operated privately by Peronist activists. Anyone may open a UB anywhere, at any time. Frequently, activists create UBs in their homes and literally become their "owners." Local party bureaucracies thus have no influence over the number or location of UBs. Indeed, most have no record of the UBs under their jurisdiction. Only a minority of UBs take the form of standard party offices, with most taking the form of informal "working groups" based out of activists' homes or operating informally out of unions, clubs, or community centers (Levitsky 2003b, 68–69). Although these subunits do not formally exist (they are not recognized by the party bureaucracy), they recruit members, compete in primaries, and campaign in elections.

The PJ's boundaries are fluid and ill-defined. Peronism's membership criteria were never clear or widely enforced. Historically, individuals and groups simply declared their affiliation. As a result, the party has at times contained individuals and groups—including leftist and fascist paramilitary organizations—whose affiliation is disputed. Indeed, the Montonero guerrillas made a point of *not* joining the party during the 1970s. Although individuals or groups are sometimes expelled, these expulsions are often ignored and are rarely permanent. Thus, Perón twice expelled Catamarca party boss Vicente Saadi, but Saadi never lost control over Catamarca Peronism, and although the Montoneros were "expelled" in 1974, most Montonero networks never left Peronism. At the same time, individuals and factions routinely float in and out of Peronism, abandoning the party for an election or two, only to return a few years later. In 1985, for example, "Renovation" factions in several provinces abandoned the PJ and competed against it in elections, but returned to take over the party leadership a few months later. Due to these temporary schisms, it is not unusual for two or more Peronist parties to compete in an election.

Peronist career paths are decidedly nonbureaucratic. During the party's formative years, careers hinged on individuals' personal ties to Perón (Zorrilla 1983). Although the PJ formally adopted a primary system in 1987, contemporary career paths are shaped more by patronage networks than by elections. Peronists ascend through the ranks via *agrupaciones* controlled by local and provincial bosses. Primaries are routinely undercut by "unity lists" imposed by party bosses (De Luca et al. 2002).[11] In the absence of bureaucratic procedure, movement into, up, and out of the PJ hierarchy is quite fluid. Juan Manuel Abal Medina (in 1972), Isabel Perón (1974), and José María Vernet (1984) ascended to the top of the Peronist hierarchy without ever holding a party post, and, between 1983 and 1990, none of the PJ's four presidents completed his mandate.

Justicialista Party membership is largely informal. During the 1990s, the party's membership—3.85 million, or 18 percent of the electorate—exceeded memberships of most European social democratic parties (Levitsky 2003b, 61). However, PJ membership entails a lower level of commitment than does membership in many European parties. No application or screening process exists. Members do not pay dues or attend regular meetings. Prospective members simply sign a form, and in the absence of official oversight or enforcement, many registration forms are forged. Given the lack of reliable membership rolls, many affiliates are not even aware of their status.

Peronism maintains strong ties to a variety of working- and lower-class organizations, but these linkages are almost entirely informal. Historically, the PJ's closest ties were to unions (Torre 1990; McGuire 1997). However, unlike most European social democratic parties, these linkages were never formalized. Traditionally, the party-union linkage was based on two informal mechanisms: the "62 Organizations" (or "62") and the *tercio* system. The "62," which functioned as the PJ's "labor branch," nominating unionists for candidacies and leadership posts, was not mentioned in Peronist statutes and had no formal position in the party leadership (McGuire 1997, 98–99). Similarly, the *tercio* tradition of granting unions a third of candidacies and leadership posts was not found in the statutes. The PJ also maintains informal linkages to a variety of other working- and lower-class organizations, including squatters' organizations, neighborhood associations, clubs, church groups, and a variety of other civic and nonprofit groups (Levitsky 2003b, 62–65). Of particular importance are ties to local soccer clubs. Soccer clubs are a central part of social life in working-class zones, and links to these clubs allow the PJ to tap into organized fan clubs to mobilize youth for electoral campaigns. Soccer fan clubs are mobilized to attend rallies, paint campaign graffiti, and, in some cases, engage in thuggish activities aimed at rival factions or parties.

Finally, the PJ is financed largely through informal channels. On paper, the PJ is financed through a combination of state subsidies and private contributions, which are channeled through the party bureaucracy. However, these regulated forms of finance are dwarfed by unregulated contributions. In 1989, for example, the PJ officially reported taking in a total of US$1.8 million in contributions, but one businessman claimed to have given US$3 million to the Menem campaign (Ferreira Rubio 1997, 19). The most important sources of party finance, however, are patronage and other unregulated forms of public finance. Tens of thousands of PJ activists are on local and provincial government payrolls (Gibson and Calvo 2000). A 1997 survey of UBs in the Federal Capital and Greater Buenos Aires found that 69 percent were run by activists with government jobs (Levitsky 2003b, 195). Local PJ organizations also finance themselves via embezzled state resources. These resources are channeled through individuals and *agrupaciones*, not the party treasury.

In sum, an examination of Peronist statutes reveals little about the party's local organization, finances, mechanisms of decision-making and career advancement, or linkages to society. Although the PJ is formally structured as a European-style mass bureaucratic party, in practice, this formal structure is an empty shell. The real party structure is fluid, decentralized, and increasingly organized around patronage.

The Ecuadorian Roldosista Party

Ecuador's Roldosista Party is a charismatic party, built around Abdalá Bucaram following the death of Jaime Roldós and the demise of the populist Concentration of Popular Forces. Concentrated in the coastal city of Guayaquil, the party draws its support mainly from the marginal poor and emerging "new rich" entrepreneurs (often of Lebanese descent) who have been excluded from the traditional coastal oligarchy. Bucaram has remained the party's charismatic leader—serving as a source of cohesion for a heterogeneous collection of local and provincial bosses—even after his 1997 removal from power and subsequent exile.[12]

The locus of authority in the PRE is Bucaram, who remains the organization's supreme director despite his self-imposed exile in Panama. Bucaram's power is undisputed. As one Ecuadorian politician put it, Bucaram "is the owner of the PRE . . . All the others are his servants."[13] The PRE's formal leadership bodies, the National Command and the National Convention, lack independent authority. No matter what the composition of these bodies, Bucaram remains the ultimate decision-maker, interpreter of intraparty rules, mediator of internal disputes, and candidate selector. In a survey of PRE leaders and activists, a majority said that if they had to make an important party decision, they would personally consult Bucaram (Freidenberg 2003, 188). Indeed, during Bucaram's exile, party leaders have routinely consulted him by telephone (or traveled to Panama to consult him directly) before making decisions. Annual meetings of the National Convention were held in Panama.

Due to Bucaram's near-total discretion in decision-making, there is a vast gap between the PRE's formal rules and actual intraparty behavior. For example, when Marco Proaño Maya, a party leader with substantial territorial and legislative support, launched a bid for the post of supreme director without Bucaram's blessing during the 1997 National Convention, Bucaram declared that the position was no longer up for contestation and that party authorities would remain in their posts for another year (Freidenberg 2003, 171). This response openly violated party statutes, which called for an annual renovation of the leadership.

The PRE's central bureaucracy is weak and ineffective. According to its 1982 statutes, the PRE is organized in a bureaucratic manner: national, provincial, and local commands integrate the party's membership and diverse internal groups into a formal hierarchical relationship. In practice, however, this structure is ignored. The central bureaucracy is an empty shell. Local and provincial commands exist only in the few districts where the PRE is particularly strong (Freidenberg 2003). Most local party offices are not integrated into the bureaucracy, but rather are privately owned or rented. Party subunits are often located in local bosses' homes or businesses. Each local leader possesses the autonomy to create offices where he wishes, and to finance and manage them as his own. The PRE's national headquarters in Guayaquil has no record of these local branches and thus cannot coordinate or control them.

The PRE's local infrastructure is based almost entirely on personal and patronage networks. Local bosses build personal followings—through family, commercial, or sports ties—at the margins of the party bureaucracy (Freidenberg 2002). Particularly in the PRE's electoral strongholds along the coast, these networks are critical to the party's electoral success: they deliver votes, money, local media influence, contacts with the local elite, and, crucially, groups of supporters who carry out party work. Local bosses enjoy substantial autonomy in organizing the party in each district, although this autonomy is ultimately limited by their subordination to Bucaram.

Career paths in the PRE also diverge from bureaucratic norms. Advancement within the party depends largely on personal relationships, particularly to Bucaram and his family (Freidenberg 2003, 198–206). Most top party officials are family members, longtime cronies, or business partners of Bucaram. For example, Bucaram's wife has served as PRE supreme director (the only person other than Bucaram to hold this post); his brother Adolfo has served as national subdirector during his exile; another brother, Jacobo, was the PRE presidential candidate in 2002; his sister Elsa is a member of the National Command and has been PRE mayor of Guayaquil; and his eldest son, Jacobito, is the de facto leader of the PRE's parliamentary bloc—even though he is not even a member of Congress. Several of Bucaram's children, nephews and nieces, cousins, and in-laws also occupy positions in the party hierarchy. Bucaram's longtime business partner Eduardo Azar Mejía is responsible (along with Bucaram and his brothers) for the PRE's finances.

Notwithstanding the existence of party caucuses and other formal leadership and candidate selection processes, Bucaram and his family dominate the hierarchy and are usually decisive in shaping career paths. The PRE's candidate lists are routinely altered—usually at Bucaram's request—after they have been selected by party leaders (Freidenberg 2003). Party bosses play a similar role at the local and provincial levels. According to Bucaram, "the provincial commands know nothing about internal elections. They run them, but they don't care about them. It is always the director, the provincial leader, who chooses the names" for candidacies and party leadership posts.[14]

The PRE's organizational boundaries are ambiguous. More than a party, members belong to the Roldosista "family," which is viewed as broader than the PRE itself. The party lacks clear criteria for membership or updated membership rolls. As a result, membership in the PRE is largely a matter of self-declaration. Joining the party—at virtually any level—is simple, especially if one has financial resources, a clientelistic base, media access, or ties to the supreme leader (Freidenberg 2001, 2002). Indeed, local *caciques* ("political brokers") move with relative ease between the PRE and other clientelistic parties. Unlike Argentina's PJ, affiliations and expulsions are subject to the ultimate approval of Bucaram, but this vetting process—even if later ratified by the party's National Convention—is thoroughly informal.

The PRE has no formal membership requirements or selection criteria, collects no dues, and possesses no record of its own membership. Activists are generally recruited through clientelistic networks, joining the party in the hope of gaining access to material benefits. Particularly in low-income zones, many party members view the Roldosista family as a salvation in a context of social anomie and scarcity of resources. Membership may entail a relatively high level of commitment. To gain access to material benefits, new members must prove themselves to local party bosses by carrying out a variety of organizational tasks during electoral campaigns. There is also a charismatic element to party-activist linkages: party loyalties are reinforced by followers' belief in the extraordinary qualities of Bucaram's leadership.[15]

The PRE maintains strong informal ties to diverse social organizations in low-income regions, particularly along the coastal region of Guayaquil. These include food kitchens, human rights groups, and associations of small retailers, banana growers, lawyers, and social workers. Though not formally linked to the PRE, many of these organizations carry out intensive party work. In addition, many PRE bosses either directly own or maintain close ties to soccer clubs, using members of soccer fan clubs as advisors, bodyguards, and rank-and-file activists. Soccer players themselves often work in PRE offices, campaign for the PRE, and serve as bodyguards for PRE legislators.

The PRE finances itself through both formal and informal channels. Like all Ecuadorian parties, the PRE receives financing from the state's Permanent Party Fund. Although party statutes stipulate that these monies be channeled into the party bureaucracy via an economic commission in the National Command, party leaders acknowledge that no such commission exists. It is the supreme leader and his close associates—including private business partners—who control the party's finances and coordinate the bulk of its fundraising. Although it is impossible to measure accurately the unregulated finance received by the PRE, it is clear that this quantity exceeds that of regulated finance. The PRE makes massive use of illicit state finance, including government jobs, food, medicine, public housing access, and a variety of social programs to reward activists and voters (Freidenberg 2001). State resources are complemented by the private contributions of local bosses. In many cases, it is the local bosses themselves (and not the party) who pay for local advertising and finance transportation for activists, hire graffiti-painting brigades, and provide food and live music for party rallies.

Like Argentina's PJ, then, the PRE's formal statutes tell us little about how it makes decisions, selects its leaders and candidates, organizes its activists, or raises money. The major difference between the PRE and the PJ is that the former combines an informal structure with a charismatic leadership. Whereas contemporary Peronism is organized along patronage lines, Bucaram's charismatic leadership—like Perón's in the original Peronist Party—is critical to the PRE's electoral mobilization, its activist base, and its linkages to society.

CONCLUSION

This chapter has sought to (re)introduce the dimension of informality into contemporary analyses of party organization. Although this dimension has long been central to research on political clientelism and machine politics, informal institutions have been confined to the margins of contemporary conceptual and theoretical work on party organization.

Informal organization matters because it shapes how parties work. Thus, a crucial area for future research lies in exploring ways in which informality affects party behavior. For example, recent studies suggest that informally structured parties may be more flexible and adaptable in the face of environmental change than are bureaucratic parties (Roberts 1998; Levitsky 2003b). Informality also affects candidate selection. Studies of parties in the United States suggest that primary systems may encourage the nomination of ideologically polarizing candidates, as turnout tends to be higher among ideologically committed voters (Wright and Berkman 1986). Yet in clientelistic or patronage-based parties, in which local brokers bring voters to the polls, primaries produce very different results: elections are almost always won by candidates backed by the largest patronage organization or machine. Similar questions may be asked about legislative cohesion, coalition formation, activist recruitment, intraparty democracy, and public policymaking in informally organized parties.

Another potential area for research is how informal party organization affects the quality of democracy. At first blush, these effects seem to be uniformly negative. Informal party structures are often rooted in particularistic relationships, which tend to erode the kinds of programmatic linkages that many scholars view as critical to effective democratic representation. In addition, the nontransparent nature of most informal party structures limits democratic accountability. Where decision-making power lies outside formal authority structures, formal mechanisms of democracy and accountability—such as party caucuses, congresses, and primaries—tend to be undercut. (This is clearly seen in Langston's chapter, in this volume, on the PRI.) Where finance is unregulated and undocumented, and parties' real power brokers thus obscured from public view, voters' capacity to discern who and what those parties represent is limited. Hence, informally organized parties may be less oriented toward public goods provision and more vulnerable to capture by private—even illicit—interests.

Informality may not always be inimical to democracy, however. In the context of repressive or exclusionary regimes, informal party structures may be critical to the survival or mobilization of disadvantaged groups. For example, Peronism's informal structure helped it survive two decades of proscription and several periods of military repression, and informal networks helped sustain resistance to Polish communism, South African apartheid, martial law in Taiwan, and various other dictatorships. Informal organization may also provide channels of access to groups that have traditionally been excluded from the political process. In Ecuador, for example, the populist Concentration of Popular Forces incorporated previously marginal sectors during the 1960s (Menéndez Carrión 1986), and Pachakutic—which mixes elements of formality and informality—vastly expanded indigenous peoples' electoral and legislative representation during the 1990s.

Latin American parties are now being studied with increasing comparative breadth and theoretical sophistication. Theories that for years were limited to studies of advanced industrialized countries are now being applied and tested in Latin American cases. Although these are indeed positive developments, efforts to theorize Latin American parties must be based on an accurate understanding of how those parties work on the ground. The gap between how parties are organized on paper and how they function in practice is much wider in Latin America than in most advanced industrialized countries. Bridging that gap requires that scholars move beyond party statutes and enter the murky world of informal politics—a world than in many cases revolves around patron-client ties, corruption, and other less-than-transparent activities. This is difficult empirical terrain. Yet as long as scholars steer clear of it, they will be left with an incomplete (and inaccurate) picture of how political parties work.

PART IV

Informal Judicial Institutions and the Rule of Law

CHAPTER TEN

The Rule of (Non)Law

Prosecuting Police Killings in Brazil and Argentina

DANIEL M. BRINKS

Democracy, most students of the region agree, has swept across Latin America since the 1970s and early 1980s. But most also agree that democracy in the region suffers significant shortcomings, and one of the shortcomings most often cited is the failure of the rule of law. Thus, Michael Shifter points to two key components of a democratic rule of law: "Latin American Democracy is most seriously stalled on two key fronts. The first is a drive for a legal system that guarantees both the equality of all citizens before the law and basic personal rights. The second has to do with the separation of powers and the imposition of effective checks on executive authority" (1997, 116). One of the critical components of what Guillermo O'Donnell has called the "brown areas" of democracy is precisely this failure. O'Donnell argues that in most countries of Latin America, "huge gaps exist, both across their territories and in relation to various social categories, in the effectiveness of whatever we may agree that the rule of law means" (1999c, 311).

This chapter examines one area in which the legal systems of Brazil and Argentina have failed to check executive authority (in the sense that the police are agents of the executive) and failed to guarantee basic personal rights: the police in both Brazil and Argentina, with some variation across and within the countries, continue to kill with impunity, despite laws that purport to limit their use of lethal force. In 1992, for example, the police in São Paulo killed more than fourteen hundred people. Over the course of the 1990s, this police force averaged nearly seven hundred homicides per year. While these absolute numbers are virtually unparalleled in the region, per capita, the police in Salvador da Bahia (in northeastern Brazil) kill three times as often, while the police in Buenos Aires kill almost as often as those in São Paulo. Meanwhile, conviction rates for police officers accused of homicide hover around 7 percent in São Paulo, less than 5 percent in Salvador da Bahia, and below 20 percent in Buenos Aires.

The main goal of this chapter, then, is to examine the mechanisms and processes that give rise to the high levels of impunity for police officers who kill in the course of their duties. One of the arguments that have been put forth to account for the failure of the rule of law generally (as well as the failure of various other institutions to produce their intended results) is the presence of informal institutions. From the pattern described above, one might conclude—and many human rights activists in the region argue—that there is an informal institution that gives the police broad latitude in the use of lethal force: the police may kill whom they must, so long as they maintain some minimum of social stability. The hypothesized informal institution, therefore, is one that grants the police broad or even unlimited discretion in the use of lethal force.

If (formal) institutions are made up of (formal) rules, then informal institutions must also be made up of (informal) rules. Thus, if informal institutions are driving police impunity, we should be able to detect informal rules that, at a minimum, permit this behavior. With due apologies to Méndez, O'Donnell, and Pinheiro (1999), then, the presence of informal institutions might be labeled "the rule of (non)law." Rules that are not laws determine outcomes. But before we can evaluate this argument, we need a more precise definition of informal institutions (and perhaps even of rules) and a more precise notion of how to operationalize these concepts.

The second goal of this chapter, therefore, is to specify and apply a rigorous definition of informal rules and informal institutions, and to propose some standards for operationalizing informal institutions. This second goal necessarily must be dealt with first, so I begin by expanding upon some of the theoretical developments already anticipated in Helmke and Levitsky's introduction to this volume, and then apply this theoretical framework to the institution at issue here. I conclude by examining an instance of institutional change affecting Salvador da Bahia and placing the institution at issue within the classification scheme proposed in the introduction.

DEFINING AND OPERATIONALIZING INFORMAL INSTITUTIONS

The introduction to this volume and an earlier essay (Brinks 2003b) develop much of the definition of informal institutions. I will not repeat that discussion here, but will sketch out the basic elements of this definition and, along the way, propose a series of questions that can guide researchers in determining whether certain behavior responds to an informal institution.

As noted in Helmke and Levitsky's survey of the concept, the study of informal institutions generally requires a more ethnographic approach and needs to be more data intensive than a survey of formal institutions. The first two questions posed here will permit researchers to quickly determine whether we need bother to look for an informal institution at all.

> Question 1: Do we observe outcomes in accordance with the hypothesized informal rule (i.e., regularities that cannot be explained by reference to the formal rules)?

If the answer to this question is no, we need go no further. Informal rules derive their existence in part from the very fact of their operation (Brinks 2003b). While laws and other formal rules may, in some sense, continue to be laws even if they are never enforced, it makes little sense to say there is an informal rule but it is never applied. And it makes little sense to waste research resources on a hypothetical institution that ultimately makes no difference. We may come to this research from a different and equally valid starting point, however, if we find that relevant actors consistently ascribe certain outcomes to informal rules.

> Question 2: Do people describe certain behavior in terms of an enforceable rule of conduct?

Depending on the rule, of course, informants may not be willing to acknowledge its existence. On the other hand, informants are often more than willing to describe widespread illegal practices as the norm. In either event, they may be completely sincere—and completely mistaken. As a result, while the description of an informal rule can form the starting point for the inquiry, we still need to find more objective evidence of its existence.[1]

Once we are on the lookout for an informal institution, however, we need to be precise about what we mean by the concept. There is broad agreement that informal institutions, like formal ones, are made up of rules. Helmke and Levitsky define informal institutions, in contrast to formal ones, as "*socially shared rules, usually unwritten, that are created, communicated, and enforced outside officially sanctioned channels.*" In an earlier essay (Brinks 2003b), my distinction between formal and informal institutions focused purely on the way in which informal rules are created, not on the means of communication and enforcement. I argued that informal rules are those that are not enacted in accordance with the second-order rules that govern the creation of formal rules in a given organizational context (which is, I think, simply a more cumbersome way of saying "outside officially sanctioned channels"). While I am substantially in agreement, then, with the definition in Helmke and Levitsky's introduction, it may be too restrictive by going beyond the extraofficial manner of the rule's creation to its communication or enforcement (though it is undoubtedly true that these will usually follow). In this chapter, for instance, I present evidence of an informal rule that is enforced through both official and unofficial instances.

A point on which we all agree is that a rule is more than a behavioral regularity. To describe this added component, Helmke and Levitsky argue for "defining [informal institutions] in terms of shared expectations or beliefs rather than shared values." This statement leaves open exactly what it is that we must expect. Clearly it is not enough simply to expect that all or most people will behave in accordance with the proposed rule. What is distinctive about a rule is that it is *prescriptive*, not merely descriptive (Hart 1961; Ellickson 1991; Brinks 2003b). The expectations, therefore, must be normative ones: a shared understanding of how people *ought* to behave, whether they actually behave this way or not.

This is not to say that all of society (or anybody) approves of the rule in a normative sense: a given rule may be viewed as abhorrent, even as it is understood to be the dominant one. Thus Helmke and Levitsky are correct in rejecting shared values as the touchstone. But a rule must be held by some agent of social control to state a standard of conduct that this agent will enforce (O'Donnell makes this point also in the afterword to this volume). The key point is that actors expect that deviations from the purported rule will be met with some sort of sanction (Hart 1961; Ellickson 1991).[2] Institutions, then, imply the potential for what Ellickson labeled "secondary behavior": "Social control activity (such as the administration of sanctions) carried out in response to (or in anticipation of) primary behavior." Primary behavior is "ordinary human conduct" (1991, 128).

In other words, rules must have both normativity (in the limited sense that they state a standard of conduct) and facticity (in the sense that they are actually enforced). This is implicit in Helmke and Levitsky's discussion of what is *not* an informal institution. On the one hand, they acknowledge that there may be strong regularities that are not the result of a rule—formal or informal. Clearly, such regularities would lead us to expect certain behavior without causing us to consider that a deviation is worthy of sanction. On the other hand, a weak institution might only weakly structure expectations of that behavior without losing its character as a rule. Thus, an informal institution exists if a deviation from a certain informally prescribed standard of conduct is likely to generate some "external sanction," applied by the relevant agents of social control.[3] This leads to the crucial question for identifying such an institution.

Question 3: Are deviations from the hypothesized informal rule punished by the relevant agents of social control?

This evidence, where available, is the acid test for the presence of an informal institution. As Ellickson (1991) notes, people might regularly behave in a certain manner for any number of reasons, unrelated to the presence or absence of rules governing that behavior. The very best evidence of the existence of a rule is the punishment of deviant behavior by third-party agents of social control (Hart 1961, 9–25; Ellickson 1991, 128). These agents could be neighbors, bosses, the police, the courts, or many others, depending on the type of institution at issue.

This apparently simple matter requires a little more elaboration, however. Superficially, rules can take three forms: they can permit, require, or prohibit certain behavior (Crawford and Ostrom 1995, 585). The latter two are self-evidently equivalent: a rule that requires x prohibits not-x. In either case, the search for deviant behavior is quite simple, as the deviant actor is the one engaged in the primary behavior that the rule addresses. But a permissive rule generates a different kind of deviant behavior. The actor to whom the rule is apparently addressed cannot transgress, as both x and not-x are permissible. In this chapter, for example, I hypothesize a rule that permits but does not require the killing of violent criminals. In a given incident, a police officer has a choice whether or not to kill and, I argue, will not be punished either way. If this is true, the decision to kill can be made without factoring in the cost of a sanction for violating the rules against homicide.

A rule that permits either x or not-x is in reality directed at agents of control and prohibits punishing either of these choices. It could be restated as: "You may not punish agent A for doing either x or not-x." Deviant behavior for such a rule, therefore, is the attempt to punish behavior that falls within the protection of the informal rule. The best evidence of a permissive rule is proof that someone in a position of authority tried to enforce a contrary rule and was punished for doing so. In the case I am considering here, then, the best evidence of a permissive rule regarding police homicides would be finding that a prosecutor or judge was punished for attempting to prosecute a police officer who exceeded formal limits on the use of lethal force, but was acting within the hypothesized informal rule.

But the effectiveness of a rule may well be measured precisely by the infrequency with which it is violated, so that, paradoxically, the strongest rules will show the least evidence of enforcement—at least once they are well established. If we cannot

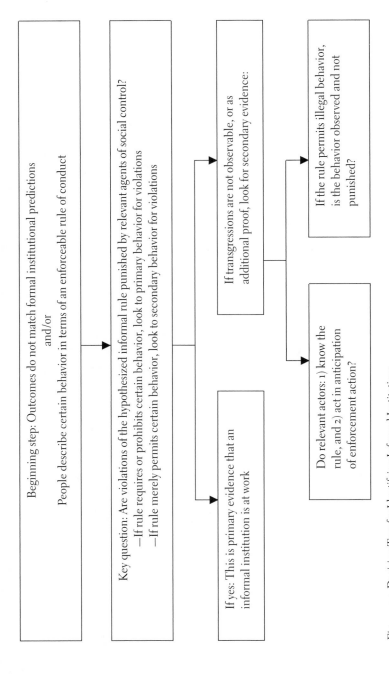

Figure 10.1. Decision Tree for Identifying Informal Institutions

The content within the figure reads:

Beginning step: Outcomes do not match formal institutional predictions
and/or
People describe certain behavior in terms of an enforceable rule of conduct

Key question: Are violations of the hypothesized informal rule punished by relevant agents of social control?
—If rule requires or prohibits certain behavior, look to primary behavior for violations
—If rule merely permits certain behavior, look to secondary behavior for violations

If transgressions are not observable, or as additional proof, look for secondary evidence:

If the rule permits illegal behavior, is the behavior observed and not punished?

If yes: This is primary evidence that an informal institution is at work

Do relevant actors: 1) know the rule, and 2) act in anticipation of enforcement action?

identify other reasons why behavior might be so universally consistent—indeed, if we conclude that difficulties of coordination, self-interest, or other motives would prompt different behavior in the absence of such a rule—then we might reasonably take this as evidence that an unwritten rule is at work. However, this is dangerously close to casting informal institutions back into the residual category formerly reserved for culture: we will attribute to an informal institution any behavior that is sufficiently puzzling to us, without adding anything to our understanding of what is really behind the pattern of behavior. Thus we must push the inquiry further, if at all possible. One way to do this, in cases in which the informal rule permits illegal behavior, is to look beyond a mere failure to enforce the formal rule.

Question 4: Is the behavior at issue observed and not punished by official enforcement instances?

No negative sanctions should be applied to those who act under the aegis of the informal rule, even if it permits or requires formally illegal conduct. Here, we must be careful to distinguish between weak or nonexistent enforcement of a rule and actual tolerance of violations by those in a position of authority. Assuming that enforcement agents are at least minimally capable of exercising their function, the key will lie in determining whether these agents observed the behavior in question, or if it simply went undetected. Failing this, or as additional proof, we might resort to indirect evidence of the existence of an informal institution.

Question 5: Is there evidence that relevant actors know the rule, anticipate the consequences of a transgression, and guide their conduct accordingly?

One of the functions of a rule is precisely to use the threat of sanctions to prevent repeated violations. Thus, if actors acknowledge that their behavior is constrained by the anticipated secondary consequences of failing to follow the rule, we may conclude that a rule is at work. Here, in essence, we are looking for direct testimonial or other evidence of the shared normative expectations called for in the definition of rules. In my case, in which the proposed rule permits otherwise illegal conduct, we should see the actors in question not only engaging in this conduct, but doing so very openly, taking little or no pains to hide their illegal conduct from formal enforcement agents.

All these questions can be organized into a decision tree for the identification of informal institutions that permit otherwise illegal behavior (figure 10.1).

In the next section, I apply these questions to an observable behavioral regularity: the use of lethal force by the police in five South American cities: São Paulo and Salvador da Bahia in Brazil, Buenos Aires and Córdoba in Argentina, and Montevideo in Uruguay. I conclude that on the one hand, there is no evidence to suggest that an informal institution protects this practice in Uruguay and in Córdoba, while at the other extreme, in Salvador da Bahia, there is broad permission for police killings of marginal social characters. Between these extremes, in Buenos Aires and São Paulo, the rule permits the killing of particularly violent criminals.

APPLYING THE DEFINITION

As noted, the first step is to identify a regularity that is not attributable to a formal institution, a structural condition, or other identifiable feature of the sociopolitical landscape. The second step is to determine whether the observed regularity constitutes an informal institution. In order to make this determination I go through the five questions presented above for each of the locations in the study.

Question 1: Regularities Not Explained by Formal Institutions

The most visible behavior prompting this research is the regular and illegal use of lethal force by the police, despite laws that purport to outlaw the practice. And the hypothesis proposed to explain this behavior is the existence of an informal institution that permits the indiscriminate use of lethal force by the police in the various countries of Latin America. As explained above, however, because the rule is a permissive one, the actual conduct that the hypothesized rule purports to proscribe is punishment on the part of agents of social control (e.g., judges and prosecutors) of police officers who act under the protection of the rule. I take the first behavior—the police killings themselves—as a given, without seeking to explain it, in order to explore the second aspect—the failure of enforcement mechanisms to punish murders committed by the police.[4]

Clearly, the police conduct at issue is inconsistent with the formal rules. The substantive laws on this matter are essentially the same in Argentina and Brazil. Both countries have signed international conventions that protect human rights, including the right to due process, the right to access the legal system, and the right to be free from summary execution. Both countries have incorporated these laws into the domestic legal framework. Recent constitutional changes in both countries have elevated basic civil rights and human rights treaties to constitutional status, including protections against arbitrary police violence. Uruguay is also a signatory to the main international human rights treaties and has the standard protections in its laws against arbitrary killing, though it has done less in the postdictatorial period to strengthen its domestic laws in this area than either Argentina or Brazil.

Despite these laws, in the last decade, the number of civilians killed in São Paulo and Buenos Aires has been very high and shows signs of worsening. On average, the police in the Buenos Aires metropolitan area killed 160 persons every year from 1990 through 2000. The worst year was 1999, when they killed 277 persons—more than 5 people every week. The trend has been generally rising. In São Paulo the numbers are even higher, averaging 680 victims annually from 1990 through 2000. The number peaked in 1992, at a stunning 1,428 persons. Even considering the immense population of the state of São Paulo—around thirty-six million—this number of casualties is reminiscent of a civil war. The difference in the size of the two cities obscures the similarity between per capita figures for Buenos Aires and São Paulo. From 1990 to 1994, São Paulo's police homicide rate was twice as high as that of Buenos Aires: 2.2 deaths per 100,000 versus 1 per 100,000. But from 1995 through 2000, the rates are nearly identical: 1.61 and 1.63 per 100,000.[5]

By way of contrast, other cities with large populations and police forces and with notorious violent crime problems show indices that are orders of magnitude lower in both absolute and relative terms. In 1992, São Paulo police killed thirty-one people for every one shot to death in Los Angeles, the city whose police "kill more people in proportion to the size of the force than any other major U.S. police department" (Chevigny 1995, 46). Los Angeles reported approximately 0.5 killings per 100,000 in 1991 and 1992. New York's figures are lower: an average of about 0.34 per 100,000 persons killed per year between 1991 and 1993. The best available number for a single year for Mexico City, an urban area larger even than São Paulo, is less than 1 per 100,000, though this is likely due, at least in part, to undercounting (Chevigny 1995).

Complete information on police homicides in Salvador da Bahia is hard to come by. There is no official oversight agency other than the regular prosecutor's office, and the relevant nongovernmental organizations (NGOs) do not regularly collect systematic information on the subject. But what we know about police homicides in Salvador suggests that the incidence of violations is even higher, and that judicial results are possibly worse, than in São Paulo. A study by the Justice and Peace Commission of the Archdiocese of Salvador, based on a survey of daily press reports, counted 623 deaths at the hands of police officers in the Salvador metropolitan area between January 1996 and December 1999 (de Oliveira et al. 2000). Given a population of 2.5 million, the average annual rate of deaths per 100,000 for these four years in this metropolitan area was 6.23, nearly three times higher than São Paulo's average for the most violent half of the last decade.[6]

In Uruguay and in Córdoba, Argentina, the situation is quite different. A search of online archives for the main newspapers in Uruguay, plus a review of the human rights reports by international NGOs and the police violence reports prepared by the

Peace and Justice Service, a Uruguayan NGO, reveal only a little more than twenty killings from 1992 to 2000 in all of Uruguay. In Córdoba, the Council against Police and Institutional Repression, an NGO that is devoted exclusively to killings committed by state agents, reports an average of about ten cases per year over the course of the 1990s.

The legal response to this activity strongly suggests that, at least in some instances, the courts are prepared to tolerate this level of violence. In Salvador da Bahia, São Paulo, and Buenos Aires, the conviction rate is so low that it can be readily construed as official complicity in the conduct in question.[7] Figure 10.2 compares the proportion of convictions for all five locations, based on a database I compiled of more than five hundred prosecutions of police homicides in São Paulo, Buenos Aires, Salvador da Bahia, Córdoba, and Uruguay, to the per capita rates of police homicides.[8] The conviction rates include only cases that involved official police conduct, whether in or out of uniform, and exclude cases in which police officers killed someone in a quarrel or similar private dispute.

Note that the locations with the highest rates of police homicides have the lowest conviction rates. If the formal rules were the only ones at work and the enforcement capacities of all these systems were even remotely similar, we might have expected quite the opposite: the more restrained police forces should be using force only under more justified circumstances, thus producing a lower conviction rate, while the more violent forces in Salvador da Bahia, São Paulo, and Buenos Aires should be punished more often. The answer to the first question, then, is yes, there is a behavioral regularity—the failure to convict police officers who kill—that cannot be explained by differences in the formal rules of the game, in at least three of the cities at issue.

But the exact contours of the rule are not so clear. On the one hand, there seems to be little reason to believe that a permissive rule is present at all in Córdoba and Uruguay. Conviction rates there are quite high, despite what seem to be less violent police forces. Moreover, not all of these cases go completely unpunished in even the worst systems—this is more true in Buenos Aires, but is even true in São Paulo, where 6 percent or so of the cases end in a conviction. Thus a blanket permissive rule is somewhat inconsistent with the evidence. Based on comments made by various activists whom I interviewed in May through December 2000 and my own observation of a few prominent cases in Buenos Aires that could not be otherwise explained, the rule might work only in cases in which the victim had forfeited the right to legal protection by taking up arms against society.

I set out to test for the existence of this informal rule of decision, using the database described earlier. I coded all the cases to identify those that would fit within

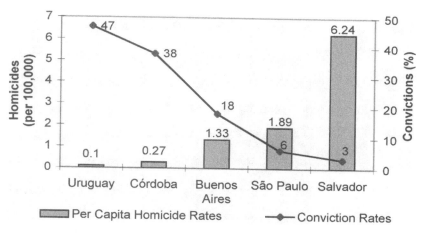

Figure 10.2. Police Homicides and Conviction Rates in the 1990s. *Sources:* Data from multiple official and unofficial sources; see note 8.

the parameters of the rule, and compared judicial outcomes across the categories defined by the rule. The hypothesized rule, broadly speaking, frees the police to kill individuals perceived as being violent criminals, whether they shoot them in the course of a gun battle or execute them in cold blood after they have been apprehended. For ease of reference, I call this the Violent Victim exception.

In practice, of course, victims may be more or less tainted by a connection with violence, and the evidence of that involvement may be more or less firm, so the rule works more as a sliding scale, with the level of prosecutorial and judicial resources devoted to a case going down, producing a lower conviction rate, as the cases approach the extreme. For purposes of this discussion, however, I included only clearcut cases in this category, coding as Violent Victim cases those in which there was strong third-party evidence—in the form of eyewitness reports, criminal records, or detailed news coverage—that the victim had a close connection to a violent crime, whether or not the killing occurred in connection with that crime. Table 10.1 compares results in these cases with all other cases in the database, for all sites except Salvador da Bahia.[9]

In São Paulo and Buenos Aires, none of the cases involving Violent Victims led to a conviction. In Uruguay and Córdoba, on the other hand, there is no evidence that this rule drives the outcomes. The Uruguayan system actually shows a higher conviction rate in Violent Victim cases, but because of the small number of cases, the rather large percentage difference across the two groups is not statistically significant. In Córdoba there are simply not enough of these cases to ground a conclusion one

TABLE 10.1
Conviction Rates in Violent Victim cases

| | Conviction rate (total no.) | | |
| | Non-Violent Victim cases | Violent Victim cases | All cases |
City			
Buenos Aires	26% (256)	0% (16)	24% (272)
São Paulo	11% (149)	0% (70)	7% (219)
Córdoba	44% (90)	50% (2)	44% (92)
Montevideo	30% (20)	80% (10)	47% (30)

way or the other. Two facts suggest that the rule does not operate in this city: first, one of only two cases in this category ended in a conviction; and second, if the police felt they had license to kill, we might expect more of these cases. Thus, in São Paulo and Buenos Aires at least, there is a regularity that is more precisely explained by the proposed informal rule: security agents who kill Violent Victims are not punished, even though the law suggests they ought to be.[10]

Moreover, I coded all the cases for evidence that the killing was an execution in cold blood—that is, the victim was shot and killed *after* being reduced to custody and control. In legal terms, these are extreme cases and should result more often, if not always, in a conviction. As we might expect, there is a higher percentage of executions in the Violent Victim cases than in other cases: in both São Paulo and Buenos Aires, 37 percent of all Violent Victims were executed, compared with 25 percent of all others. But even in these extreme cases there are no convictions. In short, the formal laws cannot account for this result, nor can it be explained by the strength of the enforcement agencies, as the difference is repeated within each system. This striking pattern, so neatly predicted by the informal rule and so difficult to explain by reference to other variables, is already evidence in support of finding an informal institution at work.

The pattern of impunity seems much broader in Salvador da Bahia. A study by Lemos-Nelson (2001) shows that members of the civil police who kill a suspect are rarely investigated by internal disciplinary instances. Lemos-Nelson finds that in most cases the very first step in a judicial investigation, the *inquérito*, is never completed, so the case does not even reach the prosecutor's office or the judiciary. The activists who spoke to me all agreed that only in the very rarest cases—cases that for one reason or another served a political purpose—was an effective judicial response likely. Moreover, I selected about thirty cases that received media attention in the second half of the 1990s and traced the judicial response to them. With the exception of recent cases involving minors (addressed in more detail later in the chapter), I found no convictions at all among these cases. I will be describing many of these cases in more detail.

In addition to these regularities, as I have suggested already, there is abundant testimonial evidence that an informal rule of some kind is operative in this regard, which brings us to the next question.

Question 2: Describing the Behavior in Terms of an Enforceable Rule of Conduct

In the course of fieldwork in Argentina and Brazil, I often came across statements suggesting that the killing of a civilian by a police officer would be punished only if the *victim* were somehow worthy of legal protection, independent of the facts surrounding the killing. In fact, it is not uncommon to find statements in which victims' relatives, the police, or even elected officials seem to approve of a policy of killing those who constitute a danger to society.

Two different prosecutors in São Paulo whom I interviewed argued, for example, that policemen who killed criminals would not be convicted in the courts, no matter what the legalities of the case. Within the police corporation, police officers who kill (and are assumed to have killed violent criminals) are often promoted—Gilson Lopes in São Paulo, for example, consistently climbed the ranks of the military police, in no small part due to his role in at least forty-two killings over the course of a decade, before finally being convicted of homicide and removed from the force (Chevigny 1995, 167). Carlos Ruckauf, when he was governor of the province of Buenos Aires, became a notorious advocate of a *meta bala* approach to crime control (roughly translated, a "shoot 'em up" approach). He offered a bonus of up to five times their salary to police officers involved in "acts of bravery," which he loosely defined as the detention or killing of violent criminals.[11] This gesture echoes the actions of the commander of the São Paulo military police, who also offered a reward and a five-day leave to those who distinguished themselves by killing criminals (Chevigny 1995).

Even the relatives of victims show that they understand public acceptance of the use of violence against violent criminals. They always emphasize that *their* relative was not a *marginal*. It is not uncommon to hear them justifying the killing of "lawless" criminals, even while protesting the unjustified murder of their own relative. A mother decrying the killing of her son, whose story is related by de Oliveira and coauthors, says: "Why didn't they go after misguided children? Because if they went after misguided children, and took their lives, they wouldn't cause such hardship, but they took a life that had nothing to do with crime!" (de Oliveira et al. 2000, 142). I heard echoes of this complaint in Salvador da Bahia, São Paulo, and Buenos Aires, but not in Uruguay. In Córdoba, the issue was presented more as a matter of class than criminal records; and indeed, in some convictions the victim had an extensive record.

In Salvador, there is other testimonial evidence describing the rule. In a dossier prepared by a group of human rights entities, the investigator in charge of the homicide division in that city makes the point explicitly. He relates that whenever he arrives at a police outpost to investigate the killing of someone who had a criminal record, "they say 'we have better things to do than to clear up the death of a criminal.'" Leo Ornéllas, the head of an Afro-Brazilian civil rights group, agrees: "In Bahia, before investigating, [police investigators] first check to see if the deceased victim had a criminal record, and then they decide whether or not to investigate." A priest who works in one of the most violent neighborhoods in Salvador relates similar responses by police investigators. In one case, he says, the *delegado* refused to investigate the shooting of a young girl, simply because the girl's *mother* was involved with drugs.[12]

The unidentified killers who execute *marginais* are known as *justiceiros*, a word that can be translated as "vigilante," but carries an obvious connotation of meting out "justice." In interviews, people, especially those of lower socioeconomic standing, often say "marginal tem que morrer mesmo"—criminals must simply die (de Oliveira et al. 2000, 35). Even the media are to some degree complicit in justifying these killings. Commenting on the newspapers' persistent habit of noting the criminal history of victims (even if unrelated to the incident itself), the Bahian sociologist Carlos Espinheira says: "It is as if there is a tacit understanding that a habitual criminal *can be eliminated*, while one who has never been arrested was, in fact, *murdered*, with the full moral and legal import society assigns to such an event" (de Oliveira et al. 2000, 35; my translation). Thus several sources would suggest there is an informal exception to the rule against the killing of civilians by the police: the rule would permit the killing of criminals, though not, presumably, of "honest citizens."

It is at least a plausible hypothesis, therefore, that policemen who kill in the course of their duties are protected by a broad and generous rule against their prosecution in Salvador da Bahia, and that those who kill Violent Victims are protected by a similar rule in Buenos Aires and São Paulo. But we need to test this hypothesis with more than simply the presence of a behavioral regularity and some testimonial evidence.

Question 3: Punishing Deviations from the Hypothesized Informal Rule

The third question brings us to the enforcement activity surrounding the rule. As noted earlier, because the rule in question here is permissive, we must look for deviance and enforcement at the secondary level. What we are looking for is not merely a lack of enforcement that is consistent with the informal rule and not with the law, but, more importantly, the punishment of deviations from that pattern. This information, as we will see, is not always easy to come by. Precisely because actors anticipate and avoid negative consequences, we should expect these instances to be rare. The absolute lack of convictions among Violent Victim cases in São Paulo and Buenos Aires makes it difficult to determine what adverse consequences might flow from an attempt to strictly enforce the law. One lawyer in Buenos Aires suggested that a particular judge, whom she viewed as sympathetic to the victims' cause, was repeatedly passed over for advancement. While in both Buenos Aires and São Paulo appellate courts intervened occasionally in favor of the defendants (and never in favor of the victim) in these cases, the number of appellate interventions is too low to support a firm conclusion on this issue.

I did obtain from one prosecutor and several other lawyers in Buenos Aires a suggestion of how the rule might be enforced from below. They argued that if the police viewed certain prosecutors or judges as being overly aggressive about enforcing the law in cases in which the police felt they were simply doing their job, they would simply stop cooperating with them. In Buenos Aires the courts depend on the regular police for all the everyday tasks associated with the investigation and prosecution of individual cases.[13] Judges and prosecutors rely on the police to serve warrants, locate witnesses and bring them into court, and serve the hundreds of *oficios*—a sort of general-purpose writ requesting that something be done—that arise in the ordinary course of business. When judges or prosecutors are pushing a case that the police hierarchy thinks should go no further, my informants told me, they will find that their *oficios* never arrive, witnesses are never home, documents cannot be found, and police officers cannot be spared to carry out their requests. In São Paulo, where ordinary investigations are carried out by the civil police, I did not hear similar complaints.

In Salvador I found clearer evidence that the rule is enforced in both official and unofficial instances, in ways both subtle and forceful. The occasional investigators and prosecutors who are serious about investigating these cases are subject to career sanctions. Marília Veloso, a former prosecutor in the military justice system, related in a personal interview in 2001 that her attempts to pursue violent military police officers were impeded by her superiors, until she quit out of frustration. Nilton José Costa Ferreiro, a former police investigator with the homicide division, also quit. Costa Ferreiro was actively pursuing an investigation into military police participation in extermination groups. He had weathered various death threats and other forms of intimidation by the police; he left when his efforts to investigate were met with the warning that he himself would be prosecuted for abuse of power if he continued (de Oliveira et al. 2000).

In summary, in Salvador da Bahia, there is evidence that a general rule permitting the relatively indiscriminate use of force by the police is enforced. Prosecutors and judges who seek to enforce the law are harassed not only by the police but also by elected officials and their superiors in the legal system itself. The proof is less clear-cut in the case of Buenos Aires, but there is some evidence that both the police and the oversight institutions take measures to impede the effective prosecution of cases in which the police have killed someone they perceive to be a violent criminal. In the case of São Paulo, I have thus far presented little evidence that the pattern detected is due to the application of an alternative rule of decision. Thus it is still possible that in these cases, the failure to enforce the law is due to weak courts or prosecutors who are unable to gather the evidence necessary for a full investigation and prosecution (though it is difficult to explain why this weakness would affect so peculiarly the Violent Victim cases). For further proof we will have to turn to the remaining questions.

Question 4: Observing and Failing to Punish the Behavior at Issue

A closer look at individual cases suggests that the negative outcomes are not the result of the legal system's failure to observe the violations in question. The killing of a person believed to have taken up arms against society often goes unpunished whether or not all the information that might be needed to produce a conviction is present.

In São Paulo, it is the case of Regiane Dos Santos that makes this point most clearly. Regiane and her husband attempted to rob a home, taking the family hostage when the police interrupted the robbery. In the subsequent exchange of gunfire the police killed her husband and one of the hostages, a child. At this point, Regiane surrendered herself and her gun to the owner of the house. The police entered the house at the invitation of the owner, took Regiane to the bathroom, and summarily executed her. The policemen were tried and acquitted on the basis of self-defense. According to the attorney who represented Regiane's children and mother, the judges blamed Regiane for the death of the hostage and ignored the testimony of the owner of the house, who said she had surrendered and relinquished her gun before the police took her away to be killed. The court of appeals affirmed the acquittal.[14]

In Argentina there are several similar cases. The best known is probably the "Villa Ramallo" case. In 1999, the police surrounded and incapacitated a car carrying four people away from a bank robbery. They pulled the occupants out of the car and executed all but the sole woman in the group. One of the three executed was a robber, but the other two were hostages—employees of the bank. The same evidence supports the conclusion that all three men were killed while unarmed and defenseless *after* being pulled from the car. But the prosecution proceeds only as to the killing of the two bankers, not the killing of the hostage-taker, who, while undoubtedly an unappealing individual, was also entitled to the benefit of due process.[15]

The evidence from Salvador da Bahia is even more compelling, as the fate of several well-publicized cases argues for an alternative rule of decision rather than a failure of enforcement resources. One such case involves the killing of Robélio Lima dos Santos. On October 11, 1999, Robélio was apprehended after he and three others committed a bank robbery that resulted in one police officer being seriously wounded. Robélio was photographed as he was handcuffed and placed in the back of a police wagon. In the photograph, taken from no more than six feet away, one can clearly see that he has only a single wound in the pelvic region. Some time later he arrived at the emergency room of the local hospital. He was dead, shot in the chest with at least two different weapons.[16]

The local press published an editorial reporting the justification offered by other police officers in defense of those who had killed this *bandido*. They noted that the arresting officers were aware that one of their colleagues had been shot and seriously wounded, and that it was likely they had acted out of vengeance. This attitude is "wrong, but accepted at an emotional level," the officers argued. The editorial concludes: "Policemen do not act as these Bahian ones did if they do not feel protected."[17] The four police officers who were in the car when Robélio was murdered were initially arrested for the crime, but when last I checked (nearly three and a half years after the event), no convictions had resulted. So far, it does not seem that the police officers involved in this case misjudged the normative expectations of their superiors, or the legal system as a whole.[18]

A more typical case, and one that received considerably less media attention, is that of Sérgio Silva Santos, a physically handicapped youth who lived in one of the *favelas* around Salvador. On January 22, 1999, five police officers on midnight rounds decided to question a group of men standing around a street-side vending post. One of the police officers had drawn his gun as he approached the men, and he accidentally fired a shot, wounding Sérgio in the neck. Not knowing what to do, they loaded Sérgio, who was still alive, in the police car, took him to a remote region, debated briefly about their course of action, and executed him, with at least two officers taking part in the actual shooting. Then they placed a gun in Sérgio's hand and prepared a report that said he had died in an exchange of gunfire with the police.[19]

Eventually, confronted with witnesses to the initial wounding, the victim's physical disability, and other damning evidence, one of the five police officers disclosed what had actually happened, and testified to the entire sequence of events. In spite of all this, at last report the accused are still employed by the police, and remain free. The judge's office reports that the difficulty in moving forward with the case lies in locating the witnesses to the initial event. This should come as no surprise, as in April 2000 we read that "one of the main witnesses in the killing of the physically handicapped Sérgio Silva Santos . . . was beaten to death in Nordeste de Amaralina, the neighborhood where he lived."[20] As noted below, the less publicized killings are, ironically, surrounded by much less violence. There are few complaints, even fewer investigations, and the cases are routinely ignored.

While no prosecutor or judge I interviewed stated directly that a police officer *should not* be convicted under these circumstances, in many of these cases there is no doubt that the violation of the formal rule was observed by the system, and still there was no sanction, suggesting the application of an alternative rule of decision. The decisions themselves are couched in more general language and use formal legal categories to decide adversely, citing a lack of evidence to support a finding that the police acted in excess of their legal authority. At worst, the courts simply fail to rule at all. In Buenos Aires and Salvador da Bahia, there are cases that simply languish until they are forgotten or until the statute of limitations expires. Moreover, it is clear that in many of these cases, judicial officials have not undertaken the most minimal efforts to uncover what really happened, despite gaping inconsistencies in the police version of events. In short, the evidence suggests that the courts will not convict in these cases even when the available evidence abundantly requires it.

Question 5: *Affected Individuals Know the Rule, Anticipate the Likelihood of Enforcement, and Guide Their Conduct Accordingly*

As noted in the case of the Salvadoran bank robber, the police show considerable reliance on, and expectation of, the lack of enforcement of the official rule in cases involving violent criminals. In many cases they carefully create the appearance that the victim was a menace to society. For more than half the cases in Argentina and nearly two-thirds of all cases in Brazil, I was given some indication—either because judicial proceedings uncovered police deception or because advocates for the victim made a concrete allegation—that the police had staged a confrontation after the death of the victim, planted a gun, threatened witnesses, produced false forensic reports, or tampered with the process in some similar way. The methods are diverse and creative: one former policeman testified that the São Paulo police will place a gun in the dead victim's hand and pull the trigger so the skin will show gunpowder residue; in one of the cases, the police shot their own car to simulate a confrontation; in several, they were observed transporting the victim's body to a different place where they could stage a confrontation.

Often the evidence of tampering is irrefutable, as when a second report confirms that the shots entered the back of the head, rather than the front of the body, or when a gun attributed to the victim is traced to the *comisario* who had charge of the operation. Other times it is simply the claim of an advocate for the victim. Sometimes the evidence is more subtle, but nevertheless persuasive, as in the case of Darcy Ferreira dos Santos and Fábio Mário Saraiva Rodrigues. The indictment against the São Paulo police officer who killed these men was dismissed, on the grounds that they had entered a bar, drunkenly confronted the police officer, taken out guns, and started shooting. The ability of the policeman to successfully repel the aggression was somewhat surprising, since the two had allegedly started shooting first. But the exculpatory evidence was provided by the owner of the bar, who claimed to witness the event, and by the owner of an adjacent bar, who said the victims had indeed been in his establishment drinking and brandishing guns immediately before the incident.[21] That is typically as far as the investigation goes.

A closer look casts strong doubt on this version of events. The bar owner who provided the exculpatory evidence is a relative of the police officer. The victims' relatives, who talked to the police but were not called in by the prosecutor, claim that the two young men left home only fifteen minutes before the shooting, were not drunk, and were unarmed. The details of the autopsy report, which can be found in the case file but are not discussed in any of the prosecutor's filings before the judge, show that in addition to one and two frontal wounds, respectively, each of the victims had a gunshot wound in the same spot in the middle of the back, suggesting a coup de grâce. The motive for the execution becomes clear when we learn that one of the two men was on conditional release pending trial in the killing of a police officer. An aggressive prosecutor could have uncovered these facts, ordered expert reports, and put together at least a semblance of an effective prosecution. Instead, one wonders why the prosecutor bothered to indict at all, when the indictment accepts without question and repeats the allegations that the victims initiated the shooting, and makes no reference to any inconsistencies between the facts and the official story. The outcome is predictable.

In Salvador da Bahia, the police also behave in a manner suggesting that they know and rely on this rule: they are especially casual about killing, so long as it is within the course of their duties, and seem to expect impunity. Witnesses and relatives often report that police officers accused of a killing openly taunt them, to the point that neighbors and relatives discourage complainants from going forward, and the complainants themselves desist. The case of Sérgio Silva Santos, the disabled youth who was first wounded and then summarily executed, makes this point clearly: the police preferred to kill someone in cold blood, in an attempt to set up an "ordinary course of duties" killing, than to be caught having wounded someone by mistake. Moreover, it was not one panicked police officer who did this, but no less than five, after some deliberation. Similarly, it was not one enraged police officer who shot and killed Robélio Lima dos Santos in the back of the police wagon, but at least two, while two others were in the car with them. These are not individual "rogue cops"; they are acting in accordance with accepted and established patterns of conduct.

Thus far all the evidence suggests that the permissive rule is quite broad in Salvador. But some evidence to the contrary suggests the permissive rule actually applied by judicial officers is limited to killings committed in the course of official police duties. The case of Heloísa Gomes dos Santos and her partner, Manuel Ferreira dos Santos, shows that the police feel that violence is necessary to keep information from the courts when the killing was committed in furtherance of criminal activity on the part of the police. Manuel's son Valdemir was killed by a group of military police officers when he resisted attempts at extortion. Heloísa and Manuel carried out a very public campaign to bring these policemen to justice. They brought their complaints to the media, spoke to and joined various human rights organizations, and spoke to state and federal legislators about police abuses in Salvador. They even identified the alleged killers by name.[22]

Soon after they began their campaign, Heloísa and Manuel began to receive death threats. On June 21, 1998, they were shot to death as they sat in their car in front of the hospital where Heloísa worked as a nurse. Since then, of the four witnesses who testified against this group of policemen, along with Heloísa and Manuel, two were murdered, one disappeared and is presumed murdered, and one is in hiding under the auspices of Bahia's witness protection program. There have been no convictions in connection with the original extortion attempts, the murder of Manuel's son, the murder of Heloísa and Manuel, or the murder of the other three witnesses. The use of such extreme measures to impede the prosecution is clear evidence that the implicated police officers thought they could not rely on official complicity but had to take self-help steps to ensure their impunity. In short, the evidence suggests the application of a rule that is broad but not unbounded in Salvador, and is limited to Violent Victims in São Paulo and Buenos Aires.

CHANGE OF AN INFORMAL INSTITUTION

We might expect the informal rule that permits killings by police to be the hardest to change in Salvador da Bahia, where it seems to be so widespread and supported by so many at all levels of the state. But it is precisely here that there is some evidence of a change in the rules, as evidenced by a few convictions in cases involving minors over the last six or eight years. The Center for the Defense of the Child and Adolescent (CEDECA), an organization fighting violence against children in Bahia, selects particularly egregious cases involving poor children from marginal neighborhoods and attempts to pressure the legal system to respond effectively. An interview with its director suggests an instance in which the informal rules of the game changed, in response to a change in the enforcement structure of the formal rules. At the same time, a gross disparity of power between those who were negatively affected by the new rules and those who benefited from them prevented a dramatic change in actual outcomes, largely preserving the behavioral regularity.

Before the creation of a specialized juvenile justice system, police killings of children and adolescents were open and frequent in Salvador. Many of the killings fit the mold of the informal institution described above: a kind of social cleansing carried out by, or with the cooperation of, the police against "undesirable" social elements. In 1992, for example, a military police patrol confronted a band of youths that engaged in petty crime in Liberdade, a peripheral neighborhood of Salvador. The next day the police returned out of uniform and picked up two children they suspected of belonging to the gang. One day later, the parents found their children's savagely mutilated bodies. The parents knew who had picked up the children, and these police officers were initially charged with the crime. But the file on the case mysteriously disappeared from the court records, and the case has gone nowhere in ten years.[23]

In another case, in 1991, a child from one of the *invasões* (shantytowns) around Salvador tried to beg a ride from a bus driver. The driver refused to let him on, and as he drove away the child threw a stone, hitting the bus on the side. The bus stopped, and a policeman descended with his gun drawn and shot the child in the back as he ran away. This case never even triggered a formal investigation by the prosecutor's office and so did not make it into the courts at all. In 1992, another policeman stabbed a child to death for hitting his dog with a stone. When representatives of CEDECA confronted the police investigator in charge about his failure to open a formal inquiry in this last case, his only response was: "When are people like CEDECA going to establish a center for the defense of the police?"[24]

The stories are chilling; the killings were almost casual, perpetrators did very little to hide their participation, the justice system did not investigate them, and no one was ever punished for the crimes. CEDECA's director told me in May 2001 that the organization's first systematic investigation revealed that eighty children were murdered in 1991 in Salvador, most of them poor. Of those cases, only eleven led to a formal judicial proceeding; only one of these led to a trial, and that single trial ended in an acquittal. Though he could not say exactly how many, he noted that the police were involved in a large percentage of these homicides. At this point the police made little or no attempt to hide the facts, and the operative rule by all appearances dictated that these crimes would not be prosecuted.

But the legal apparatus that attended these crimes in Salvador da Bahia was reformed following the passage in 1990 of the (federal) Estatuto da Criança e do Adolescente. This statute authorized the creation of the Vara Criminal Especializada da Infância e da Juventude, a juvenile justice system that acts in criminal cases involving acts by or against minors. The investigators, prosecutors, and judges in this system work only on cases involving minors.

According to the director of CEDECA, since cases began to be processed by the new system, beginning around 1992, there has been a marked difference in the way child homicides are treated. Whereas before it was difficult to find a police investigator, prosecutor, or judge who might show even a minimal interest, now the prosecutors and judges, who deal only with children, are much more aggressive. Today, a specialized investigative office (*delegacia*) opens formal inquiries for all the cases. They are somewhat slow, they do not have a great many resources, and the *inquéritos* often have errors, but at least the investigations are done in good faith, according to CEDECA's director. Similarly, one of the two judges in the juvenile system noted many changes in the treatment of minors since the early 1990s, all of which permit monitoring their safety from the time they come in contact with law enforcement.

Interestingly, the new official agency does two things. On the one hand, it offers a more effective agency to control under-age crime, by ensuring there are facilities that can process and house youthful offenders more quickly and effectively. This neutralizes the proffered justification for dealing with these children extrajudicially and undermines the claim that routinely permitting their murder is a necessary substitutive institution. On the other, it strengthens the enforcement of laws protecting children from extrajudicial punishment by creating a corps of judicial and law enforcement officers at all levels whose sole task is to ensure that the laws protecting and governing children are respected. The performance of this corps will be judged on the basis of how well it does this, and only this, task. Moreover, the statute itself signals a national reaction to a perceived problem that would no longer be tolerated: violence against children was singled out for special treatment and declared to be unacceptable. Thus there is reason to hope that the informal institution permitting the murder of socially marginal children might disappear altogether.

The behavioral regularity, however, may not disappear quite so quickly. As the formal system became more aggressive in protecting the rights of children, a new problem has come to the fore. Since the police can no longer count on benign neglect by the justice system, the rate of threats and violence against complainants and witnesses has vastly increased. Now, CEDECA's director reports, relatives of the victims come into his office in the initial days after the event, impelled by anger and grief at the harm to or loss of a child, and asking the center to take some action to ensure that the perpetrators are held accountable. But often they call back some days later to withdraw the complaint, citing threats of violence against them if they persist: "His father has three other children to raise," said a mother recently. "Even the judge is afraid." Witnesses cease cooperating with prosecutors and withdraw earlier statements about police participation in the crime. In short, the police involved in these killings now exploit the weaknesses of the system—primarily the vulnerability of the lower classes that are the most frequent targets of violence—to close down the flow of essential information to the system. As in the case of Heloísa Gomes dos Santos and Manuel Ferreira dos Santos, violence against complainants increases when the certainty of impunity decreases.

The end result is a slight improvement in outcomes, but far less than what the advocates of reform had hoped for. CEDECA can now point to several cases in the last five or six years in which the courts convicted a police officer for killing a minor. But there are still a large number of cases in which the prosecutions failed because the police intimidated the witnesses or the complainants themselves. And CEDECA can attest to an increase in the level of secondary violence, as the police respond to stricter enforcement by taking more extreme measures to ensure that their illegal behavior is not officially detected. This example shows why we should not extrapolate rules from mere regularities, or assume that a change of rules will necessarily effect a change in behavior. It also sounds a cautionary note about the possible negative consequences of changing the rules in the face of a continuing and serious imbalance in resources between those who benefit from and those who are constrained by the new rules. The failure to protect the new rights-bearers ultimately exposes them to more violence, as the rules constrain the behavior of those who are accustomed to impunity.

CONCLUSION

In summary, there is considerable evidence that an informal institution that permits the killing of perceived violent criminals is the operative rule in Buenos Aires and São Paulo. The rule of conduct included in this institution is applied by actors within the legal system—including the police, prosecutors, and judges—as evidenced by cases in which clear violations of the law come to the attention of the legal system and are not punished. The police enforce the rule through the use of violence against complainants and witnesses, and by withdrawing cooperation from the courts that are supposed to supervise them. Higher-level courts and judicial superiors may also enforce it, but I have less evidence of this than I would like, especially in the case of São Paulo. The rule is confirmed, however, by flagrant police behavior that suggests reliance on such a permissive rule.

In Salvador da Bahia, it is clear that a similar informal rule permitting the killing of *marginais* rules the streets and is applied in the courts. First, we can observe a high number of actions in accordance with the hypothesized informal rule—the rate at which the police kill is three times higher than in São Paulo, the next highest, and a city with an already exceptionally violent police force. Then there is the absence of secondary conduct enforcing the contrary, formal, rule—there are virtually no reports of convictions of police officers for killing someone in the course of their duties. Those who try to run counter to the rule, as did certain prosecutors and investigators, are punished, while those who act within the rule enjoy nearly complete impunity. In short, those suffering from rights violations do not seem to have effective recourse to an enforcement agent that is not co-opted by the informal rule; the enforcement agents within the system who attempt to enforce the law are themselves punished for doing so. For all practical purposes, then, the rule that governs is one of impunity for police officers who kill, at least so long as they are seen to be carrying out their social cleansing function.

One aspect of this rule has changed in Salvador, with the reform of the juvenile justice system. A change in the design of formal institutions to offer greater protection to child offenders and greater effectiveness in fighting juvenile crime led actors within these institutions to cease applying the informal rule in the case of children. This resulted in an increase in the effectiveness of the formal institutions, though not as great a change as we might have hoped for. The poor outcomes will no doubt continue until the beneficiaries of the change in the formal rules—impoverished parents of murdered children—acquire the resources to stand up to the violence and intimidation of police officers who continue to abuse their power, or until the state itself devotes more resources to this task.

The outbreak of violence against claimants, precisely when their rights seem to be strengthened by institutional change, prompts a more general observation. Institutions—rules—define who the winners and losers will be under certain conditions. The a priori balance of power in this particular context—the relationship between police and policed in marginal neighborhoods—was congruent with an informal rule that permitted the police to act at will, without owing any duty to the policed. The newly effective rule purports to change the balance of power by creating new rights, and clashes with an entire concatenation of power resources that essentially point in the opposite direction: the police have more coercive power, greater legitimacy, and more access to political power than their victims. This suggests that the new winners will not be able to protect their winnings without an additional investment by the state and, specifically, the state's decision to allocate some of its resources to protecting the new rights-bearers. Institutional change in this area requires a series of changes in related areas before it can produce the desired effect. The outbreak of violence against claimants highlights the need for witness protection programs, specialized investigative agencies, perhaps even different rules permitting the detention of suspects, and a more aggressive prosecution of obstruction of justice.

So far, I have not addressed what may seem like a basic question, given the typology set forth in the introduction to this volume: what kind of institution is this, complementary or substitutive, accommodating or competing? The answer depends on how we define the outcomes of the formal and informal institutions at issue (see figure I.1 in the introduction). One overarching goal of the criminal justice system is the preservation of social order. Those who defend the practice of using excessive force against actual or suspected offenders argue that the formal institutional structure has failed to produce sufficient order, and the only way to fight crime in the context of this perceived state failure is, in essence, *meta bala*—"shoot 'em up." If we accept this at face value, then the informal institution I have described is designed as a substitute for an effective criminal justice system and arises as a response to state weakness.

But the criminal justice system includes a subset of rules intended to protect individual rights to due process and physical integrity. These, too, are valued social goals, despite the fact that they are persistently flouted in practice. The outcome foreseen under these rules is an individual prosecution under standards of due process. As to these rules, the institution I have outlined here is clearly competing: it short-circuits due process and shows no regard for the physical integrity of those who come in contact with the police. In the final analysis, then, the outcomes of these cases would be different if they were judged according to the formal rules, and therefore we should classify this informal institution as a competing one.

As this example shows, informal institutions can substitute for some formal institutions while simultaneously competing with others, and it may not always be easy to determine precisely what role they are playing. As should be clear by now, informal institutions often prove difficult to identify, describe, and categorize. This only highlights the valuable contributions that remain to be made as we struggle to understand the missing links between formal institutions and unexpected outcomes.

CHAPTER ELEVEN

Mexico's Postelectoral *Concertacesiones*

The Rise and Demise of a Substitutive Informal Institution

TODD A. EISENSTADT

During the 1980s and 1990s, Mexico transformed from a hegemonic single-party regime into a competitive democracy, culminating in Vicente Fox's victory in the 2000 presidential election. Although the transition brought far-reaching change to the country's formal institutional architecture (Eisenstadt 2004), it was also marked by the use of distinctive informal norms of interparty bargaining. During Mexico's protracted transition, dozens of postelectoral conflicts were settled through informally negotiated *concertacesiones*, or gentleman's agreements. Invoked in nearly a dozen national high-profile cases—and scores of lesser ones—during the 1990s, these informal bargaining tables became the principal arena of negotiation between the governing Party of the Institutional Revolution (PRI) and the opposition National Action Party (PAN). The PAN usually lost in the PRI-state's famously corrupt elections, but it was given something back—an interim mayorship or, at the very least, a proportional-representation city council seat—as a reward for continued participation. The preferences of the electorate were put aside, as mayors- and governors-elect resigned, under pressure from the PRI, to make way for negotiated "interim" executives from the losing PAN and "plural" municipal cabinets were shuffled in closed-door negotiations to include an opposition co-mayor or city manager.

Concertacesiones operated at the margins of—and in lieu of—formal institutions (such as electoral commissions and courts) that were designed to resolve electoral disputes. Indeed, the demand for informal postelectoral bargaining tables was rooted in the ineffectiveness of formal electoral and judicial institutions, as well as in PRI and PAN leaders' recognition that informal institutions offered them much more flexibility in tailoring electoral outcomes to the parties' mutual needs. Once the PRI and PAN learned of the discretion afforded them by the informal institution, without any of the inflexible legalism or transparency required by formal institutions, *concertacesiones* supplanted formal electoral institutions for a decade. The evolution of *concertacesiones* thus offers an excellent opportunity to explore the rise and fall of a substitutive informal institution (Helmke and Levitsky, introduction to this volume; see also Lauth 2000). At a time when electoral courts were still widely viewed with suspicion, *concertacesiones* provided politicians with a temporary, but highly flexible, means of adjudicating electoral disputes. The bargaining tables did not give way to reformed formal electoral institutions until the end of the 1990s, as increasing political competition fostered more calls for clean elections and far-sighted opposition leaders pushed the one-party state to accept ever-more constraining electoral rules.

The term *concertacesión* (originating in a Mexican slang combination of the words for "concertation" and "concession") has gained such cachet as a concept of Mexican political culture as to merit inclusion in the country's most important electoral dictionary. The definition given is an "act by which, in cases where official electoral results do not correspond to a reality sensed and witnessed by the electorate, the official winner steps down and cedes to the candidate of the party which was really thought to have won . . . This process offers a political out to severe electoral conflicts" (Martínez Silva and Salcedo Aquino 2002, 99). This definition exaggerates the role of voters in the process. Rather than responding to the electorate's perceptions of who won, *concertacesiones* were a product of the PAN's growing leverage vis-à-vis the PRI at key postelectoral moments, which the PRI used to activate PRI-state discretion in installing losing PAN candidates in local office (at the expense of local PRI leaders). Voters and opposition activists played a role in making *concertacesión* credible in two ways. First, they ensured a sufficiently close race that the PAN could claim fraud on political grounds (even if not on legal grounds). Second, they provided "bread and circuses" for a visible local postelectoral mobilization, which, while not of primary importance in negotiations, helped make *concertacesión* easier for the public to swallow.

The chapter examines the rise and eventual collapse of *concertacesiones*. It shows how an equilibrium was reached in which PRI and PAN leaders possessed incentives to continue trying their luck at informal bargaining tables, rather than binding themselves to formal institutions, and how this equilibrium unraveled as the incentives of both actors changed. I argue that *concertacesiones* evolved out of preexisting informal behavior patterns employed by the PRI to co-opt allies and repress threats.[1]

During the 1980s and 1990s, they became an integral part of the PRI's effort to appear more democratic without actually opening the electoral system. The PRI negotiated away "consolation prize" spoils from its banquet of riches, allowing the party, in the waning years of its seven decades of continuous rule, to maintain the PAN's interest in participating in elections. PAN participation gave the PRI-state—deeply embarrassed in 1976 when the PAN withdrew the only opposition presidential candidate and the PRI still only managed to get 82 percent of the vote—a cover of legitimacy. For the PAN, complicity with the PRI-state ensured access to local governance, which allowed the party to establish a record of accountability otherwise unheard of in Mexico. It also spurred the PAN's legislative advocacy of electoral reforms, which slowly leveled the electoral playing field and made way for the PAN's strategic shift to supporting only formal institutions when negotiation with the PRI grew less essential.

Successful *concertacesión* required the confluence of six necessary factors: (1) a PAN loss, but in a close enough race that the victory could credibly be "given" to it as runner-up; (2) a PRI-state willingness to engage in postelectoral negotiations when the PAN held a bargaining chip of national interest to the ruling party; (3) a willingness of the local PRI to sacrifice electoral victory to make good on the national PRI-state's promises to the national leadership of the opposition party; (4) a disciplined opposition with national leadership that could deliver on its promises and could faithfully negotiate on behalf of local candidates; (5) local protests and mobilizations of a magnitude sufficient to lead the electorate to believe that *concertacesión* was the only solution to intractable local conflicts unresolvable by other means; and, perhaps most importantly for the analysis of substitutive institutions, (6) the willingness of participants to subvert formal institutions by relying on informal ones, and to abide by agreements reached at informal bargaining tables, despite the adverse effects on the credibility of formal institutions.

These conditions existed between the PRI and the PAN, but not the leftist Party of the Democratic Revolution (PRD), from the late 1980s to mid-1990s. While the PRD and other left-wing parties were involved in hundreds of postelectoral conflicts during Mexico's democratic transition,[2] the PRI, whose strategy was to co-opt the conservative PAN and repress the left, utterly refused to engage with the PRD national leadership. In any case, the national PRD lacked the discipline to deliver the compliance of its local activists.[3] Hence, it was the PAN, which prioritized winning regional governance positions in the short term as a segue to national governance in the longer term, that benefited from *concertacesión*. PAN leaders readily undermined formal institutions throughout the 1990s, but with the zealous belief that, by accepting what they called "partial restitution" of electoral injustices now, they could pave the way for truly autonomous and transparent electoral institutions (Eisenstadt 2004, 177–79).

Once the PAN had leveraged its postelectoral prizes to create a more competitive party and to force the creation of more effective formal electoral and judicial institutions, it abandoned postelectoral bargaining tables—even though the PRI desperately wanted to keep them open. The demise of *concertacesión* can thus be traced to two requisite factors: first, the growing credibility of formal institutions and, second, the defection of the PAN, which reordered its preferences after winning the presidency for the first time in 2000. Thus, when the PAN was strong enough to gain national public office without the assistance of informal bargaining tables, and when electoral commissions and courts gained credibility as genuine third-party enforcers, the informal institution of *concertacesión* collapsed.

The chapter draws on original ethnographic research to elaborate the evolution of *concertacesiones*. I break the rise and demise of *concertacesión* into four periods, designated according to changes in the incentives of the national PAN and PRI directorates. I conclude by situating the importance of *concertacesión* in the Mexican transition, arguing that it was a crucial way station between the creation of equitable formal electoral institutions and their acquisition of credibility (measured as the observance of their dictates by relevant actors). Indeed, while *concertacesiones* crowded out (and even delegitimized) formal institutions in the short term, in the longer term they allowed actors to adjust their expectations regarding formal institutions, moving from the perception that formal institutions were fraudulent and inferior to ad hoc settlements, to a period of dueling focal points in which both formal and informal institutions were used, to full compliance with formal institutions and delegitimation of substitutive informal institutions. Hence, the PAN's strategic choice to use informal institutions in conjunction with constant efforts to bolster the formal ones helped ensure that *concertacesiones* would eventually be replaced by genuinely autonomous formal institutions.

PERIOD I: THE UNDERPINNINGS OF *CONCERTACESIÓN*

The origins of *concertacesión* can be traced back to the heyday of the PRI's "soft" authoritarian regime. The PRI-state's legitimacy after its 1929 consolidation stemmed from an ideological mission of institutionalizing objectives derived from the demands of the Mexican Revolution: land reform, labor rights, and political enfranchisement. By the 1970s, that platform had been diluted into symbolism and pageantry, with few public policies attached. Nevertheless, the PRI maintained a corporatist system that mobilized citizens in official labor and peasant unions, and managed a high level of popular support based on appeals to the ideals of a Revolution decades away. As long as the party-state could offer constituency services—albeit discretionary and conditional—citizens would support (or at least acquiesce with) the "catchall" PRI. Although the PRI-state at times violently repressed those, usually on the left, who refused to go along with the system, the success of corporatism was rooted in the effective co-optation of potential challengers. Thus, Mexico's formal electoral institutions, which were democratic on paper but corrupt and biased in practice, coexisted with informal patterns of bargaining and co-optation.

Among the informal authoritarian institutions that emerged during this period was the interim municipal council, a mechanism for resolving the many intraparty conflicts that emerged after controversial candidate selection processes (Langston, this volume). In municipal councils, interim mayors and/or city council members were selected according to purely political criteria, rather than based on who won the corrupt (but always held) popular elections—a pattern that would later be replicated in *concertacesiones*. Hundreds of municipal councils were formed between the 1930s and the 1980s. By the early 1980s, they were governors' legal solutions of choice for postelectoral conflicts.[4] Between 1978 and 1981, for example, some twenty-five plural municipal councils were formed after controversial local elections—a period in which only 41 opposition victories were allowed nationwide (Assad and Ziccardi 1988, 41). By comparison, during the three-year period between 1990 and 1992, fifty-seven municipal councils were formed, but 202 opposition victories were recorded, and between 1993 and 1995, only nineteen municipal councils were created, compared with 557 opposition local electoral victories.[5] During this period, postelectoral conflicts were responsible for the creation of some 70 percent of the municipal councils, while internal PRI conflicts provoked authorities to declare 10 percent and other causes (e.g., corruption scandals, formation of new municipalities) triggered 20 percent.[6]

While *concertacesión* was not really established until 1989, when the PAN "won" its first interim governorship in Baja California and its first mayoral substitution in Mazatlán, two precursors to postelectoral conflict processes became routine by the early 1980s. First, losing parties staged mass demonstrations, blocked freeways, burned ballots, occupied public buildings, declared "parallel municipal governments" to sabotage public works by the winning party, and initiated mob brawls when demonstrations were dissipated by local authorities or challenged by PRI counterdemonstrations. Second, to ensure at least a modicum of electoral competition, the PRI-state began to concede some power, especially at the local level. Thus, municipal reforms in 1977 and 1983 guaranteed proportional-representation city council seats for opposition parties and devolved to the localities a little more control over the distribution of public resources. These reforms—together with the relegalization of communist parties—generated unprecedented opposition interest in local elections and gave rise to new patterns of participation and protest.

This surge in opposition political activity was fueled by economic crisis and mismanagement, which shrank the PRI-state's support base significantly during the 1980s and triggered important new challenges on both the right and the left. Although the regime ignored the left's postelectoral demonstrations, it paid attention to those by moneyed PANistas in Mexico's industrial north, who conveyed their growing opposition to the PRI's statist economic model by sending tens of billions of dollars out of the country (Barkin 1990, 109). The PAN, in existence since 1939, had made strong electoral showings in isolated cases in the 1960s and 1970s and had been stripped of several mayoral victories by the PRI's legendary electoral fraud machine—such as in the notorious Mexicali and Tijuana races of 1968, where the PRI-state annulled elections rather than declare PAN victories, and a corrupt governor's race in Yucatán in 1969 (Eisenstadt 2004, 167–72). In response to the fraud, the PAN withdrew candidates from several local elections in the early 1970s, and the party's refusal to nominate a candidate to oppose the PRI in 1976 was the lynchpin of defiance, which, along with the need to channel into the electoral arena insurgents on the left (Klesner 1988, 391), catalyzed the regime's granting of electoral reforms in 1977. But the reforms did little to change the tilted electoral playing field, and the PRI continued to resort to fraud whenever even staged elections went awry. Moreover, the PRI's domination (and corruption) of electoral bodies and the judiciary meant that formal institutions lacked the credibility to act as third-party arbiter in disputed elections. Consequently, the PAN, like the left, turned to protest. Although the PRI would eventually domesticate these postelection mobilizational strategies into *concertacesión*, the PAN launched a few genuine, widespread and disruptive social movements in the mid-1980s, attracting cross-class support and international media attention.

Meanwhile, imaginative opposition leaders, eager to appropriate claims of real legality from the PRI-state's arsenal of "window-dressing" formal judicial institutions, established propaganda "people's courts," highlighting differences between opposition positions and those of the PRI-state. By framing electoral justice as commonsense arbiters of intuitive "fair play," in contrast to the formal institutions' unintelligible and even suspicious legalisms, regime critics could claim that their admittedly biased "courts" were no further removed from reality than those constructed by the official arbiters. The protests began in Puebla in 1982 with a poorly publicized effort by the PAN to take election certification into its own hands. The party fared better in Chihuahua in 1986, where a "People's Jury" of local notables was formed by critical (pro-PAN but allegedly nonpartisan) opposition civic groups, to monitor elections and issue the predictable conclusion that the election warranted annulment due to its "great number of irregularities and vices" (Lau 1989, 87).[7] Another similar "People's Electoral Court" was formed in Michoacán in 1989, which declared, contrary to the state electoral commission, that the PRD (chartered that year to unite the previously disparate left) had won a vast majority of the state legislative races (Zamarripa 1989). Also along these lines were the "Electoral Defender of the People of Chiapas" and the "Electoral Tribunal of the People of Chiapas," which consisted of local and national notables convened through nongovernmental channels to "judge" the 1994 governor's race (Vargas Manríquez and Moreno Corzo 1994). Headed by an actress rather than a jurist, the publicity-seeking intentions of this body were more transparent than its administration of justice. But the opposition made its point.

These informal institutions of "cardboard commissions and courts" galvanized public opinion, but held little sway with the authoritarian PRI-state until the left and right united. For a fleeting moment in Chihuahua in 1986, and for a few resounding weeks in 1988, the PRI-state faced the threat of a grand coalition against its decades of ossifying "catchall" populism, but with dwindling state resources to distribute. After the 1986 Chihuahua governor's race was stripped from the PAN by the PRI-state, the moralistic patron of Mexico's recalcitrant left, Heberto Castillo, participated in PAN marches and protests and argued that the PRI-state had a choice: "Either it respects the popular will or else we engage in violence. I am ready to die" (L. Gómez 1991, 372). Castillo stepped aside as a 1988 presidential candidate to make way for Cuauhtémoc Cárdenas, the left-of-center scion of one of Mexico's most fondly remembered generals and presidents. Although the PRI-state summoned all its electoral "alchemy" (to use the common Mexican slang term) to push candidate Carlos Salinas's vote total to 50 percent (to Cárdenas's 31 percent), Cárdenas was perceived by many and, perhaps most importantly, by 1988 PAN candidate Manuel Clouthier (who placed third, with 17 percent of the vote) to have been robbed of the presidency. Clouthier temporarily bucked the conservative PAN establishment to join Cárdenas in decrying the results (Loaeza 1999, 461).

The nightmare of a left-right coalition against Salinas's fragile credibility—placed in the service of Cárdenas's opposition to the Salinas (and the PAN's) neoliberal platform—was said to have motivated many of the president's actions, as well as those of the conservative PAN hierarchy (Loaeza 1999, 462; Eisenstadt 2004, 175–82, 262). The common threat posed to the PAN and PRI and the realignment of these parties' preferences were propitious to the golden years of *concertacesión*. In siding with the

PRI in an alliance for Mexico's economic opening, after dalliances with the PRD that only increased the PRI's zeal to compromise and work with the PAN, the PAN evolved from a more passive party seeking to win (or even just run in) local races, publicize its conservative platform, and pursue only gradual and stable change, to one threatened by the left and intent, first, on blocking radical change (by collaborating with the PRI-state in an anti-PRD alliance) and only secondarily on winning local races. In period II (1988-96), starting immediately after the threat of the right-left coalition first emerged, the PRI was marked both by the PAN's aversion to radical change and by its new partner's desire to implement compatible economic reforms.

PERIOD II: THE *CONCERTACESIÓN* SOLUTION

The 1988 election was so fraudulent that, even with vast majorities in both legislative chambers, the PRI-state needed PAN complicity in the Electoral College (the lower chamber of Congress) to ratify President Carlos Salinas's victory without extreme embarrassment. Thus, during the summer-long postelectoral controversy, Salinas dramatically increased the payoffs of *concertacesión*. The president-elect, in need of PAN support against his PRD challenger, signed a letter of intent with the PAN promising to enact the PANista-backed electoral reform in exchange for his opponents' complicity in certifying the 1988 election. While the PRD did not join the PAN's enduring electoral reform crusade—and then halfheartedly—until the mid-1990s, the PAN seized its opportunity in 1989 not only to push its legislative agenda but also to force Salinas to, in effect, rescind local PRI victories and throw them to the opposition (Eisenstadt 2004, 176).

The PAN's escalating costs of co-optation were also driven by the fact that the PRI no longer possessed the two-thirds majority in both legislative chambers required for constitutional reforms. In addition to needing a coalition partner and an opposition party legitimizer, Salinas also personally feared and deplored PRD leader Cuauhtémoc Cárdenas. As late as 1994, Salinas was thought to have an almost irrational fear of the PRD,[8] and that party's early-1995 insistence that Salinas's successor, Ernesto Zedillo, resign so that the PRD might lead a "government of national salvation" hardly endeared it to that president either.

The choice was thus clear to the authoritarian incumbents by the end of the 1980s. Either they would have to take their chances on further reforming the electoral institution monster they had created, and at least gain a partner with whom to finalize Mexico's neoliberal economic reforms, or they would have to rely on their increasingly belligerent regional PRI machines to defeat the antiregime PRD. The PRI-state consciously chose the former—*concertacesión*. In 1989, Salinas sided with the PAN's neoliberals over the populist machine bosses in his own party, and the PRI leadership did not backtrack until two years before the 2000 electoral watershed, when some activists realized that the party's electoral firewall had been dismantled and that its era of complete hegemony was over. Mexico's most notorious *concertacesiones* followed this 1989 move (table 11.1), as the substitutive informal institution was used to supplant formal electoral courts and commissions on dozens of occasions, including a half-dozen with profound national implications.

Some of the *concertacesiones* were shocking in their subversion of formal institutions—and the popular vote—to whitewash PAN-PRI deals. Several agreements stand out during period II, but the most blatant case of subversion that I documented, and the one that set the standard for *concertacesión* as a substitutive institution, was the 1993 election in Mérida, Yucatán. The problem began when the local chapter of the PRI in Mérida declared its candidate victorious, prompting the PAN to launch an extensive postelectoral mobilization led by Diego Fernández de Cevallos, the party's just-named 1994 presidential candidate. In an effort to "undo" the local PRI's disobedience of the national PRI, which was increasingly more concerned with garnering PAN cooperation than with who governed in Mérida, the national Interior Secretariat composed an electoral court case to annul PRI votes so that victory would pass to the PAN. After being flown to Mexico City for briefings on the national PRI's case, the Yucatán electoral court magistrates returned to Mérida, heard the case, and did not revert the victory to the PAN (Eisenstadt 2004, 183–86). Making no headway with the electoral court magistrates, the national PRI flew the party's Yucatán state legislators to Mexico City for discussions. According to Rodríguez Lozano: "They spent a tormented twenty-four hours" being convinced to overturn the mayoral race in the state electoral college. The resulting settlement, an electoral college vote to designate the "runner-up" PANista to fill the term when the PRI victor resigned under protest, clearly violated the Yucatán state constitution.[9]

The settlement was acknowledged as "illegal" and "antidemocratic" by the PRI mayoral candidate who conceded, and by a national PRI negotiator who said he was overruled by the Interior Secretariat.[10] It discredited the Yucatán state legislature (which, when convened as electoral college, certified the election for the PRI but awarded the post to the PAN) and the Yucatán state electoral court in favor of the national and local directorates of the PAN and the PRI and the mayor of Mérida.

The official electoral college statement selecting the PAN runner-up, however, lauded PRI candidate Orlando Paredes's resignation as "an act of the highest civic value, which puts the interests of Mérida and the State of Yucatán ahead of those of any person, interest, or party."[11] Furthermore, "given this overwhelming circumstance, this Commission considers that to maintain political stability, social harmony

TABLE 11.1
Deals behind Prominent Concertacesión *Agreements, 1988–96 (Period II)*

City or state election (population governed, per 1990 census, to nearest 10,000)	What the PRI allegedly got	What the PAN allegedly got	Formal institution said to have been replaced by informal institutions	Probable mechanism of *concertacesión*
Presidential election 1988 (81.25 million)	PAN national support in certifying Salinas as president	Pledges from Salinas for electoral reform; predisposition to recognize subnational PAN victories	Electoral College's certification of presidential election subverted by side deals	Salinas wrote a letter on behalf of PRI to PAN leadership formalizing deal; PAN leadership agreed, over objections of maverick candidate Clouthier
Guanajuato state governor 1991 (3.98 million)	PAN support for constitutional agricultural and economic reforms	Interim governor from PAN, Carlos Medina Plascencia (now prominent senator)	Electoral Court; PAN officials recognized they did not have legal grounds, although they filed cases to state electoral court	PRI governor-elect "retired" under PRI pressure by losing PAN candidate Vicente Fox; federal Interior Secretariat brokered deal
Mérida, Yucatán, mayor 1993 (0.56 million)	PAN 1994 presidential candidate's pledge to keep running (after he threatened to withdraw)	Sacrifice of PRI mayor-elect in favor of PAN candidate	Electoral college of the Yucatán state legislature, which illegally granted victory to number 2 finisher to preserve social order	State legislators under national PRI pressure committed *concertacesión* after electoral court refused to annul PRI victory; federal Interior Secretariat brokered deal
Monterrey, Nuevo León, mayor 1994 (1.07 million)	Pledge by PAN not to withdraw from Electoral College's certification of PRI presidential victor Ernesto Zedillo	Sacrifice of PRI mayor-elect in favor of PAN candidate	Nuevo León state electoral court overturned by appeals chamber, but under extensive pressure from national PRI-state	"Whitewashing" of election through appeals chamber of state electoral court; federal attorney general and national PRI and PAN brokered deal
Huejotzingo, Puebla, mayor 1996 (0.04 million)	Pledge by PAN to return to the negotiating table where PRI-state wanted consensus electoral reform	Sacrifice of PRI mayor-elect in favor of PAN candidate	The Puebla state electoral court (which possessed no appeals chamber) was overturned by bargaining table of national and local PRI-PAN negotiators	State electoral court set aside after months of national PAN protests and national negotiations determined outcome without any legal "cover" whatsoever

Source: Eisenstadt (2004), 105–9, 183–93.

Note: Reports of *concertacesión* were widespread, but reported here are only those that I corroborated via both primary and secondary sources. Attempts were made in each instance to interview both PAN and PRI protagonists. Other notable alleged cases, such as the Mazatlán, Sinaloa, mayorship 1989, the Guaymas, Sonora, mayorship 1991, and the San Luis Potosí governorship 1991 are omitted because I did not corroborate them firsthand.

and an acknowledgment of the political participation and maturity of Mérida's citizenry, it is necessary to give the triumph to the party which won second place in the election, in this case, the National Action Party" (Yucatán State Legislature 1993, 369). Thus, although the national PRI-state's arm-twisting had failed to convince local electoral court magistrates to annul the race through formal institutions, the PRI-state had managed to usurp the court and implement its *concertacesión* with the national PAN through proper electoral procedures and preserve the form, if not the substance, of a formal legal resolution. The Mérida mayoral election of 1993 was the procedural high water mark of *concertacesión*, and one of the most embarrassing moments ever for advocates of formal institutions and the rule of law in Mexico.

The Mérida *concertacesión* was also indicative of how powerful the national PAN grew during period II. Yet, even as it increasingly settled postelectoral conflicts at the bargaining table, the PAN continued pursuing fortification of legal institutions for dispute adjudication. Informal institutions were simply seen as a suboptimal way station between authoritarianism and democracy. Even as the PAN battled hard for its scraps from the table of power, it pushed for reforms of the formal electoral institutions that would enhance its viability and hence allow the PAN to stop having to submit its postelectoral fortunes to fickle PRI discretion. For example, efforts to establish an independent electoral court—which date back to 1947—were among the PAN's highest electoral reform priorities in 1989 and again in 1996. The first Salinas-era reform of formal institutions, mandated in 1989–90 by the president's commitment to the PAN for facilitating the certification of his election in 1988, constructed the first electoral institution independent of the executive branch for mediating the fairness of the electoral playing field: the Federal Electoral Institute (IFE). The previous election-monitoring institution, the highly controversial Federal Electoral Commission, had been run directly by the Interior Secretariat, which was part of the (PRI-dominated) executive branch. The Federal Electoral Tribunal was created in 1989 as a more autonomous body capable of challenging most IFE decisions. An antecedent body, the Tribunal of Electoral Contention, had been inaugurated for the 1988 elections, but its decisions were widely ignored and largely irrelevant (Eisenstadt 2004, 66–69).

Urged on by the PAN, the PRI-state tolerated two more rounds of electoral reform, extending the autonomy and jurisdiction of the IFE, further scaling back PRI overrepresentation—this time in both houses of Congress—and codifying a role for electoral observers. Concrete (though very high) limits were placed on party campaign spending and election-related media coverage, and electoral registry reforms continued with the introduction of a voter photo identification card. The Federal Electoral Tribunal was also fortified, and the Electoral College's role in certifying federal elections was eliminated in all but the presidential race.[12] The most important anti-*concertacesión* reform, however, was the 1996 incorporation of local postelectoral disputes into the jurisdiction of the fortified federal electoral court, subsumed under the judicial power. The Electoral Tribunal of the Judicial Power of the Federation (TEPJF) owed its creation at least partly to the mayoral *concertacesión* in Huejotzingo, Puebla, and to the aborted Tabasco gubernatorial *concertacesión* (to the PRD this time) at the beginning of period III.

PERIOD III: THE BEGINNING OF THE END OF *CONCERTACESIÓN*

Concertacesión had never been the solution of choice for local PRI chapters, which preferred to win elections at all costs, and then submit the results to sham electoral commissions and politically driven electoral colleges, just as they always had. During the Salinas administration (1988–94), the PRI's local activists bided their time, silently watching as the president and his national technocrats recruited the PAN to help privatize and streamline Mexico's previously bloated state, while trading away the local elections they had fought so hard to win or steal.

In 1994, Salinas's politically weaker successor, Ernesto Zedillo, sought to extend the practice of *concertacesión* to the PRD in the aftermath of a fraud-ridden gubernatorial election in Tabasco. As in the Salinas years, Zedillo's interior secretary and the national PRI engaged pragmatic PRD representative Andrés Manuel López Obrador (Mexico City mayor and a leading 2006 presidential aspirant) in an effort to end two months of PRD-led oilfield blockages, street protests, and work stoppages. The Tabasco PRI had violated campaign spending limitations fifty-fold with impunity, jammed the state's electoral apparatus with biased officials who committed flagrant election-day "engineering" (including a mysterious blackout of the vote-tallying computer, which turned back on with 4 percent fewer votes cast), and engaged in the usual "get out the vote'" promotions and petty ballot-stuffing (Eisenstadt 1999, 281). The PRD never expected electoral justice, but López Obrador, taking his lesson from the PAN, explained: "Whatever we do, it will be construed as acting outside the law, so we must proceed through strict legal channels [in addition to extralegal channels] to avoid these criticisms. We must follow this legal course, even as we mobilize citizens, knowing that it [the law] does not work."[13]

This PAN-like dual strategy of legal challenge and mobilization (a departure for the PRD, which had dedicated most of its effort to the latter) was particularly salient because hundreds of Tabasco PRD activists marched to Mexico City and occupied the city's central square, threatening to interrupt Zedillo's presidential inauguration

(López Obrador 1996, 170). As dialogue over Tabasco lagged in January 1995, the PRD forced the PRI to agree to at least "reconsider" 1994 postelectoral controversies in several states in exchange for PRD participation in reform talks.

The Tabasco *concertacesión* ultimately fell apart, however. When word of a possible *concertacesión* reached Tabasco, local PRI leaders preempted the PRD by taking to the streets themselves. The Tabasco legislature's PRI leadership declared that the local party had been abandoned by Mexico City, and the PRIistas agreed among themselves to refuse any resignation tendered by the governor-elect and, furthermore, to adopt the PRD's mobilization tactics to get Mexico City's attention. They succeeded. When the "rebellion of the PRI" threatened widespread violence and ungovernability, Zedillo rescinded the forced resignation of governor-elect Roberto Madrazo (who had already been offered a cushy federal cabinet position in exchange for his projected personal sacrifice) (Eisenstadt 1999, 285–87). The politically inexperienced Zedillo, apparently lacking the authority to impose such legal shenanigans on the local PRI machine, distanced himself from the PRD's *concertacesión* gone sour and reaffirmed his staunch advocacy of the rule of law.

The Tabasco episode marked the emergence of a more moderate and pragmatic PRD that was willing to use both formal and informal institutions. But more important to the future of *concertacesión*, the "rebellion of the PRI" drew attention to the growing breach between the incentives of election-driven local PRI activists and their policy-driven national leaders. It also demonstrated to local PRI factions that, unlike in the Salinas era of strong party discipline, rejection of national PRI dictates was an option under Zedillo. Condition 4 of the six necessary conditions for *concertacesión* outlined earlier—a disciplined opposition party with a national leadership that could deliver on its end of informal bargains—had been violated, but by the PRI rather than the PAN.

PAN activists, however, continued to view *concertacesión* as a viable, if second-best, option during the mid-1990s. Taking advantage of Zedillo's interest in including the PAN in a definitive electoral reform, the national PAN activists found cause in a small town where electoral court rulings were an abomination, even to reformers in the PRI. With the rallying cry "democracy passes through Huejotzingo!" the national PAN shone light on sham formal institutional rulings not witnessed since the 1993 Mérida mayoral ruling by the Yucatán state legislature. Local PRI efforts to fix the PAN's 1995 Huejotzingo victory resulted in an electoral tribunal's whitewashing of the outcome by overturning the PAN, on shaky legal grounds, in favor of the PRI (Eisenstadt 2004, 190–91). The national PAN mobilized, finessing the PRI mayor's resignation in favor of a PAN-selected interim mayor. The interior subsecretary, Arturo Nuñez, acknowledged that who was mayor in Huejotzingo was deemed less important than disarming PAN threats to derail President Zedillo's negotiation of a "definitive" electoral reform.[14]

The PAN had again managed to prevail over the egregious manipulation of the Puebla state electoral court, and the party used its victory to advocate for a crucial federal electoral reform to prevent future Huejotzingos. It managed, as part of a broader package of reforms in 1996, to transfer jurisdiction over local elections to the fortified TEPJF, which was less susceptible to "capture" by local interests. Indeed, in its subsequent record on tackling difficult cases and annulling elections won by all parties and on judicial arguments gleaned from case law, the TEPJF demonstrated that the norm of electoral justice would henceforth be better served by formal institutions alone.

The Federal Electoral Institute, created in 1989 and fortified by reforms in 1993, was also given new autonomy in 1996, as its ombudsmen, or "electoral counselors," were selected—for the first time—entirely by the political parties in Congress, with no executive branch participation. One of the new electoral ombudsmen noted that immediately after being named, late in 1996, the IFE's scholars-turned-ombudsmen defied PRI-state expectations that they would be malleable and docile.[15] IFE's policymakers immediately dispelled such notions, investigating campaign spending violations against the PRI's most controversial machine boss, Governor Madrazo of Tabasco. Reminiscent of the PAN's successful departures from the bargaining table of national reforms in 1996 over Huejotzingo, the PRI withdrew its party representative from the IFE General Council in 1998, arguing that the body had no jurisdiction over alleged Tabasco campaign spending improprieties in 1994.

The PRI's five-month IFE walkout was the beginning of the PRI's transformation from confident rulers to beleaguered opponents. In a strategy suggestive of an opposition party more than of the dominant party that had presided over the IFE's very creation, the PRI-state exacted a heavy public relations cost. How could an electoral institute established to mediate party interests function without the presence of the largest party? The PRI's boycott lasted months, but dissipated in March 1999, when party moderates, seeking to bolster the electoral institutions they still thought would legitimize their projected 2000 victory, realized that the party's interest was in reinforcing IFE's authority. As PRI campaign advisor Sandra Fuentes-Berain put it: "We don't want to shoot our own foot by discrediting IFE."[16]

PRI leaders decided they were vested in the formal institutions they had tolerated, but only as long as they thought that the legitimacy brought by autonomous formal electoral institutions would work to their favor. The desperate appeals by the national PRI hierarchy after 2000 to the discretion of *concertacesión*—even with the tables turned, with the PAN-as-government getting to make the discretionary Solomonic choices—would undermine a decade of PRI-state rhetoric about the rule of law and electoral transparency.

Farsighted PRI strategists, however, began to see, even before the 2000 electoral defeat, that they were losing the discretion and control that *concertacesión* had given them. During period IV, the PRI would learn that the PAN was no longer willing to fulfill necessary condition 6 of *concertacesión*: unlike the PRI-state, the PAN-as-government would not sully formal institutions with the credibility loss from *concertacesión*. To the contrary, the new PAN administration was composed of *concertacesión* veterans—such as President Vicente Fox—who disliked negotiating votes at bargaining tables almost as much as they disliked losing to PRI-committed fraud.[17]

PERIOD IV: *CONCERTACESIÓN* COLLAPSE— THE NEW TURN TO COURTS

Dislodged from the state apparatus that had nourished it for seventy-one years, the PRI grew even more desperate in the months following its July 2000 presidential defeat. Casting aside the formal electoral institutions it had tolerated—and even promoted—as part of the PRI-state, the PRI's national leadership backpedaled strategically to the heyday of *concertacesión* with the PAN. Reminiscent of the PAN's threats to boycott Zedillo's inauguration if its Monterrey mayoral candidate was not recognized (another notorious *concertacesión*; see table 11.1), the PRI threatened to boycott Fox's inaugural if the PAN did not agree to a ballot-by-ballot recount of the Jalisco election for governor, which the PRI had lost. Although initially the PRI and PAN sat down at a bargaining table with the outgoing interior secretary to hammer out a deal, the PANistas, entering office in a matter of days, stalled negotiations. Having finally gained the upper hand, they referred the angry national PRI leadership to the federal electoral court, where the PRI clamored for "relief" to the electoral magistrates, who, freed of any ties to their nominators (Zedillo and his Supreme Court) were more interested in continuing to develop their growing reputation for impartial electoral justice than in placating the PRI.

In sharp contrast to the Monterrey mayoral election of 1994, the federal electoral court refused to whitewash the Jalisco gubernatorial election. After months of verbal recriminations, the PRI's poorly argued case (in which the party violated the appeals process by changing its argument between the time of the initial hearings in the Jalisco electoral court and the federal appeal) was ruled as mostly unfounded in February 2001, leading to further—unfounded—attacks against the electoral court

(Granados Chapa 2001). By the admission of their own legal advisor,[18] the PRIistas were the last to realize that the electoral courts had become real, independent arbiters, whatever the PRI-state's intentions when it allowed for their creation.

The PAN had long used the idealized norm of electoral justice and parliamentary persistence to push for creation of an electoral court.[19] By the late 1990s, the PRD had also finally resolved to use the courts effectively as a check against the most heinous regional PRI machine bosses, spearheading legal—rather than political— efforts in 2000 and 2001 to overthrow PRI-rigged elections in Tabasco and Yucatán. The federal electoral court's inscrutably legal and politically dispassionate Jalisco ruling confirmed its professionalism,[20] and exposed the widening breach between the diehard local PRIistas' efforts to cling to the past and the national policymaker moderates' escalating embarrassment with their own party. Rather than being pulled together by an emerging leader, the internal division only pushed PRI partisans further apart, prompting postponement of the election of a new national leadership (originally slated for 2000) to 2002.

Also in 2000, the federal electoral court annulled that year's PRI gubernatorial victory in Tabasco. The electoral court cited several "indicators of electoral fraud": electoral authorities' insistence on opening all the preliminary results statewide without justification, the dramatic PRI monopoly on television publicity and news coverage, the location of contraband electoral materials such as ballots at a PRI-contracted survey research firm, and compelling but circumstantial evidence that Governor Roberto Madrazo had mobilized public resources for the campaign. As the electoral court magistrates argued that they had been gradually amassing tools of judicial activism to render the powerful verdict,[21] the political parties—and especially the PRI, accustomed to a servile electoral court—were shocked.

Having indirectly defied the PRI's perhaps most powerful governor (the PRI's national president and a leading 2006 presidential aspirant), the federal electoral court then directly challenged another PRI stalwart boss, Víctor Cervera Pacheco, the governor of Yucatán. If the Tabasco ruling helped quell last-ditch efforts at *concertacesión*, the court's Yucatán actions in defense of formal institutions ended most talk of *concertacesión* once and for all, especially since the Fox administration wanted nothing to do with negotiating electoral outcomes or even any appearance of intervention in local politics.[22] Governor Cervera Pacheco's argument that the electoral court's intervention in December 2000 to select a slate of state electoral-commission citizen counselors was a violation of federal law was unsubstantiated. Contrary to widely circulated claims within Yucatán that the federal electoral court overstepped its bounds by selecting Yucatán's citizen counselors in Mexico City, the federal electoral court was empowered to do so under Mexico's Constitution. Judi-

cial authorities insisted that unchallenged precedents existed for direct federal interpretation of state electoral laws and of election-related state legislature acts.[23] The
original violation of the Yucatán electoral code was self-evident: the electoral commission ombudsmen required approval by a four-fifths majority of the state legislature (or twenty of twenty-five members), and only fifteen legislators approved the
initial slate. In October 2000, the TEPJF ruled that the Yucatán legislature had
selected its electoral commissioners illegally and called for a new selection.

The Yucatán legislature agreed initially to uphold the electoral court decision,
reselecting the same slate of electoral commissioners, but with the needed twenty
votes. However, irregularities in this process prompted the electoral court to intervene again to request stricter adherence to the original verdict, which the Yucatán
legislators refused. Cervera Pacheco and his legislative leaders were not deterred
by the contradiction of first accepting the electoral court decision and then back-
tracking and declaring it unconstitutional. Nor was PRI national president Dulce
María Sauri, the former Yucatán governor who resigned over the 1993 *concertacesión*
of Mérida with the PAN and who sided in 2001 with Cervera Pacheco against
Mexico City.

Waving the banner of state autonomy and even threatening secession from the
union, Cervera Pacheco found further political resonance in defying a late 2000
federal electoral court verdict to block the Yucatán governor from stacking the state
electoral commission in favor of his party in the run-up to the 2001 gubernatorial
election. His *"yucatecos* versus the Mexico City bureaucrats" campaign, resound-
ingly endorsed by 95 of the state's 106 mayors, boosted the governor's popularity and
caught the federal electoral authorities between two poor options: ordering enforcement of their verdict via public force, or failing to intervene, losing credibility,
and opening future decisions to second-guessing by emboldened *caciques*, or local
bosses. Fox, himself a victim of the 1991 *concertacesión* in Guanajuato (table 11.1),
insisted that the Yucatán legislature was responsible for following the federal electoral court's dictates and that his government planned not to intervene, since "the
yucatecos have the ability to resolve their own issues and I'm sure they are going to do
so" (quoted in Olvera Aguirre 2001, 5).

The proposed solution, which allowed federal authorities to bide their time while
Cervera Pacheco played out all options short of violence, was for the federal electoral court to name a "legal" Yucatán electoral commission to compete with the
"illegal" Yucatán legislature–ratified electoral commission. Not unlike the Puebla
1983 "People's Tribunal" to publicize electoral fraud, the Chihuahua 1986 "Peoples'
Jury," and the 1994 "Electoral Defender of the People of Chiapas," dueling institutional focal points were found to be the best means of distending conflict. However,

the key difference between the Yucatán 2001 electoral commissions and the Puebla, Chihuahua, and Chiapas "peoples' electoral courts" was that this time the legal authorities had opted for the duality as a means of stemming conflict, whereas, in the prior cases, opposition parties and other societal interests had initially chosen to vent conflict only through the parallel institutions. The resort to dual institutions provided a procedural symmetry.

The solution to the Yucatán conflict was political, as the legislatively appointed electoral commission received the $4 million budget for conducting the May 2001 elections, but a second, federal electoral court–appointed commission received the federal voter list (usually "lent" by the federal electoral authorities to each state's electoral commission). Still, Cervera Pacheco did not desist until the Mexican Supreme Court ruled in April 2001 that combining the two electoral commissions into one "super-commission" was illegal. The Cervera Pacheco–backed commission (formally named by the PRI-dominated legislature) finally stood down, to allow the naming of a compromise electoral commission to organize elections some six weeks hence.

The Yucatán conflict broke with previous *concertacesión* patterns in several ways. First, the protesters who occupied the state electoral commission for two months were all PRIistas, breaking the opposition-led protest dynamic of the past. Second, the hard-liner–led national PRI was united with the local Cervera Pacheco machine in opposing the federal electoral court ruling, against the PAN-led federal government and PRI moderates. Third, contrary to past patterns of Interior Secretariat intervention, the national government was loath to take sides. Fourth, the protesters' ire targeted a legal decision, justified by an emerging field of law and legal institutions, rather than the usual arbitrary *concertacesión* (or lack thereof, in PRD cases). In managing to move the public discourse from debate over the arbitrariness of a *concertacesión* to debate over the legality of an electoral court decision, federal electoral authorities won even before the case was decided.

The electoral court's decision to select its own Yucatán electoral commission was all the more powerful coming on the heels of the landmark Tabasco gubernatorial case. National PRI president Sauri inconsistently accepted the federal electoral court's annulment of the Tabasco governor's race, though refusing to allow federal electoral court meddling in her home state's gubernatorial race, and the national PRI largely heeded her position. A few moderates bucked the PRI leadership, but most remaining PRIistas unquestioningly toed the party line. The contradictions with decades of PRI rhetoric praising law, reason, and restraint by those who had stewarded the development of autonomous electoral institutions (even while seeking not to actually use them) were exposed. At their worst, the PRI's new leaders appealed to the base instincts of mob rule; at their best, they enlisted the populist anti–Mexico City themes of regionalism, federalism, and sovereignty to justify disobeying federal mandates. Either way, the powerful and unobstructed defiance by the electoral court of what just a few years before had been "untouchable" forces signaled the final demise of *concertacesión*. Once in power, Fox and the PAN were unwilling to indulge the PRI's engagement with informal institutions, and the success of Mexico's electoral institutions meant that subversion via *concertacesión* was destructive of the formal institutional architecture the PAN-as-opposition had worked so hard to construct.

IMPLICATIONS OF SUBSTITUTIVE INFORMAL INSTITUTIONS FOR DEMOCRATIZATION

Leaders of the PAN made a moral choice during the peak of *concertacesión* during the late 1980s and early 1990s. On deciding to seat the party's members in the Chamber of Deputies to certify PRI candidate Carlos Salinas's irregular election as president in 1988, the PAN party president, Luis H. Alvarez, set a precedent for partial co-optation with the PRI, declaring that "we have to be capable of negotiating and accepting partial and provisional formulas of transition" (Loaeza 1999, 462). This was a controversial conclusion, as the early PAN activists—especially the party's distinguished lawyers and parliamentarians—were directly responsible for proposing and stewarding the electoral reforms that the PRI-state had allowed. Whereas PAN purists sought to fortify the credibility of formal electoral institutions only, Alvarez and the pragmatists—who led the party from its early decades as a doctrinaire debating society to its politically crucial role as the engine of Mexican democratization—settled for a second-best strategy. They would seek to create and fortify strong formal electoral institutions in the long run, but accept informal bargaining tables in the short run.

The PAN's strategy, known as "partial restitution" of electoral improprieties through bargaining tables, ran counter to the legal purists' argument that *jus ex injuria non oritur* ("rights do not arise from wrongs"). Clearly, participation in informal electoral institutions—especially substitutive ones, which undermined the credibility of formal institutions—was inconsistent with the PAN's advocacy for the rule of law. But by the early 1990s, the pragmatists had defeated the purists. Acknowledging the moral compromise involved, an interim 1991 PAN Guanajuato state governor averred that *concertacesión* had been used to "partially restore" fairness after fraud in that state had cost now-President Vicente Fox the governorship. According to a PAN National Council release: "National Action considered the extreme dichotomy drawn by purists between dialogue and confrontation to be false, simplistic, and sterile; that the party could conduct legitimate negotiations or justified protest movements in defense of Mexicans' human rights without violating party doctrine precepts" (Reynoso 1993, 146).

Much of the impetus underlying *concertacesión* stemmed from the fact that formal judicial institutions did not work at the time. The only way to achieve electoral justice in the 1991 Guanajuato governor's race was to side-step the very formal institutions the PAN had borne the burden of creating. The PAN succeeded in the use of the substitutive institution of *concertacesión* because such agreements were also in the PRI-state's interest before Mexico's 2000 power alternation (at least until about 1998, when some PRI activists realized they were reforming themselves out of power), and would have been strongly in the PRI-as-party's interests post 2000 had the PAN-in-government allowed the pattern to continue. But with the combination of formal institutions sufficiently fortified to level the playing field and certify PAN victories, and electoral strength sufficient to make such a possibility real rather than just hypothetical, there was no longer a normative trade-off to be made between informal institutions that undermined the rule of law and formal institutions that short-changed them. When the balance was tipped decisively in 2000, the PAN jettisoned the substitutive institutions immediately.

The broader normative question raised by the PAN's dilemma is whether substitutive institutions are antithetical to democratic decision-making. While the answer is an open one, it is probably affirmative (at least in regard to "transparent decision-making"), since informal institutions in general—and perhaps by definition —encourage the utilization of information beyond that which is publicly available and, in the case of substitutive institutions, seem to exploit power asymmetries between actors. The substitutive electoral institutions did not arise spontaneously, but rather were actors' adaptations to weak formal institutions established by the early 1980s. The PAN's dilemma of needing to right crooked elections, even as this process undermined the rule of law, captured the broader dilemma posed by the use of informal institutions at the expense of formal ones. Still, to their credit, the PAN leaders never lost sight of the broader objective of establishing strong formal institutions to substitute, in turn, for the informal institutions they had acceded to for over a decade.

The substitutive institutions of Mexico's democratic transition were crucial to the PAN's incremental—election-by-election—but persistent inroads to power. But they ultimately proved ephemeral. Once in power, and at a moment when the PRI lacked bargaining chips that could force the PAN back to the informal bargaining table, the

PAN quickly cast these institutions aside. The vital legacy of these substitutive institutions was in tipping the balance of forces toward the PAN even before the 2000 alternation, not in the design of their formal institutional counterparts. The PANistas were too disciplined to allow the substitutive institutions to ever replace formal institutions, which they always used in tandem with their substitutive analogues. After a few iterations, expectations converged with those of PRIistas about how the *concertacesión* bargaining tables would be run. But, apparently contrary to the PRI (which sought *concertacesión* unsuccessfully several times in 2000 and 2001), the PAN never considered *concertacesiones* as more than a second-best option and always kept the goal of perfecting the formal institutions of the rule of law within its sights.

Of the six necessary conditions for *concertacesión* listed earlier, the final condition—that actors be willing to accept the subversion of formal institutions inherent in their being substituted by *concertacesión*—thus provided the greatest impetus for change. The parties' incentives changed during each period in the evolution of *concertacesión*, but the PAN did not lose sight of its primary goal of long-term stakes in the creation of autonomous formal institutions, and maintained great discipline in "settling" for partial restitution ad hoc while longing for systematic electoral justice.

A broader theoretical point is worth noting. The substitutive *concertacesión* bargaining tables did temporarily crowd out or undermine formal institutional resolutions, as suggested by Helmke and Levitsky in the introduction to this volume, but they did so only as long as the formal institutions failed to impart justice. By clearly perceiving when they no longer needed *concertacesión*, the PANistas were able to disregard the practice as a rung in the ladder they had already climbed. The PRI-state allowed the PAN (and, after the mid-1990s, the PRD) reformers to gradually empower formal institutions, electoral reform by electoral reform, in a feedback loop that was also driven by the PAN's improving electoral competitiveness, especially in traditional opposition strongholds (the same areas that had been tainted by *concertacesión*).

By the time PRI strategists realized, in the late 1990s, that they had empowered the electoral institutions beyond their ability to control them, it was too late. The PRIistas did not realize (and probably could not fathom) that the PAN would stop submitting to *concertacesión* and switch to a policy of exclusive reliance on formal institutions at the earliest opportunity. The mutually reinforcing trends of improved PAN electoral performance and fortified formal electoral institutional autonomy allowed Mexico's oldest opposition party and the electoral institutions it had imagined to prosper in tandem. When the formal electoral institutions showed themselves to be sufficiently autonomous and transparent to be worthy of compliance, the post-2000 PAN-government vested itself completely in them, exposing the hard-liners in the PRI as the only remaining proponents of *concertacesión*. To the PAN, *concertacesión* was just a means to the end of powerful formal institutions, but to the PRI's hard-liners, it brought the end of their means.

CHAPTER TWELVE

Dispensing Justice at the Margins of Formality

The Informal Rule of Law in Latin America

DONNA LEE VAN COTT

Informal institutions often emerge in the vacuum created by weak formal institutions. In Latin America, formal institutions may be weakest with respect to the rule of law. For centuries, segments of Latin American geography and society have existed outside the reach of the state. As Guillermo O'Donnell (1993) has observed, large swaths of Latin America may be considered "brown areas," in which most citizens are not protected by the courts and police. In the absence of judicial control, corruption and impunity are endemic, and conflicts are resolved and order maintained through extrajudicial means. Such problems have captured the attention not only of scholars. Policymakers are likewise concerned that the weakness of judicial institutions severely inhibits the achievement of economic, political, and social progress. The World Bank recently declared that justice administration in Latin America is "inefficient and ineffectual," arbitrary, inaccessible to many citizens, underfunded and lacking in modern facilities and practices, and not subject to external review. As a result, public confidence in judicial systems is low throughout the region (Malik and Martínez 1999, 827). The quality of Latin American justice administration is so poor that even powerful economic interests are seeking alternatives in private arbitration fora. In this context, it is tempting to view informal justice institutions as uniformly benign—albeit imperfect—solutions to the demand for justice.

Yet, while informal justice institutions often emerge or persist in the vacuum created by the weakness of state law, I argue that the relationship between informal and formal legal institutions is more varied and complex than the conventional wisdom suggests. Indeed, informal justice systems may fall into all four of the categories discussed in Helmke and Levitsky's introduction to this volume. Although many are fully consistent with state law or substitute for absent or incompetent state institutions, others directly compete with penal laws.

Modifying slightly the typology developed in the introduction, I explore informal justice institutions along two dimensions. The first is the degree of contact with and coordination between a particular informal institution and the state. At one end of the spectrum, informal authorities act as purely *substitutive* institutions, in that they are wholly responsible for justice administration and dispute resolution. At the other end of the spectrum, informal institutions *complement* formal institutions by sharing responsibilities with the police and courts, particularly for issues not addressed by the state. As the chapter demonstrates, most cases fall somewhere in between these two ideal types. The second dimension is the propensity of the informal and state authorities to alter their institutions to adjust to the presence of the other. On this dimension, institutions may range from *competing* to *accommodating*. Where informal practices violate penal law and no mutual adjustment occurs, the relationship may be described as competing. However, instances of pure competition are decreasing because more than a dozen Latin American states now legally recognize some informal justice systems. In addition, community authorities are reshaping their own norms and procedures to adjust to the new regime of "legal pluralism": the coexistence of distinct legal systems in one geographic space (von Benda-Beckmann 1997, 1). In some cases, formal justice institutions are being accommodated to community cultures and customs, and the police, courts, and community authorities work together to detain suspects, investigate offenses, and select the appropriate venue for the administration of justice.[1]

The two continua described above are neither mutually exclusive nor interdependent. A given informal institution can be classified on both dimensions (i.e., the extent of the role of formal institutions and the degree of mutual accommodation between formal and informal authorities), and the location of a particular community's informal justice administration system on one continuum does not necessarily determine its location on the other.[2]

I begin by examining diverse examples of informal systems of community justice administration, explaining how and why these informal legal institutions emerged, how they have evolved over time, and their relationship(s) to the state. I then examine efforts in the last decade to legally recognize informal justice institutions and to link their jurisdictions to that of the state, and the reasons for the growing trend toward formal recognition. I also discuss the theoretical and practical challenges generated by efforts to establish legal pluralism. Because the Andean countries (particularly Bolivia, Colombia, Ecuador, and Peru, and Venezuela) are most advanced in recognizing the authority of informal legal systems, they receive more attention.

THREE CASES OF INFORMAL JUSTICE INSTITUTIONS

In this section I describe three types of informal community justice institutions: indigenous law, the *rondas campesinas* of rural northern Peru, and the *juntas vecinales* of urban Bolivia. Because the latter two types were created recently, they allow us to observe the origin of informal institutions, something that is usually difficult to do. The *rondas* case also is illuminating because it demonstrates marked changes in function in an informal institution over time.

Indigenous Peoples' Law

The norms and procedures of indigenous law vary so greatly among cultures, even within regions of particular countries, that cogent generalizations about them are difficult. Indigenous law encompasses "the uncodified concepts, beliefs and norms which, within a given community, define prejudicial actions or crimes; the selection of authorities and processes by which these should be resolved; and the sanctions or resolutions decided and applied" (Sieder 1998, 98). For example, indigenous law typically determines who will resolve disputes within the community and the procedures for hearing and resolving these disputes; the acceptable standards for the use of coercion in domestic relations; and who should have access to agricultural and pasture land within a community's collectively owned territory.

Nonspecialists often receive an essentialized and static version of indigenous law, which is purported to protect centuries-old traditions—a vision often propagated by indigenous leaders themselves as a strategy to defend their autonomy. This view of indigenous law also was propagated during the twentieth century by positivist state officials, who view indigenous justice systems to be "customary law," an essentially static, subordinate, and less authoritative form of law. In fact, however, contemporary indigenous systems are flexible and dynamic, and many practices and norms are of recent vintage. Indigenous legal systems are constantly adapting to changing circumstances (Orellana Halkyer 1998, 232; Sánchez Botero 2000, 224; Yrigoyen Fajardo 2000, 198). A second misconception about indigenous law is derived from the statements of some anthropologists and indigenous movement leaders, who portray indigenous communities as harmonious, homogeneous, and unified collectivities. In fact, indigenous communities typically are rent by internal conflicts, and we must resist the temptation to romanticize them (Jackson 2002, 120).

Origins. Before the arrival of Europeans, the peoples indigenous to the Americas established systems of self-government, including norms of acceptable behavior and procedures for enforcing them. Thus, indigenous law has a special character with respect to state law: its existence and authority precede the creation of the state (M. Gómez 2000, 5). The imposition of colonial rule, however, had an enormous impact on these systems. In some cases they were destroyed. Others were transformed and adapted to colonial power relations. Colonial administrators tolerated the normative, administrative, and jurisdictional activities of indigenous authorities for the management of minor, internal matters that did not impinge on state or divine law (Yrigoyen Fajardo 2000, 206). Indigenous authorities served as useful intermediaries between colonial authorities and the native population and as an efficient means of indirect social control. Some indigenous legal systems originated in the colonial period in order to link community and colonial authorities. In cases where they were designed and imposed by colonial authorities, over time, Indians appropriated and adapted them, and made them their own.

Evolution. After independence, with few exceptions, such as Colombia and Guatemala, states influenced by liberalism and positivism outlawed indigenous legal systems and enacted policies to forcibly assimilate indigenous peoples and destroy legal distinctions among ethnic groups. Despite the formal ban, however, indigenous legal systems continued to operate where indigenous communities survived. As a rule, the more remote the geographic location of indigenous cultures, the greater the relative isolation in which such authority systems developed and the greater their autonomy. In locations closer to state power structures, indigenous peoples incorporated more aspects of Western law and were more likely to coordinate their justice systems with those of the state, particularly in cases involving outsiders or serious offenses.

Indigenous legal systems survived for two reasons. First, they helped to perpetuate and defend the autonomy of indigenous cultures and the sovereignty of indigenous nations and their authorities. This function is distinct from some of the other informal institutions described in this book, which were developed by elite members of the dominant culture. Second, state legal systems, in addition to discriminating against the indigenous, tend to be inefficient, inaccessible, and culturally inappropriate for dispensing justice in indigenous communities. Indigenous justice institutions emphasize resolving conflict and restoring social harmony, thereby strengthening the community's system of reciprocal assistance and mutual responsibility. Because they are based on commonly held indigenous values and norms, they have greater legitimacy. They use indigenous languages and are socially, culturally, and geographically closer to the communities they serve. They also act faster and are less costly than the state system, since they do not require lawyers and there are usually no fees (Ochoa García n.d., 13; Yrigoyen Fajardo 1999, 44–45).

The survival of indigenous law, however, is due as much to its adaptation to new circumstances as to its retention of long-standing practices. Indigenous legal systems underwent significant transformations in the twentieth century as they adjusted to changing relations with outside actors, as well as changes within their communities. Beginning in the 1960s, in many highland areas indigenous authority systems were replaced with or subordinated to *campesino* unions. In the past decade or so, however, as indigenous identity has increased in prestige and become the subject of advantageous rights, many indigenous authority systems have been revived (Yrigoyen Fajardo 2000, 204). The pace of change increased in response to the active recuperation of indigenous authority structures, which was provoked by the emergence of strong regional and national indigenous peoples' social movements in most Latin American countries in the mid-1970s and 1980s.

For example, in two Ecuadorian Quichua communities during the past decade, communal assemblies have reformulated their internal rules, which now are reviewed annually (García Serrano 2000, 15). In one Quichua community, García found that community authorities, together with representatives from the Catholic, evangelical, and Mormon churches, had established a new justice institution—the Autonomous Social Justice Commission—that was neither a part of traditional Quichua culture nor contemplated in the 1937 Ley de Comunas. In fact, in the Quichua communities of Ecuador that he studied in the late 1990s, García found that the revived systems of indigenous justice administration had completely replaced the formal state system: lawyers and judges in cities near indigenous communities that had recently strengthened their own systems reported a "total absence of claims" by indigenous people in their offices and courts (García Serrano 2000, 15). Moreover, the superiority of indigenous justice systems to state fora was not just based on their cultural appropriateness. García's informants reported that it is common for *mestizos* and Indians from communities lacking such systems to take their disputes to the newly strengthened indigenous tribunals, particularly those disputes that the state is unable or unwilling to resolve. As the president of the Unión de Pueblos Chibuleos observed: "Even when the problem is only among *mestizos*, they come here to resolve the problem and they leave tranquilly" (García Serrano 2000, 20).

Relationship to the State. Though not officially recognized by most Latin American states until the 1990s, indigenous law has long been influenced by the state. As

Orellana Halkyer (1998) shows in the case of Bolivia, many indigenous communities are eager to learn more about state law and to obtain documents concerning legislation that affects them. Access to these laws often prompts changes that replace traditional norms. Orellana Halkyer (1998, 233) also observes an increasing tendency for indigenous authorities to mimic formal law by writing down their decisions and registering and codifying their norms, usually as a means of enhancing the legitimacy of community proceedings and decisions.

The impact of state law and the extent of cooperation between state and indigenous authorities vary, depending on the geographic proximity, strength, and effectiveness of formal legal institutions, the seriousness of the case, and the threat of state repression of indigenous authorities. All of these variables help determine whether indigenous law will compete with, complement, or substitute for state law. The most common source of competition or conflict is the fact that indigenous and Western justice institutions are based on distinct sets of cultural meanings and values (Stavenhagen 1988, 102). A key normative conflict is the priority given in indigenous law to restoring the harmony of the community, which may infringe on the rights of individuals. There are crimes in Western law that are not considered such in some indigenous communities, such as the marriage of minors, violence by husbands against their wives, and the use of corporal punishment and the death penalty. Conversely, there are transgressions in indigenous law that are not considered crimes in Western law, such as gossip and religious dissent, which are sanctioned because they disrupt the social order. Indigenous law may sanction the alleged use of supernatural powers, which Western cultures do not recognize: the burning to death of suspected witches is the classic example.

Collier (1998, 203–17) describes a case involving supernatural forces that occurred in the community of Zinacantan, Chiapas, Mexico. According to local superstition, engineers routinely use human sacrifices to ensure that their constructions endure, particularly highway bridges, which must include several human bodies or body parts. Despite the absence of evidence against seven young men accused of killing Indians and selling their bodies to engineers, they were found guilty and required to admit their guilt and to pay the transportation costs for the authorities and witnesses attending the trial in the municipal capital. Collier argues that the indigenous judges achieved their goal of protecting the accused against mob violence and calming fears in the community. Nevertheless, from a Western liberal perspective, the accused did not receive justice, since they were convicted of actions that did not even occur.

Where indigenous law complements state law, it is typically due to efforts by indigenous authorities to avoid conflict with state authorities. Indigenous authorities have learned to select from their own and state systems according to their needs, choosing the venue where they believe they will get the desired result. Indigenous authorities use remittance to state authorities as an implicit threat should transgressors wish to challenge their authority, just as the threat of state intervention causes indigenous authorities to exercise their powers with discretion (Assies 2001, 87). Authorities are likely to use state procedures and remedies if they are not sure how to proceed, when nonindigenous outsiders are involved, when their own law is incomplete or unclear, or if they are worried about the penalties for breaking state law (Orellana Halkyer 1998, 233). Indigenous authorities may serve as the first instance of adjudication for grave matters, which may subsequently be referred to the state system. They often bring the most serious offenses to state authorities, because these usually are the result of conflicts that could not be reconciled within the community or are instances of repeated violations. These are punished severely, often with banishment, because they demonstrate a rejection of the indigenous society's norms. Going to outside authorities indicates that the community no longer seeks to reintegrate the offender (M. Gómez 2000, 13–15).

Indigenous law at times substitutes for state law, particularly in remote rural areas or in urban slums founded by migrants, where state institutions have failed to establish jurisdiction. Here, indigenous law operates without interference unless some party to the dispute—or a concerned outsider—summons state authorities. In such cases, relations may become competitive or accommodating, depending on the inclination of the state and indigenous authorities to seek a mutually satisfactory solution. For example, in lowland Bolivia, the Guaraní of Alto y Bajo Izozog burned to death a suspected witch. Hearing of the incident, state authorities visited the community to apprehend and punish "those responsible." The entire community claimed responsibility, so the police had no alternative but to leave, since the jail would not accommodate hundreds of people. The incident prompted the Guaraní to write down their laws. The written version, however, does not include execution as a punishment for witchcraft, although anthropologists observe that the practice continues.[3]

Rondas Campesinas

Northern Peru's *rondas campesinas* began as community patrols that compensated for the lack of effective police protection during a time of increased criminal activity. As their effectiveness in fighting crime increased, their functions expanded. Communities came to feel a great sense of pride and ownership with respect to the *rondas,* which were imbued with the cultural symbols of Peru's northern, rural, *cam-*

pesino communities. As Starn observes, their importance transcended their functional role: "A society ripped apart by mistrust, jealousy, robbery, fighting, misery, and corruption was being recomposed. Periodization of history in the hell of 'before the ronda' and the redemption of 'after the ronda' equated order with a politics of emancipation" (1999, 96).

Ronda justice assemblies usually proceed as follows. Three or four cases are heard each night. Villagers—mostly men—gather and sit or stand in a circle, with *ronda* authorities sitting at a table together within the circle. Unlike the courts they replaced, assemblies were intended to facilitate the participation of the community, and all attendees are encouraged to speak, which is important in a culture where state authorities had imposed centuries of silence. The circle implies that no one is placed before or above anyone else. Proceedings typically begin with the *ronda* president presenting a case. The main accusing witness and the accused then state their positions. Next, anyone may offer an opinion. At first, the accused and the accuser take extreme and adamant positions; over time the crowd pressures them to be more conciliatory, ultimately demanding that they find agreement. Rather than impose a verdict, the *ronda* president attempts to find the sense of the crowd and to suggest this as a solution. Proceedings may continue until dawn or until a resolution is found. In some cases, further meetings may be required. In keeping with the Peruvian obsession with bureaucracy and documentation, northern *ronda* assemblies keep detailed written records of their activities, which are housed in community archives. Minutes are always taken, and decisions are written down and signed by all parties and witnesses to the assemblies. *Ronda* steering committees affix their personal seals to each piece of paper (Starn 1999, 126–31).

Corporal punishment was common in the first years of the *rondas* and was effective in dramatically reducing theft. Punishments incorporated sanctions common to indigenous law, such as bathing in freezing water at night, as well as punishments imposed by local police and now-defunct *hacienda* guards. For example, Starn (1999, 87) witnessed with horror the use of the "little bird" torture,[4] which had been learned from the local police, along with other abusive methods for extracting confessions that villagers believe to be part of correct police procedure. Whipping and the use of stocks were taken from *hacienda* justice. Whipping became synonymous with the *rondas*, although it usually is used only for serious or repeat offenses. To reduce the possibility of abuse of this sanction, a relative or friend of the transgressor does the whipping, which also reduces the likelihood of police intervention. An admonishment from the relative to live better in the future precedes the punishment, and afterward the punished person thanks the whipper and the community. As

the crime situation became less desperate, the *rondas'* use of violence in the northern villages studied by Starn decreased (Starn 1999, 89, 135; Degregori and Mariños
2000, 406; Ardito Vega 2001, 14).[5]

Origins. The first *rondas campesinas* were formed in 1976 in the northern Peruvian department of Cajamarca to prevent and sanction the theft of livestock, which
was rampant and had increased with an economic crisis that pushed many peasant
families to the edge. The agrarian reform of the early 1970s had rapidly destroyed the
private *hacienda* authority structures prevailing in the *sierra*, without replacing them
with a system of effective public authority. Criminals had corrupted police and
judges, leaving *campesinos* to fend for themselves. In much of the northern *sierra*,
traditional cultural authority systems had long since broken down. Thus, the *rondas*
filled a vacuum of public and private authority. The absence of traditional, culturally
based authority structures, such as those persisting in the south, required the creation
of a totally new justice institution. The form it took was based less on ethnic traditions than on the *hacienda* guards that had been organized by landowners to protect
their property in an earlier era, on perceived police procedure, and on *ronderos'*
experience of military service. In the late 1970s, hundreds of Cajamarca communities formed *rondas*. The model also was disseminated to the department of Piura,
particularly after the El Niño of 1983 caused economic devastation that forced many
peasants to steal in order to survive. By the late 1980s, *rondas* had formed in the
departments of Amazonas, Lambayeque, and Ancash, involved more than thirty-four
hundred villages and more than four hundred thousand *ronderos*, and covered more
than sixty thousand square miles of the northern Andes (Starn 1999, 4, 18, 43, 109;
Degregori and Mariños 2000, 392–403).

Evolution. As crime diminished and the authority and prestige of the *rondas*
increased, at the insistence of villagers, *rondas* increasingly took on conflict resolution functions. *Ronda* assemblies were convened to administer justice in local criminal matters and to reduce "bickering and infighting" (Starn 1999, 113). There were
several reasons why the *rondas* were more effective than the state. First, they possessed the local knowledge and resources to investigate the facts of a case, whereas
local police and judges did not know the community and lacked the resources and
interest to make on-site investigations. Second, justice was speedy in *ronda* assemblies, which in the 1980s were held once a month, on average. Three-quarters of
cases heard in Tunnel Six, Piura, were resolved in one night, whereas in the state
system cases typically took three to four years to resolve. The threat of conveying a
transgressor to the police was usually enough to get that person to accept the author-

ity of the *ronda*, since *ronda* justice is preferable to languishing in jail for years before trial. Third, trials were typically free, although Starn heard of isolated cases of *ronda* presidents charging fees or demanding bribes. The state system required fees, notaries, travel expenses, and lawyers, as well as time away from economic activities. Finally, assemblies occurred in the disputants' own community; it was not necessary to travel to the foreign, intimidating environment of the city, where humiliation and abuse were common. As the *ronda* assemblies became widely used in the northern *sierra*—each village hearing approximately a hundred disputes each year—the local police and courts saw a dramatic reduction in their caseload (Starn 1999, 123–38).

The *rondas* continued to evolve in the 1990s. By the end of the decade, they had fallen into disuse in some areas: nightly patrols had been suspended and assemblies were seldom held. This occurred in Piura, where state justice administration improved dramatically in the 1990s and community leaders were tired of the unpaid, thankless job of running the *rondas* (Starn 1999, 264). Elsewhere, in addition to controlling crime, *rondas* act as political representatives before municipal authorities and have become involved in important political issues, such as land titling. In some areas they perform some of the roles assigned to municipal governments, usually without conflict from the latter (Degregori and Mariños 2000, 407-9).[6]

Relationship to the State. The *rondas* of Peru are "substitutive" institutions, in that they filled a vacuum of policing and judicial authority. But they were not intended to take the place of the state. Rather, the goal of creating the *rondas* was to link *campesino* communities to the state and thus to "complement" formal judicial authority (Starn 1999, 60). Starn reports how the *rondas* borrowed the symbols and artifacts they associated with state authority for their activities: an old table might serve as a judge's bench; "grimy legal statutes, dispersed papers and at times a Bible" are frequently placed on the table; decisions and proceedings are recorded in a book and notarized; leaders are chosen through a secret ballot in imitation of the state political system (Starn 1991, 48, cited in Degregori and Mariños 2000, 403). But the *rondas* were not just copies of formal justice systems: villagers adapted what they perceived to be good legal practice to local values, authority structures, resources, and needs (Starn 1999, 71).

As the *rondas* grew in strength and stature, the state attempted to control and co-opt them. Efforts to legalize the *rondas* began with the 1980 democratic transition, but opposition from center-right political parties without *ronda* affiliation (such as Popular Action and the Popular Christian Party) thwarted these initial attempts. By this time, other parties, such as the center-left American Popular Revolutionary Alliance (APRA) and the leftist Red Fatherland, had infiltrated many *rondas* and organized rival *ronda* federations. In 1986, APRA president Alan García promulgated the Rondas Campesinas Law, which gave *rondas* legal standing to resist attacks from police and the authority to protect individual and community property.

The army used the *ronda* model in the late 1980s and early 1990s to organize southern *campesinos* against Sendero Luminoso (the Shining Path). By the mid-1980s, the southern Andes, the center of fighting between the army and Sendero, had become militarized. Those who suffered most were *campesino* communities, which increasingly sought means to protect themselves from both sides. In the southern highlands, traditional authorities and cultures were stronger than in the north and these provided a resource for collective resistance. In fact, the first anti-Sendero *campesino* rebellions occurred in response to attacks on indigenous community authorities, particularly when these substituted young *senderistas* for older authorities. To assist the *campesinos* in fighting Sendero, in 1991 the army distributed more than ten thousand Winchester shotguns to the new *rondas*. But these antiinsurgency *rondas* had an origin and purpose distinct from the ones described above, and they were subordinate to existing forms of traditional authority (Starn 1992, 90).

Legal projects to define and constrain the *rondas* followed, and continue to this day. Peru's 1993 Constitution recognized their jurisdiction but, thus far, legal recognition has been confined to protection of property and self-defense (Starn 1992, 105; Degregori and Mariños 2000, 404). Degregori and Mariños (2000, 407) argue that the Peruvian state has failed to take advantage of the potential of the *rondas* to fill the huge gap in the availability of justice administration by formally linking them to the local police, to local government, or to the system of justices of the peace. Perhaps this is just as well, since the informality of the *rondas* continues to be an important part of their identity and, perhaps, their strongest source of legitimacy and autonomy. This situation may change as a result of Law 27908 (2003), which recognized the jurisdiction of the *rondas* with respect to conflict resolution and called for local public authorities to establish relations of coordination with them.

Juntas Vecinales

Most informal legal systems exist in rural, usually isolated communities, but in Bolivia, migrants to squatter settlements on the outskirts of Cochabamba and La Paz have constructed their own justice systems at the margins of state law. These systems are deeply rooted in the Andean cultures of the rural sending communities, but their written, internal rules incorporate Western norms, structures, and procedures.

This section is based on a 1997 Bolivian government study of four urban barrios (Ministerio de Justicia 1997a, 1997b),[7] two in El Alto (on the outskirts of La Paz) and two in the city of Cochabamba, that developed their own informal legal systems within the quasi-formal institution of the *junta vecinal* (neighborhood junta) (1997b). More than a system of justice administration or dispute resolution, the *juntas* provide a highly legitimate form of local government that represents the will of the community. In all four cases there are two parallel, linked fora for conflict resolution: the disciplinary tribunal, composed of a few of the most honest and respected members of the community, and the direct action of the president and the secretary of conflicts/justice. Although the duties of *junta* authorities are broad and explicit—encompassing disputes over private property, abuse of public authority, crime and delinquency, and domestic relations—the norms of justice administration that they implement are not. The tribunal investigates complaints and offers a solution or mediates an accord among the disputing parties. The solution is then recorded in the Libro de Actas. In Villa Adela, El Alto, the tribunal conducts the investigation and then forwards its report to the General Assembly of Neighbors, which discusses the issues raised and chooses a sanction. The Federation of Juntas Vecinales of the municipality might be asked to review the decision in cases where the *junta* is unsure of itself (1997b, 65).

Frequently, people seek the direct intervention of the *junta* president or secretary of conflicts. The written duties of these officials are typically to negotiate and find consensus with respect to disputes over the boundaries of urban plots and the buildings upon them, to negotiate disputes over the use of land, to assist in drawing district limits, and to serve as an intermediary in disputes among neighbors or between them and another private or public entity. Most of these duties are actually illegal—*juntas* do not have the legal authority to settle property issues, which are the purview of municipal authorities. Nevertheless, the majority of disputes addressed by the secretary of conflicts and the *junta* president are related to property disputes, which also are the main source of intracommunity conflict in rural Aymara communities. Since most urban property claims are not based on legal rights (claimants are squatters), the *juntas* are the preferred venue (1997a, 23; 1997b, 39, 43).

Junta procedures incorporate Andean spirituality. In the Cochabamba barrio of Alto Sebastián Pagador, it is common for the aggrieved party to consult a *yatiri* (seer) to ascertain the truth of a matter, the person responsible (if unknown), or the appropriate sanction. In El Alto, aggrieved parties also may privately seek the advice of a *yatiri*, and *junta* authorities will invoke the norms of their ancestors as they begin the task of conflict resolution. Sanctioning takes place in the rural fashion, before a crucifix and Bible, which are set upon a block of salt. The accused apologizes, promises not to make the mistake again, and asks forgiveness. The sanctioning phase, over which the oldest community member presides, most often draws on

Andean culture. The community elder's ritual participation "seals the act with more validity than a written paper" (1997b, 65; my translation). A fine is usually imposed and registered in the Libro de Actas. The most common punishments are verbal warnings (public or private), economic restitution and/or fines, and temporary suspension of political rights. In the most serious cases or for repeated offenses—and this happens only rarely—a person might be expelled from the community. Instead of physical punishment there is a marked preference for resolving the problem with a warning or nonpunitive agreement, or for the imposition of a fine (1997b, 63–64). However, since punishments expected to elicit state condemnation or retribution may not be entered in the *juntas'* records, the government's study may in fact understate the incidence of corporal punishment.

Origins and Evolution. The origins of the *juntas* are similar to those of the *rondas.* Communities in Bolivia formed the *juntas* to address the lack of state attention to urgent community needs. Whereas the *rondas* reduced theft, the role of the *juntas* was to defend, before the municipal government, the communities' demands for property and for access to urban infrastructure and public services to meet basic housing, health, education, and transportation needs. Thus, in both cases, justice administration was a subsidiary, albeit important, function at the time of origin.

Whereas the *rondas* were invented anew in the absence of traditional ethnic authority structures, the *juntas* adapted contemporary rural Aymara and Quechua cultural and authority institutions. Thus, the *juntas* may be considered either a new informal institution or a relatively sudden transformation and transplantation of an existing one. Although there is considerable variation, in many places urban barrios are essentially mono-ethnic and may even be composed predominantly of migrants from one province. Ethnic norms and authority structures are more predominant in El Alto's Aymara migrant communities, because their rural authority structures (*ayllus*) are relatively strong. For example, the barrio of Alto Lima exhibits all the traits of Aymara culture fused with the labor union experience of many Aymara ex-miners. The urban justice system is quite similar to the rural Aymara justice system, except that formal procedures are more strictly followed in order to lend a "greater veneer of legality in an 'illegal' environment" (1997b, 69; my translation). In the Quechua barrios around Cochabamba, by contrast, customs are as likely to be adapted from *campesino* union norms and procedures, since most of the *ayllus* in the Cochabamba valley have been destroyed and the region has experienced a greater degree of *mestizaje* (cultural mixing) (1997b, 28).

In some respects, *juntas vecinales* are highly bureaucratized institutions. Authorities are differentiated and ranked, and their functions and duties are carefully written down in by-laws. The selection of authorities is based not on age or knowledge of culture, as in indigenous communities, but rather on traits that increase their effectiveness in the urban environment, such as wealth, social status, and Spanish literacy. Some *juntas* require authorities to have served in the military and/or to be heads of household, which excludes women. *Junta* presidents and vice presidents are usually the most influential, wealthiest men of the community (1997b, 35-39). Detailed notes of meetings, resolutions of conflicts, sanctions, and other business of the *junta* are carefully recorded in a Libro de Actas, as occurs today in rural Andean communities. In both settings, if the authorities believe that certain procedures or sanctions violate state law, they may omit them from the written record.

Relationship with the State. Relations between the *juntas* and municipal authorities vary. In Villa Adela, El Alto, the *junta* has "fluid" relations with the police, and these have improved in recent years. In Alto Lima Primera Sección, El Alto, where there is no police presence despite the repeated entreaties of the *junta*, the *junta* carries out police functions itself, using a system of whistles that alert the community to a problem. If one or more of the parties to a dispute is not satisfied with the *junta*'s decision, he or she may bring the dispute to the state authorities, but not before requesting the permission of the *junta*. This is an unlikely event, since state justice institutions are more costly and likely to be less helpful to culturally distinct migrants. Conversely, *junta* authorities may decline to handle serious problems, such as rape or murder, and refer them to the state (1997b, 58–71). An estimated four to eight thousand *juntas vecinales* throughout Bolivia gained legal standing through the 1994 Law of Popular Participation, which conferred collective participation rights on *campesino* communities, indigenous communities, and *juntas vecinales*. These new rights, however, are related to community planning and budgeting, rather than justice administration. The *juntas*' justice administration function is not recognized in the 1994 constitutional language that officially sanctioned indigenous customary law. Thus, like the *rondas*, the *juntas vecinales* are not formally permitted to administer justice.

Table 12.1 summarizes the most important features of the three types of informal justice institution discussed above. The commonality of norms, sanctions, duties, and procedures among these types is attributable to the fact that all three systems are based on the interplay of two features common to Latin America: long-standing practices and cultural norms common to indigenous peoples in its rural areas, and state procedures and norms that share similar features throughout the region. In all three types of justice system, authorities have a broad mandate to resolve disputes

TABLE 12.1
A Comparison of Informal Justice Administration Systems

	Indigenous law	*Rondas campesinas*	*Juntas vecinales*
Reasons for original emergence	Regulate social life; perpetuate culture; relate to colonial authorities	Protect against theft	Replicate rural culture in urban space; present collective demands to local public authorities; mediate property disputes
Current purposes served	Preserve political and territorial autonomy; complement or substitute for state justice system	Deter and punish crime; resolve internal conflicts; provide more efficient, effective justice administration; represent community to outsiders	Same as above
Scope of issues considered	Broad, including penal, domestic, and religious issues, administrative law, and dispute resolution	Broad, including penal and domestic issues and dispute resolution	Most commonly concerns access to land and public services; also penal and domestic issues
Typical sanctions imposed	Mild corporal punishment, brief detention, economic restitution, community labor; more serious offenses: expulsion, severe corporal punishment, death, remit to state system	Mild, ritual whipping, economic restitution, community service, brief detention; more serious offenses: expulsion, death, remit to state justice system	Verbal warning, fines, loss of property or political rights; most serious cases: expulsion
Authorities and organizational structures	Juridical authorities fused with religious and political authorities, chosen through community customs	Village men elect authorities; decisions made by consensus of community, with guidance of president	Highly bureaucratized and hierarchical system of Western-style authorities, with differentiation of functions
Relationship to formal system	Varies, depending on status of state recognition	De jure subordination to police and local courts; de facto autonomy, with varying levels of coordination with state	Judicial functions not recognized by the state; degree of coordination varies

and to restore the harmony of the community in the absence of a more authoritative and accessible institution. The relationship of these informal justice institutions to the state varies according to the geographic and cultural distance of the state authorities, as well as the propensity of community-state relations to be cooperative or conflictual. The main difference among the systems is the extent to which traditional indigenous cultural identities and norms permeate the provision of justice. Indigenous law tends to reflect modern-day interpretations of traditional indigenous culture and typically is practiced in the traditional rural community setting. *Rondas campesinas* tend to adopt more features from state institutions to be used in traditional rural settings, whereas *juntas vecinales* bring traditional cultural practices to a nontraditional, urban setting, which requires some adaptation to a new environment and closer proximity to state institutions and formal politics.

THE FORMAL RECOGNITION OF INFORMAL JUSTICE
ADMINISTRATION: CHALLENGES AND IMPLICATIONS

The development of indigenous legal institutions entered a new era in the 1990s, when Latin American constitutions began to formally recognize their public authority and legal jurisdiction as part of a larger effort to recognize ethnic diversity and collective rights for indigenous peoples. Bolivia, Colombia, Ecuador, Mexico, Nicaragua, Paraguay, Peru, and Venezuela explicitly recognized the multicultural or multiethnic nature of societies in their revised constitutions. This recognition provides the normative framework for the recognition of legal pluralism. Bolivia, Colombia, Ecuador, Peru, and Venezuela have extended the most constitutional or statutory recognition to indigenous legal institutions, with Mexico also extending at least formal recognition in the 1990 and 2001 constitutional reforms. In addition, the constitutions of Guatemala, Nicaragua, Panama, and Paraguay make some reference to customary law (Assies 2001, 83) (see table 12.2).

There are three main reasons for this formal recognition. First, states responded to intense pressure from indigenous organizations to recognize their collective rights as peoples, following decades of activism and political organization by indigenous peoples' organizations. The demand for official recognition of indigenous law is an integral part of the articulation of the demand of all indigenous movements in the Americas: the demand for *self-determination* as peoples. This term encompasses the right to self-government and the autonomy to freely develop their political, legal, economic, social, and cultural institutions, while achieving full representation in the state political system. In the face of centuries of state *injustice* directed toward indigenous communities, the demand for autonomy in the administration of justice is particularly important (Sieder 1999, 111).

Second, international norms for the treatment of indigenous peoples developed in the 1980s require states to recognize indigenous law. Most important among them is International Labor Organization Convention 169 (1989) on the rights of indigenous and tribal peoples. Among the broad set of rights that ILO Convention 169 codifies, it requires that states allow indigenous communities to conserve their legal customs and institutions, provided that they do not violate fundamental rights as defined by national or international law (art. 8, art. 9). Mexico (1990), Colombia (1991), Bolivia (1991), Costa Rica (1993), Paraguay (1993), Peru (1994), Honduras (1995), Guatemala (1996), Ecuador (1998), Argentina (1999), Brazil (2002), Dominica (2002), and Venezuela (2002) have ratified the convention, which also requires that states adjust their national legislation to apply its norms, although the

TABLE 12.2
State Recognition of Indigenous Law in Latin America

Bolivia: 1967 Constitution, reformed 1995, art. 171. The natural authorities of the indigenous and *campesino* communities may exercise functions of administration and application of their own norms as an alternative solution in conflicts, in conformity with their customs and procedures, always providing that they are not contrary to the Constitution and the laws.

Brazil: 1988 Constitution and 1999 reforms, art. 231. The Indians' social organization, customs, languages, beliefs, and traditions are recognized, and the original rights over the lands that they traditionally occupy.

Chile: Law 19,253(1993), art. 54. Custom shall be taken into account in judgments among Indians belonging to the same ethnic group, it shall constitute law, provided that it is not incompatible with the Political Constitution of the Republic. In penal law it shall be considered when it can serve as an antecedent for the application of an exemption or extenuating circumstance.

Colombia: 1991 Constitution, art. 246. The authorities among the native peoples may exercise judicial functions within their territorial areas in accordance with their own rules and procedures, which must not be contrary to the Constitution and laws of the Republic.

Ecuador: 1998 Constitution, art. 191. The authorities of the indigenous peoples may exercise functions of justice, applying their own norms and procedures for the solution of internal conflicts in conformity with their customs or customary law, provided that they are not contrary to the Constitution and the laws.

Guatemala: 1995 Accord on the Identity and Rights of the Indigenous Peoples, IV, E, 3. "In order to strengthen the juridical security of the indigenous communities, the government promises to promote before the legislative organism, with the participation of the indigenous organizations, the development of legal norms recognizing the indigenous communities and the management of their internal issues in accord with their customary norms, provided that these are not incompatible with the fundamental rights defined by the national juridical system nor with internationally recognized human rights" (Yrigoyen Fajardo 1999, 67–68).

Mexico: 1917 Constitution, mod. 2001, art. 2. This Constitution recognizes and guarantees the right of the indigenous peoples and communities to self-determination and, in consequence, to the autonomy to: I. Decide the internal forms of social, economic, political, and cultural organization. II. To apply their own normative systems in the regulation and solution of their internal conflicts, subjecting these to the general principles of this Constitution, respecting individual guarantees, human rights, and in the manner relevant, the dignity and integrity of women.

Nicaragua: 1987 Constitution, art. 89. The communities of the Atlantic Coast have the right . . . to have their own forms of social organization and to administer their internal issues according to their traditions.

Panama: Recognized through ordinary legislation regulating the indigenous comarcas (autonomous reserves), especially Law 16 of 1953, creating the first Kuna comarca.

Paraguay: 1992 Constitution, art. 63. The right of indigenous peoples to preserve and develop their identity within their respective habitat is recognized and guaranteed. They have the right, as well, to freely apply their systems of political, social, economic, cultural, and religious organization, as well as the voluntary subjection to their customary norms for the regulation of their internal lifestyle, provided that these do not violate the fundamental rights established in this Constitution.

Peru: 1993 Constitution, art. 149. The authorities of the *Campesino* and Native Communities, with the support of the *Rondas Campesinas*, may exercise jurisdictional functions within their territorial ambit in conformity with the customary law, always provided that they do not violate the fundamental rights of the person.

Venezuela: 1999 Constitution, art. 260. The legitimate authorities of the indigenous peoples may apply in their habitat instances of justice based in their ancestral traditions, and that only affect their own members, according to their own norms and procedures, provided that they are not contrary to the Constitution, to the law, and to public order.

Note: All language is my own translation from the original Spanish or Portuguese, except where noted.

convention is automatically in effect without such legislation. The broad set of indigenous rights recognized by ILO Convention 169, together with domestic pressure from indigenous organizations and their allies, resulted in the codification of an unprecedented number of indigenous rights in Latin American constitutions during the 1990s (Van Cott 2000a).

Finally, states recognizing indigenous law sought to extend the presence of public law throughout their territories, particularly in rural areas. In the 1980s, Latin American states and international organizations began to focus attention on serious deficiencies in the region's justice systems. In Colombia—the first country to constitutionally recognize, in 1991, indigenous legal jurisdiction—constitution-makers sought to extend public law and authority into the one-quarter of Colombian territory covered by indigenous reserves. This was intended as a counterweight to control by guerrillas, paramilitaries, and drug traffickers. Influenced by the Colombian example, Bolivian constitution-makers sought to extend the rule of law into vast rural areas unserved by police or courts (Van Cott 2000a, 2000b). Many of the projects now underway to recognize indigenous law are sponsored by international organizations (United Nations, United Nations Development Program, International Development Bank, Organization of American States, World Bank), and bilateral aid is part of a larger international effort to improve the administration of justice in Latin America, while conforming to contemporary standards for the treatment of disadvantaged groups (Sieder 1998, 112; 2003, 142; García Serrano 2000; Assies 2003). Thus, constitution-makers believed that linking existing, effective, authoritative, and highly legitimate informal justice institutions to the state would lend effectiveness, authority, and legitimacy to the state justice system—both through the very act of recognition and through the increased supply of justice available to society's most marginalized and underserved groups. Informal justice institutions relieve the overburdened and resource-deficient police and courts of cases that can be solved with fewer resources by informal authorities.

At the insistence of indigenous peoples' organizations, in most cases indigenous law remains within a zone of autonomy that can be entered by the state only in cases of serious violations of human or high-ranking constitutional rights. The *formal recognition* of indigenous law or other community justice administration institutions, therefore, should not be confused with the *formalization* of those institutions, since they continue to operate in a sphere that is not regulated by the state and not subject to its values and norms, except in a narrow range of unusual cases. Formal recognition actually decreased the propensity of the state to interfere with indigenous authorities, since it made these activities legal. In sum, from the perspective of the state, formal recognition made indigenous law public rather than private, and legal rather than illegal, but not *formal*, since it remains beyond the regulatory reach of a centrally controlled, normatively distinct legal system.

From the perspective of indigenous peoples, however, indigenous law is formal law—binding, authoritative, and deeply rooted in indigenous norms and cultures, even when some practices are of recent origin. Indigenous law constitutes, orders, and preserves the sovereignty of indigenous society and forms of self-government, just as state law constitutes, orders, and preserves the larger state and society. And this is the perspective promoted by the new multicultural constitutions, which hold indigenous law to be equal to state law by virtue of the equality of the cultures from which both emanate and by virtue of the equal contribution of all cultures to the nation. In addition, because of the underlying context of ethnic domination, indigenous law is an expression and an affirmation of indigenous peoples' right to self-determination and, thus, may be better described from the indigenous point of view as a "counter-formal" institution.

THE CHALLENGE OF COORDINATION

Extending formal recognition to informal justice institutions and linking them to the state raises important theoretical and practical issues. To a certain extent, the value of informal justice institutions is their informality: their authority deriving from social values and meanings that have great authority, as well as the flexibility and dynamism afforded by their (mostly) uncodified status (Sieder 1998, 107). Is this authority, flexibility, and dynamism lost if community authorities are authorized to act as agents of the state? Formal recognition has led in some cases to the writing down of indigenous customary law by experts hired by the state, or by indigenous peoples themselves. But recognition and codification may have negative effects. Codification tends to give the law a static nature that is not characteristic of informal law and ignores the fact that the claim being recognized is not to a particular set of norms that are practiced faithfully but rather to the right of distinct peoples to make their own norms (von Benda-Beckmann 1997, 30). Disruptive internal debates emerge as certain aspects of the law are selected and become the "official version." On the positive side, recognition has caused some indigenous organizations to seek to avoid interference by nonindigenous courts by strengthening their own justice practices, particularly with regard to respect for human rights, and by creating new mechanisms for appeals in controversial cases (Assies 2003, 15).

All five Andean constitutions (Bolivia, Colombia, Ecuador, Peru, and Venezuela) call for the creation of a law to "compatibilize" or "coordinate" the potentially competing jurisdictions of state and indigenous law, but this has proved difficult to achieve in practice, given the lack of knowledge about indigenous law among Western legal scholars and judges and the complexity of the issues involved. These difficulties can be divided into conflicts related to process, norms, and sanctions.

Conflicts Related to Process. Western systems, in order to provide consistent administration of justice across society, are based on written rules and precedent. Indigenous systems, by contrast, are flexible and dynamic. It is more important to indigenous communities to provide the appropriate resolution in a specific case than to provide a justice "product" that is consistent over time and space. Indigenous legal procedures may violate liberal-democratic standards of due process, such as the right to an attorney, and may discriminate against women, since the vast majority of indigenous authorities are men.

Conflicts of Norms. The conflict between a state's liberal tradition, which privileges individual rights, and indigenous peoples' emphasis on collective rights has prevented or delayed the writing of implementing legislation satisfactory to both parties (Sierra 1998, 25). Often it is difficult for courts to determine what indigenous norms are, since many Western norms and procedures have been incorporated into indigenous cultures over the years. Another source of normative conflict is the use of religion. In indigenous systems, religious beliefs may be central to the judgment, investigation, and punishment of transgressions, since there is no distinction between religious and politico-juridical authority (Stavenhagen 1988, 101). Crimes may be attributed to supernatural forces, which may conceal and perpetuate power imbalances.

Conflicts over Sanctions. Sanctions imposed by indigenous authorities typically involve some combination of brief confinement, mild forms of corporal punishment, compulsory community labor, and indemnification of the victim or the victim's family. Expulsion from the community and death are reserved for repeated instances of the most serious offenses, after lighter sanctions have failed to moderate the transgressor's behavior. Indeed, it is not uncommon for a victim's family to seek to move the proceedings to state courts because indigenous sanctions are likely to be lighter. The state most often intervenes when defendants or observers claim that sanctions violate the defendant's human or constitutional rights. Such accusations have been troubling to indigenous organizations, since most recognize the authority of international human rights conventions and, indeed, regularly make claims based upon them (Kymlicka 1995, 169; Assies 2003, 15). The accusations have generated internal debates within the communities. In some cases, practices that could not bear scrutiny have been altered.

Legislators in Bolivia, Ecuador, Peru, and Venezuela have drafted legislation implementing indigenous jurisdiction. All of these projects were pending in 2003, mainly due to conflicts regarding three issues in particular. (1) Should indigenous jurisdiction be mandatory or optional? (2) Should crimes or disputes involving non-Indians or Indians from distinct cultures be handled differently or remitted to the state? (3) Should indigenous jurisdiction be defined geographically or personally? In addition, indigenous peoples' representatives usually resist any limitation on the scope of their autonomy, such as the national constitution and ordinary laws and judicial bodies such as the constitutional or supreme court, since they view indigenous law and state law as inherently equal. This position elides the fact that indigenous peoples are part of a larger political community that is governed by a constitution and that, with few exceptions, indigenous communities demand participation in that larger political community. Indeed, indigenous delegates participated in constituent assemblies in Colombia, Ecuador, Paraguay, and Venezuela. However, as Kymlicka (1995, 169) observes, most indigenous peoples did not participate in the drafting of their national constitutions, and they object to having their own norms subject to review by nonindigenous justices who interpret the constitutions of their conquerors.

The draft proposals coordinating indigenous and state jurisdictions address these questions in various ways. The Bolivian, Ecuadorian, and Venezuelan projects view indigenous justice as mandatory, although in Bolivia non-Indians in indigenous territories are exempt from indigenous law. The Ecuadorian proposal expressly includes non-Indians but includes stipulations for handling these cases. In Venezuela, all persons within indigenous territories are subject to indigenous jurisdiction, and indigenous authorities have jurisdiction, if they choose to exercise it, over Indians outside indigenous territory. Similarly, in the draft Peruvian law, any person within the territorial jurisdiction of native or *campesino* communities is subject to these authorities (*rondas* gained this authority in Law $27908/_{2002}$).

NONLEGISLATIVE MEANS OF RECOGNIZING AND LINKING INFORMAL JUSTICE INSTITUTIONS

In the absence of legislation specifying the relationship of indigenous to state law, states have developed other means of implementing the constitutional recognition of indigenous law: through the development of (1) jurisprudence, as cases are brought before the courts, and (2) institutional relations between the state and indigenous justice systems. Colombia's Constitutional Court has acted as a de facto legislator in the absence of implementing legislation. No other higher court has yet done this (Cabedo Mallol 1998, 7).[8] Although often contradictory, taken together the Court's rulings have established a broad scope for the exercise of indigenous law. Because nearly all the issues that may be expected to arise have reached the Court in the last decade, Colombia provides an interesting model for states trying to implement legal pluralism.

A 1994 case (Sentence T-254) established three important principles for linking state and indigenous law. First, cultural traditions are to be respected to the extent that those traditions have been preserved; that is, the less contact with and permeation by Western culture, the greater the scope for cultural autonomy in the application of special indigenous jurisdiction. Second, indigenous authorities must not in their decisions or sanctions violate international human rights or fundamental constitutional rights of a higher rank than cultural diversity. Third, indigenous law ranks above ordinary civil law and ordinary legislation that does not protect fundamental constitutional rights. The issue of conflicting views of due process was raised in a 1996 case (Sentence T-349) in which an indigenous defendant claimed his rights had been violated because he had not been allowed to use an attorney before community justice authorities and because the authorities had sentenced him to confinement in a state jail, an unusual sentence for this community. The Court ruled against the claimant, arguing that use of an attorney was not a community norm. In that case the Court established an important rule: when limitations are necessary to defend constitutional rights of a higher rank, such limitations must have the minimum possible impact on indigenous autonomy and cultural integrity. The Court concluded that these "intangible rights" are confined to "the right to life, the prohibition on slavery and the prohibition of torture," because there is an "intercultural consensus" on these rights (Assies 2003, 4).

The most sensational indigenous jurisdiction case in Colombia occurred in 1996–97. Seven men were accused of being the "intellectual authors" of the murder of the indigenous mayor of the mainly Páez (also called Nasa) town of Jambaló. The Jambaló *cabildo* (community government) found the accused guilty and sentenced them to whippings with a leather whip, expelled them from the community, and stripped them of their political rights as Indians. The principal defendant took the case to the municipal criminal court in Santander de Quilichao, which ruled that the *cabildo* had denied the defendants the opportunity to defend themselves, that the judges in the case were politically biased, and that the whipping constituted torture and thus was illegal under international law. A higher court affirmed the lower court ruling. The Páez Cabildo Association of the North then took the case to the Constitutional Court, which ruled that whipping, although incorporated from Spanish colonial culture, had become part of Páez culture and that its use inflicted no permanent, serious harm (Sentence T-523/1997). Moreover, its object was not to cause pain or humiliation but to purify the accused and thus facilitate his or her reintegration into the community (an argument that conflicts with the simultaneous expulsion of the accused in this case). Sánchez Botero deems this ruling to be "truly paradigmatic from the hermeneutical point of view" (2000, 232), because it recognized a broad scope of autonomy for indigenous authorities based on recognition of the existence of non-Western symbolic orders that give meaning to non-Western cultures.

In essence, Colombia's Constitutional Court sustained Kymlicka's "multicultural" interpretation (1995, 167) of the responsibility of liberal states with respect to violations of individual rights by illiberal national minorities: they must not impose liberal values on groups that do not share those values, but must endeavor instead to negotiate peacefully with illiberal national minorities, as they would with foreign countries, except in cases of severe violations of human rights, such as slavery or genocide. In fact, in Colombia, state agencies often intervene to negotiate a compromise when an indigenous individual seeks protection against the illiberal rulings of indigenous authorities. Sánchez Botero relates an enlightening example. The mother and maternal uncle of a Wayúu girl who had been educated outside her community instructed her to return to the community to be married following her first menstruation. The girl filed a writ of protection with a court "to protect her fundamental rights to education and free development of the person" (Sánchez Botero 2000, 228). The court did not impose a solution; instead, representatives of the girl and officials of the state Service for the Protection of the Minor negotiated with the community authorities. The girl was allowed to stay in school and to decide in five years whether she wished to return to the community, at which time her status would be reevaluated. An exchange of animals occurred to compensate the family for the loss of wealth that would have accrued from the girl's marriage. This solution restored the economic equilibrium of the tribe while protecting the minor from an early forced marriage.

Another way of linking indigenous and state justice systems is through the creation of community justices of the peace, who work with indigenous authorities while representing the state. Such projects are underway in Guatemala and Peru. In Peru, justices of the peace sometimes incorporate local indigenous customs and norms into their procedures and decisions or divide the work of justice administration with native or *campesino* authorities (Ardito Vega 2001, 10). Where local authorities are effective and legitimate, justices may perform a mainly ceremonial or notarial role and relegate most of the administration of justice to the *rondas campesinas*, and even participate in *ronda* activities. In some cases, community authorities may refer cases to the justices of the peace, while, in turn, justices may ask community authorities to act as guarantors of their decisions or sanctions—for example, making sure that the transgressor completes his community service—or to capture a community member to be brought before the judge. In Guatemala, the United Nations is sponsoring a project to create community justices of the peace to serve in Mayan communities where there is no formal authority. These community justices of the peace are not an organic part of Mayan social and political organization and, because the communities themselves did not select them, they may lack legitimacy. They also challenge existing traditional authorities and indigenous mayors, and they create a separation of political and juridical powers that does not exist in indigenous culture (Murgas Armas 1999, 326-41). Nevertheless, the new community justices of the peace have improved access to bilingual justice administration in Mayan communities, while making it more culturally sensitive (Sieder 2003, 144–45).

CONCLUSION

Where the state has extended formal recognition to informal institutions, they take on a somewhat ambiguous status as autonomous informal institutions that are protected from state regulation, subject to certain limitations. From the perspective of indigenous peoples and the region's most "multicultural" constitutions, informal institutions derived from indigenous cultures may be considered "counter-formal" institutions, because of their legal equality and historical precedence with respect to the state. But in most places, where there has been little or no legal recognition, community justice institutions remain informal and relations may be competing and conflictual.

What are the implications of the foregoing for the quality of democracy, particularly in the region's most multiethnic countries? Latin American legal systems that recognize indigenous law and other forms of informal justice administration better correspond to their heterogeneous social reality. They are less discriminatory, more flexible, and thus more just (Yrigoyen Fajardo 1999, 9). Improved access to appropriate legal protection helps construct citizenship for society's most excluded groups, particularly in societies that have a long history of discrimination (Sieder 1998, 98). O'Donnell (1993) acknowledges this when he links "low-intensity citizenship" to the inability of the state to establish the rule of law. Where states are too weak to provide justice, informal institutions can substitute for state efforts and thereby improve the quality of citizenship. Although formal recognition seems to be necessary to avoid jurisdictional conflicts, it also seems necessary that informal institutions retain a good deal of the "informality" from which their autonomy and authority are derived.

Many scholars observe that the autonomy and authority of informal justice institutions enable them to serve as spaces of empowerment. Moore (1986) writes of "semi-autonomous circles of power" or "semi-autonomous social fields," while Nader (1980) uses the term "subaltern counter-publics." Assies (2001, 93) and Yrigoyen Fajardo (1999, 41) view indigenous law as spaces of autonomy from which subaltern groups can engage in an equitable intercultural dialogue with the state and the dominant culture. Others argue that informal institutions may improve the quality of state law. For example, Sierra (1998, 39) argues that indigenous peoples' quest for autonomous spheres of self-government can serve as a model of decentralized democratization for Latin American societies, and Chambers (1997, 426–27) holds that recognizing cultural diversity and human rights provides a source of legitimacy to states that have lost the moral center previously derived from constitutional invocations of God and Catholicism.

Legal pluralism advocates may overestimate the macrosocietal benefit of recognizing informal justice institutions: first, because the deficiencies in democracy and the rule of law in Latin America are so vast that many other reforms are needed to achieve improvement; and second, because informal justice institutions have many flaws that reflect the jealousies, power imbalances, cruelty, and ignorance that are common to all human groups. Connecting informal and formal institutions, however, has provoked a constructive intercultural debate on the flaws of both, and their increasing mutual accountability should draw attention to these flaws and the need to rectify them.

Conclusion

GRETCHEN HELMKE AND STEVEN LEVITSKY

It is by now widely accepted among students of democratic institutions that informal rules matter. Indeed, as scholarly and policy debates about Latin American politics have shifted from issues of democratization to those of democratic governance and quality, the impact of informal institutions has become increasingly salient. Informal rules shape how—and how well—electoral systems, legislatures, judiciaries, and other democratic institutions work. In some cases, they reinforce democratic institutions by enhancing their effectiveness or stability; in other cases, they weaken democratic institutions by creating incentives to subvert them. For this reason, scholars seeking to explain formal institutional outcomes—as well as policymakers seeking to craft effective democratic institutions—must take informal institutions seriously.

The prevalence of informal institutions in the developing world suggests a need to broaden the scope of institutionalist analysis in comparative politics. As we noted in the introduction to this volume, the contemporary literature on political institutions in Latin America focuses largely on formal rules, and much of it simply assumes a direct causal link between parchment rules and political behavior. Parchment rules *do*, of course, matter in Latin America, and recent studies of formal institutions in the region have generated a wealth of important new knowledge. However, formal rule-driven behavior hardly exhausts the universe of institutional life in the region. Rather, the rules of the game that structure politics vary along two dimensions: strength (or enforcement) and formality. Formal rules may be routinely enforced or complied with, but they may also be widely ignored.[1] And the rules that actors enforce or comply with may be formal or informal. Instead of taking for granted that formal rules are both effective and predominant, then, it is more accurate to treat formal institutional predominance as one of several possible institutional scenarios. Actors may operate in a context of strong formal and informal rules, as the chapters on Chile show. Alternatively, weakly enforced formal rules may be trumped by informal ones, as in the case of campaign finance in Brazil, norms of police violence in Brazil, and candidate selection during the heyday of Mexico's Party of the Institutional Revolution (PRI). Finally, both formal and informal rules may be weak, in that neither effectively guides actors' behavior.[2] Scholars of Latin American politics who assume away these latter institutional scenarios do so at great peril.

The chapters in this volume challenge widely held conceptions about informal institutions in Latin America. For example, whereas informal institutions are often viewed as deeply entrenched and slow to change, many are in fact quite dynamic. As the Eisenstadt and Langston chapters on Mexico show (and as Carey and Siavelis predict in the case of Chile), informal institutional change may occur quite suddenly. Moreover, as Van Cott's chapter makes clear, even apparently long-standing indigenous laws have, in many cases, been repeatedly modified and reinvented as indigenous communities interacted with state authorities. An important lesson is that informal institutions should not be treated as permanent fixtures in the political landscape. Even where informal institutions prove highly robust (e.g., clientelism in Honduras), it is essential to examine the *sources* of that stability.

The chapters also challenge the notion that informality is uniformly corrosive of democratic institutions. Although corruption, clientelism, and patrimonialism remain widespread—and highly consequential—in Latin America, their pervasiveness should not obscure the existence of informal institutions that strengthen the performance or quality of democracy. These include unwritten power-sharing arrangements that promote multiparty or executive-legislative cooperation in presidential democracies (Siavelis; Carey and Siavelis), norms that sustain or enhance electoral accountability (Stokes), and informal legal systems that deliver justice in communities where the rule of law is weak (Van Cott). To this list we might add numerous informal institutions with ambiguous or double-edged effects. "Ghost coalitions" eroded transparency and accountability in the Ecuadorian legislature, but they also enhanced governability (Mejía Acosta). Mexican *concertacesiones* undermined the electoral process and circumvented the judiciary, but they also facilitated the resolution of postelectoral conflicts and helped the opposition National Action Party (PAN) break down the PRI's monopoly of power (Eisenstadt). And as Taylor-Robinson argues, Honduran clientelism plays an important "substitutive" role by inducing otherwise nationally oriented politicians to attend to local needs.

BEYOND LATIN AMERICA: INFORMAL INSTITUTIONS AND POLITICS IN THE DEVELOPING WORLD

The central themes of this volume travel beyond Latin America. Although we cannot possibly do justice to the growing body of literature on informal institutions in Africa, Asia, the Middle East, and postcommunist Eurasia, this section briefly sketches out how the typology discussed in the introduction—complementary, accommodating, competing, and substitutive informal institutions—might be applied elsewhere.[3]

As in Latin America, the bulk of the research on informal institutions in the developing and postcommunist worlds has focused on competing informal institutions, or those that directly subvert formal rules. Two types of competing informal institution may be identified. The first is particularism—that is, particularistic norms such as corruption, clientelism, and patrimonialism, which, as in Latin America, are said to be both widespread and highly corrosive of new democratic institutions throughout the developing world.[4] This is especially true in sub-Saharan Africa, where neopatrimonialism, or "personalized rule . . . organized through clientelistic networks of patronage, personal loyalty and coercion" (Lindberg 2003, 123), is said to be a defining characteristic of most emerging multiparty regimes (Bratton and van de Walle 1994). In Ghana, for example, pervasive neopatrimonialism is said to have undermined the formal checks on executive power outlined in the 1992 Constitution (Sandbrook and Oelbaum 1999), and the clientelistic practice of "chop," in which members of parliament are expected to distribute particularistic resources to supporters, is seen to "threaten the very heart of parliament as an institution" (Lindberg 2003, 136).

Particularism is also pervasive in postcommunist Eurasia. According to Joszef Borocz, clientelism, graft, and other particularistic practices are so widespread in Central Europe "that conducting any business, economic or otherwise, is virtually impossible without bowing, or even succumbing, to" such practices (2000, 348).[5] In the countries of the former Soviet Union, "particularistic rules and norms" routinely trump the formal rule of law, and, in extreme cases, formal rules "serve as merely a 'façade' covering informal dominance" (Gel'man 2003, 92–93).[6] In Central Asia, for example, clan politics so subverted formal institutions during the 1990s that "informal mechanisms of network-controlled exchange and norms . . . became the rules of the game" (Collins 2002b, 23). Consequently, the formal political regimes that emerged in the region following the collapse of the Soviet Union became "deinstitutionalized and inconsequential" (Collins 2002b, 30).

Another type of competing informal institution that has received widespread attention in studies of developing regions (but which is less common in Latin America) is "traditional" or indigenous institutions. As the literature on legal pluralism has shown, the imposition of colonial legal systems created "multiple systems of legal obligation" in many societies (Hooker 1975, 3).[7] Because Western and indigenous systems of law frequently "embodied very different principles and procedures" (Merry 1988, 869), adherence to custom law at times required a violation of state law (and vice versa). The survival of competing indigenous institutions seems to be particularly widespread in sub-Saharan Africa, where colonialism was more recent and state authority is generally weaker than in Latin America (Hyden 1980, 2002; Dia 1996; Galvan 2004).

Substitutive informal institutions are also widespread in the developing and post-communist worlds, particularly where state and other political institutions are weak. Thus, in much of Africa, where pervasive state weakness limits governments' ability to provide public goods, and where formal secondary associations are largely absent, informal institutions such as "pooling" (voluntary cooperation in informal rotating credit associations or labor groups, which are often embedded in family or kinship networks) help provide localized public goods (Hyden 2002, 20–21). In Russia, where political parties were notoriously underdeveloped in the aftermath of Soviet rule, incumbent politicians used informal "party substitutes" such as state-run patronage machines and "politicized financial-industrial groups" to provide organization, reputation, and material resources (Hale 2005). In parts of the Middle East, the absence of effective formal channels of participation or access to the state may help foster or sustain informally institutionalized forms of political participation. Thus, in her study of Yemen, Lisa Wedeen (2003) links the vibrancy of *qat*-chews—informally institutionalized gatherings in which men chew *qat* leaves and engage in lively political debate—to the fragility of the state.

Scholars have also pointed to the importance of substitutive informal institutions in China. According to Lily Tsai, local officials in rural China often compensate for the state's inability to raise revenue and provide public goods by mobilizing resources informally through temple and lineage associations, effectively "substituting the use of these informal institutions for . . . formal political institutional channels of public goods provision" (2001, 16; see also L. Tsai 2004). In a somewhat similar vein, Hongying Wang argues that informal networks play an important role in attracting foreign investment where Chinese state institutions are "either ineffective or irrelevant." According to Wang, the weakness of Chinese legal institutions generates high levels of uncertainty and provides few "mechanisms for foreign investors to minimize transaction costs and protect their business interests." This role is filled by informal personal relationships, or *guanxi*. Although *guanxi* tend to "contradict and undermine formal institutions," they promote foreign investment by fostering trust and providing mechanisms of coordination, enforcement, and dispute settlement (Wang 2000, 531–39).

Accommodating informal institutions generally emerge in brittle formal institutional contexts, in which the formal rules of the game are widely disliked but are costly to openly violate or change. Such institutions have been widely observed in state socialist regimes. Because many formal institutions in such regimes are unpopular and/or difficult to comply with, but open defiance of the rules is extremely costly, actors have an incentive to create what Kellee Tsai (2003) calls "adaptive" informal institutions.[8] Such institutions were a central feature of political and economic life in the Soviet Union, where strict adherence to formal procedure made it virtually impossible for individuals to meet their daily needs or for enterprises to fulfill state targets (Ledeneva 1998). In this context, a set of informal norms—commonly known as *blat*—emerged in which individuals met these goals through personal networks (Bauer et al. 1956, 74-81; Berliner 1957, 182–230; Ledeneva 1998). Though not strictly illegal, *blat* allowed factory managers, workers, and bureaucrats to "find a way around formal procedures" (Ledeneva 1998, 1).[9]

Similar informal patterns have been observed in China and Vietnam. For example, norms of "gift-giving," rooted in personal relationships (or *guanxi*), proliferated in China in the period after Mao's death, facilitating the exchange of goods and services in the formally socialist economy (Yang 1994). As the gap between China's formal (Leninist and socialist) institutions and de facto (capitalist) economy widened, such adaptive informal institutions became increasingly central to Chinese economic life (K. Tsai 2003). Because socialist laws banning private property relations remained on the books, economic agents—with the collusion of local state officials—developed a variety of informal, "quasi-legal" arrangements to operate private firms, obtain credit, and raise capital (K. Tsai 2003, 9-21). Similarly, in Vietnam, an influx of foreign investment—despite the formal persistence of state socialist institutions—during the 1990s led to a "de facto decentralization," as officials in provinces with high concentrations of foreign capital undertook—with the acquiescence of central authorities—"fence breaking" liberalization measures that circumvented, to varying degrees, the national government's official laws and policies (Malesky 2005, 12).

If the dearth of research on the subject is a valid indicator, complementary informal institutions seem to be scarce in the developing world. As in Latin America, such institutions are most common in countries with relatively stable and effective formal institutions—such as Singapore. Thus, Natasha Hamilton-Hart (2000) has pointed to the centrality of informal institutions in the operation of Singapore's notoriously effective state bureaucracy. According to Hamilton-Hart, the formal structure of Singapore's postcolonial public administration was similar to those of Indonesia and the Philippines. What differed was the informal institutional context within which the administration was embedded: in Singapore, state bureaucrats and private sector entrepreneurs operated in a context of shared norms of meritocracy and discipline that were largely absent in the other two countries (Hamilton-Hart 2000, 202–8). Lily Tsai (2004) makes a somewhat similar argument in her comparative study of local government performance in rural China. Tsai found that village governments were more likely to provide public goods where there were informal norms of social obligation generated by membership in local temple associations.

Anna Grzymala-Busse (2004) has identified several complementary informal institutions in postsocialist Central Europe. Much like Siavelis and Carey's and Siavelis's analysis of how power-sharing norms helped sustain multiparty coalitions in Chile's presidential democracy (this volume), Grzymala-Busse (2004, 24–25) argues that informal norms regarding which parties were acceptable alliance partners and how government positions would be allocated facilitated parliamentary coalition-building in new Central European democracies during the 1990s. By lowering information costs and providing "distributive guidelines" for parties, these informal institutions streamlined decision-making in ways that enhanced the functioning of new parliamentary democracies in, for example, Hungary and Poland (Grzymala-Busse 2004, 23–36).

Two observations emerge from this brief sketch of research on informal institutions in other parts of the developing world. First, in contrast to the literature on informal institutions in the United States and western Europe, much of which focuses on informal norms that complement formal institutions, research on the developing world focuses largely on those that *subvert* formal institutions. Several factors seem to account for this pattern. One is that many formal institutions in the developing world are imported from the West, rather than indigenously created. As Mamadou Dia writes, colonial and postcolonial institutions were "transplanted from outside" and "superimposed upon indigenous institutions" (1996, 3), often without taking the latter into account. As a result, many of them were "at odds with societal behavior, expectations, and incentive systems" (Dia 1996, 1; see also Riggs 1964; Galvan 2004).

Another reason for the prevalence of subversive informal institutions in the developing world is state weakness. With few exceptions, states in Africa, Latin America, and much of Asia and the former Soviet Union are significantly weaker than those in the advanced industrialized countries. They often lack the capacity to enforce the rule of law or provide even basic public goods across the national territory (O'Donnell 1993). In many countries, much of the national territory—especially rural areas—is characterized by the "unrule of law" (O'Donnell 1993, 1999c). The absence of effective state enforcement of formal rules and laws allows for the survival of indigenous institutions, as well as the emergence and persistence of particularistic institutions such as clientelism, corruption, and mafias and clan networks.

Furthermore, many developing countries are characterized by severe socioeconomic, ethnic, and/or regional stratification, which makes it more likely that certain groups—for example, ethnic minorities—will be denied access to (or protection from) formal state institutions. As Van Cott's chapter suggests, such exclusion may lead these groups to maintain or (re)create substitutive informal institutions at the margins of the state legal system.

A second observation concerns the flip side of the coin: the relative absence in the developing world of underlying informal institutions that reinforce formal ones. Although the ineffectiveness of formal institutions is usually attributed to the presence of subversive informal institutions, such an outcome may also be rooted in the *absence of complementary ones.* Functioning formal institutions do not operate in a vacuum. Rather, they tend to be embedded in shared norms and expectations that facilitate or encourage compliance with them (North et al. 2000; Galvan 2004; Stokes, this volume). As Dennis Galvan (2004, 18–19) has noted, liberal democratic constitutions work effectively when they are embedded in underlying norms such as gracious losing and a strict public-private boundary. Similarly, as Stokes argues in her chapter, elections serve as mechanisms of vertical accountability only where there exists a shared expectation that voters will follow retrospective decision rules.

In the absence of such underlying norms, even systematically enforced formal institutions may not work well. Consider presidentialism. Juan Linz (1990) has argued that the constitutional arrangements of presidentialism (separately elected executives and legislatures, fixed presidential terms in office) generate political behavior (such as zero-sum politics and executive-legislative conflict) that can destabilize new democracies. Indeed, the United States is the only country in the world in which presidential democracy did not break down during the twentieth century. This outcome is explained, in part, by the array of "paraconstitutional" norms and practices in which U.S. presidentialism has long been embedded (Riggs 1988). Indeed, as Stokes (2003, 5–6) has noted, the authors of the *Federalist Papers* were keenly aware of how their proposed constitutional arrangements would interact with existing social norms. In Latin America, by contrast, postcolonial elites essentially transplanted U.S.-style presidentialist constitutions, grafting them onto very different informal institutional contexts. From this perspective, then, the failure of presidentialism in many developing countries may be rooted not only in the existence of subversive informal institutions such as patrimonialism (Hartlyn 1998; Sandbrook and Oelbaum 1999) but also in the absence of the complementary informal institutions needed to sustain it.

This discussion has important implications for scholars and policymakers who are interested in how institutional design affects the stability and quality of new democracies. Crafting effective democratic institutions entails not (only) importing successful models from abroad, but also reconfiguring formal and informal institutions in ways that enhance their compatibility (Dia 1996; Sil 2002; Galvan 2004; Van Cott, this volume). To cite an example, Dia (1996, 105–6) argues that whereas most postcolonial African governments officially abolished the indigenous institution of local chieftancy, governments in Botswana and Ghana preserved it (eventually enshrining it in their constitutions). By working through local chiefs and customary law, Dia (1996, 106–11) claims, the governments enhanced the legitimacy and effectiveness of both public-goods provision and local justice systems. Similarly, in his work on formal and informal institutional arrangements governing peasant land use in Senegal, Galvan (2004) shows how peasants adapted "traditional" norms in ways that would potentially reinforce formal state institutions and policies. During the 1970s, local farmers used newly introduced elected rural councils to administer "remembered practices of resource management" (Galvan 2004, 3). Although these syncretic arrangements collapsed when state authorities attempted to impose centralized control, Galvan's work suggests that both "modern" (formal) and "traditional" (informal) institutions may be reconfigured in ways that enhance the stability and/or effectiveness of formal state and regime institutions. Indeed, such efforts at institutional syncretism may be critical to making democratic institutions work in much of the developing world. At a minimum, successful formal institutional engineering requires understanding the incentives and constraints that existing informal institutions impose.

ISSUES FOR FUTURE RESEARCH

As scholarly debates turn increasingly to issues of "deepening" or enhancing the quality of democracy in Latin America and elsewhere (O'Donnell et al. 2004), informal institutions are almost certain to gain greater salience. This volume has examined several areas in which informal rules affect the performance of demo-

cratic institutions, including electoral politics, candidate selection, campaign finance, executive-legislative relations, and judicial politics and the rule of law. However, numerous areas remain inadequately explored.

One important area for research is how informal institutions affect public transparency and accountability. A lesson of the 1980s and 1990s in Latin America was
that competitive elections are insufficient to ensure transparency in public policy. In
most contemporary Latin American democracies, much of what transpires within
public institutions—from the clientelistic distribution of favors, backroom candidate
selection, and legislative deal-making to illicit party finance, bribery, and mafia
activity—continues to evade public scrutiny. Enhancing transparency is often seen as
central to reducing corruption and increasing accountability in the region.[10]

At first glance, the impact of informal institutions on transparency seems to be
almost uniformly negative. By definition, informal institutions lie outside the scope
of official rules and authorities. Rules are unwritten, privately communicated and
enforced, and almost never subject to public oversight. Corruption, clientelism,
concertacesiones, legislative "ghost coalitions," the *dedazo*, norms of police violence,
and other informal institutions discussed in this book all hinge on—and arguably
reinforce—the absence of such oversight. This is true even of positively evaluated
informal institutions such as the power-sharing arrangements discussed by Siavelis
and by Carey and Siavelis. Not surprisingly, then, greater transparency is frequently
associated with the adoption of more formal procedures: the replacement of smoke-
filled rooms with primary elections (Langston, this volume), a shift from *concertacesiones* to electoral courts (Eisenstadt), the adoption of roll-call voting in legislatures
(Desposato), or the elimination of discretionary spending accounts within the executive branch (Mejía Acosta).

Yet the relationship between formality and transparency may not be quite so
simple. As several chapters in this volume show, simply creating formal rules or
mechanisms of oversight does not ensure greater transparency in practice. Roll-call
voting may be introduced to legislatures but not used (Desposato); campaign finance rules may be systematically ignored (Samuels); party primaries may be rigged
or orchestrated by clientelistic machines (Freidenberg and Levitsky). Indeed, following Stokes, the effectiveness of formal mechanisms of transparency and accountability may hinge on shared underlying norms or expectations that reinforce transparent behavior. In other words, enhancing transparency may involve more than a
shift from informal to formal rules. It may also require encouraging the emergence
or maintenance of the "right" informal rules.

A second area for research is whether informal norms of restraint emerge to
temper formal institutions. Most successful democracies are characterized not only

by widespread compliance with democratic rules but also by widespread agreement on the appropriate—and, in many cases, limited—use of those rules. If applied in full force, majoritarian institutions (such as parliaments in Westminster systems) could seriously threaten political minorities, and the institutional checks and balances of U.S.-style presidentialism could effectively paralyze governments. In both cases, then, the smooth functioning—indeed, the survival—of democratic institutions hinges on actors' willingness to underutilize certain rules and procedures. However, there is considerable evidence that in many new democracies in Latin America and elsewhere, norms of institutional restraint either do not exist or are at best weakly institutionalized.[11] Hence, identifying the conditions under which such norms emerge—or fail to emerge—is critical.

Finally, informal institutions seem to play an increasingly important role in *nondemocratic regimes*. Following the collapse of the Soviet Union, the unprecedented power of the West and the absence of viable regime alternatives created strong incentives for developing-world elites to adopt formal democratic institutions.[12] Nevertheless, the demise of military and Leninist dictatorships did not always lead to full-fledged polyarchy. Indeed, regimes in Belarus, Cambodia, Croatia, Kenya, Malaysia, Mexico, Peru, Russia, Ukraine, Zimbabwe, and numerous other countries combined formal democratic institutions with autocratic rule during the 1990s (Levitsky and Way 2002; Ottaway 2003). Due to the prohibitive external cost of eliminating democratic institutions (i.e., canceling elections or banning opposition parties), post–Cold War autocrats increasingly turned to informal mechanisms of coercion. Thus, instead of banning opponents, they employed "informal repression," or state violence undertaken by nominally private militias, paramilitaries, and party "youth wings," to weaken opposition groups (Kirschke 2000; Roessler 2005); rather than ban the independent media, they established informal control of the private media via proxy ownership and widespread co-optation and bribery of editors and journalists (Lawson 2002; Rodan 2004); and rather than cancel elections, they employed state and media resources to tilt the electoral playing field against opposition parties (Schedler 2002; Ottaway 2003). For scholars of contemporary regimes in sub-Saharan Africa, the former Soviet Union, and elsewhere, a key challenge lies in identifying these informal institutions of authoritarianism and evaluating their effects, as well as in exploring the conditions that facilitate their emergence, persistence, and collapse.

Unwritten rules continue to shape political processes and outcomes throughout the world. The analysis of informal institutions thus belongs at the forefront of research in comparative politics. A key contribution of this volume has been to identify and elaborate a set of issues that are central to the study of informal institutions in Latin America and elsewhere. These include questions of why and how informal institutions are created, the sources of informal institutional stability and change, and the conditions under which informal institutions are formalized. They also include the dynamics of interaction between formal and informal rules: how informal institutions contribute to formal institutional stability or change—and vice versa. Compared with the study of formal institutions, the "learning curve" in informal institutional analysis—particularly in terms of establishing their existence—is fairly steep. However, because the identification of informal institutions requires that scholars look closely at the actors and mechanisms that sustain them, the very process of identification may go a long way toward identifying sources of continuity and change.

Although political scientists have long recognized that informal institutions matter, systematic research on the subject remains at an incipient stage. As this volume has shown, advances in these areas are likely to take place on a variety of methodological fronts, ranging from abstract formal modeling to fine-grained historical or ethnographic studies. Theoretical insights into the origins, dynamics, and effects of informal political institutions will likely draw from a range of disciplines, including anthropology, economics, law, and sociology. It is therefore essential to maintain a broad and pluralistic research agenda that encourages fertilization across disciplines, theoretical traditions, and methods. It is this spirit that gave rise to this volume—and to which we hope the volume will contribute.

On Informal Institutions, Once Again

GUILLERMO O'DONNELL

Although focused on Latin America, the present volume is an important step forward for the study of informal rules and institutions in political science generally. In their introduction to this volume, the editors, Gretchen Helmke and Steven Levitsky, are gracious to acknowledge my early contributions to this topic (O'Donnell 1994, 1996b). Now, with the benefit of this introduction and of the varied and very interesting chapters contained herein, I want to add some further reflections. I hope they will concur with the rest of this volume in enriching a research agenda that, among other things, hinges crucially on how we study democracy and democratization.

I begin with a story. Twenty years ago I published a paper that dealt with differences in how one is supposed to drive a car in South Bend (Indiana), Rio de Janeiro, and Buenos Aires (O'Donnell 1984). The point I want to recall here is that in certain Latin American cities (and, indeed, other cities in the developing world), you have to be nuts (or a very naive foreigner) to drive according to the formal rules of transit. In most parts of the city, and during the night in practically all of it, it is perfectly obvious that you should *not* stop at a red light, not to mention a yellow light or a stop sign. If you do this, you are subjecting yourself to serious risks. The first is being run over by the car behind you; *of course* the driver of this car does not expect you to stop. The second risk is that without, or before, or, even more, after the accident, you will be robbed.

Everyone knows this—where *everyone* means all the actors involved in the relevant context of interaction. This leads to a first suggestion: Helmke and Levitsky propose a useful definition of an informal institution, as *"socially shared rules, usually unwritten, that are created, communicated, and enforced outside officially sanctioned channels."* However, even if it is implied in this definition, I would stress that the set of informal rules that constitute an informal institution is *common knowledge*; that is, each actor knows the rules and knows that everyone else, in the relevant context of interaction, also knows those same rules. As a consequence, there exists the generalized expectation that "everyone" will follow the rules and that, in case of failure to do so, some kind of punishment or ill will follow, even though, as my example illustrates, no predesignated agent may exist for applying such sanction. As the editors assert, these rules may be nontransparent, but certainly they are well known to the relevant actors.

But the picture is more complicated—and interesting. In the kind of city I am depicting,[1] there are times and areas (most of the day in downtown and in affluent quarters) where you *do* follow the formal rules of transit. Otherwise you will be fined, formally or informally (i.e., paying a bribe to the policeman who stops you). So, if you want to drive without major problems, you must know when the rules to be followed change. Local fools and naive foreigners risk both serious accidents and heavy (formal and informal) fines.

That in certain areas of the city you follow the formal rules is also common knowledge. Yet, as I add in my 1984 article, in many cities, even where formal rules predominate there are also other, common-knowledge informal rules, such as the order of precedence at intersections: trucks and buses over regular cars, say, or rusty cars over new ones, or the almost unsolvable problem of knowing what to do when in the other car there are those most reputedly unreliable drivers, women. But I do not need to delve into these details for the point I am making here.

The point is (and this is my second suggestion) that arguably one of the more interesting aspects to investigate in the future is the *shifting movements* to and from formal and informal rules *by the same actors* as they change contexts and as they assume (correctly, most of the time) that this shift is common knowledge. In politics we observe this all the time: President X or Congressperson Z solemnly acting according to formally prescribed rules, and soon afterward behaving in ways that are clearly divergent from those rules. This does not license utter cynicism, as it does in vast sectors of public opinion in Western countries, where many know that when political leaders dress themselves in formal rules they are "only" playing one of their roles. Even in the worst of cases, such public behavior is the tribute that vice pays to virtue: the enactment, even if temporary and suspect, of the formal rules and rituals of democracy is a reminder of these rules and their underlying values. This opens opportunities for the public invocation of those same rules and values, and eventually for the condemnation of those informal institutions that most egregiously transgress them. In this convoluted and admittedly less than optimal way, democratizing discourses and demands are anchored in and by the formal rules that even very informal rulers cannot cease to evoke.[2] This happens repeatedly under democratic regimes, and this is one of their main, if seldom acknowledged, advantages in relation to other kinds of regimes—democracy, even if "formal" or "electoral," has some discursive and ritual requirements that not even scarcely democratic leaders can fully bypass.

It seems to me that these strategic shifts from and to formal and informal are the stuff of politics, particularly where regimes are poorly institutionalized. Thus, the typology proposed in the introduction might be complemented by a focus on how and why some actors adapt, skillfully and recurrently, to codes embodying various sets of rules, and on how and why the relevant others in the respective contexts respond to these shifts. In this perspective, the focus would be not so much on the *institutions* themselves (formal and/or informal) but on how *actors* "within" these institutions behave, and on how they strategically shift according to varying contexts.[3]

Now I take a step back in these reflections. In my early articles on this matter, I expressed concern with the excessive formalism of many of the works in the first wave of institutionalist studies on Latin America (and, in fact, elsewhere). I was (and am) persuaded that, as the editors note and the chapters in this volume amply show, "analyses of democratic institutions that focus exclusively on formal rules thus risk missing much of what shapes and constrains political behavior, which can yield an incomplete—if not wholly inaccurate—picture of how politics works." My concern was centered on *competing* informal institutions: those that through various sets of informal rules (clientelism, nepotism, corruption, and others) guide behaviors that are inconsistent with, if not opposed to, the formal rules of democracy. Seen from this angle, it seems to me that the first question to be asked in these matters is, to what extent do the formal rules predict actual, observed behavior (and in some cases omissions)? In some cities, as we saw, the formal rules of transit are very poor predictors in most situations, albeit pretty good ones in others. Based on an admittedly nonscientific observation of politicians, congresspersons, and some presidents in Argentina and Brazil, I believed that this was also true of them. Several chapters in this volume support, from various angles, this view.

On the other hand, it is trivial to assert that informal rules and institutions exist everywhere. The matter is, to what extent and in what areas (the political one, in the case of this volume and my articles) informal rules and institutions actually govern behavior, and to what extent and in what areas such behavior is inconsistent with, or opposed to, the formal rules of democracy. As several contributors to this volume note,[4] these deviations may not necessarily be harmful to the workings of a given political regime, but if they are importantly influential, then something significant has been found that cannot be accounted for by views that presuppose the predominance of formal rules. Of course, studying these matters is empirically difficult, but, as this volume illustrates, various methods can deal with them in quite satisfactory ways.

Still, these matters need a bit more conceptual precision, for which the typology proposed by Helmke and Levitsky is apposite. One matter, of course, is what contemporary political scientists know about the role of *complementary* and *accommodating* institutions in facilitating or partially correcting the workings of formal institutions.[5] In fact, this role was detected earlier, and abundantly discussed, by sociologists, so much so that the contemporary sociology of the organization was born precisely with this discovery.[6] Thus, the existence of these kinds of informal institution does not entail a valid objection to the study of other kinds, including *competing* and *substitutive* ones. One is free to study whatever kind of institution seems interesting, although it may not come as a surprise that many students of democratization choose the latter types, precisely because they are critically interested in how to improve the workings of these highly informalized democracies.

This disagreement points to the need for another bit of conceptual precision, which is my third suggestion. The editors take good care in stipulating what informal institutions are not. Perhaps it may be added, in more detail, that such institutions are constituted by sets of informal rules. These rules, as such, have at least three characteristics: (1) they entail some kind of sanction in case of being violated or grossly ignored, even though there may not be a predesignated actor to apply the sanction; (2) they are common knowledge in the relevant context of interaction; and (3) they prescribe some kind of action (or, in some cases, omission) on the part of the subjects acting in the relevant context. Thus, in addition to the differentiations of informal institutions vis-à-vis other phenomena that the editors correctly stipulate, it would be useful to add that informal rules are not simply *expectations*, even though, obviously, they generate them. This may dispel confusions such as the assertion that voters' beliefs that candidates will honor their campaign promises are informal rules[7]—these beliefs are *expectations*, not rules in any reasonable definition of the term of which I am aware.

Following the useful typology proposed in the introduction, we may note that *complementary, accommodating,* and *competing* informal institutions are all in some kind of relationship with formal ones. As Helmke and Levitsky note, in many cases the informal may be endogenous to the formal, in the sense that they originate in and through the workings of the latter. Yet an intriguing possibility is the reverse. Particularistic practices in informal institutions have been central to the trade of many Latin American politicians before and during authoritarian regimes.[8] Thus, even though this does not make the formal institutions of democracy endogenous to the informal ones, they may have been, as it were, plunged into a deep sea of preexisting informal rules and institutions. This may account for the resilience of these informalities in spite of so many efforts (and money from international institutions) to "modernize" parties, congress, the judiciary, and the like. This might also be helpful in finding clues for reducing the weight of those informalities. One way or the other, we do not know much about the mechanisms through which each kind of institution relates to any other, and even less about the consequences of the temporal sequences in which they are effected,[9] but one useful characteristic of this volume is to open the way for this kind of inquiry.

The lack of endogeneity of informal institutions in relation to formal ones is also illustrated, albeit from a different angle, by Van Cott's chapter. As this author shows, indigenous legal systems, although influenced by the state and sometimes forced to partially adapt to it, have mostly developed on the basis of a dynamic of their own. Furthermore, I doubt that the institutions that Van Cott discusses should be dubbed *informal*. Truly, most of their rules are not written (although Van Cott shows an increasing movement toward written law), but these indigenous legal systems and institutions are quite formally effected, including publicly appointed and legitimized authorities, detailed procedures, elaborate rituals, regularized sanctions, and the like. Consequently, these institutions are not only public knowledge but also transparent, not just for those directly involved in the relevant context of interaction but also for outsiders. In any event, this chapter suggests that in some cases there may be a gray zone between formal and informal institutions—as the use of any dichotomy in the social sciences would unfailingly find.

As springs, I hope, from the preceding discussion, in addition to its obvious intrinsic merits this volume is a welcome challenge. It would have been nice if implanting new formal rules and institutions had sufficed for producing the "consolidation" of democracy, in Latin America and elsewhere. The problem is that, as this volume abundantly illustrates, those rules and institutions often are poor predictors of behavior. This defies us, not to neglect formal rules and institutions, but to undertake careful studies of, as the editors propose, the interactions between the formal and the informal and, as I suggest here, the ways in which actors strategically navigate formal and informal contexts. The progress of social knowledge does not admit the shortcuts implied by simplistic formalists, importers of ready-made models, or hurried consultants.

Notes

INTRODUCTION

1. For an excellent survey of this literature, see Carey (2000).

2. We borrow this term from Carey (2000).

3. On informal institutions in Latin America, see Taylor (1992), O'Donnell (1993, 1996a, 1999c), Siavelis (1997b, 2002a), Hartlyn (1998), Starn (1999), Van Cott (2000b), Langston (2001, 2003), Brinks (2003a, 2003b), Eisenstadt (2003), Levitsky (2003b), and Helmke (2004). On informal institutions in sub-Saharan Africa, see Dia (1996), Sandbrook and Oelbaum (1999), Hyden (2002), Lindberg (2003), Erdmann (2004), and Galvan (2004). On informal institutions in East Asia, see Yang (1994), Hamilton-Hart (2000), Wang (2000), Gobel (2001), L. Tsai (2002, 2004), Colignon and Usui (2003), and K. Tsai (2003). On East-Central Europe and the former Soviet Union, see Clarke (1995), Ledeneva (1998), Borocz (2000), Easter (2000), Sil (2001), Collins (2002a, 2003, 2004), Darden (2002), Grzymala-Busse and Jones Luong (2002), Way (2002), and Gel'man (2003, 2004). For general surveys of this literature, see Lauth (2000) and Helmke and Levitsky (2004).

4. On legislative politics, see Mershon (1994); on judicial politics, Helmke (2002, 2004), Brinks (2003b), and Bill Chavez (2004); on electoral systems, Taylor (1992); on party politics, Langston (2001, 2003), Freidenberg (2003), and Levitsky (2003b); on political regimes, Collins (2002b, 2004) and Ottaway (2003); on federalism, Way (2002); on public administration, Della Porta and Vannucci (1999), Hamilton-Hart (2000), Darden (2002), Grzymala-Busse and Jones Luong (2002), and Colignon and Usui (2003).

5. As applied to culture, see Dia (1996) and Pejovich (1999); to civil society, Boussard (2000) and Manor (2001); to personal networks, Wang (2000); to clans and mafias, Lauth (2000) and Collins (2002b, 2003); to corruption and clientelism, O'Donnell (1996b), Borocz (2000), and Lauth (2000); and to bureaucratic and legislative norms, Hamilton-Hart (2000).

6. See Katzenstein (1996), Della Porta and Vannucci (1999), Hamilton-Hart (2000), Darden (2002), and Colignon and Usui (2003); see also chapters by Brinks and Langston in this volume.

7. This definition borrows from Brinks (2003a) and is consistent with North (1990), O'Donnell (1996b), Carey (2000), and Lauth (2000). We treat informal *institutions* and *norms* synonymously. However, it should be noted that norms have been defined in a variety of ways and that some conceptualizations do not include external enforcement (see Elster 1989).

8. This latter category encompasses state institutions (courts, legislatures, bureaucracies)

and state-enforced rules (constitutions, laws, regulations), as well as Ellickson's "organization rules" (1991).

9. An exception, discussed in the text below, is what Brinks (this volume) calls "permissive rules."

10. In particular, see the chapters by Brinks and Langston.

11. See, e.g., Huntington (1968, 8–9) and Mainwaring and Scully (1995).

12. See, e.g., O'Donnell (1996b), Hartlyn (1998), Sandbrook and Oelbaum (1999), Borocz (2000), Lauth (2000), Gobel (2001), Collins (2002b, 2003), and Lindberg (2003).

13. See Mainwaring (1993), Linz and Valenzuela (1994), O'Donnell (1994), Mainwaring and Shugart (1997), Pérez Liñan (2003), and Kenney (2004).

14. See Mainwaring (1993), Mainwaring and Scully (1995), Mainwaring and Shugart (1997), and Kenney (2004).

15. This typology builds on the work of Lauth (2000), who distinguishes among three types of formal-informal institutional relationships: complementary, substitutive, and conflicting.

16. By *effectiveness* we do not mean efficiency. History is littered with examples of inefficient institutions that nevertheless effectively shaped actors' expectations (North 1990).

17. On efficiency-enhancing norms in the U.S. legislature, see Mathews (1959), Weingast (1979), and Weingast and Marshall (1988). On efficiency-enhancing norms in the U.S. Supreme Court, see Maltzman and Wahlbeck (1986) and Epstein and Knight (1998, 118–36).

18. We borrow this term from Lauth (2000, 25).

19. See Ullman-Margalit (1978), Weingast (1979), Axelrod (1986), and, from a more sociological perspective, March and Olsen (1989).

20. See O'Donnell (1996b), Borocz (2000), Lauth (2000), Gobel (2001), and Lindberg (2003).

21. In Brinks's case, norms encouraging killing by police compete with state laws protecting criminals' rights, but they may be said to substitute for a notoriously ineffective public security system.

22. Other scholars have characterized clientelism as substituting for weak state institutions (Scott 1972; Auyero 2000b).

23. We thank Gerald Gamm for this example.

24. U.S. prohibition laws are an example.

25. Such an effect has been noted by Wang (2000, 548) and L. Tsai (2001).

26. Not all substitutive informal institutions produce such a crowding-out dynamic, however. As Eisenstadt (this volume) notes, Mexican opposition leaders used *concertacesiones* only as a temporary "second-best" strategy—or "way station"—as they pushed for the development of more effective electoral institutions.

27. For an alternative approach, see Grzymala-Busse (2004).

28. We thank an anonymous reviewer for making this excellent suggestion.

29. For recent work on formal institutional emergence and change, see Boix (1999), Thelen (1999, 2003, 2004), Boylan (2001b), and Pierson (2004).

30. Exceptions include Mershon (1994), Farrell and Héritier (2002), and K. Tsai (2003). These issues are the subject of a large literature within formal political theory; see Schotter (1981), J. Knight (1992), Calvert (1995), and Greif and Laitin (2004).

31. For a critique, see J. Knight (1992).

32. See, e.g., Starn's (1999, 36–69) account of the disputed origins of the *rondas campesinas* in Peru and Ledeneva's analysis (1998) of the origins of *blat* in the Soviet Union.

33. See, e.g., Weingast (1979), March and Olsen (1989), R. Nelson and Winter (1982, 99–136), Weingast and Marshall (1988), and Farrell and Héritier (2002).

34. Langston (this volume) makes a related, if slightly different, argument about the origins of the *dedazo*, claiming that PRI elites opted for informal rules in part because they were less costly to *maintain*.

35. Mershon (1994, 50) makes a similar point.

36. On path dependence in formal institutional analysis, see Pierson (2000).

37. See, e.g., Katzenstein's analysis (1996, 197–200) of the origins of the norms of restraint and flexibility within Japan's security forces.

38. We thank an anonymous reviewer for this suggestion.

39. For endogenous arguments about how institutions change, see Pierson (2000) and Greif and Laitin (2004).

40. See Price (1975), Dia (1996), Colignon and Usui (2003), Collins (2004), and Galvan (2004).

41. Thus, the 1974 Bill of Rights of subcommittees in the House of Representatives "produced a sharp change in formal rules that overrode previous informal committee structures" (North 1990, 88).

42. The challenge in both cases, however, is to pin down *ex ante* the thresholds at which such change is likely. Although formal modeling can provide a useful set of theoretical tools for this task, scholars with empirical ambitions will have to think carefully about how to operationalize and test such arguments. For an excellent example of how such work may proceed, see Greif and Laitin (2004).

43. See, e.g., Starn's work (1999) on the *rondas campesinas* in northern Peru, Gay's work (1994, 1999) on clientelism in Brazil, and Auyero's work (2000b) on clientelism in Argentina.

44. This is the very logic of the credible-threat argument, which underlies a rational-choice view of institutions.

45. On the subnational comparative method, see Snyder (2001).

46. In the original study from which Desposato's chapter was drawn, he compares five different Brazilian states.

CHAPTER 1. ACCOMMODATING INFORMAL INSTITUTIONS AND CHILEAN DEMOCRACY

The author thanks John Carey, Gretchen Helmke, Steven Levitsky, Maria Victoria Murillo, and Ignacio Walker for their many comments and suggestions, which improved this chapter.

1. The Spanish terms are used here because they are used in the press and in everyday parlance in Chile—attesting to their centrality in Chilean political life.

2. In dozens of interviews with members of the legislative and executive branches during the Aylwin government, few interviewees failed to cite the "special conditions" and/or "special circumstances" of the transition that affected their behavior (see Siavelis 2000, 51–52).

3. *Cuoteo* carries a negative connotation, and an implicit suggestion that the quota is reached behind closed doors.

4. Exceptions include Deheza (1997) and Amorim Neto (2000).

5. Usually said to include SEGPRES (Ministry of the General Presidency) and the ministries of Interior, Government, Defense, and Foreign Relations.

6. For a small sampling of the controversy surrounding the *cuoteo* in ministerial appointments and some of its negative consequences, see *Qué Pasa* (2000), and *El Mercurio de Valparaíso* (2003).

7. While this is an account from negotiations on the right, as is the example cited in the text below, the electoral system provides these same incentives and logic of pairings across the political spectrum; Andrés Allamand, interview, Washington, DC, July 13, 1998. On the significance of the role of small parties in general, see *El Mercurio* (1993b).

8. For a complete discussion of the rules governing candidate selection, and the incentives they generate depending on party size, see Siavelis (2002b).

9. For some of the many examples of this phenomenon, see *El Mercurio* (1993a) and *La Epoca* (1993a, 1993b).

10. Ignacio Walker, telephone interview, March 3, 2004.

11. Carlos Carmona, interview, Santiago, Chile, April 23, 1993.

12. Ignacio Walker, telephone interview, March 4, 2004.

13. Cesar Ladrón de Guevara, interview, Santiago, Chile, May 13, 1999.

14. Correa quoted by Ignacio Walker, interview, March 3, 2004.

15. Concertación leaders also often engaged in direct negotiations with influential actors on the left, primarily trade unions, when drafting and advocating the passage of controversial legislation, pointing to a consistent pattern of pact-making even when attempting to satisfy the coalition's natural constituencies.

CHAPTER 2. HOW INFORMAL ELECTORAL INSTITUTIONS SHAPE THE BRAZILIAN LEGISLATIVE ARENA

1. State coffers may directly provide jobs or even public services that can be distributed—for example, enrollment in a public school or access to a public health clinic offered to supporters. Others have suggested that politicians deliver pork projects in exchange for kickbacks from construction firms (Samuels 2001a, 2001b).

2. Note that in many clientelistic systems, parties play very important roles in politics. But in Brazil, budget power is vested in strong executives, so parties' role in clientelistic electoral markets is minimal.

3. The interviews in Piauí were conducted in April 1999.

4. The interviews in São Paulo were conducted between December 1998 and March 1999.

5. Deputy Leal Junior, interview, Piauí State Legislative Assembly, May 1999; Leal Junior quoted in Ana Cláudia Coelho, "'Oposição se faz com dois, três, cinco, ou dez,' afirma Leal Júnior," *Meio Norte*, March 5, 2000.

6. Deputy Tonin, interview, and Deputy Dias, interview, São Paulo State Legislative Assembly, January 1999.

CHAPTER 3. CRAFTING LEGISLATIVE GHOST COALITIONS IN ECUADOR

The author thanks Daniel Brinks, Max Cameron, Michael Coppedge, Fran Hagopian, Gretchen Helmke, Steven Levitsky, and Michelle Taylor-Robinson for their insightful comments and valuable feedback

1. For a broader review of alternative theories explaining the success and failure of market-oriented reforms in Ecuador, see Mejía Acosta (2004, 3–9).

2. In 1999 alone, Ecuador's economy was severely affected by El Niño–related floodings (with an estimated loss of 13% of 1998 gross domestic product), a drop in international oil prices (from $20.45 a barrel in 1996 to $6.95 in 1998), and the contagion effect from the Russian crisis (drying up of international credit, soaring interest rates).

3. In the mid-1990s, several reforms were passed to abolish term limits, eliminate midterm elections, and adopt a peculiar open-list proportional representation system that allowed for personalized voting. For a more complete review of the implications of institutional reform for coalition formation, see Mejía Acosta (2004).

4. Presidents have exclusive authority to initiate the budgetary process and other economic-related legislation, to contract and acquire foreign debt, and to grant the required licenses and contracts for the administration of the public sector (Political Constitution of Ecuador, art. 171). They also have some judicial prerogatives to pardon and reduce sentences and pass controversial legislation by plebiscite.

5. The data reported are net public approval rates (all favorable minus unfavorable) for the president. Support for congressional performance (not reported here) consistently remains in the negative numbers as well.

6. Wilfrido Lucero, ID congressman, interview, Quito, July 19, 1999.

7. Jamil Mahuad Witt, former DP (Popular Democracy) party member and former president, interview, Cambridge, MA, July 9, 2002. According to Mahuad, one party leader and former president of Ecuador explained that criticizing him (Mahuad) was a matter of public reputation, since "he could not [seem to] be less tough on the president than political leaders from other parties."

8. Interviews with members of Ecuadorian National Congress, Quito, July 1999.

9. Some interesting examples are *camisetazo*, shameless change of political party with rent-seeking purposes; *colaboracionismo*, an accusation made against parties that accept government appointments without belonging to the president's party; *liborios*, legislators subservient to the government; *teta*, compensations received for government collaboration; and *chuchumecos*, last-minute government allies.

10. The first bill included some basic reforms needed to implement dollarization in Ecuador; it was approved at the end of February, only fourteen days after its initiation (for a full report, see Economist Intelligence Unit 2000, 16). In mid-March, Noboa proposed additional amendments demanded by the International Monetary Fund in order to sign the stand-by agreement with Ecuador, and although the congressional majority did not fully approve of those reforms, it accepted the government's partial veto.

11. The index is an aggregate measure of commercial, financial, capital accounts, privatiza-

tion, and tax reforms between 1970 and 1995; it ranges from 0 (complete state intervention in these policy areas) to 1 (economic liberalization) (Morley et al. 1999).

12. For an interesting exception to this trend, see Gibson and Calvo (2000); they claim that clientelistic practices were efficiently used to produce cheap legislative coalitions for economic reform in Argentina.

13. Mainwaring (1999, 180) rightly points out that neither clientelism nor patrimonialism is coterminous with corruption. Obtaining state resources for a specific region or distributing government positions to political partners can be legitimate practices, or not proscribed by the constitution. However, operating in poorly institutionalized polyarchies with eroding legal authority and no (vertical and horizontal) links of accountability, clientelistic exchanges created huge temptations for corruption.

14. Alexandra Vela, DP congresswoman, interview, Quito, July 11, 2001.

15. This is, however, not exclusive of Latin American presidential systems, as other scholars have illustrated the roles of clientelistic exchanges in parliamentary systems as well.

16. Another concealed strategy to "support without supporting" was applied by the ID, when it enabled Esparza's election by annulling its vote, thus adding support to the winning candidate according to internal congressional rules. "La convergencia al revés," *Vistazo* (Guayaquil), August 26, 1983.

17. Quoted in Mills 1984. After his term in congress, Gary Esparza was given control over the Customs Administration, presumably as compensation for his role in facilitating legislative cooperation with the Hurtado government.

18. *Diario Hoy* (Quito), January 24, 2001.

19. According to the Internal Legislative Rules, any legislator—with the support of ten colleagues—can request a roll-call vote (Reglamento Interno de la Función Legislativa, chap. IV). This is an unusual procedure used for controversial votes. A more common voting mechanism is the simple vote, in which legislators raise hands to support a motion on the floor.

20. Interview with anonymous congressman from the independent MIN, Quito, April 11, 2001. The congressman added: "It's like former Mexican President Echeverría used to say to his chauffeur, 'always signal to the left when you are going to turn to the right.'"

21. In Ecuador, for instance, a newly appointed health or public works minister would, in turn, have the authority to appoint provincial directors, allocate government contracts, and include her own political cronies on the government payroll.

22. After the 1998 constitutional reforms, congressional authorities were elected every two years, and there was an explicit provision to select the president of Congress from among the two largest parties.

23. Agendas could include (1) administration of justice through the joint presidential and party nomination of Supreme Court judges (between 1979 and 1996) or the nomination of Constitutional Tribunal members (since 1997); (2) election oversight through the designation of the members of the directorate of the Supreme Electoral Tribunal and those of its provincial branches; (3) control and oversight of government administration through the appointment of such authorities as the attorney general, the general comptroller, and the superintendents of banking and telecommunications, as well as various directors of state-owned enterprises.

24. Pro-government coalitions are those composed of parties that vote for the executive branch's candidate in annual congressional leadership elections.

25. Roughly speaking, Ecuadorian presidents had the authority to appoint at least two hundred or so government officials, including cabinet ministers and their subcabinet secretaries, for all ministries.

26. Similarly, in her work on coalition making in Italy, Mershon (1996, 538) argues that politicians were able to "raise" the payoffs of coalitions by expanding—among other things—the number of subcabinet positions available to coalition partners.

27. Interview with former Ecuadorian president, held anonymous at his request, Quito, April 2001.

28. Through these positions, political parties gain access to significant provincial-level or area-specific resources, grant concessions and licenses to diverse interest groups, negotiate the channeling of funding for a locality, appoint and remove lower government bureaucrats, and use their diplomatic status to further trade, tourism, and cultural policies.

29. The increment was especially significant in the most flexible spending accounts: transferences, (local) allocations, general spending, and public works (Araujo 1998, 145).

30. A 1996 survey of Ecuadorian legislators confirms this clientelistic connection. When asked how important it was for them to obtain resources for their communities, more than 90 percent of legislators from center or right-wing parties, and more than 80 percent from center-left parties, responded that it was "very important."

31. It seems that President Noboa bought individual votes to push a fiscal reform through Congress in 2001. On May 4, he blocked a congressional override and passed a 2 percent VAT (value-added tax) increase, with the help of several legislators who failed to vote or voted against their party leadership. In subsequent weeks, the media reported the nature of payoffs received by defecting legislators: Reynaldo Yanchapaxi (a veteran DP legislator from Cotopaxi) obtained better roads for his province; Raúl Andrade (a legislator from the Ecuadorian Roldosista Party [PRE]) obtained a fast-track credit for his native province, Manabí; Fulton Serrano (PRE) bargained to get the governorship of his province for his son and directorship of the Health Ministry for another family member. "Noboa relies on political quotas," *Diario El Comercio* (Quito), July 8, 2001.

32. Alexandra Vela, DP congresswoman, interview, Quito, July 1999.

33. On average, only one in ten legislators in Ecuador abandoned their parties in a given year, despite the nonexistent or ineffectual punishments for party defection. By contrast, Brazilian legislators, operating in an equally fragmented and polarized legislature, switched parties two or three times more often than their Ecuadorian counterparts (Mainwaring 1999).

34. See Sánchez-Parga (1998, 84, 101, 106).

35. Detailed information about the party affiliation of such government officials is mostly nonexistent or incomplete.

36. After 1998, legal provisions were set in place to raise the threshold required to impeach and censure members of the cabinet.

37. I thank Michel Rowland for sharing with me his cabinet survival dataset (1979–2002).

38. Perhaps a classic example is that of PSC Deputy León Febres Cordero (1979–84), who launched several cabinet impeachment initiatives before earning an electoral reputation that helped him gain the presidency in 1984.

39. In this "letter of commitment," legislators also requested that the president pass—or not

block—necessary reforms to allow immediate legislative reelection. *Diario Hoy* (Quito), August 13, 1993 (cited in Landau 2001, 128).

40. In the case of Montero, switching sides did not affect the electoral support in his small southern province of Loja, as he returned to Congress under a different party label (CFP) in 1996.

41. "Government-Congress Relationship Sours," *Weekly Analysis*, August 19, 1993, 6 (cited in Landau 2001, 45).

42. *Revista Vistazo* (Quito), May 19, 1994 (cited in Hey and Klak 1999, 78).

43. When the PSC lost the election for president of Congress to Carlos Vallejo (ID) in August 1992 (Burbano de Lara and Rowland 1998), a government alliance helped it regain control of the courts and Electoral Tribunals until 1994 (Congreso Nacional del Ecuador 1995).

44. Party switching rates reached a record high of nearly 25 percent of legislators during this period. At some point, the "group of independents" became the second largest contingent in Congress after the PSC, giving them great bargaining leverage vis-à-vis the executive (Mejía Acosta 2003).

45. *Diario Hoy* (Quito), August 13, 1993 (cited in Landau 2001, 128).

46. Alberto Dahik, telephone interview with David Landau, January 30, 2001 (cited in Landau 2001, 47).

47. Dahik interview (by Vivanco) and Febres Cordero's comments on Dahik in *Diario Hoy* (Quito), July 7, 1995; Castello's comments in Congreso Nacional del Ecuador (1995).

48. In Ecuador, some corruption watchdogs, such as the Civic Committee against Corruption, have been endowed with some jurisdictional powers, and important legislation has been approved to mandate disclosure of campaign financing, government contracting, and access to government information. Finally, several civic organizations promoting transparency and accountability have appeared in the Ecuadorian context, but none that act as legislative watchdogs.

49. The first two reforms are included in the 1998 Constitution; the third is codified in the 1998 Legislative Ethics Code.

50. Indeed, since the constitutional reform, not a single elected president has successfully completed his mandate.

51. Ramiro Rivera, DP congressman, interview, Quito, July 1999.

CHAPTER 4. INFORMAL INSTITUTIONS WHEN FORMAL CONTRACTING IS PROHIBITED

1. A worthy question is the extent to which other informal institutions emerge in contexts where no formal institution whatsoever regulates the question at hand.

2. I am excluding, for tractability, the possibility that a politician provides services in exchange for expected financial support at some undetermined later time.

3. This argument holds independent of whether corruption exists and/or whether those with money also attempt to influence nonelected officials. Only if elected officials are mere window dressing will access-seekers not see them as potential investment targets.

4. Of course, recent scandals in Mexico, Germany, and elsewhere point to the likelihood that even where campaigns are publicly funded, politicians will seek additional sources of money illicitly, whether for campaigns or for personal enrichment.

5. This hypothesis holds independent of whether suppliers believe that it matters who wins; only if contributors believe candidates are interchangeable *and* that politicians cannot affect their interests will they *not* supply funds.

6. These factors are too numerous to explore here, but include the costs of newspaper and television advertisements, other publicity efforts such as the manufacturing of pamphlets, banners, and tee-shirts, transportation costs, get-out-the-vote efforts, and the costs of running a campaign organization. These costs vary with local conditions.

7. I discuss elsewhere the reliability and validity of the data (Samuels 2001a, 2001b, 2001c, 2002). Cox and Thies, defending the use of campaign finance data from Japan, concluded that "if these data have been fabricated, they have been fabricated so as to preserve a number of expected correlations and even to fit the theories of political scientists—which does not seem too likely" (2000, 45). The same holds for the Brazilian data, justifying their use.

8. For 1994 and 1998, candidates were required to report only contributions, not expenditures. I assume that candidates spent all they raised, because by law candidates are required to hand over all "leftover" funds to their national party organization.

9. Television and radio time is free, distributed according to parties' proportion of seats in the lower chamber of Congress.

10. In-depth field research might find that family relations extend to in-laws, cousins, and others who do not carry the candidate's family name, and might also reveal that corporate contributions come from firms for which the candidate had previously worked or which he owns, or in which he holds a large stockholding share.

CHAPTER 5. THE DIFFICULT ROAD FROM *CAUDILLISMO* TO DEMOCRACY

1. What *representation* means is a matter of debate: it has been defined as the act of representing the interests of the electorate as delegates or as trustees, or of granting all groups a place at the table where policy is deliberated, among other formulations (Pitkin 1967; Mansbridge 2003).

2. This would mean that patron-client relations are the foundation for the rootedness of parties in society that Mainwaring and Scully (1995) offer as one characteristic of an institutionalized party system.

3. This literature summary draws primarily on the theory presented by Carey and Shugart (1995), but also on Lancaster (1986), Carey (1996), Mainwaring and Shugart (1997), and Shugart (2001).

4. See Rothstein (1979) for a discussion of how Mexico's PRI (Party of the Institutional Revolution) used patron-client relations to allocate scarce resources for local infrastructure development.

5. Despite its name, the Liberal Party has always been relatively conservative. Both traditional parties defend traditional elite interests, and neither is ideological.

6. Interview with PLH deputy, Tegucigalpa, Honduras, July 30, 1997.

7. In the 2002–5 Congress, the three small parties won twelve seats, and for the first time the president's party lacks an absolute majority in Congress (his National Party holds 61 of 128 seats).

8. Until 1993, municipal elections were also fused with the presidential and congressional elections.

9. I could not verify these claims, but they are an indication that local support matters to aspiring politicians.

10. For a detailed explanation of the coding scheme for bill targets, see Taylor-Robinson and Diaz (1999). For bills with multiple authors, the bill is counted in the legislative record of each author, because records in the Honduran Congress do not indicate a "primary" author or "cosponsors." Multiauthored bills are very rare in Honduras and typically have only two authors, so this will have little impact on the analysis.

11. It is hard for an individual legislator to claim credit for curbing inflation or for a national highway program (Mayhew 1974, 59–60). Big projects require the support of many members, so credit must be shared. There is also an informational challenge to claiming credit for such projects. As Mayhew writes: "For typical voters Capitol Hill is a distant and mysterious place; few have anything like a working knowledge of its maneuverings. Hence there is no easy way of knowing whether a congressman is staking a valid claim or not . . . [and for] a voter lacking an easy way to sort out valid from invalid claims the sensible recourse is skepticism" (1974, 60). If lack of information makes it difficult for U.S. congressional representatives to claim credit for their legislative activities, it is likely even more difficult for Honduran deputies, given the country's low level of education.

12. In this way, politics in Honduras differs from that in Brazil. In Brazil, opposition legislators "sell" their support for bills initiated by the executive in exchange for pork projects and other resources (Ames 2001; Desposato 2001). They have this opportunity because the president or governor rarely has a majority in the legislature, due to the fragmented party system. The executive needs to "purchase" support in the legislature to pass bills, and deputies can trade their votes for resources controlled by the executive branch. In Honduras, until 2002, the president's party always had a majority in Congress, and the president's strong partisan powers ensure backbencher loyalty. Under these circumstances, opposition deputies do not have the opportunity to "sell" their votes to the executive in exchange for access to pork and patronage, because the governing party has not needed their votes to pass legislation and does not want to share resources.

13. Scott argues that an urban machine "dealt almost exclusively in *particularistic, material rewards* to maintain and extend its control over its personnel. Although pork-barrel legislation provided inducements for ethnic groups as a whole, the machine did most of its favors for individuals and families" (1969, 1144). He also contends that patrons deliver many benefits to clients during the enforcement stage of policy implementation, when the patron secures an exception to a rule for the client.

14. This deputy is an outlier in many ways. He was a frequent initiator not only of locally targeted bills but of all other types of bills as well. He also held leadership positions in Congress and in his party. To make certain that this deputy and other Congress and party leaders were not biasing the analysis, I ran all models excluding members of the congressional leadership, and the results remained the same.

15. Since *suplentes* are not included in the analysis, a *suplente* elected for two consecutive terms is not included in the count of reelected deputies. A *suplente* who became a *propietario* in the next election was counted as reelected. A *propietario* reelected as a *suplente* was not counted as reelected.

16. I also ran the analysis using other indicators: population with less than three years, and less than six years, of schooling, and a composite indicator of the prosperity of a department (based on the percentage of households with access to electricity, running water, and television). The results did not change, and all indicators are strongly correlated.

17. The PINU and PDCH competed in the 1993 elections but did not win any municipalities. Small parties did not begin to win municipal elections until 1997.

18. There is one exception to the "wealthy" department–high population rule. The Bay Islands are a small department in terms of population (DM = 1), but prosperous because of tourism (only 11.6% of the population has no education). Despite its prosperity, in-migration to that department has been low.

19. Hypothesis 1 predicts that politicians will perform more constituency service when they are elected by open-list rather than closed-list rules. This is a routine expectation in the electoral institution literature, but it cannot be tested here, as Honduras has always used closed-list elections. The results thus begin with a test of hypothesis 2.

20. Most party and congressional leaders are elected from the two largest departments. In the 1994–97 Congress, the Congress president, three of four vice presidents, one of two secretaries, and the faction leader of one of the major parties were elected from the two largest departments.

21. The only substantive difference between models 1 and 2 is that the *department dominance* variable is not significant in model 1. However, theory does not predict a relationship between district competitiveness and the incentive created by the size of DM in closed-list PR electoral systems.

22. However, with a *p* value of .498, the sign for *marginal list position* has little meaning.

23. Simulations based on model 2 are almost identical to those for model 3.

24. However, overlapping confidence intervals between new and senior deputies make it difficult to draw conclusions here.

25. All findings are substantively the same. The sign on *average percentage of deputies reelected in department* becomes negative, but it never comes close to conventional significance levels in any model.

26. There are signs that this support is eroding, as small parties won 12 of 128 seats in the 2001 elections, and for the first time even won seats outside the two largest departments. Even in the 2001 elections, however, the traditional parties won 80 percent of the vote in the congressional elections and 92 percent in the presidential election.

27. This was most noticeable in the 1993 election, when PNH supporters were reported to have stayed home to protest the lack of benefits from their party when it was in power, from 1990 to 1993. Both traditional parties should have learned from that election that while poor clients may be reluctant to switch parties, they will not continue to vote for patrons who do not deliver when they control executive-branch resources. This example of experiential learning, even in long-established clientelistic political parties, illustrates how new "rules of the game" can be transmitted in informal institutions (Helmke and Levitsky, introduction to this volume). In this case, clients communicated rules to patrons.

CHAPTER 6. DO INFORMAL RULES MAKE DEMOCRACY WORK?

1. One might object that grammatical rules do not govern, but simply describe, behavior. Yet these rules, in fact, are as prescriptive as they are descriptive; the point of their formalization is to police people's usage, which is prone to stray from the rules.

2. I mean by *accountability* the ability and tendency of voters to turn out of office those governments and politicians that, at the end of their term, are deemed by voters to have performed below a threshold that the voters set. I mean by *responsiveness* a tendency for governments and politicians to adopt policies preferred by (a majority of) their constituents. Democratic theorists often hold that accountability causes responsiveness, but responsiveness can be achieved through other mechanisms as well.

3. On sociotropic and egocentric rules, see Ferejohn (1986); on socialization voting, Campbell et al. (1964); on spatial voting, Downs (1957); on strategic voting, Cox (1997); on directional voting, Rabinowitz and McDonald (1989); on ethnic voting, Chandra (2004); on clientelistic voting, Stokes (2005).

4. Peronist party member, interview by Valeria Brusco, Marcelo Nazareno, and the author, Córdoba, Argentina, January 2003.

5. Peronist party member, interview by Valeria Brusco, Marcelo Nazareno, and the author, Córdoba, Argentina, January 2003.

6. See Gibson and Calvo (2000), Remmer and Wibbels (2000), UNDP (2002), Calvo and Murillo (2004), Amaral and Stokes (2005), and Cleary and Stokes (forthcoming).

7. The surveys were carried out in December 2001 and January 2002. We instructed the polling firm Consultores en Políticas Públicas, S.A., to conduct face-to-face interviews with 480 adults, aged eighteen or older, in each of the four regions. To select our sample, we used multistage cluster sampling procedures, based on census tracks.

8. The models in table 6.2 include dummy variables for respondents who lived in all three regions other than Mar del Plata. Negative signs on the Buenos Aires, Córdoba, and Misiones dummies indicate that people in these provinces were less likely than others to offer "accountability" answers to the question.

9. Here and later I generated the simulations using the Clarify program (King et al. 2000; Tomz et al. 2003). This program draws simulations of parameters of statistical models (in this case, logit regressions) from their sampling distribution and then converts these simulated parameters into expected values, such as expected probabilities of an answer to a survey question, given hypothetical values of explanatory variables. For this simulation we held household income, educational level, quality of housing, age, and population size of the respondents' community at their sample means, and assumed a female Peronist supporter.

10. I did study the effect of the proportion of poor people in a municipality—measured as either the proportion of houses that are substandard or the proportion of people in a municipality with "unsatisfied basic needs"—on the beliefs and expectations discussed in this chapter. Unfortunately, these data come from the 1991 census and hence are not very reliable measures of poverty rates in 2001–2, when we conducted the survey. Furthermore, poverty rates are a very uncertain measure of the distribution of income: two communities with identical poverty rates may have very different Gini indices, for example. With both caveats, the effect of poverty

rates was the reverse of what we might have expected: the *higher* the poverty rate in the community, the more likely a person was (all else being equal) to offer "accountability" responses to various questions. Nor did poverty rates make regional effects disappear; indeed, poverty rates, if anything, brought out these regional effects more strongly.

CHAPTER 7. THE BIRTH AND TRANSFORMATION OF THE *DEDAZO* IN MEXICO

The author thanks Gretchen Helmke, Steven Levitsky, and Ignacio Marván Laborde for their help with this chapter.

1. The PRI was created in 1929 by then-president Plutarco Elías Calles, and was placed on a mass base by President Lázaro Cárdenas in the 1930s. For several decades, the party won presidential elections by more than 70 percent of the national vote.

2. One obvious exception to this rule was Luis Donaldo Colosio, who was assassinated in a campaign event after being named the PRI's presidential candidate in the 1994 race.

3. The nonconsecutive reelection clause was changed several times before the final 1933 edict. In 1917, the representatives to the Constitutional Convention determined that there would be no reelection for presidents and the term of office would last four years. In January 1927, General Álvaro Obregón changed the articles and allowed for the reelection of the president after one term out of office, so revolutionary strongmen Álvaro Obregón and Plutarco Elías Calles could alternate in the presidency. In January 1928, the presidential term was lengthened to six years. In 1933, under the guidance of former president and then–*jefe máximo* Elías Calles, the article was again reformed to prohibit consecutive reelection for congressmen, local deputies, and municipal presidents and any reelection of presidents and governors (including, for the first time, provisional and interim executives). With three constitutional changes in fifteen years, it was entirely credible that the article could be changed once again at the whim of a new president or strongman, so one cannot argue that the informal prerogatives grew up around an entrenched formal rule. Cárdenas could have at least attempted to reverse the nonreelection clause back to its 1927 phrasing to give him another chance to win the presidency after a term out of office. The 1933 prohibition of reelection was not a rock-solid formal institution until President Miguel Alemán (1946–52) challenged it by starting a whispering campaign favoring his reelection (and a change in the Constitution), and failed (see Nieto 1993). On Alemán's failed attempt at reelection, see Paoli Bolio (1985).

4. The 1946 challenger had been the secretary of foreign relations in the then-current administration.

5. In practice, only a few secretariats were considered important enough to field a possible presidential candidate. These included the Treasury (Hacienda), Spending (Presupuesto), Home Office (Gobernación), and, early on, the Labor ministry.

6. Some argue that de la Madrid and his aides simply did not take the CD leaders, Porfirio Muñoz Ledo and Cuauhtémoc Cárdenas, seriously and, for this reason, never believed that their break with the party would constitute such a serious threat to the electoral fortunes of the PRI's presidential candidate. Jorge de la Vega Domínguez, then-leader of the PRI, interview, Mexico City, March 1996.

7. One should also point out that during the late 1990s, some changes in nomination practices were not carried out through formal statutory reform—for example, gubernato-

rial nominations went from presidential imposition to open state primaries without any real change in the formal party rules. The statutes were so ambiguous that the change could be made without a formal rewriting.

8. Because of the particular electoral calendar in Mexico, with governors elected on a staggered calendar, President Zedillo had not appointed many of the governors serving under him in 1996. Few if any of the state executives were Zedillo allies, and they had no special reason to protect his ability to place his own successor. Finally, two of the most independent PRI governors, Manuel Bartlett of Puebla and Roberto Madrazo of Tabasco, attended the statutory working group and helped instigate the rebellion that would remove the president's technocrats from the nomination race.

9. A large number of publications have described the changing nature of the regime's elite during the last two decades of its rule. The discussion centered on the growing importance of technocratic, elite-educated leaders, who had never held elected posts and who rose to positions of power. The positions of bureaucrats and politicians were considered political careers that held increasingly little promise (Camp 1985; Centeno 1994).

10. For more on Zedillo's statements on the succession process, see *Reforma* (Mexico City), June 10, 1998, and *El Universal* (Mexico City), October 13, 1998.

11. One should not exaggerate the fairness of the new nomination method. In Mexico, the Federal Electoral Commission does not regulate party primaries, so each party must take responsibility for managing its own nominations. This constitutes a problem when the de facto leader of the party (in this case, President Zedillo) clearly has a favorite—and the resources to tip the balance. The electoral method was designed to minimize the ability of any pre-candidate to use fraud to win the contest (the winner had to capture a majority of the nation's three hundred electoral districts, so winning a million extra votes in a geographic region would not decide the primary). Explicit rules to guarantee that nominees would receive equal treatment and resources were, by and large, ignored, because the enforcement of these rules was largely impossible. This is an important issue: to this day (2006), primaries are still not the only method for choosing candidates, and there are no clear rules for the presidential nomination. This has begun to provoke conflict within the PRI as groups look for leverage to choose the nominating procedure for 2005. Formal rules still do not dictate all political outcomes within the PRI.

12. Closed primaries, consisting of only registered party members, could not be held because there was no reliable membership list acceptable to the pre-candidates.

CHAPTER 8. ELECTION INSURANCE AND COALITION SURVIVAL

A related paper based on this research was originally published as "Insurance for Good Losers and the Survival of Chile's *Concertación*," by John M. Carey and Peter M. Siavelis, *Latin American Politics and Society*, vol. 47, no. 2 (Summer 2005), pp. 1–22.

1. This is true for the Chamber of Deputies, whose 120 members are elected from sixty two-member districts, and for the *elected* members of the Senate, who are chosen, two each, from nineteen districts.

2. The frequent result, as noted in many accounts of posttransition elections in Chile, is that the second-place candidate in a district, in terms of preference votes, is not elected to

Congress. This happens when the first- and second-place candidates are on the same list, but that list's total does not double the total of the second-place list.

3. The Alianza por Chile has also been known as Democracia y Progreso and Unión por el Progreso. The Union of the Center-Center (UCC) aligned formally with the Right for the 1993 election. Party key: PDC, Christian Democratic Party (Partido Demócrata Cristiano); PRSD, Radical Social Democratic Party (Partido Radical Social Demócrata); PPD, Party for Democracy (Partido Por La Democracia); PS, Socialist Party (Partido Socialista); RN, National Renewal (Renovación Nacional); UDI, Independent Democratic Union (Unión Demócrata Independiente).

4. For a more comprehensive discussion of the intricacies of the Chilean party system and the empirical conditions that bear on coalition formation, see Siavelis (2002b).

5. The mean shares of the two-coalition vote were, respectively, 59 and 41 percent, with a standard deviation of 9 percent. Thus, the Concertación could double with a performance one standard deviation above the mean, whereas the Right had to perform three standard deviations above the mean.

6. The legislators wish to remain anonymous. The conversations took place in April 2003 with a former deputy from the Christian Democrats, and in December 2003 with an incumbent deputy from the UDI, the latter conducted by Adam Brinegar, who provided research assistance for this project.

7. Concertación lists that successfully double, of course, produce no good losers, because both their candidates are elected, so these lists are not included in the analysis.

8. www.elecciones.gov.cl/full/indexf.htm.

9. Including these Senate good losers should bias against supporting our model, as we are beefing up the "least likelies" category with Senate candidates, who are more likely than Chamber candidates to secure appointments.

10. "Most likelies" and "least likelies" were subject to an exhaustive search, beginning with our appointment database, followed by an extensive search of the entire Government of Chile website (including current and past legislators). We followed up with combined searches of first name, last name, and political party, then first and last names, and then simply last names, using the Google search engine (widely acknowledged as the most complete and accurate). We examined every hit and followed up to ensure that we had identified the correct person, paired with the correct postelection position. One could contend that the probable higher visibility of "most likelies" makes them more likely to be found, skewing results in favor of our hypothesis. To the extent that this was the case, however, our search efforts were asymmetric, with greater effort devoted to the "least likelies," for whom postelectoral career information was generally more sparse. In the end, we are confident that the information we collected accurately reflects the postelectoral fates of both groups.

11. UDI deputy, Congress of Chile, interview by Adam Brinegar, Valparaiso, December 9, 2003.

12. UDI deputy, Congress of Chile, interview by Adam Brinegar, Valparaiso, December 9, 2003.

13. Indeed, scrapping the two-member system has been on and off the Chilean agenda since it was first imposed, over the objections of the parties that went on to form the Concerta-

ción. In the early 1990s, supporters of the former Pinochet regime defended this particular formal institution against Concertación attacks. Over time, the Concertación adapted to the two-member system, and its objections diminished. If the Chilean electoral landscape changes, and Concertación dominance is shaken, the coalition's discomfort with the two-member system should revive.

CHAPTER 9. INFORMAL INSTITUTIONS AND PARTY ORGANIZATION IN LATIN AMERICA

A modified version of this chapter is scheduled to be published in *Party Politics*. The authors thank Manuel Alcántara, Gretchen Helmke, David Scott Palmer, and Guillermo O'Donnell for comments on earlier drafts of the chapter.

1. Recent exceptions include Mainwaring (1999) and Erdmann (2004).

2. See Duverger (1954), Kirchheimer (1966), Panebianco (1988), Kitschelt (1994), and Katz and Mair (1994, 1995).

3. See Roberts (1998), Mainwaring (1999), Freidenberg (2003), Levitsky (2003b), and the chapters by Desposato, Taylor-Robinson, and Langston in this volume.

4. Eduardo Rollano, PJ legislator, interview by Levitsky, June 24, 1997. All interviews by Levitsky were conducted in Buenos Aires.

5. Raúl Roa, ex-treasurer of the PJ Federal Capital branch, interview by Levitsky, May 12, 1997.

6. Daniel Checker, interview by Levitsky, September 9, 1997.

7. José Luis Gioja, PJ senator, interview by Levitsky, September 18, 1997.

8. Roberto Garcia, interview by Levitsky, June 23, 1997.

9. Ibid.

10. Raúl Roa, interview by Levitsky, May 12, 1997.

11. The PJ has never held a competitive primary to select its national leadership and has only once (in 1988) held a competitive primary to select its presidential candidate.

12. Bucaram has been self-exiled on three different occasions due to corruption charges. He has lived outside Ecuador (currently in Panama) for more than ten years.

13. Interview with anonymous politician, by Freidenberg, Quito, June 20, 1999.

14. Abdalá Bucaram, interview by Freidenberg, Panama City, August 16, 1999.

15. Many party activists describe themselves as *abdalacistas* rather than *roldosistas*.

CHAPTER 10. THE RULE OF (NON)LAW

1. Here we need to distinguish between an observer's belief that the conduct in question responds to a written rule and a shared belief among the relevant actors that their behavior is required by an unwritten rule of some kind, which may be enforced if violated. As discussed in the following paragraphs, the latter is precisely the sort of shared *normative* expectation that defines an informal rule.

2. Some rules are enforced through a combination of negative sanctions for violations and positive rewards for compliance. For a discussion of when a society might choose to reward compliance rather than simply punish a breach, see Ellickson (1991, 124–26). For simplicity, in

this chapter I speak as if—as is usually the case—enforcement implies punishment rather than reward, though it should be understood that they are merely opposite sides of the same coin.

3. In fact, it is the potential for enforcement behavior that makes informal institutions an interesting concept. Without that, they add nothing to an explanation that could simply list the various first-order incentives that cause actors to choose one course of conduct over another. The corollary to this observation is that, just as we must define the organizational context in which an informal rule operates, we must also identify the relevant enforcement instances that are charged with ensuring that the informal institution is respected. It is these agents that must hold some sort of normative attachment to the rule, in the relatively thin sense that they will apply sanctions to deviant behavior in order to uphold the rule.

4. There are others who do explore the roots of the problem; see, e.g., Skolnick and Fyfe (1993), Chevigny (1995), and Holston and Caldeira (1998).

5. I used a figure of thirty-six million inhabitants for the state of São Paulo, as reported on the state government's official website, and a figure of twelve million for the Buenos Aires Metro area, from the *Encyclopaedia Britannica*'s list of largest metropolitan areas. The available figures for São Paulo suggest that the proportion of killings in the capital versus the rest of the state roughly corresponds to the capital's relative population.

6. This figure of 6.23 per 100,000 does not include an additional 85 annual victims of *grupos de extermínio*, even though all accounts of these groups confirm a high participation of police officers. See, e.g., interview with Costa Ferreira in Oiticica (2001); see also de Oliveira et al. (2000).

7. The point is not that the conviction rate should be 100 percent. The other side of the coin is the success of the institution in protecting the rights of those who are accused on the basis of flimsy or inaccurate evidence. Thus a certain number of acquittals are to be expected and are, indeed, a sign of health. But the rate of appropriate convictions should be higher where the investigative, prosecutorial, and judicial functions are most effective.

8. Data on *per capita police homicides* are compiled from unofficial sources in Argentina (Center for Legal and Social Studies [CELS] in Buenos Aires; Council against Police and Institutional Repression [CORREPI] in Córdoba), and in São Paulo from the Ouvidoria da Polícia, a state-run ombudsman organization. In Uruguay, data are from human rights reports, especially the Peace and Justice Service (SERPAJ) and U.S. State Department, and my own search of newspaper archives. In Salvador da Bahia, the data are from a study by the Archdiocese of Salvador and a number of other organizations. The *conviction rates* are from samples of cases that I gathered and tracked through the courts. In Argentina, the points of departure for the samples are lists of victims compiled by civil society organizations (primarily CORREPI) that conduct daily newspaper reviews and have networks of informants in marginal areas. In São Paulo, the starting point is a list compiled by the Ouvidoria da Polícia. In Uruguay, I conducted my own search of newspaper archives, as well as reviewing all the available human rights reports that dealt with police violence during the 1990s. In Salvador, I was unable to piece together a representative sample of police homicide prosecutions. Instead, I interviewed a number of representatives of NGOs, prosecutors, and lawyers, and reviewed newspaper accounts, estimating a conviction rate about half that of São Paulo, based on my own qualitative impression of the judicial response. Descriptive details of the performance of the courts in Salvador that support this low evaluation are set forth at length in later sections of the chapter.

9. While the evidence suggests that the rule applies in Salvador as well, I have not included that city in table 10.1, for two reasons. First, the evidence from Salvador is more qualitative and not based on a representative sample, so simple percentages are misleading. Second, though it includes Violent Victims, the rule seems broader in Salvador, as discussed in more detail in the text.

10. Note that the conviction rates in non–Violent Victim cases are still quite low in Buenos Aires and São Paulo. I have argued elsewhere (Brinks 2003a, 2003b) that these low conviction rates are the result not of an informal rule but rather of other limitations of the legal system. Due to space constraints, this chapter focuses on the Violent Victim cases in Buenos Aires and São Paulo.

11. *La Nación* (Buenos Aires), October 4, 2000, p. 17.

12. Yulo Oiticica, Dossiê Grupos de Extermínio, unpublished legislative briefing material, 2000, on file with author.

13. Even after a separate judicial police force was authorized in the province of Buenos Aires, investigators remained part of, and under the control and supervision of, the regular police hierarchy. And in the federal system, the federal police continue to carry out all the investigations and forensic tests required by the courts.

14. Case documents and interviews with Beatriz Sinisgalli of the Centro Santo Dias de Direitos Humanos, São Paulo, 2001.

15. "Tras cinco años de concluída la tragedia, concluyó el juicio oral [Five years after the tragedy, the oral trial concludes]," *La Nación* (Buenos Aires), December 8, 2004; and interviews with lawyers from CORREPI, 2000–2001.

16. "Policiais militares acusados de executar assaltante na Bahia camburtao [Military police accused of executing bank robber in police wagon]," *A Tarde* (Salvador), October 14, 1999.

17. "Mais que mil palavras [Worth a thousand words]," *A Tarde* (Salvador), October 13, 1999.

18. As of December 2005, extensive searches of the online archives of *A Tarde* do not reveal any news items regarding a trial or conviction of these police officers.

19. "PM s matam jovem e ficam impunes [Military police kill youth with impunity]," *A Tarde* (Salvador), December 31, 2000.

20. *A Tarde* (Salvador), April 16, 2000, p. 7.

21. Author's review of case file, Case No. 1908-1998, vara 1ª do júri, São Paulo.

22. José Antonio Carvalho, Cidade Repartida, Salvador, Gráfica do Sindicato dos Bancários, Salvador, 2001, on file with author.

23. Valdemar Oliveira, director of CEDECA, interview, Salvador, Bahia, May 22, 2001; CEDECA report, January 17, 2001, on file with author.

24. Ibid.

CHAPTER 11. MEXICO'S POSTELECTORAL *CONCERTACESIONES*

The author thanks Gretchen Helmke and Steven Levitsky for helpful comments, and acknowledges research funding from the United States Agency for International Development Grant 523-A-00-00-00030-00.

1. See, e.g., Aguilar Camín and Meyer (1993, 178–83) on consolidation of the PRI-state's Janus-faced policies toward dissenters, fully developed by the 1960s.

2. Between 1989 and 2000, the PRD staged 750 postelectoral conflicts, while the PAN staged only 200 (Eisenstadt 2004, 141).

3. As PRD leader Javier González Garza (federal deputy and former national PRD director of electoral affairs) put it: "The PRD is an optical illusion rather than a party," and "every day, there are a hundred acts in the country in the name of the party about which the national directorate knows nothing." Interview, Mexico City, August 25, 1996.

4. Any worthy governor followed this judicially inscrutable and politically expedient formula, perfected, perhaps, by Puebla state's ruthless Maximino Ávila Camacho (1937–41), whose "intervention . . . in local elections assured that most of the municipalities would be composed of allies sympathetic to the 'political line' of the governor," prone to "dissolving municipalities that remained outside his yoke, and naming, in their place, municipal council governments" (Valencia Castrejón 1996, 106–7).

5. This database covers all mayoral races in Mexico's thirty-one states between 1989 and 2000, based on coding of national and local print media. The numbers cited refer only to municipal councils formed specifically to alleviate postelectoral conflicts (as opposed to those formed to stem corruption, or because a mayor died, or for other reasons).

6. The federal documents used for this analysis were incomplete, accounting for only 103 municipal councils in fifteen of Mexico's thirty-one states, between 1989 and 1996. Reasons for creation of each municipal council were given in only 60 of these cases (Federal Secretary of the Interior 1996). Percentages are based on an N of 60, which, as I argue elsewhere (Eisenstadt 2004, 121), vastly underrepresents the actual number of occurrences.

7. An earlier "People's Tribunal" in the state of Puebla was actually established as part of the PAN's Puebla 1983 postelectoral mobilization (Alvarez de Vicencio 1995, 142), but it did not seem to have much transcendence.

8. Boylan quotes long-time Salinas confidant Manuel Camacho: "My impression is that the president never stopped worrying about the possibility that [Cuauhtémoc] Cárdenas' popularity might grow and that he might win in 1994 . . . This was true even after 1991 and continued right until the very end" (2001a, 16).

9. Amador Rodríguez Lozano, former national PRI electoral affairs secretary and Baja California senator, interview, Mexico City, August 12, 1996. Article 9 of the Yucatán state constitution calls for naming a temporary replacement, but only until a new election is convened.

10. Rodríguez Lozano, interview; Orlando Paredes, Yucatán gubernatorial candidate and former Mérida mayoral candidate, interview, Mérida, Mexico, May 25, 2001.

11. An embittered Paredes denounced the agreement even in 2001, insisting that he had never resigned. Interview, May 25, 2001.

12. The 1994 electoral process was deemed transparent by most observers, despite persistent complaints, largely by the PRD, about subtle forms of manipulation of the electoral registry and gerrymandering of congressional districts.

13. Andrés Manuel López Obrador, PRD Tabasco formal gubernatorial candidate, interview, Villahermosa, Mexico, January 14, 1996.

14. Arturo Núñez Jiménez, former subsecretary of the Interior Secretariat of the Mexican federal government, interview, Mexico City, August 28, 1996.

15. Jaime Cárdenas, former Federal Electoral Institute citizen counselor, interview, Mexico City, July 19, 2000.

16. Sandra Fuentes-Berain, PRI international coordinator, with Carter Center delegation, interview, Mexico City, June 14, 2000.

17. Fox was the 1991 Guanajuato gubernatorial candidate who contested his dubious loss and negotiated an interim governorship for fellow Guanajuato PANista Carlos Medina Plascencia (now a prominent senator). Interior secretary Santiago Creel, the most powerful cabinet member, was a clutch mediator in the attempted *concertacesión* with the PRD, Tabasco, 1994. And Senator Diego Fernández de Cevallos, the PAN's interlocutor with Salinas during most *concertacesión* negotiations of that era, was the PAN's 1994 presidential candidate and continues (as of 2006) to serve as one of the party's most prominent senators. Federal controller Francisco Barrio, probable victor of the Chihuahua 1986 governor's race, tried to negotiate a political solution to that fraud-riddled election but found no interlocutor in the presidential administration of Miguel de la Madrid (1982–88).

18. Marco A. Zazueta Félix, PRI representative at the Federal Electoral Institute, interview, Mexico City, July 18, 2000.

19. More than 10 percent of the PAN's 321 legislative initiatives in the pre-1988 years were electoral reform proposals, and it had advocated for the creation of an electoral court starting in 1947 (Eisenstadt 204, 168).

20. The ruling was disseminated via the internet (www.trife.gob.mx).

21. Mauro Miguel Reyes Zapata, magistrate of the Electoral Court of the Judicial Power of the Federation, interview, Mexico City, January 16, 2001.

22. For example, during the Tabasco controversy, Fox announced: "This is an issue for Tabasco to decide and not for the Federal Executive, which has powers clearly delineated in the constitution, which nowhere states that we should go around sticking our noses in to see what happens in the states. Other presidents were accustomed to doing that, but it is not happening now, nor will it" (Garduño 2001, 3).

23. José de Jesús Orozco Henríquez, magistrate of the Electoral Court of the Judicial Power of the Federation, interview, Mexico City, January 18, 2001.

CHAPTER 12. DISPENSING JUSTICE AT THE MARGINS OF FORMALITY

The author is indebted to Willem Assies and Raquel Yrigoyen for help with obtaining documents, to Fernando García and René Kuppe for conveying information on the status of relevant legislation, and to René Kuppe and Rachel Sieder for comments on a previous draft of this chapter. She gratefully acknowledges funding support for field research from a 1997 Fulbright dissertation fellowship and two University of Tennessee Professional Development Awards.

1. Where states officially have codified multiculturalism as a principle of the political system and established regimes of legal pluralism, the category of *competing* is open to interpretation. Sanctions imposed by culturally distinct indigenous authorities that may seem to violate state law—such as corporal punishment—may be interpreted as not competing if one evaluates them in the context of indigenous cultures, which are held to be equally valid sources of law.

2. But in practice, as we shall see, those institutions that are more complementary than

substitutive tend also to be more accommodating than competing, since coordination and cooperation are more likely to entail some accommodation. The converse is not true, however: institutions closer to the substitutive end are not necessarily more competing, since they typically have less contact with the state.

3. René Orellana Halkyer, interview, Santa Cruz, Bolivia, July 18, 1997; Isabelle Combes, interview, Santa Cruz, Bolivia, July 18, 1997.

4. The accused is suspended in the air by his arms, which are tied behind his back.

5. *Ronda* violence must be evaluated in context. Starn (1999, 88–89) compares the approximately five thousand murders committed by police and the military in the south-central Andes during the 1980s with only eleven *ronda* murders committed between 1976 and 1992, despite the more than half a million *ronderos* active during that period.

6. Also, interviews with representatives of municipal authorities in Cuzco, Peru, July 2002.

7. All references in this section on *juntas vecinales* are to these Ministerio de Justicia y Derechos Humanos publications (1997a, 1997b).

8. Costa Rica has produced a small amount of jurisprudence. However, whereas Costa Rica's Constitutional Court recognizes the *private* nature of indigenous authorities (Chacón Castro 1999, 129), Colombia's Court views them as *public* authorities.

CONCLUSION

1. On variation in institutional strength in Latin America, see Levitsky and Murillo (2005).

2. For example, no recognizable (formal or informal) rule governed presidential mandates in Argentina between 1928 and 2003. During that period, only two elected presidents completed their constitutional mandate, and both of them (Juan Perón and Carlos Menem) modified the Constitution to grant themselves an additional term.

3. Other typologies of informal institutions in the developing world include those of Lauth (2000), Hyden (2002), and Grzymala-Busse (2004).

4. Indeed, "clientelism may be the most prolific informal institution around the world" (Hyden 2002, 18).

5. According to Anna Grzymala-Busse (2004), patronage distribution and illicit party finance became particularly widespread in postsocialist countries that lacked robust partisan competition.

6. See also Ledeneva (1998), Darden (2002), Collins (2003, 2004), and Gel'man (2004).

7. See also Griffiths (1986), Moore (1986), and Merry (1988).

8. According to K. Tsai, such informal norms emerge in "formal institutional environments that fail to reflect the implicit demands of both political and economic actors" (2003, 3).

9. Interestingly, some Soviet-era norms survived the transition to a market economy (Clarke 1995; Ledeneva 1998; Sil 2001). As Rudra Sil (2001) has shown, for example, workers and managers in many privatized Russian firms continued to adhere to preexisting "nonmarket norms" during the 1990s in an effort to cope with new market institutions that they were unable to change.

10. See, e.g., John Carey's recent work (2003, 2004) on transparency in legislative voting.

11. As Siavelis suggests (this volume), Chile may be an exception in this regard.

12. Thus, whereas thirty-nine of forty-five sub-Saharan African countries were governed by one-party regimes in 1989 (Olukoshi 1998, 9), five years later "single-party rule had been at least formally abolished throughout almost the entire region" (Kirschke 2000, 386).

AFTERWORD

1. Which, for that matter, could also be South Chicago or the Bronx, which shows that these problems do not refer only to "underdeveloped" countries. But the issue, to which I will return, is the relative weight of the respective informal rules, and the degree to which, and the number or type of occasions in which, they are effective.

2. On this subtle but important matter, see Bourdieu (1999).

3. Of course, I am not proposing this shifting *actor* perspective as an alternative to the study of informal *rules* and *institutions*. I just believe that such a perspective would provide additional valuable information on this whole matter.

4. See the chapters by Siavelis, Mejía Acosta, Samuels, Taylor-Robinson, Carey and Siavelis, and Freidenberg and Levitsky.

5. This knowledge dates back to the authors of the *Federalist Papers*—and, for that matter, even before them, to Montesquieu and Machiavelli, among others.

6. For the seminal work, see March and Simon (1958). A huge literature on various sides of this matter followed.

7. See, e.g., Stokes's chapter in this volume.

8. See the chapters by Desposato, Taylor-Robinson, Langston, Freidenberg and Levitsky, Brinks, and Eisenstadt. For an apposite detailed study, see Hagopian (1996).

9. This remark points to a topic that has generated enormous attention and many polemics in several disciplines and regions: the complex interactions between "imported" formal institutions and developing countries' institutions, rules, and practices. Of course, I cannot deal with this matter here.

References

Abrúcio, Fernando. 1998. *Os Barões da Federação*. São Paulo, Brazil: Departamento de Ciên-cia Política da Universidade de São Paulo–Editora Hucitec.

Acemoglu, Daron, and James Robinson. 2002. "The Political Economy of the Kuznets Curve." *Journal of Public Economics* 84: 341–56.

——. 2005. *Economic Origins of Dictatorship and Democracy*. New York: Cambridge University Press.

Agüero, Felipe. 2003. "Chile: Unfinished Transition and Increased Political Competition." In Jorge I. Domínguez and Michael Shifter, eds., *Constructing Democratic Governance in Latin America*. 2nd ed. Baltimore: Johns Hopkins University Press.

Aguilar Camín, Hector, and Lorenzo Meyer. 1993. *In the Shadow of the Mexican Revolution—Contemporary Mexican History, 1910–1989*. Austin: University of Texas Press.

Akerlof, George A. 1970. "The Market for 'Lemons': Quality Uncertainty and the Market Mechanism." *Quarterly Journal of Economics* 84, no. 3: 488–500.

Alcántara Sáez, Manuel. 2004. *Instituciones o máquinas ideológicas? Origen, programa y organización de los partidos latinoamericanos*. Barcelona, Spain: Institut de Ciènces Politiques i Socials.

Alcántara Sáez, Manuel, and Flavia Freidenberg, eds. 2001. *Partidos Políticos de América Latina*. Salamanca, Spain: Ediciones Universidad de Salamanca.

Alvarez de Vicencio, María Elena. 1995. *Municipio y Democracia—Tesis y prácticas de gobierno del Partido Acción Nacional*. Mexico City: Epessa.

Amaral, Samuel, and Susan C. Stokes. 2005. *La democracia local en Argentina: Clientelismo, capital social, e innovación en Argentina*. Buenos Aires, Argentina: Universidad Tres de Febrero.

Ames, Barry. 1987. *Political Survival: Politicians and Public Policy in Latin America*. California Series on Social Choice and Political Economy 12. Berkeley: University of California Press.

——. 1995a. "Electoral Rules, Constituency Pressures, and Pork Barrel: Bases of Voting in the Brazilian Congress." *Journal of Politics* 57, no. 2: 324–43.

——. 1995b. "Electoral Strategy under Open-List Proportional Representation." *American Journal of Political Science* 39, no. 2: 406–33.

——. 2001. *The Deadlock of Democracy in Brazil*. Ann Arbor: University of Michigan Press.

Amorim Neto, Octavio. 1998. "Of President, Parties, and Ministers: Cabinet Formation and Legislative Decision-making under Separation of Powers." Ph.D. diss., Department of Political Science, University of California, San Diego.

———. 2000. "Gabinetes presidenciais, ciclos eleitorais e disiplina legislative no Brasil." *Dados* 43, no. 3: 479–519.

———. 2002. "Presidential Cabinets and Legislative Cohesion in Brazil." In S. Morgenstern and B. Nacif, eds., *Legislative Politics in Latin America*. Cambridge: Cambridge University Press.

Amorim-Neto, Octavio, and Fabiano Santos. 2001. "The Executive Connection: Presidentially Defined Factions and Party Discipline in Brazil." *Party Politics* 7, no. 2: 213–34.

Araujo, Caridad. 1998. *Gobernabilidad durante la crisis y políticas de ajuste*. Quito, Ecuador: Corporation of Development Studies (CORDES)–Konrad Adenauer Foundation.

Ardito Vega, Wilfredo. 2001. "Cambios culturales en la justica de paz." Paper presented at Red Latinoamericana de Antropología Jurídica-Sección Perú, Conferencia en Lima, Feb. 7. Available at www.alertanet.org.

Assad, Carlos Martínez, and Alicia Ziccardi. 1988. *Política y gestión municipal en México*. Mexico City: National Autonomous University of Mexico, Instituto de Investigaciones Sociales.

Assies, Willem. 2001. "La oficialización de lo no oficial: (re)encuentro de dos mundos?" *Alteridades* 11, no. 21: 83–96.

———. 2003. "Indian Justice in the Andes: Re-rooting or Re-routing?" In Ton Salman and Annalies Zoomers, eds., *Imagining the Andes: Shifting Margins of a Marginal World?* Amsterdam: Center for Latin American Research and Documentation.

Austen-Smith, David, and Jeffrey Banks. 1990. "Stable Governments and the Allocation of Policy Portfolios." *American Political Science Review* 84, no. 3: 891–906.

Auyero, Javier. 2000a. "The Logic of Clientelism in Argentina: An Ethnographic Account." *Latin American Research Review* 35, no. 3: 55–81.

———. 2000b. *Poor People's Politics: Peronist Survival Networks and the Legacy of Evita*. Durham, NC: Duke University Press.

Axelrod, Robert. 1984. *The Evolution of Cooperation*. New York: Basic Books.

———. 1986. "An Evolutionary Approach to Norms." *American Political Science Review* 80, no. 4: 1095–1112.

Bailey, John. 1988. *Governing Mexico: The Statecraft of Crisis Management*. New York: St. Martin's Press.

Baldez, Lisa, and John Carey. 1996. "The Chilean Budget Process." Unpublished ms., paper presented at the World Bank Conference on Policy Making in Latin America, University of California, San Diego, May.

Banfield, Edward C., and James Q. Wilson. 1965. *City Politics*. Cambridge, MA: Harvard University Press.

Barkin, David. 1990. *Distorted Development—Mexico in the World Economy*. Boulder, CO: Westview Press.

Bauer, Raymond A., Alex Inkeles, and Clyde Kluckhorn. 1956. *How the Soviet System Works: Cultural, Psychological, and Social Themes*. Cambridge, MA: Harvard University Press.

Berliner, Joseph S. 1957. *Factory and Manager in the USSR*. Cambridge, MA: Harvard University Press.

Bezerra, Marcos Otávio. 1999. *Em Nome das "Bases": Política, Favor e Dependência Pessoal*. Rio de Janeiro, Brazil: Relume Dumará–Núcleo de Antropologia da Política.

Bill Chavez, Rebecca. 2004. *The Rule of Law in Nascent Democracies: Judicial Politics in Argentina*. Palo Alto, CA: Stanford University Press.

Boeninger, Edgardo. 1989. "Gestión de gobierno y proceso de decisiones públicas." Internal memo circulated in Chilean presidential palace, Santiago.

Boix, Carles. 1999. "Setting the Rules of the Game: The Choice of Electoral Systems in Advanced Democracies." *American Political Science Review* 93, no. 3: 609–24.

———. 2003. *Democracy and Redistribution*. New York: Cambridge University Press.

Borocz, Joszef. 2000. "Informality Rules." *East European Politics and Societies* 14, no. 2: 348–80.

Bourdieu, Pierre. 1999. "Rethinking the State: Genesis and Structure of the Bureaucratic Field." In George Steinmetz, ed., *State/Culture: State Formation after the Cultural Turn*. Ithaca, NY: Cornell University Press.

Boussard, Caroline. 2000. "Democratic Consolidation: The Role of Informal Institutions: Illustrations from Central America." Paper presented at the twenty-second International Congress of the Latin American Studies Association, Miami, Mar. 16–18.

Boylan, Delia. 1996. "Taxation and Transition: The Politics of the 1990 Chilean Tax Reform." *Latin American Research Review* 31, no. 1: 7–31.

———. 2001a. "Democratization and Institutional Change in Mexico: The Logic of Partial Insulation." *Comparative Political Studies* 34, no. 1: 3–29.

———. 2001b. *Diffusing Democracy: Central Bank Autonomy and the Transition from Authoritarian Rule*. Ann Arbor: University of Michigan Press.

Bratton, Michael, and Nicolas van de Walle. 1994. "Neopatrimonial Regimes and Political Transitions in Africa. *World Politics* 46, no. 4: 453–89.

Brazil Tribunal Superior Eleitoral. 2002a. "Divulagação de Prestação de Contas 2002." Computer files, Tribunal Superior Eleitoral, Brasília.

———. 2002b. "Resultados das Eleições de 2002." Computer files, Tribunal Superior Eleitoral, Brasília.

Brinks, Daniel. 2003a. "Courts, Norms, and Laws: Competing Rules and Legal Rights in Salvador, São Paolo, and Buenos Aires." Paper presented at the conference Informal Institutions and Politics in Latin America, Kellogg Institute for International Studies, University of Notre Dame, IN, Apr. 24-25.

———. 2003b. "Informal Institutions and the Rule of Law: The Judicial Response to State Killings in Buenos Aires and São Paolo in the 1990s." *Comparative Politics* 36, no. 1: 1–19.

———. 2003c. "Legal Equality and Effectiveness in the Courts of Argentina, Uruguay and Brazil." Paper presented at the sixty-first annual meeting of the Midwest Political Science Association, Chicago, Apr. 3–6.

Bruhn, Kathleen. 1977. *Taking on Goliath: The Emergence of a New Left Party and the Struggle for Democracy in Mexico*. University Park: Pennsylvania State University Press.

Brusco, Valeria, Marcelo Nazereno, and Susan C. Stokes. 2004. "Vote Buying in Argentina." *Latin American Research Review* 39, no. 2: 66–88.

Burbano de Lara, Felipe, and Michel Rowland. 1998. *Pugna de Poderes: Presidencialismo y Partidos en el Ecuador: 1979–1997*. Quito, Ecuador: Corporation of Development Studies (CORDES)–Konrad Adenauer Foundation and Spanish Cooperation.

Butler, Edgar W., and Jorge Bustamante, eds. 1991. *Sucesión Presidencial: The 1988 Presidential Election*. Boulder, CO: Westview Press.

Cabedo Mallol, Vincente José. 1998. "El Pluralismo Jurídico en Colombia, Peru, Bolivia y Ecuador: Derecho Consuetudinario y Jurisdicción Indígena." *Cuadernos constitucionales* (Valencia, Spain), no. 25 (autumn). Available at www.geocities.com/alertanet.

Cain, Bruce E., John Ferejohn, and Morris Fiorina. 1987. *The Personal Vote: Constituency Service and Electoral Independence.* Cambridge, MA: Harvard University Press.

Calvert, Randall. 1995. "The Rational Choice Theory of Social Institutions: Cooperation, Coordination, and Communication." In Jeffrey S. Banks and Eric A. Hanushek, eds., *Modern Political Economy.* New York: Cambridge University Press.

Calvo, Ernesto, and Victoria Murillo. 2004. "Who Delivers? Partisan Clients in the Argentine Electoral Market." *American Journal of Political Science* 48, no. 4: 742–57.

Camp, Roderic A. 1980. *Mexico's Leaders, Their Education and Recruitment.* Tucson: University of Arizona Press.

———. 1985. "The Political Technocrat in Mexico and the Survival of the Political System." *Latin American Research Review* 20, no. 1: 97–118.

Campbell, Angus, Philip E. Converse, Warren E. Miller, and Donald E. Stokes. 1964. *The American Voter.* New York: John Wiley and Sons.

Carey, John M. 1996. *Term Limits and Legislative Representation.* New York: Cambridge University Press.

———. 2000. "Parchment, Equilibria, and Institutions." *Comparative Political Studies* 33, nos. 6–7: 735–61.

———. 2002. "Parties and Coalitions in Chile in the 1990s." In Scott Morgenstern and Benito Nacif, eds., *Legislative Politics in Latin America.* Cambridge: Cambridge University Press.

———. 2003. "Transparency versus Collective Action: The Fujimori Legacy and the Peruvian Congress." *Comparative Political Studies* 36, no. 9: 983–1006.

———. 2004. "Visible Votes: Recorded Voting and Legislative Accountability in Latin America." Unpublished ms., Dartmouth College, Hanover, NH.

Carey, John M., and Matthew Soberg Shugart. 1995. "Incentives to Cultivate a Personal Vote: A Rank Ordering of Electoral Formulas." *Electoral Studies* 14, no. 4: 417–39.

Carey, John M., and Peter Siavelis. 2003. "El 'seguro' para los subcampeones y la sobrevivencia la la Concertación." *Estudios Políticos* 90 (fall): 5–27.

———. 2005. "Insurance for Good Losers and the Survival of Chile's Concertación." *Latin American Politics and Society* 47, no. 2: 1–22.

Castañeda, Jorge G. 1999. *La herencia: Arqueología de la sucesión presidencial en México.* Mexico City: Extra Alfaguara.

Castillo, Pilar del, and Daniel Zovatto, eds. 1998. *La Financiación de la Política en Iberoamérica.* San José, Costa Rica: Instituto Interamericano de Derechos Humanos.

Centeno, Miguel. 1994. *Democracy within Reason: Technocratic Revolution in Mexico.* University Park: Pennsylvania State University Press.

Centro de Estudios Públicos. 2003. "Puntos Salientes: Encuesta nacional de opinión pública." Santiago, Chile: Centro de Estudios Públicos. Available at www.cepchile.cl.

Chacón Castro, Rubén. 1999. "Comentario a la presentación de Rodolfo Piza E.: Análisis de jurisprudencia constitucional emergente en materia indígena en el caso de Costa Rica: poder estatal y pueblos indígenas." In *Memoria: II Seminario Internacional sobre Admin-*

istración de Justicia y Pueblos Indígenas. San José, Costa Rica: Instituto Interamericano de Derechos Humanos.

Chambers, Ian. 1997. Untitled comments. In Magdalena Gómez, ed., *Derecho Indígena.* Mexico City: Instituto Nacional Indigenista.

Chandra, Kanchan. 2004. *Why Ethnic Parties Succeed: Patronage and Ethnic Headcounts in India.* Cambridge: Cambridge University Press.

Chevigny, Paul. 1995. *Edge of the Knife: Police Violence in the Americas.* New York: New Press.

Chull Shin, Doh. 1994. "On the Third Wave of Democratization: A Synthesis and Evaluation of Recent Theory and Research." *World Politics* 47, no. 1: 135-70.

Clarke, Simon, ed. 1995. *Management and Industry in Russia: Formal and Informal Relations in the Period of Transition.* Aldershot, England: Edward Elgar.

Cleary, Matthew, and Susan C. Stokes. Forthcoming. *Democracy and the Culture of Skepticism: Political Trust in Argentina and Mexico.* New York: Russell Sage Foundation.

Colignon, Richard A., and Chikako Usui. 2003. *Amadukari: The Hidden Fabric of Japan's Economy.* Ithaca, NY: Cornell University Press.

Collier, Jane. 1998. "The Peaceful Resolution of a Cortacabezas Case in the Toztzil Maya Community of Zinacantan, Chiapas, México." *América Indígena* 58, nos. 1–2: 203–20.

Collins, Kathleen. 2002a. "Clans, Pacts and Politics in Central Asia." *Journal of Democracy* 13, no. 3: 137–52.

———. 2002b. "Clans, Pacts, and Regime Transitions in Central Asia." Paper presented at the conference Informal Institutions and Politics in the Developing World, Harvard University, Cambridge, MA, Apr. 5–6.

———. 2003. "The Political Role of Clans in Central Asia." *Comparative Politics* 35, no. 2: 171–90.

———. 2004. "The Logic of Clan Politics: Evidence from the Central Asian Trajectories." *World Politics* 56, no. 2: 224–61.

Conaghan, Catherine. 1995. "Politicians against Parties: Discord and Disconnection in Ecuador's Party System." In Scott Mainwaring and Timothy R. Scully, eds., *Building Democratic Institutions: Party Systems in Latin America.* Stanford, CA: Stanford University Press.

Congreso Nacional del Ecuador. 1995. *Impeachment Proceedings of Vice-President Alberto Dahik.* Quito, Ecuador: Congreso Nacional del Ecuador.

Cordova, Arnaldo. 1992. *La formación del poder político en México.* Mexico City: Era Publishers.

Cornelius, Wayne A. 1996. *Mexican Politics in Transition: The Breakdown of a One-Party-Dominant Regime.* Monograph Series, 41. San Diego: University of California, Center for U.S.-Mexican Studies.

Cox, Gary. 1987. *The Efficient Secret.* New York: Cambridge University Press.

———. 1997. *Making Votes Count.* Cambridge: Cambridge University Press.

Cox, Gary W., and Scott Morgenstern. 2002a. "Epilogue: Latin America's Reactive Assemblies and Proactive Presidents." In Scott Morgenstern and Benito Nacif, eds., *Legislative Politics in Latin America.* Cambridge: Cambridge University Press.

———. 2002b. "Reactive Assemblies and Proactive Presidents: A Typology of Latin American Presidents and Legislatures." In Scott Morgenstern and Benito Nacif, eds., *Legislative Politics in Latin America.* Cambridge: Cambridge University Press.

Cox, Gary, and Michael Thies. 1998. "The Cost of Intra-Party Competition: The Single, Non-transferable Vote and Money Politics in Japan." *Comparative Political Studies* 31 (June): 267–91.

———. 2000. "How Much Does Money Matter? 'Buying' Votes in Japan, 1967–1990." *Comparative Political Studies* 33, no. 1: 37–57.

Craig, Ann L., and Wayne A. Cornelius. 1995. "Houses Divided: Parties and Political Reform in Mexico." In Scott Mainwaring and Timothy R. Scully, eds., *Building Democratic Institutions: Party Systems in Latin America*. Stanford, CA: Stanford University Press.

Crain, W. Mark. 1977. "On the Structure and Stability of Political Markets." *Journal of Political Economy* 85 (Aug.): 829–42.

Crawford, Sue E. S., and Elinor Ostrom. 1995. "A Grammar of Institutions." *American Political Science Review* 89, no. 3: 582–600.

Darden, Keith. 2002. "Graft and Governance: Corruption as an Informal Mechanism of State Control." Paper presented at the conference Informal Institutions and Politics in the Developing World, Weatherhead Center for International Affairs, Harvard University, Cambridge, MA, Apr. 5–6.

Degregori, Carlos Iván, and María Ponce Mariños. 2000. "Movimientos sociales y estado: El caso de las rondas campesinas de Cajamarca y Piura." In Carlos Iván Degregori, ed., *No Hay País Más Diverso: Compendio de antroloplogía peruana*. Lima: Pontificia Universidad Catolíca del Peru, Instituto de Estudios Peruanos.

Deheza, Grace Ivana. 1997. "Gobiernos de coalición en el sistema presidencial: América del Sur." Ph.D. diss., Political Science Department, European University Institute, Florence, Italy.

De la Torre, Augusto, Roberto García-Saltos, and Yira Mascaró. 2001. *Banking, Currency, and Debt Meltdown: Ecuador Crisis in the Late 1990s*. World Bank working paper. Washington, DC: World Bank.

Della Porta, Donatella, and Alberto Vannucci. 1999. *Corrupt Exchanges: Actors, Resources, and Mechanisms of Political Corruption*. New York: Aldine de Gruyter.

De Luca, Miguel, Mark P. Jones, and María Inés Tula. 2002. "Back Rooms or Ballot Boxes? Candidate Nomination in Argentina." *Comparative Political Studies* 35, no. 4: 413–36.

de Oliveira, Nelson, Lutz Mulert Sousa Ribeiro, and Jose Carlos Zanetti, eds. 2000. *A Outra Face da Moeda*. Salvador, Bahia, Brazil: CommisSão de Justiça e Paz da Arquidiocese de Salvador.

Desposato, Scott W. 2001. "Institutional Theories, Societal Realities, and Party Politics in Brazil." Ph.D. diss., University of California, Los Angeles.

———. 2004. "The Impact of Federalism on National Political Parties in Brazil." *Legislative Studies Quarterly* 29: 259–85.

Dia, Mamadou. 1996. *Africa's Management in the 1990s: Reconciling Indigenous and Transplanted Institutions*. Washington, DC: World Bank.

Domínguez, Jorge I., and Michael Shifter, eds. 2003. *Constructing Democratic Governance in Latin America*. 2nd ed. Baltimore: Johns Hopkins University Press.

Downs, Anthony. 1957. *An Economic Theory of Democracy*. New York: Harper and Row.

Duverger, Maurice. 1954. *Political Parties: Their Organization and Activity in the Modern State*. New York: John Wiley and Sons.

Easter, Gerald. 2000. *Reconstructing the State: Personal Networks and Elite Identity in Soviet Russia.* New York: Cambridge University Press.

Economist Intelligence Unit. 2000. *Country Profile: Ecuador.* London: Economist Intelligence Unit.

Eisenstadt, Todd A. 1999. "Electoral Federalism or Abdication of Presidential Authority? Gubernatorial Elections in Tabasco." In Wayne Cornelius, Todd Eisenstadt, and Jane Hindley, eds., *Subnational Politics and Democratization in Mexico.* La Jolla, CA: Center for U.S.-Mexican Studies.

———. 2003. "Thinking Outside the (Ballot) Box: Mexico's Informal Electoral Institutions." *Latin American Politics and Society* 45, no. 1: 25–54.

———. 2004. *Courting Democracy in Mexico.* Cambridge: Cambridge University Press.

Ellickson, Robert C. 1991. *Order without Law: How Neighbors Settle Disputes.* Cambridge, MA: Harvard University Press.

Elster, Jon. 1989. *The Cement of Society: A Survey of Social Order.* New York: Cambridge University Press.

Epoca, La (Santiago). 1993a. "RN anunció definitivamente no dará más concesiones a la UDI." Mar. 27.

———. 1993b. "La DC quiere que Eduardo Frei sea el árbitro del pacto parlamentario." June 22.

Epstein, Lee, and Jack Knight. 1998. *The Choices Judges Make.* Washington, DC: Congressional Quarterly Press.

Erdmann, Gero. 2004. "Party Research: Western European Bias and the 'African Labyrinth.'" *Democratization* 11, no. 3: 63–87.

Estévez, Federico, Beatriz Magaloni, and Alberto Diaz-Cayeros. 2003. *A Portfolio Diversification Model of Policy Choice.* Paper presented at the conference Clientelism in Latin America: Theoretical and Comparative Perspectives, Stanford University, CA, May 17–18.

Euraque, Darío E. 2000. "Los políticos hondureños y la Costa Norte (1876-1950): narrativa e interpretación." *Revista Política de Honduras* 2: 113–56.

Farrell, Henry, and Adrienne Héritier. 2002. "Formal and Informal Institutions under Codecision: Continuous Constitution Building in Europe." *European Integration Online Papers* 6, no. 3. Available at http://eiop.or.at/erpa/OAI/eiopxx/EIoP-Poo76.html.

Fearon, James. 1999. "Electoral Accountability and the Control of Politicians: Selecting Good Types versus Sanctioning Poor Performance." In Adam Przeworski, Susan C. Stokes, and Bernard Manin, eds., *Democracy, Accountability, and Representation.* Cambridge: Cambridge University Press.

Federal Secretary of the Interior, Mexico. 1996. "Relación de Concejos Municipales Instalados en el País Durante los Ultimos Tres Periodos de los Ayuntamientos." Internal ms., Secretaría de Gobernación, Mexico City.

Fenno, Richard F., Jr. 1978. *Homestyle.* Boston: Little Brown.

Ferejohn, John. 1986. "Incumbent Performance and Electoral Control." *Public Choice* 50, nos. 1–3: 5–25.

———. 1999. "Accountability and Authority: Toward a Theory of Political Accountability." In Adam Przeworski, Susan C. Stokes, and Bernard Manin, eds., *Democracy, Accountability, and Representation.* Cambridge: Cambridge University Press.

Ferreira Rubio, Delia, ed. 1997. *Financiamiento de Partidos Políticos.* Buenos Aires, Argentina:

Centro Interdisciplinario de Estudios sobre el Desarrollo Latinamericano–Konrad Adenauer Stiftung.

Ferreira Rubio, Delia, and Matteo Goretti. 1998. "When the President Governs Alone: The Decretazo in Argentina, 1989–93." In John M. Carey and Matthew Soberg Shugart, eds., *Executive Decree Authority.* New York: Cambridge University Press.

Fleischer, David. 1997. "Political Corruption in Brazil." *Crime, Law, and Social Change* 25, no. 4: 297–321.

Fox, Jonathan. 1994. "The Difficult Transition from Clientelism to Citizenship: Lessons from México." *World Politics* 46, no. 2: 151–84.

Freidenberg, Flavia. 2001. "Ecuador." In Manuel Alcántara Sáez and Flavia Freidenberg, eds., *Partidos Políticos de América Latina.* Salamanca, Spain: Ediciones Universidad de Salamanca.

———. 2002. "Incentivos electorales y selección de candidatos en organizaciones neopopulistas en organizaciones neopopulistas: El Partido Roldosista Ecuatoriano (1984–2000)." *Ciencias de Gobierno* 12 (Dec.): 32–62.

———. 2003. *Jama, caleta y camello: Las estrategias de Abdalá Bucaram y el PRE para ganar las elecciones.* Quito, Ecuador: Universidad Andina Simón Bolívar.

Fuentes, Claudio. 1999. "Partidos coaliciones en el Chile de los '90: Entre pactos y proyectos." In Paul Drake and Iván Jaksic, eds., *El modelo chileno: democracia y desarrollo en los noventa.* Santiago: LOM Ediciones.

Galvan, Dennis. 2004. *The State Must Be Our Master of Fire: How Peasants Craft Sustainable Development in Senegal.* Berkeley: University of California Press.

García Serrano, Fernando. 2000. "Formas indígenas de administración de justicia: Tres estudios de caso de la nacionalidad quichua de la sierra y amazonía ecuatoriana." Paper presented at the twelfth International Congress of the Comisión de Derecho Consuetudinario y Pluralismo Legal, Arica, Chile, Mar. 13–17. Available at http://geocities.com/alertanet/index.html.

Garduño, Roberto. 2001. "En el Caso Tabasco 'No Andaremos de Metiches,' Expresa Vicente Fox." *La Jornada* (Mexico City), Jan. 3.

Garrido, Luis Javier. 1982. *El partido de la revolución institucionalizada: la formación del nuevo estado en México (1928–1945).* Mexico City: Siglo Veintiuno.

———. 1993. *La ruptura: La Corriente Democrática del PRI.* Mexico City: Editorial Grijalbo.

Gay, Robert. 1994. *Popular Organization and Democracy in Rio de Janeiro: A Tale of Two Favelas.* Philadelphia: Temple University Press.

———. 1999. "Rethinking Clientelism: Demands, Discourses and Practices in Contemporary Brazil." *European Review of Latin American and Caribbean Studies* 65: 7–24.

Gel'man, Vladimir. 2003. "Post-Soviet Transitions and Democratization: Toward Theory Building." *Democratization* 10, no. 2: 87–104.

———. 2004. "The Unrule of Law in the Making: The Politics of Informal Institution Building in Russia." *Europe-Asia Studies* 56, no. 7: 1021–40.

Gibson, Edward, and Ernesto Calvo. 2000. "Federalism and Low-Maintenance Constituencies: Territorial Dimensions of Economic Reform in Argentina." *Studies in Comparative International Development* 35, no. 3: 32–55.

Gobel, Christian. 2001. "Towards a Consolidated Democracy? Informal and Formal Institutions in Taiwan's Political Process." Paper presented at the annual meeting of the American Political Science Association, San Francisco, Aug. 30–Sept. 2.

Gómez, Leopoldo. 1991. "Elections, Legitimacy, and Political Change in Mexico, 1977–1988." Ph.D. diss., Georgetown University, Washington, DC.

Gómez, Magdalena. 2000. "Derecho Indígena y constitucionalidad." Paper presented at the twelfth International Congress of the Comisión de Derecho Consuetudinario y Pluralismo Legal, Arica, Chile, Mar. 13–17. Available at www.geocities.com/alertanet/index.html.

González Casanova, Pablo. 1965. *La democracia en México*. Mexico City: Era Publishers.

———. 1981. *El Estado y los partidos políticos en México*. Mexico City: Era Publishers.

Graeff, E. 2000. "The Flight of the Beetle: Party Politics and the Decision-Making Process in the Cardoso Government." Paper presented at the fifth Congress of the Brazilian Studies Association, Recife, Brazil, June.

Graham, Richard. 1990. *Patronage and Politics in Nineteenth-Century Brazil*. Stanford, CA: Stanford University Press.

Granados Chapa, Miguel Angel. 2001. "Jalisco en el Trife." *Reforma* (Mexico City), Feb. 20, p. 15A.

Greif, Avner, and David D. Laitin. 2004. "A Theory of Endogenous Institutional Change." *American Political Science Review* 98, no. 4: 633–53.

Griffiths, John. 1986. "What Is Legal Pluralism?" *Journal of Legal Pluralism and Unofficial Law* 24: 1–55.

Grindle, Merilee, and Francisco E. Thoumi. 1993. "Muddling toward Adjustment: The Political Economy of Economic Policy Change in Ecuador." In R. H. Bates and A. O. Krueger, eds., *Political and Economic Interactions in Economic Policy Reform: Evidence from Eight Countries*. Oxford: Blackwell.

Grzymala-Busse, Anna. 2004. "Informal Institutions and the Post-Communist State." Unpublished ms., Department of Political Science, Yale University, New Haven, CT.

Grzymala-Busse, Anna, and Pauline Jones Luong. 2002. "Reconceptualizing the State: Lessons from Post-Communism." *Politics and Society* 30, no. 4: 529–54.

Hagopian, Frances. 1993. "After Regime Change: Authoritarian Legacies, Political Representation, and the Democratic Future of South America." *World Politics* 45, no. 3: 464–500.

———. 1996. *Traditional Politics and Regime Change in Brazil*. New York: Cambridge University Press.

———. 1998. "Democracy and Political Representation in Latin America in the 1990s: Pause, Reorganization, or Decline?" In Felipe Agüero and Jeffrey Stark, eds., *Fault Lines of Democracy in Post-Transition Latin America*. Miami: North-South Center Press.

Hale, Henry E. 2005. "Why Not Parties? Electoral Markets, Party Substitutes, and Stalled Democratization in Russia." *Comparative Politics* 37, no. 2: 147–66.

Hamilton-Hart, Natasha. 2000. "The Singapore State Revisited." *Pacific Review* 13, no. 2: 195–216.

Handy, Jim. 2004. "Chicken Thieves, Witches, and Judges: Vigilante Justice and Customary Law in Guatemala." *Journal of Latin American Studies* 36, no. 3: 533–61.

Hart, H. L. A. 1961. *The Concept of Law*. New York: Oxford University Press.

Hartlyn, Jonathan. 1998. *The Struggle for Democratic Politics in the Dominican Republic*. Chapel Hill: University of North Carolina Press.

Heath, Roseanna Michelle, and Michelle M. Taylor-Robinson. 2003. "All Dressed up with No Place to Go? Political Ambition in Unitary Political Systems with Unicameral Legislatures." Paper presented at the annual meeting of the American Political Science Association, Philadelphia, Aug. 28–31.

Helmke, Gretchen. 2002. "The Logic of Strategic Defection: Court-Executive Relations in Argentina under Dictatorship and Democracy." *American Political Science Review* 96, no. 2: 291–304.

———. 2004. *Courts under Constraints: Judges, Generals, and Presidents in Argentina.* New York: Cambridge University Press.

Helmke, Gretchen, and Steven Levitsky. 2003. "Informal Institutions and Comparative Politics: A Research Agenda." Paper presented at the conference Informal Institutions in Latin America, University of Notre Dame, IN, Apr. 23–24.

———. 2004. "Informal Institutions and Comparative Politics: A Research Agenda." *Perspectives on Politics* 2, no. 4: 725–40.

Hey, Jeanne A. K., and Thomas Klak. 1999. "From Protectionism towards Neoliberalism: Ecuador across Four Administrations (1981–1996)." *Studies in Comparative International Development* 34, no. 3: 66–97.

Hillman, Richard. 1994. *Democracy for the Privileged: Crisis and Transition in Venezuela.* Boulder, CO: Lynne Reinner.

Holston, James, and Teresa P. R. Caldeira. 1998. "Democracy, Law, and Violence: Disjunctions of Brazilian Citizenship." In Felipe Agüero and Jeffrey Stark, eds., *Fault Lines of Democracy in Post-Transition Latin America.* Coral Gables, FL: North-South Center Press.

Honaker, James, Anne Joseph, Gary King, Kenneth Scheve, and Naunihal Singh. 2001. Amelia: A Program for Missing Data. Windows version. Harvard University. Available at http://gking.harvard.edu.

Hooker, M. B. 1975. *Legal Pluralism: An Introduction to Colonial and Neo-Colonial Laws.* Oxford: Clarendon Press.

Huntington, Samuel P. 1968. *Political Order in Changing Societies.* New Haven, CT: Yale University Press.

Hurtado, Osvaldo. 1990. *Política Democrática: los últimos veinte y cinco años.* Quito, Ecuador: Fundación Ecuatoriana de Estudios Sociales y Corporación Editora Nacional.

Hyden, Goran. 1980. *Beyond Ujamaa in Tanzania: Underdevelopment and an Uncaptured Peasantry.* London: Heinemann.

———. 2002. "Why Africa Finds It So Hard to Develop." Paper presented at the conference Culture, Democracy, and Development: Cultural and Political Foundations of Socio-Economic Development in Africa and Asia, Monte Verita, Ascona, Switzerland, Oct. 6–11.

Jackson, Jean. 2002. "Caught in the Crossfire: Colombia's Indigenous Peoples during the 1990s." In David Maybury-Lewis, ed., *The Politics of Ethnicity: Indigenous Peoples in Latin American States.* Cambridge, MA: Harvard University Press.

Johannes, John R. 1984. *To Serve the People: Congress and Constituency Service.* Lincoln: University of Nebraska Press.

Johnson, Kenneth. 1971. *Mexican Democracy: A Critical View.* Boston: Allyn and Bacon.

Jones, Mark. 1995. *Electoral Laws and the Survival of Presidential Democracies.* Notre Dame, IN: University of Notre Dame Press.

Katz, Richard S., and Peter Mair, eds. 1994. *How Parties Organize: Change and Adaptation in Party Organizations in Western Democracies.* London: Sage.

———. 1995. "Changing Models of Party Democracy: The Emergence of the Cartel Party." *Party Politics* 1, no. 1: 5–28.

Katzenstein, Peter J. 1996. *Cultural Norms and National Security: Police and Military in Postwar Japan.* Ithaca, NY: Cornell University Press.

Keech, William R. 1995. *Economic Politics: The Costs of Democracy.* New York: Cambridge University Press.

Kenney, Charles. 2004. *Fujimori's Coup and the Breakdown of Democracy in Latin America.* Notre Dame, IN: University of Notre Dame Press.

King, Gary, Michael Tomz, and Jason Wittenberg. 2000. "Making the Most of Statistical Analyses: Improving Interpretation and Presentation." *American Journal of Political Science* 44, no. 2: 347–55.

King, Gary, James Honaker, Anne Joseph, and Kenneth Scheve. 2001. "Analyzing Incomplete Political Science Data: An Alternative Algorithm for Multiple Imputation." *American Political Science Review* 95, no. 1: 49–69.

Kirchheimer, Otto. 1966. "The Transformation of Western European Party Systems." In Joseph LaPalombara and Myron Weiner, eds., *Political Parties and Political Development.* Princeton, NJ: Princeton University Press.

Kirschke, Linda. 2000. "Informal Repression, Zero-Sum Politics and Late Third Wave Transitions." *Journal of Modern African Studies* 38, no. 3: 383-405.

Kitschelt, Herbert. 1994. *The Transformation of European Social Democracy.* Cambridge: Cambridge University Press.

———. 2000. "Linkages between Citizens and Politicians in Democratic Politics." *Comparative Political Studies* 33, nos. 6–7: 845–79.

Klesner, Joseph L. 1988. "Electoral Reform in an Authoritarian Regime: The Case of Mexico." Ph.D. diss., Massachusetts Institute of Technology, Cambridge.

Knight, Alan. 1990. "Mexico, c. 1930–1946." In Leslie Bethell, ed., *Cambridge History of Latin America*, vol. 7. Cambridge: Cambridge University Press.

———. 1992. "Mexico's Elite Settlement: Conjuncture and Consequences." In John Higley and Richard Gunther, eds., *Elites and Democratic Consolidation in Latin America and Southern Europe.* Cambridge: Cambridge University Press.

Knight, Jack. 1992. *Institutions and Social Conflict.* New York: Cambridge University Press.

Kroszner, Randall, and Thomas Stratmann. 1998. "Interest-Group Competition and the Organization of Congress: Theory and Evidence from Financial Services' Political Action Committees." *American Economic Review* 88 (Dec.): 1163–87.

Kymlicka, Will. 1995. *Multicultural Citizenship.* Oxford: Oxford University Press.

Lancaster, Thomas D. 1986. "Electoral Structures and Pork Barrel Politics." *International Political Science Review* 7, no. 1: 67–81.

Landau, David. 2001. "Policy or Pork? Presidential Strategy Choice and the Legislature in Ecuador." B.A. thesis, Faculty of Arts and Sciences, Harvard University, Cambridge, MA.

Langston, Joy. 2001." Why Rules Matter: Changes in Candidate Selection in Mexico's PRI, 1988–2000." *Journal of Latin American Studies* 33, no. 3: 485-512.

———. 2003. "The Formal Bases of Informal Power: Mexico's PRI." Paper presented at the conference Informal Institutions and Politics in Latin America, Kellogg Institute for International Studies, University of Notre Dame, IN, Apr. 24–25.

Latin America Advisor. 2002. "Chilean Lawmakers Decry Leader's Statement on Ruling Coalition." Washington, DC: Inter-American Dialogue. Dec. 11.

Lau, Rubén. 1989. *Cuadernos del Norte—Las Elecciones en Chihuahua (1983-1988).* Chihuahua, Mexico: Centro de Estudios Libres Ignacio Rodríguez Terrazas, A.C.

Lauth, Hans-Joachim. 2000. "Informal Institutions and Democracy." *Democratization* 7, no. 4: 21–50.

Laver, Michael, and Kenneth Shepsle. 1990. "Coalitions and Cabinet Government." *American Political Science Review* 84, no. 3: 873–90.

Lawson, Chappell H. 2002. *Building the Fourth Estate: Democratization and the Rise of a Free Press in Mexico.* Berkeley: University of California Press.

Ledeneva, Alena A. 1998. *Russia's Economy of Favors: Blat, Networking and Informal Exchange.* Cambridge: Cambridge University Press.

Lemarchand, René. 1981. "Comparative Political Clientelism: Structure, Process and Optic." In S. N. Eisenstadt and René Lemarchand, eds., *Political Clientelism, Patronage and Development.* Beverly Hills, CA: Sage.

Lemos-Nelson, Ana Tereza. 2001. "Judiciary Police Accountability for Gross Human Rights Violations: The Case of Bahia, Brazil." Ph.D. diss., University of Notre Dame, Notre Dame, IN.

Lerner de Sheinbaum, Bertha, and Susan Ralsky. 1976. *El poder de los presidentes.* Mexico City: National Autonomous University of Mexico, Instituto Mexicano de Estudios Políticos.

Levi, Margaret. 1997. *Consent, Dissent, and Patriotism.* New York: Cambridge University Press.

Levitsky, Steven. 2003a. "Chaos and Renovation: Institutional Weakness and the Transformation of Argentine Peronism, 1983–2002." Paper presented at the conference Rethinking Dual Transitions: Argentine Politics in the 1990s in Comparative Perspective, Weatherhead Center for International Affairs, Harvard University, Cambridge, MA, Mar. 20–22.

———. 2003b. *Transforming Labor-Based Parties in Latin America: Argentine Peronism in Comparative Perspective.* New York: Cambridge University Press.

Levitsky, Steven, and M. Victoria Murillo. 2005. "Theorizing about Weak Institutions: Lessons from the Argentine Case." In Steven Levitsky and M. Victoria Murillo, eds., *Argentine Democracy: The Politics of Institutional Weakness.* University Park: Pennsylvania State University Press.

Levitsky, Steven, and Lucan A. Way. 2002. "The Rise of Competitive Authoritarianism." *Journal of Democracy* 13, no. 2: 51–65.

Lewin, Linda. 1987. *Politics and Parentela in Paraíba: A Case Study of Family-Based Oligarchy in Brazil.* Princeton, NJ: Princeton University Press.

Lijphart, Arend. 1975. *The Politics of Accommodation: Pluralism and Democracy in the Netherlands.* 2nd ed. Berkeley: University of California Press.

Lindberg, Steffan I. 2003. "'It's Our Time to Chop: Do Elections in Africa Feed Net-Patrimonialism Rather than Counteract It?" *Democratization* 10, no. 2: 121–40.

Linz, Juan, J. 1990. "The Perils of Presidentialism." *Journal of Democracy* 1, no. 1: 51–69.

———. 1994. "Democracy: Presidential or Parliamentary: Does It Make a Difference?" In Juan Linz and Arturo Valenzuela, eds., *The Failure of Presidential Democracy*, vol. 1. Baltimore: Johns Hopkins University Press.

Linz, Juan J., and Arturo Valenzuela, eds. 1994. *Presidential or Parliamentary Democracy: Does It Make a Difference?* Baltimore: Johns Hopkins University Press.

Lipset, Seymour Martin. 1958. "Some Social Requisites of Democracy: Economic Development and Political Legitimacy." *American Political Science Review* 53: 69–105.

———. 1960. *Political Man: The Social Bases of Politics*. Garden City, NY: Doubleday.

Loaeza, Soledad. 1999. *El Partido Acción Nacional: la larga marcha, 1939-1994*. Mexico City: Fondo de Cultura Económica.

López Obrador, Andrés Manuel. 1996. *Entre la Historia y la Esperanza—corrupción y lucha democrática en Tabasco*. Mexico City: Grijalbo Editores.

Mackie, Gerry. 1996. "Ending Footbinding and Infibulation: A Convention Account." *American Sociological Review* 61, no. 6: 999–1017.

Madison, James, Alexander Hamilton, and John Jay. 2000 [1788]. *The Federalist*. Ed. William R. Brock. London: Phoenix Press.

Mahoney, James. 2001. *The Legacies of Liberalism: Path Dependence and Political Regimes in Central America*. Baltimore: Johns Hopkins University Press.

Mainwaring, Scott. 1991. "Politicians, Parties, and Electoral Systems: Brazil in Comparative Perspective." *Comparative Politics* 24, no. 1: 21–43.

———. 1993. "Presidentialism, Multipartism, and Democracy: The Difficult Combination." *Comparative Political Studies* 26, no. 2: 198–228.

———. 1997. "Multipartism, Robust Federalism, and Presidentialism in Brazil." In Scott Mainwaring and Matthew Soberg Shugart, eds., *Presidentialism and Democracy in Latin America*. New York: Cambridge University Press.

———. 1998. "Party Systems in the Third Wave." *Journal of Democracy* 10, no. 3: 67–81.

———. 1999. *Rethinking Party Systems in the Third Wave Democratization: The Case of Brazil*. Stanford, CA: Stanford University Press.

Mainwaring, Scott, and Timothy R. Scully. 1995. "Introduction: Party Systems in Latin America." In Scott Mainwaring and Timothy R. Scully, eds., *Building Democratic Institutions: Party Systems in Latin America*. Stanford, CA: Stanford University Press.

Mainwaring, Scott, and Matthew Soberg Shugart, eds. 1997. *Presidentialism and Democracy in Latin America*. New York: Cambridge University Press.

Mainwaring, Scott, and Christopher Welna, eds. 2003. *Democratic Accountability in Latin America*. New York: Oxford University Press.

Malesky, Edmund. 2005. "Straight Ahead on Red: The Impact of Foreign Direct Investment on Local Autonomy in Vietnam." Paper presented at the annual meeting of the Midwest Political Science Association, Chicago, Apr. 3–7.

Malik, Waleed H., and Juan Martínez. 1999. "Hacia la modernización en América Latina: consultas con la población indígena en Guatemala sobre administración de justicia." In *Memoria: II Seminario Internacional sobre Administración de Justicia y Pueblos Indígenas*. San José, Costa Rica: Instituto Interamericano de Derechos Humanos.

Maltzman, Forrest, and Paul J. Wahlbeck. 1996. "May It Please the Chief? Opinion Assignment in the Rehnquist Court." *American Journal of Political Science* 40, no. 2: 421–33.

Manin, Bernard. 1997. *Principles of Representative Government*. Cambridge: Cambridge University Press.

Manion, Melanie. 1996. "Corruption by Design: Bribery in Chinese Enterprise Licensing." *Journal of Law, Economics, and Organizations* 12, no. 1: 167–95.

Manor, James. 2001. "Center-State Relations." In Atul Kohli, ed., *The Success of India's Democracy*. Cambridge: Cambridge University Press.

Mansbridge, Jane. 2003. "Rethinking Representation." *American Political Science Review* 97, no. 4: 515–28.

March, James, and Johan Olsen. 1984. "The New Institutionalism: Organizational Factors in Political Life." *American Political Science Review* 78, no. 3: 734–49.

———. 1989. *Rediscovering Institutions: The Organizational Basis of Politics*. New York: Free Press.

Martínez Silva, Mario, and Roberto Salcedo Aquino. 2002. *Diccionario Electoral INEP*. Mexico City: Instituto Nacional de Estudios Políticos (INEP).

Mathews, Donald R. 1959. "The Folkways of the United States Senate: Conformity to Group Norms and Legislative Effectiveness." *American Political Science Review* 53, no. 4: 1064–89.

Mayhew, David. 1974. *Congress: The Electoral Connection*. New Haven, CT: Yale University Press.

McCarty, Nolan, and Lawrence S. Rothenberg. 1996. "Commitment and the Campaign Contribution Contract." *American Journal of Political Science* 40, no. 3: 872–904.

McGuire, James W. 1997. *Peronism without Perón: Unions, Parties and Democracy in Argentina*. Stanford, CA: Stanford University Press.

Medina, Luís. 1977. *Del cardenismo al avilacamachismo: Historia de la Revolución Mexicana, 1934–1940*. Mexico City: Colegio de Mexico.

Medina, Luis Fernando, and Susan C. Stokes. 2003. "Clientelism as Political Monopoly." Paper presented at the conference Informal Institutions in Latin America, University of Notre Dame, IN, Apr. 23–24.

Mejía Acosta, Andrés. 2003. "La Reelección Legislativa en Ecuador: conexión electoral, carreras legislativas y partidos políticos (1979–2003)." In F. F. Dworak, ed., *El legislador a examen: El debate sobre la reelección legislativa en México: una perspectiva histórica e institucional*. Mexico City: Fondo de Cultura Económica.

———. 2004. "Ghost Coalitions: Economic Reforms, Fragmented Legislatures and Informal Institutions in Ecuador." Ph.D. diss., Department of Political Science, University of Notre Dame, Notre Dame, IN.

Mejía Acosta, Andrés, Caridad Araujo, Aníbal Pérez Liñán, Sebastian M. Saiegh, and Simón Pachano. 2004. *Political Institutions, Policymaking Processes, and Policy Outcomes in Ecuador*. Quito, Ecuador: Latin American Faculty of Social Sciences–InterAmerican Development Bank.

Méndez, Juan E., Guillermo O'Donnell, and Paulo Sérgio Pinheiro, eds. 1999. *The (Un)Rule of Law and the Underprivileged in Latin America*. Notre Dame, IN: University of Notre Dame Press.

Menéndez Carrión, Amparo. 1986. *La Conquista del voto*. Quito, Ecuador: Corporación Editora Nacional.

Mercurio, El (Santiago). 1993a. "Proporcionalidad impide acuerdo entre RN y UDI sobre convención." Mar. 27.

———. 1993b. "En la Concertación tenemos enormes dificultades." Apr. 25, D20–D22.

———. 2000. "La 'democracia' de Lagos." Mar. 12.

———. 2003a. "Girardi sentencia que ya no existe la Concertación." Apr. 13.

———. 2003b. "Cargos políticos se reducirán a 760 de los actuales 3.500." Apr. 25.

———. 2003c. "Subcampeones Electorales." Sept. 28, B2.

Mercurio de Valparaíso, El. 2003. "Primó el cuoteo político." Mar. 8.

Merry, Sally Engle. 1988. "Legal Pluralism." *Law and Society Review* 22, no. 5: 869–96.

Mershon, Carol A. 1994. "Expectations and Informal Rules in Coalition Formation." *Comparative Political Studies* 27, no. 1: 40–79.

———. 1996. "The Costs of Coalition: Coalition Theories and Italian Governments." *American Political Science Review* 90, no. 3: 534–54.

Meyer, Lorenzo. 1985. "La revolución mexicana y sus elecciones presidenciales, 1911–1940." In Pablo González Casanova, ed., *Las elecciones en México: Evolución y perspectivas*. Mexico City: Siglo Veintiuno.

Mills, Nick D. 1984. *Crisis, Conflicto y Consenso: Ecuador: 1979–1984*. Quito, Ecuador: Corporación Editora Nacional.

Ministerio de Justicia y Derechos Humanos, Bolivia. 1997a. *Justicia Comunitaria 1. Los Aymaras de Machaca*. La Paz: Ministerio de Justicia y Derechos Humanos–World Bank.

———. 1997b. *Justicia Comunitaria 4. Las Zonas Urbano Marginales de La Paz y Cochabamba*. La Paz: Ministerio de Justicia y Derechos Humanos–World Bank.

Mizrahi, Yemile. 2003. *From Martyrdom to Power: The Partido Acción Nacional in Mexico*. Notre Dame, IN: University of Notre Dame Press.

Molinar, Juan. 1991. *El tiempo de la legitimidad*. Mexico City: Cal y Arena.

Moore, Sally Falk. 1986. *Social Facts and Fabrications: Customary Law on Kilimanjaro, 1880–1980*. New York: Cambridge University Press.

Morley, Samuel, Roberto Machado, and Stefano Pettinato. 1999. *Indexes of Structural Reform in Latin America*. Santiago, Chile: United Nations–Economic Commission for Latin America and the Caribbean.

Munro, Dana G. 1967. *The Five Republics of Central America: Their Political and Economic Development and Their Relations with the United States*. 2nd ed. New York: Russell and Russell.

Murgas Armas, Jorge. 1999. "Efectos de la nueva Legislación Procesal Penal para los Pueblos Indígenas de Guatemala (Los Juzgados de Paz Comunitarios)." In *Memoria: II Seminario Internacional sobre Administración de Justicia y Pueblos Indígenas*. San José, Costa Rica: Instituto Interamericano de Derechos Humanos.

Mussetta, Paula C. 2002. *El Capital Social en Argentina: Exploraciones en Torno a su Composición, Tendencia, y Determinantes*. Unpublished ms., Universidad Nacional de Villa María, Córdoba, Argentina.

Nacif, Benito. 1995. "The Mexican Chamber of Deputies, the Political Significance of Non-consecutive Re-election." Ph.D. diss., Oxford University, Oxford.

Nader, Laura. 1980. *Harmony, Ideology, Justice and Control in a Zapotec Mountain Village*. Stanford, CA: Stanford University Press.

Nelson, Joan M. 1989. *Fragile Coalitions: The Politics of Economic Adjustment.* U.S.–Third World Policy Perspectives 12. New Brunswick, NJ: Transaction Books.

Nelson, Richard R., and Sidney G. Winter. 1982. *An Evolutionary Theory of Economic Change.* Cambridge, MA: Harvard University Press.

Nicolau, Jairo M. 1997. "Notas sobre os Quatro Índices Mais Utilizados nos Estudos Eleitorais." In Olavo Brasil de Lima, Jr., ed., *O Sistema Partidário Brasileiro.* Rio de Janeiro, Brazil: Fundação Getúlio Vargas.

Nieto, José Chanes. 1993. *La designación del presidente de la República.* Mexico City: Plaza y Valdés Editores.

North, Douglass C. 1990. *Institutions, Institutional Change, and Economic Performance.* New York: Cambridge University Press.

North, Douglass C., William Summerhill, and Barry R. Weingast. 2000. "Order, Disorder, and Economic Change: Latin America versus North America." In Bruce Bueno de Mesquita and Hilton L. Root, eds., *Governing for Prosperity.* New Haven, CT: Yale University Press.

North, Douglass, and Barry Weingast. 1989. "Constitutions and Commitment: The Evolution of Institutions Governing Public Choice in 17th-Century England." *Journal of Economic History* 49, no. 4: 803–32.

Ochoa García, Carlos. n.d. "Derechos Indígenas y pluralismo legal en América Latina." Unpublished ms., Instituto Munik', Guatemala City. Available at www.geocities.com/alertanet.

O'Donnell, Guillermo. 1984. *Y a Mí, Qué Me Importa? Notas Sobre Sociabilidad y Política en Argentina y Brasil.* Buenos Aires, Argentina: Cuadernos Center for the Study of State and Society (English-language version in O'Donnell 1999a).

———. 1993. "On the State, Democratization, and Some Conceptual Problems: A Latin American View with Some Postcommunist Countries." *World Development* 21, no. 8: 1355–69.

———. 1994. "Delegative Democracy." *Journal of Democracy* 5, no. 1: 55–69.

———. 1996a. "Another Institutionalization: Latin America and Elsewhere." Kellogg Institute working paper 222. Notre Dame, IN: Kellogg Institute for International Studies. Mar.

———. 1996b. "Illusions about Consolidation." *Journal of Democracy* 7, no. 2: 34–51.

———. 1999a. *Counterpoints: Selected Essays on Authoritarianism and Democracy.* Notre Dame, IN: University of Notre Dame Press.

———. 1999b. "Horizontal Accountability in New Democracies." In Andres Schedler, Larry Diamond, and Marc C. Plattner, eds., *The Self-Restraining State: Power and Accountability in New Democracies.* Boulder, CO: Lynne Reinner.

———. 1999c. "Polyarchies and the (Un)rule of Law in Latin America: A Partial Conclusion." In Juan Méndez, Guillermo O'Donnell, and Paulo Sérgio Pinheiro, eds., *The (Un)rule of Law and the Underprivileged in Latin America.* Notre Dame, IN: University of Notre Dame Press.

O'Donnell, Guillermo, Jorge Vargas Cullel, and Osvaldo M. Iazzetta, eds. 2004. *The Quality of Democracy: Theory and Applications.* Notre Dame, IN: University of Notre Dame Press.

Oiticica, Yulo. 2001. *Dossiê Grupos de Extermínio.* Salvador, Bahia, Brazil: Human Rights Commission of the Legislative Assembly of Bahia.

Olukoshi, Adebeyo. 1998. "Introduction." In Adebeyo Olukoshi, ed., *The Politics of Opposition in Contemporary Africa.* Uppsala, Sweden: Afrika Institutet.

Olvera Aguirre, Carlos. 2001. "Fox Insta a los Yucatanos a Negociar en Tabasco?" *Milenio* (Mexico City), Jan. 15.

Orellana Halkyer, René. 1998. "Escenarios locales de resolución de conflictos: Derechos consuetudinario y recursos naturales en el Perú." *América Indígena* 58, nos. 1–2: 223–35.

Otano, Rafael. 2001. "El nuevo partido transversal." *Chile Hoy*, Jan. 6.

Ottaway, Marina. 2003. *Democracy Challenged: The Rise of Semi-Authoritarianism.* Washington, DC: Carnegie Endowment for International Peace.

Panebianco, Angelo. 1988. *Political Parties: Organization and Power.* Cambridge: Cambridge University Press.

Paoli Bolio, Francisco José. 1985. "Legislación y proceso político, 1917-1982." In Pablo González Casanova, ed., *Las elecciones en México: Evolución y perspectivas.* Mexico City: Siglo Veintiuno.

Party of the Institutional Revolution. 1993. *PRI: Documentos Básicos, 1993.* Mexico City: Party of the Institutional Revolution.

Pejovich, Svetozar. 1999. "The Effects of the Interaction of Formal and Informal Institutions on Social Stability and Economic Development." *Journal of Markets and Morality* 2, no. 2: 164–81.

Perelli, Carina. 1995. "La Personalización de la Política: Nuevos Caudillos, Outsiders, Política Mediática y Política Informal." In Carina Perelli, Sonia Picado, and Daniel Zovatto, eds., *Partidos y Clase Política en América Latina en los 90.* San José, Costa Rica: Instituto Interamericano de Derechos Humanos.

Pérez Liñan, Aníbal. 2003. "Presidential Crises and Democratic Accountability in Latin America, 1990–1999." In Susan Eva Eckstein and Timothy P. Wickham-Crowley, eds., *What Justice? Whose Justice? Fighting for Fairness in Latin America.* Berkeley: University of California Press.

Philip, George. 1992. *The Presidency in Mexican Politics.* New York: St. Martin's Press.

Pierson, Paul. 2000. "Increasing Returns, Path Dependence, and the Study of Politics." *American Political Science Review* 94, no. 2: 251–67.

———. 2004. *Politics in Time: History, Institutions, and Social Analysis.* Princeton, NJ: Princeton University Press.

Pinheiro, Filho. 1998. *Reforma Eleitoral: Voto Distrital Misto: A Soluçtao que o Brasil Quer Cohnecer.* Brasília, Brazil: Câmara dos Deputados.

Pitkin, Hanna F. 1967. *The Concept of Representation.* Berkeley: University of California Press.

Posas, Mario, and Rafael del Cid. 1983. *La Construcción del Sector Público y del Estado Nacional en Honduras, 1876–1979.* 2nd ed. San José, Costa Rica: EDUCA.

Price, Robert M. 1975. *Society and Bureaucracy in Contemporary Ghana.* Berkeley: University of California Press.

Putnam, Robert D. 1993. *Making Democracy Work: Civic Traditions in Modern Italy.* Princeton, NJ: Princeton University Press.

Qué Pasa (Santiago). 2000. "Jaime Campos, fruto del cuoteo." May 27.

———. 2002. "La tregua Lagos-Zaldívar." Mar. 9.

Rabinowitz, George, and Stewart McDonald. 1989. "A Directional Theory of Issue Voting." *American Political Science Review* 83: 93–121.

Rabkin, Rhoda. 1996. "Redemocratization, Electoral Engineering, and Party Strategies in Chile, 1989–1995." *Comparative Political Studies* 29: 335–56.

Rehren, Alfredo. 1992. "Organizing the Presidency for the Consolidation of Democracy in the Southern Cone." Paper presented at the seventeenth International Congress of the Latin American Studies Association, Los Angeles, Sept. 24–27.

Remmer, Karen, and Eric Wibbels. 2000. "The Subnational Politics of Economic Adjustment: Provincial Politics and Fiscal Performance in Argentina." *Comparative Political Studies* 33, no. 4: 419–51.

Reyna, José Luis. 1985. "Las elecciones en el México institucionalizado, 1946–1976." In Pablo González Casanova, ed., *Las elecciones en México: Evolución y perspectivas*. Mexico City: Siglo Veintiuno.

Reynoso, Víctor Manuel. 1993. "El Partido Acción Nacional: La oposición hara Gobierno?" *Revista Mexicana de Sociología* 55, no. 2: 133–51.

Riggs, Fred W. 1964. *Administration in Developing Countries: The Theory of Prismatic Society*. Boston: Houghton Mifflin.

——. 1988. "The Survival of Presidentialism in America: Para-Constitutional Practices." *International Political Science Review* 9, no 4: 247–78.

Roberts, Kenneth. 1995. "Neoliberalism and the Transformation of Populism in Latin America." *World Politics* 48, no. 1: 82–116.

——. 1998. *Deepening Democracy? The Modern Left and Social Movements in Chile and Peru*. Stanford, CA: Stanford University Press.

Roberts, Kenneth, and Erik Wibbels. 1999. "Party Systems and Electoral Volatility in Latin America: A Test of Economic, Institutional, and Structural Explanations." *American Political Science Review* 93, no. 3: 575–90.

Rodan, Garry. 2004. *Transparency and Authoritarian Rule in Southeast Asia: Singapore and Malaysia*. London: Routledge.

Rodríguez Araujo, Octavio. 1974. "El henriquismo: última disidencia política organizada en México." *Estudios políticos* 3–4: 123–36.

Roessler, Philip G. 2005. "Donor-Induced Democratization and the Privatization of State Violence in Kenya and Rwanda." *Comparative Politics* 37, no. 2: 207–25.

Rosenberg, Mark B. 1995. "Democracy in Honduras: The Electoral and the Political Reality." In Mitchell A. Seligson and John A. Booth, eds., *Elections and Democracy in Central America, Revisited*. Chapel Hill: University of North Carolina Press.

Rothstein, Frances. 1979. "The Class Basis of Patron-Client Relations." *Latin American Perspectives* 6: 25–35.

Saltos Galarza, Napoleón. 1999. *Ética y Corrupción*. Quito, Ecuador: Proyecto Respon-Dabilidad–Anticorrupción en Las Américas.

Samuels, David. 2001a. "Incumbents and Challengers on a Level Playing Field: Assessing the Impact of Campaign Finance in Brazil." *Journal of Politics* 63, no. 2: 569–84.

——. 2001b. "Money, Elections and Democracy in Brazil." *Latin American Politics and Society* 43, no. 2: 27–48.

——. 2001c. "When Does Every Penny Count? Intraparty Competition and Campaign Finance in Brazil." *Party Politics* 7, no. 1: 89–102.

———. 2002. "Pork-Barreling Is Not Credit-Claiming or Advertising: Campaign Finance and the Sources of the Personal Vote in Brazil." *Journal of Politics* 64, no. 3: 845–63.

———. 2003. *Ambition, Federalism, and Legislative Politics in Brazil.* New York: Cambridge University Press.

Sánchez Botero, Esther. 2000. "The *tutela*-System as a Means of Transforming the Relations between the State and the Indigenous Peoples of Colombia." In Willem Assies, Gemma Van Der Haar, and Andre Hoekema, eds., *The Challenge of Diversity: Indigenous Peoples and Reform of the State in Latin America.* Amsterdam: Thela Thesis.

Sánchez-Parga, José. 1998. *La Pugna de Poderes.* Quito, Ecuador: Abya-Ayala Ediciones.

Sandbrook, Richard, and Jay Oelbaum. 1999. "Reforming the Political Kingdom: Governance and Development in Ghana's Fourth Republic." Critical Perspectives paper. Legon-Accra, Ghana: Center for Democracy and Development. June.

Santos, Wanderley G. dos. 1994. *Regresso: Máscaras Institucionais do Liberalismo Oligárquico.* Rio de Janeiro, Brazil: Editora Ópera Nostra.

Sartori, Giovanni. 1976. *Parties and Party Systems: A Framework for Analysis.* New York: Cambridge University Press.

Schedler, Andreas. 2002. "The Menu of Manipulation." *Journal of Democracy* 13, no. 2: 36–50.

Schedler, Andreas, Larry Diamond, and Marc F. Plattner, eds. 1999. *The Self-Restraining State: Power and Accountability in New Democracies.* Boulder, CO: Lynne Rienner.

Schneider, Aaron. 2001. "Federalism against Markets: Local Struggles for Power and National Fiscal Adjustment in Brazil." Ph.D. diss., University of California, Berkeley.

Schotter, Andrew. 1981. *The Economic Theory of Social Institutions.* Cambridge: Cambridge University Press.

Schuessler, Alexander. 2000. *A Logic of Expressive Choice.* Princeton, NJ: Princeton University Press.

Scott, James C. 1969. "Corruption, Machine Politics, and Political Change." *American Political Science Review* 63, no. 4: 1142–58.

———. 1972. "Patron-Client Politics and Political Change in Southeast Asia." *American Political Science Review* 66, no. 1: 91–113.

Segunda, La (Santiago). 1993. "Los entretelones del consejo de RN: enfrentamientos, emociones, y resultados." July 5, p. 14.

Selcher, Wayne. 1998. "The Politics of Decentralized Federalism, National Diversification, and Regionalism in Brazil." *Journal of Interamerican Studies and World Affairs* 40, no. 4: 25–50.

Shifter, Michael. 1997. "Tensions and Trade-offs in Latin America." *Journal of Democracy* 8, no. 2: 114–28.

Shugart, Matthew Soberg. 2001. "Electoral Efficiency and the Move to Mixed-Member Systems." *Electoral Studies* 20, no. 2: 173–93.

Shugart, Matthew Soberg, and John M. Carey. 1992. *Presidents and Assemblies: Constitutional Design and Electoral Dynamics.* New York: Cambridge University Press.

Shugart, Matthew Soberg, Melody Ellis Valdini, and Kati Suominen. 2005. "Looking for Locals: Voter Information Demands and Personal Vote-Earning Attributes of Legislators under Proportional Representation." *American Journal of Political Science* 49, no. 2: 437–49.

Siavelis, Peter. 1997a. "Continuity and Change in the Chilean Party System: On the Transformational Effects of Electoral Reform." *Comparative Political Studies* 30, no. 6: 651–74.

———. 1997b. "Executive-Legislative Relations in Post-Pinochet Chile: A Preliminary Assessment." In Scott Mainwaring and Matthew Soberg Shugart, eds., *Presidentialism and Democracy in Latin America*. New York: Cambridge University Press.

———. 2000. *The President and Congress in Post-Authoritarian Chile: Institutional Constraints to Democratic Consolidation*. University Park: Pennsylvania State University Press.

———. 2002a. "Exaggerated Presidentialism and Moderate Presidents: Executive-Legislative Relations in Chile." In Scott Morgenstern and Benito Nacif, eds., *Legislative Politics in Latin America*. Cambridge: Cambridge University Press.

———. 2002b. "The Hidden Logic of Candidate Selection for Chilean Parliamentary Elections." *Comparative Politics* 34, no. 2: 419–38.

Sieder, Rachel. 1998. "Customary Law and Local Power in Guatemala." In Rachel Sieder, ed., *Guatemala after the Peace Accords*. London: Institute of Latin American Studies.

———. 1999. "Rethinking Democratization and Citizenship: Legal Pluralism and Institutional Reform in Guatemala." *Citizenship Studies* 3, no. 1: 103–18.

———. 2003. "Renegotiating 'Law and Order': Judicial Reform and Citizen Responses in Postwar Guatemala." *Democratization* 10, no. 4: 137–60.

Sierra, María Teresa. 1998. "Autonomía y Pluralismo Jurídico: El Debate Mexicano." *América Indígena* 58, nos. 1–2: 21–39.

Sil, Rudra. 2001. "Privatization, Labor Politics, and the Firm in Post-Soviet Russia: Non-market Norms, Market Institutions, and the Soviet Legacy." In Christopher Candland and Rudra Sil, eds., *The Politics of Labor in a Global Age: Continuity and Change in Late-Industrializing and Post-socialist Economies*. New York: Oxford University Press.

———. 2002. *Managing "Modernity": Work, Community, and Authority in Late-Industrializing Japan and Russia*. Ann Arbor: University of Michigan Press.

Silva, Eduardo. 1992. "Capitalist Regime Loyalties and Redemocratization in Chile." *Journal of Interamerican Studies and World Affairs* 34, no. 4: 77–117.

Skolnick, Jerome H., and James J. Fyfe. 1993. *Above the Law: Police and the Excessive Use of Force*. New York: Free Press.

Smith, Peter. 1979. *Labyrinths of Power: Political Recruitment in Twentieth Century Mexico* Princeton, NJ: Princeton University Press.

Snyder, Richard. 2001. "Scaling Down: The Subnational Comparative Method." *Studies in Comparative International Development* 36, no. 1: 93–110.

Sorauf, Frank. 1988. *Money in American Elections*. Glenview, IL: Scott, Foresman.

Souza, Celina. 1998. "Intermediação de Interesses Regionais no Brasil: O Impacto do Federalismo e da Descentralização." *Dados* 41, no. 3: 569–92.

Starn, Orin. 1992. "I Dreamed of Foxes and Hawks: Reflections on Peasant Protest, New Social Movements, and the Rondas Campesinas of Northern Peru." In Arturo Escobar and Sonia E. Alvarez, eds., *The Making of Social Movements in Latin America: Identity, Strategy and Democracy*. Boulder, CO: Westview Press.

———. 1999. *Nightwatch: The Politics of Protest in the Andes*. Durham, NC: Duke University Press.

Stavenhagen, Rodolfo. 1988. *Derecho Indígena y Derechos Humanos en América Latina*. Mexico City: Instituto Interamericano de Derechos Humanos, El Colegio de México.

Stokes, Susan C. 2001. *Mandates and Democracies: Neoliberalism by Surprise in Latin America*. New York: Cambridge University Press.

———. 2003. "Do Informal Rules Make Democracy Work? Accounting for Accountability in Argentina." Paper presented at the conference Informal Institutions in Latin America, University of Notre Dame, IN, Apr. 23–24.

———. 2005. "Perverse Accountability: A Formal Model of Machine Politics with Evidence from Argentina." *American Political Science Review* 99 (Aug.): 315–25.

Sur, El (Concepción). 2003. "Cuanta cerda le queda a la Concertación." July 20, p. 4.

Taylor, Michelle M. 1992. "Formal versus Informal Incentive Structures and Legislator Behavior: Evidence from Costa Rica." *Journal of Politics* 54, no. 4: 1053–71.

———. 1996. "When Electoral and Party Institutions Interact to Produce Caudillo Politics: The Case of Honduras." *Electoral Studies* 15, no. 3: 327-37.

Taylor-Robinson, Michelle M., and Christopher Diaz. 1999. "Who Gets Legislation Passed in a Marginal Legislature and Is the Label Marginal Legislature Still Appropriate? A Study of the Honduran Congress." *Comparative Political Studies* 32, no. 5: 590–626.

Teixeira, Tomaz, 1985. *A Outra Face da Oliguarquia do Piauí (Depoimento)*. 2nd ed. Fortaleza, Brazil: Stylus Comuncações Ltda.

Tercera, La (Santiago). 2000. "Presiones por los cupos de subsecretarios." Feb. 1.

Thelen, Kathleen. 1999. "Historical Institutionalism in Comparative Politics." *Annual Review of Political Science* 2, no. 1: 369–404.

———. 2003. "How Institutions Evolve: Insights from Comparative Historical Analysis." In James Mahoney and Dietrich Rueschemeyer, eds., *Comparative Historical Analysis in the Social Sciences*. New York: Cambridge University Press.

———. 2004. *How Institutions Evolve: The Political Economy of Skills in Germany, Britain, the United States, and Japan*. New York: Cambridge University Press.

Tomz, Michael, Jason Wittenberg, and Gary King. 2003. Clarify: Software for Interpreting and Presenting Statistical Results. Version 2.1. Stanford University, University of Wisconsin, and Harvard University. Jan. 5. Available at http://gking.harvard.edu/clarify/docs/clarify.html.

Torre, Juan Carlos. 1990. *La vieja guardia sindical y Perón: sobre los orígenes del peronismo*. Buenos Aires, Argentina: Editorial Sudamericana.

Tsai, Kellee S. 2003. "Coping by Innovating: The Formal Origins and Consequences of Informal Institutions in China." Paper presented at the annual meeting of the American Political Science Association, Philadelphia, Aug. 27–31.

Tsai, Lily Lee. 2001. "Substituting for the State? The Logic of Private Efficiency in Chinese Local Governance." Paper presented at the annual meeting of the American Political Science Association, San Francisco, Aug. 30–Sept. 2.

———. 2002. "Cadres, Temple and Lineage Institutions, and Governance in Rural China." *China Journal* 48 (July): 1–27.

———. 2004. "The Informal State: Governance and Development in Rural China." Ph.D. diss., Department of Government, Harvard University, Cambridge, MA.

Ullman-Margalit, Edna. 1978. *The Emergence of Norms*. Oxford: Oxford University Press.

United Nations Development Program (UNDP). 2002. *Hacia una integración cooperativa y solidaria del territorio nacional*. Buenos Aires, Argentina: United Nations Development Program

Valencia Castrejón, Sergio. 1996. *Poder regional y política nacional en México: El gobierno de Maximino Avila Camacho en Puebla (1937–1941)*. Mexico City: Instituto Nacional de Estudios Históricos de la Revolución Mexicana.

Valenzuela, Arturo 1994. "Party Politics and the Crisis of Presidentialism in Chile" In Juan Linz and Arturo Valenzuela, eds., *The Failure of Presidential Democracy*, vol. 2. Baltimore: Johns Hopkins University Press.

Valenzuela, J. Samuel, and Timothy Scully. 1997. "Electoral Choices and the Party System in Chile: Continuities and Changes at the Recovery of Democracy." *Comparative Politics* 29, no. 4: 511–27.

Van Cott, Donna Lee. 2000a. *The Friendly Liquidation of the Past: The Politics of Diversity in Latin America*. Pittsburgh: University of Pittsburgh Press.

———. 2000b. "A Political Analysis of Legal Pluralism in Bolivia and Colombia." *Journal of Latin American Studies* 32, no. 1: 207–34.

Vargas Manríquez, Fernando, and Guadalupe Moreno Corzo. 1994. "Legitimación Jurídica de la Procuraduría Electoral del Pueblo Chiapaneco y el Valor Jurídico de sus Actuaciones y Resoluciones." Unpublished ms.

Von Benda-Beckmann, Franz. 1997. "Citizens, Strangers and Indigenous Peoples: Conceptual Politics and Legal Pluralism." *Law and Anthropology* 9: 1-42.

Walker, Ignacio. 2003. "Chile: Three Stories of Informal Institutions in a Limited Democracy." Paper presented at the conference Informal Institutions and Politics in Latin America, University of Notre Dame, South Bend, IN, Apr. 23–24.

Wang, Hongying. 2000. "Informal Institutions and Foreign Investment in China." *Pacific Review* 13, no. 4: 525–56.

Waterbury, John. 1973. "Endemic and Planned Corruption in a Monarchical Regime." *World Politics* 25, no. 4: 533–55.

Way, Lucan A. 2002. "The Dilemmas of Reform in Weak States: The Case of Post-Soviet Fiscal Decentralization." *Politics and Society* 30, no. 4: 579–98.

Wedeen, Lisa. 2003. "Seeing Like a Citizen, Acting Like a State: Exemplary Events in Unified Yemen." *Comparative Studies in Society and History* 45, no. 4: 680–713.

Weingast, Barry. 1979. "A Rational Choice Perspective on Congressional Norms." *American Journal of Political Science* 23, no. 2: 245–62.

Weingast, Barry R., and William J. Marshall. 1988. "The Industrial Organization of Congress; or, Why Legislatures, Like Firms, Are Not Organized as Markets." *Journal of Political Economy* 96, no. 1: 132–63.

Weyland, Kurt. 1993. "The Rise and Fall of President Collor and Its Impact on Brazilian Democracy." *Journal of Interamerican Studies and World Affairs* 35, no. 1: 1–37.

———. 1996. "Neopopulism and Neoliberalism in Latin America." *Studies in Comparative International Development* 31, no. 1: 3–31.

———. 1997. "'Growth with Equity' in Chile's New Democracy." *Latin American Research Review* 32, no. 1: 37–67.

——. 1999. "Neoliberal Populism in Latin America and Eastern Europe." *Comparative Politics* 31, no. 4: 379–401.

——. 2002a. "Limitations of Rational-Choice Institutionalism for the Study of Latin American Politics." *Studies in Comparative International Development* 37, no. 3: 57–85.

——. 2002b. *The Politics of Market Reform in Fragile Democracies.* Princeton, NJ: Princeton University Press.

Whitehead, Laurence. 2002. *Democratization: Theory and Experience.* Oxford: Oxford University Press.

Wiarda, Howard, and Harvey Kline. 1996. *Latin American Politics and Development* Boulder, CO: Westview Press.

Williamson, John. 1990. *Latin American Adjustment: How Much Has Happened?* Washington, DC: Institute for International Economics.

Wright, Gerald C., Jr., and Michael B. Berkman. 1986. "Candidates and Policy in United States Senate Elections." *American Political Science Review* 80, no. 2: 567–88.

Yang, Mayfair Mei-hui. 1994. *Gifts, Favors, and Banquets: The Art of Social Relationships in China.* Ithaca, NY: Cornell University Press.

Yashar, Deborah. 1999. "Democracy, Indigenous Movements, and the Postliberal Challenge in Latin America." *World Politics* 52, no. 1: 76–104.

Yrigoyen Fajardo, Raquel. 1999. *Pautas de coordinación entre el derecho indígena y el derecho estatal.* Guatemala City: Fundación Myrna Mack.

——. 2000. "The Constitutional Recognition of Indigenous Law in Andean Countries." In Willem Assies, Gemma Van Der Haar, and Andre Hoekema, eds., *The Challenge of Diversity: Indigenous Peoples and Reform of the State in Latin America.* Amsterdam: Thela Thesis.

Yucatán State Legislature. 1993. *Diario de Debates del Estado de Yucatán, 21 de diciembre, 1993.* Mérida: Congreso Estatal de Yucatán, Mexico.

Zamarripa, Roberto. 1989. "Triunfo Perredista, según el Dictamen del Tribunal?" *La Jornada* (Mexico City), Aug. 13.

Zorrilla, Ruben H. 1983. "Líder, Elite, y Masa en el Peronismo." *Todo Es Historia,* Dec., pp. 28–37.

Contributors

EDITORS

Gretchen Helmke is Assistant Professor of Political Science at the University of Rochester. Helmke specializes in comparative political institutions, with a focus on Latin America. She has recently published *Courts under Constraints: Judges, Generals, and Presidents in Argentina* (2005). Her articles have appeared in *American Political Science Review, Comparative Politics, Desarollo Economico,* and *Perspectives in Politics.*

Steven Levitsky is John L. Loeb Associate Professor of the Social Sciences at Harvard University. He specializes in comparative and Latin American politics. Specific areas of research include political parties and party change, informal institutions, and political regimes and regime change. He is the author of *Transforming Labor-Based Parties in Latin America: Argentine Peronism in Comparative Perspective* (2003). His articles have appeared in *Comparative Politics, World Politics, Comparative Political Studies, Latin American Research Review,* and other journals.

CONTRIBUTORS

Daniel M. Brinks is Assistant Professor of Government at the University of Texas at Austin. His research focuses on the role of the law and courts in supporting or extending the full set of rights associated with democracy, with a regional interest in Latin America. His most recent projects address the judicial response to police violence in Brazil, Argentina, and Uruguay; judicial independence; the role of informal norms in the legal order; and the use of law-based approaches to extend social and economic rights in developing countries. His work has been published in *Comparative Politics, Studies in Comparative International Development,* and other journals.

John M. Carey is Professor of Government at Dartmouth College. His interests
are comparative politics, democratic institutions, and Latin American politics.
Current research is on sources of unity and divisiveness within legislative parties
and coalitions, and how the nature of legislative representation affects political
accountability. His books include *Presidents and Assemblies: Constitutional
Design and Electoral Dynamics* (with Matthew Shugart; 1992), *Term Limits and
Legislative Representation* (1996), *Executive Decree Authority* (also with Shugart;
1998), and *Term Limits in the State Legislatures* (with Richard Niemi and Lynda
Powell; 2000).

Scott W. Desposato is Assistant Professor of Political Science at the University of
California, San Diego. His research interests include democratic institutions,
quantitative methods, and voting behavior. His articles have been published in
*American Journal of Political Science, British Journal of Political Science, Journal
of Politics, Comparative Political Studies,* and other journals.

Todd A. Eisenstadt is Assistant Professor of Government at American University.
He specializes in Mexican and Latin American politics, with specific research
interests in democratization, parties and elections, and ethnic politics. He is
the author of *Courting Democracy in Mexico: Party Strategies and Electoral
Institutions* (2004). His articles have appeared in *Democratization, International
Political Science Review, Latin American Politics and Society,* and *Party Politics.*

Flavia Freidenberg is Assistant Professor of Political Science and Public
Administration at the University of Salamanca. Her areas of research include
political parties and party organizations, electoral campaigns, and mass media
and public opinion. She is the author of *Jama, Caleta y Camello: Las Estrategias
de Abdalá Bucaram y el PRE para Ganar Elecciones* (2003), coauthor of *Los
Dueños del Poder: Partidos Politícos en Ecuador* (with Manuel Alcántara; 2000),
and coeditor of *Partidos Políticos de América Latina* (also with Alcántara; 2001).

Joy Langston is Research Professor at the Center for Research and Teaching in
Economics in Mexico City. Her specialty for the past several years has been
political parties in Mexico, in particular the PRI. She has published in journals
such as *Comparative Political Studies* and *Journal of Latin American Studies.*

Andrés Mejía Acosta is Killam Research fellow in the Department of Political
Science, University of British Columbia. His research focuses on the impact of
formal and informal political institutions on the adoption of economic reforms
in Ecuador and Latin America. He is the author of *Gobernabilidad Democrática*
(2002) and has published several articles on electoral systems, legislative politics,
Christian Democracy, and democratic governance.

Guillermo O'Donnell is Professor of Political Science at the University of Notre Dame and Senior Faculty Fellow at the Kellogg Institute for International Studies. His research and teaching interests focus on democratic theory, comparative democracy and democratization, Latin American politics and society, and relationships between legal and political theory. He has published extensively on authoritarianism, democratization, and democratic theory, including *Modernization and Bureaucratic-Authoritarianism; Bureaucratic-Authoritarianism; Transitions from Authoritarian Rule*; and *The Quality of Democracy*.

David Samuels is Benjamin E. Lippincott Associate Professor of Political Science at the University of Minnesota. He specializes in Latin American politics and the comparative study of political institutions, with particular emphasis on Brazilian politics, electoral systems, political parties, legislatures, and federalism. He is the author of *Ambition, Federalism, and Legislative Politics in Brazil* (2003). His articles have appeared in *American Political Science Review, Comparative Political Studies, Comparative Politics, Journal of Politics*, and *British Journal of Political Science*.

Peter Siavelis is Associate Professor of Political Science at Wake Forest University. He is the author of *The President and Congress in Post-authoritarian Chile: Institutional Constraints to Democratic Consolidation* (2000) and various journal articles and book chapters on Chilean electoral and legislative politics. His current research focuses on political recruitment and candidate selection in Latin America.

Susan C. Stokes is John S. Saden Professor of Political Science at Yale University. Her recent studies include *Democracy and the Culture of Skepticism: Political Trust in Argentina and Mexico* (with Matthew Cleary; 2006), "Perverse Accountability" (*American Political Science Review*, 2005), *Mandates and Democracy: Neoliberalism by Surprise in Latin America* (2001), and "Endogenous Democratization" (with Carles Boix; *World Politics*, 2003).

Michelle M. Taylor-Robinson is Associate Professor at Texas A&M University. Her work focuses on the comparative study of legislatures and how the performance of legislative institutions influences the prospects of democratic consolidation. She is coauthor of *Negotiating Democracy* (with Gretchen Casper; 1996) and has published in journals such as the *American Journal of Political Science, Journal of Politics, Women and Politics*, and *Electoral Studies*.

Donna Lee Van Cott is Assistant Professor of Political Science at Tulane University. Her books include *From Movements to Parties in Latin America: The Evolution of Ethnic Politics* (2005), *The Friendly Liquidation of the Past: The Politics of Diversity in Latin America* (2000), and, as editor, *Indigenous Peoples and Democracy in Latin America* (1994). Recent articles appeared in *Comparative Political Studies, Studies in Comparative International Development,* and *Latin American Politics and Society.*

Index